Father Knickerbocker Rebels

Books by Thomas Jefferson Wertenbaker

★

FATHER KNICKERBOCKER REBELS

THE PURITAN OLIGARCHY

THE OLD SOUTH

THE FOUNDING OF AMERICAN CIVILIZATION

★

CHARLES SCRIBNER'S SONS

Father Knickerbocker Rebels

NEW YORK CITY DURING THE REVOLUTION

BY

THOMAS JEFFERSON WERTENBAKER

ILLUSTRATED

CHARLES SCRIBNER'S SONS, NEW YORK
CHARLES SCRIBNER'S SONS, LTD., LONDON
1948

TO MY WIFE
SARAH MARSHALL WERTENBAKER

PREFACE

THE HISTORY OF NEW YORK CITY from 1765 to 1783 is as fascinating as it is tragic, marked as it is by clashing interests, by heroism and baseness, by gaiety and suffering, by sudden wealth and sudden poverty, by fratricidal strife, by intense hatreds, by cruelty, by corruption. This period of eighteen years saw two distinct New Yorks— the Revolutionary New York of the Stamp Act riots, of the famous liberty pole, of the "tea party," of the committees of correspondence, of the Provincial Congress, of the appeal to arms, of the defeat of Washington's army and the evacuation by the patriots; and the Loyalist New York of Sir William Howe, Sir Henry Clinton, Sir Guy Carleton, General James Robertson, Judge William Smith and James Rivington, the New York which made a fetish of loyalty to the King.

To understand the American Revolution one must know the part played by New York City. In the trading town at the toe of Manhattan resided the commander-in-chief of the British armies in America; here was the center of naval activities, from which many an imposing flotilla went out for expeditions to Pennsylvania, or Virginia, or the Carolinas, or the West Indies; here the British generals and admirals sat around the council table to formulate their policies and plan their operations.

Loyalist New York was the focal point for the refugees to which they fled to escape the wrath of the Revolutionists. At any time from the autumn of 1776 to the autumn of 1783, one could see on the streets, or in the markets, or in the shops, or down by the wharves, farmers from upstate New York or from Connecticut or New Jersey; merchants from Philadelphia or Norfolk; South Carolina planters; shopkeepers from Boston or Newport. In New York were organized most of the Tory provincial regiments, some of which gave real assistance to Sir Henry Clinton's regulars; from New York the Associated Loyalists sent out their expeditions into New England and New Jersey to burn and plunder; here in mass meetings the refugees drew up their petitions to the King; from New York at the end of the war went tens of thousands of despairing men, women and children into exile to Nova Scotia, the Valley of the St. John's River, or the West Indies.

In writing the history of Tory New York one should not look in from the outside, to describe events as they appeared to the Revolutionists, but rather live with the people of the city themselves, to look on at their various activities, their dances, their theatre parties and celebrations; their suffering from cold and hunger; their dissatisfaction with the conduct of the war and their bitter criticisms of the British commanders; their futile pleas for the restitution of civil government. And the historian, whatever his sympathies, should be impartial in giving and explaining the Loyalist point of view.

The present is an especially opportune time for writing the history of New York City during the Revolution, since a mass of documentary material has recently been made available. This book would have been incomplete indeed had it not been for the Sir Henry Clinton Papers, the Gage Papers and the Minutes of the Associated Loyalists, in the Clements Library at the University of Michigan, and the Sir Guy Carleton Papers, in the library of Colonial Williamsburg. I should like to acknowledge my indebtedness for the mass of material gathered by Mr. I. N. Phelps Stokes and published in his *Iconography of Manhattan Island,* and to express my appreciation for grants in aid in the preparation of this book by the David Hunter McAlpin Research Fund of the Department of History, Princeton University, and by the Princeton University Research Fund. I wish, also, to thank Dr. Carl Bridenbaugh for reading the manuscript and making helpful suggestions.

T. J. W.

CONTENTS

ILLUSTRATIONS

Between Pages 14 *and* 15

Between Pages 62 *and* 63

xi

ILLUSTRATIONS

Father Knickerbocker Rebels

CHAPTER I

LIBERTY ASSAILED

ALL DAY long on November 1, 1765, New York City was in a state of suppressed excitement. Wherever people met, on the street corners, at the Old Slip Market, at the City Tavern in Broadway, there were loud denunciations of the British Ministry and open threats of violence. Many of the leading burghers wore mourning. Over at the Merchants Coffee House, near the foot of Wall Street, the backgammon boxes and even the dice were covered with crêpe.[1] The vessels in the harbor rode with colors lowered in token of "lamentation and woe." This was the day on which the Stamp Act was to go into effect.

A few days earlier two thousand determined people had gathered at the Battery to prevent the landing of the stamps, and had dispersed with angry mutterings upon learning that the King's officers had eluded them. The ship *Edward* had come up in the night under cover of the man-of-war *Coventry* and had left several packages at Fort George. The aging lieutenant governor, Cadwallader Colden, had implored Captain Kennedy, of the *Coventry*, to take the stamps on board, but Kennedy, who owned several houses in the city which the people were threatening to wreck, absolutely refused.[2] So Colden was forced to leave the stamps in the Fort.

At about seven on the evening of November 1, a great crowd began to assemble in the Common.[3] A motley group it was—blacksmiths, day laborers, shopkeepers, teamsters, barbers, tavern keepers, carpenters, several hundred armed sailors, here and there a wealthy merchant. The immediate object of their wrath was Colden. The lieutenant governor, who was filling the interim between the departure of Governor Monckton and the arrival of his successor, was a strange combination of scientist and politician. His interest in botany, astronomy, medicine, electricity, and natural history won him distinc-

1

tion in Europe as well as in America, and he corresponded regularly with Linnaeus, Gronovius, Franklin and Samuel Johnson. But his efforts to enforce the Stamp Act and his insistence upon preparing Fort George for an attack by the populace had aroused the resentment of the people. So now the mob constructed a gallows mounted on wheels, to which they suspended Colden's effigy, holding a paper of stamps in his hands, with an image of the devil at his side, who seemed "to urge him to persevere in the cause of slavery." While the leaders were busy attaching lanterns to the gallows, another great crowd poured out on the Common from Broadway, their candles and torches flickering in the night and lighting up the unfinished façade of St. Paul's and the new Presbyterian Church. They came from the "coach house of the fort," where they had seized Colden's coach and, fastening on the top of it an effigy of the lieutenant governor seated in a chair, had proceeded up town.[4]

When the two groups united, their leaders addressed them, warning them not to throw stones nor break windows, and to offer no injury to anyone. Then the signal to start was given and the mob surged down Broadway back to Fort George. Colden with his family had taken refuge aboard the *Coventry*,[5] leaving the fort in charge of Major James of the Royal Regiment of Artillery, with a garrison of 183 men. The mob, ignoring the cannon which pointed out from the bastions, crowded up to the gate and demanded that it be opened, hurled brickbats and stones against the walls, and dared the redcoats to fire on them. Had not several prominent men whom they trusted restrained them they would probably have stormed the fort. As it was, they finally turned away and crossing the street to the Bowling Green, tore down the fence, made a large pile of wood on which they placed the coach and gallows and applied a light. As the flames leapt up to engulf the effigies the crowd roared out its approval.

In the midst of the excitement a part of the mob broke away from the rest and, unknown to their leaders, moved back up Broadway and past King's College to Vauxhall,[6] a beautiful estate overlooking North River which had been leased by Major James. Upon this officer, who had gained their especial dislike by declaring that he would cram the Stamp Act down their throats, they proceeded to take revenge. Breaking down the doors of the mansion, they ripped open the mattresses, smashed the china, broke up the tables, chairs and desks and made a bonfire of them, drank all the liquor in the cellar, broke the doors and window frames, destroyed the major's library with its books, mathematical instruments, maps and papers, ruined the garden and pulled down the summer houses. When they departed at two o'clock the next morning, taking with them in triumph the colors of the Royal Regiment, they left behind a scene of desolation.[7]

The people of the colonies were so resentful at the Stamp Act because they all, from the richest merchant to the humble mechanic, realized that it was aimed at their liberty. The founders of the colonies had brought with them all the rights of Englishmen, the most important of which was the right to self-government. So they had established what in time became thirteen semi-independent little republics, each ruled by an elective Assembly. For Parliament, in which they were not represented, to attempt to govern the colonies at this late date, was to render these Assemblies nullities and reduce the people to slavery.

They loved England, it is true; were proud of her power and her wealth; were happy to be under her protection. Many of them, who had never set foot on English soil, spoke of the mother country as "home." But loyalty was one thing, subjugation quite another, especially subjugation, not to the people of England, but to a Parliament which the rotten borough system had made the organ of a small and reactionary group.

The colonists had submitted to Parliamentary regulation of their commerce, for they recognized that that was an imperial rather than a local matter. If the New York merchant wished to have free access to every port within the empire, if he expected protection from the British navy, he could not put up too strenuous a kick against the restrictions of the Navigation Acts. But when Parliament took it upon itself to tax him without the consent of the provincial Assembly, he considered that his most cherished rights were threatened. Even before the Stamp Act was passed the New York Assembly had protested vigorously. They could not without the strongest demonstrations of grief express their sentiments on the late intimation of a design to impose taxes on them by laws passed in Great Britain, they wrote King George. The right of being taxed only by themselves was "fundamentally interwoven" in their constitution.[8]

In fact it was not only interwoven in their constitution, it was its very foundation. Decade after decade the Assembly had used its control over taxation to whittle down the Governor's power and weaken

Britain's hold on the colony. If the governor, after reading over his instructions from the King, vetoed some pet bill or otherwise angered the Assembly, it had repeatedly retaliated by withholding appropriations for governmental expenses. If he proved obstinate, it might actually refuse to pay his salary. It is an old maxim that one must not quarrel with one's paymaster, and the governors usually made every effort to keep the Assemblies in good humor, even at the risk of incurring a stern rebuke from the British Ministry. The governors several times wrote the Secretary of State suggesting that their salaries be paid from the British treasury, but the King had urgent need at home for every penny he could wangle out of the Commons, so the governors had been left to the mercy of the Assemblies.

Thus it was clear that if Parliament could tax the colonists without asking leave or license, the money could, and undoubtedly would, be used to buttress the royal authority. Then colonial self-government would be undermined, then the Americans would be ruled by a body in which they had no voice, separated from them by three thousand miles of water. It was with "astonishment and terror" that the people of New York learned of the Stamp Act, declared 1,200 freemen and freeholders who assembled at the City Arms late in November. "We think it essential to the security of the liberty and prosperity of Englishmen that no taxes be imposed but by the gift of the people." [9]

The bitterness over the Stamp Act was all the more intense because it followed close upon the heels of the almost equally detested Sugar Act. The prosperity of New York City depended on commerce. Visitors who came in through the Narrows past the Governor's Island, noted with interest the mass of shipping which lay before them. Here, on her way out, was a brig, bound for the West Indies, her sails spread, the Union Jack flapping in the breeze, her hold filled with wheat, flour, bread, Indian corn, salt-beef and pork. Anchored off Cruger's Wharf was a ship just in from London, preparing to put ashore her cargo of broadcloth, silk, earthenware, cutlery, saddles and bridles, silverware, furniture, pewter, hoes and shovels. Further up East River were other vessels taking on timber, planks, masts, boards, staves and shingles, potash, copper ore and iron bars, deerskins and furs, for shipment to the mother country. In the distance at the end of Water Street could be seen the skeletons of several vessels on the ways of the shipyards. Tied up in Peck's Slip, or Beekman's Slip, or at the West Dock or East

Dock at the foot of Broad Street were sloops and other small vessels, where Dutch farmers from upper Manhattan and Long Island were unloading their corn meal, poultry, meat and butter, and carting them off for sale in one of the nearby markets.

The key to this prosperity was the trade with the French and Spanish West Indies. Great Britain, herself a food producing country, did not want the wheat and flour of New York and the other continental colonies, while the British West Indian Islands were too small to provide a satisfactory market. On the other hand, the foreign islands, with their great sugar plantations and their teeming populations, were eager to buy all the food products the English colonists could bring them. So the New York merchants had long been accustomed to load their ships with flour and biscuits, beans, peas, oats, Indian corn, salt-beef, pork, hams, bacon, butter, cheese and even venison with instructions to the masters to head for Guadeloupe, Martinique or San Domingo. The French and Spaniards gave them in exchange sugar, cotton and indigo, most of which they shipped to Great Britain to pay for their importations of manufactured goods, and rum and molasses, which they brought back to the home port.

In 1733 Parliament had aimed a blow at this traffic by passing the so-called Molasses Act, but no great harm had resulted since it had never been enforced. But when Prime Minister George Grenville decided to collect the duties and sent a bevy of revenue vessels to America to prevent smuggling, the colonial merchants faced ruin. "Discontent was painted in every man's face and the distress of the people was very great," wrote Cortlandt Skinner.

At the Merchants Coffee House, the unfortunate turn of events is the one topic of conversation. Is it possible that the Ministry does not realize that the duty is prohibitive? Are they aware that the British West Indies cannot supply half the sugar demanded by the British and American trade.[10] If we are cut off from the foreign islands, who is to buy our wheat, flour and lumber? Without the sugar of the French and Spanish islands, how are we to pay for our imports from Great Britain? It will force us to make our own cloth, clothing, utensils, paper, glass and other articles, to the detriment of the British artificers and will strike a blow at the trade, wealth, and power of the mother country.[10]

The passage of the Sugar Act in 1764, reducing the duty on sugar to five shillings the hundredweight, gave no relief at all. The merchants who paid it found that they were losing money; while those who resorted to smuggling ran the risk of having their ships and cargoes confiscated by the royal revenue officers. In November, 1765, 227 New York merchants petitioned the House of Commons for relief. The act, which was bringing ruin to the commerce of the colonies, would soon react upon the merchants and manufacturers of Great Britain, they said. Would it not be wise to substitute a moderate duty on sugar for the prohibitive five shillings? This would increase the royal revenue, bring prosperity to the colonies and make it possible for them to resume their imports from the mother country.

But Grenville held his ground. As the shipments of sugar to Great Britain sank lower and lower, the New York merchants were forced to pay their balances in specie. This drained off the silver from the city, creating a shortage of money, stagnating trade, lowering prices and sending many debtors to jail. It was the hope of merchants, store-keepers, artisans, in fact everyone in the colony, that an issue of paper money would bring relief, but this the British government absolutely forbade. Again the Assembly protested. If Parliament put a ban on all colonial paper currency, it would "not only highly reflect on the credit, honour and punctuality of this colony, but also reduce it to a state of bankruptcy." [11]

For large numbers bankruptcy had already come. "Our business of all kinds is stopped," said the *Post Boy*. "Great numbers of our poor people and seamen without employment and without support . . . many families which used to live in comfortable plenty daily falling to decay for want of business." [12] "Trade in this part of the world is come to so wretched a pass that you would imagine the plague had been here," wrote a New Yorker, "the grass growing in the most trading streets, and the best traders, so far from wanting the assistance of a clerk, rather want employment for themselves." [13] Two years later the situation had not improved. "I am a tradesman and depend upon my daily labor for the support of my family," wrote one distressed correspondent to the *New York Journal*. "Are our circumstances altered? Is money grown more plenty? Have our tradesmen full employment? . . . What a dismal prospect is before us! A long winter and no work; many unprovided with firewood or money to buy it; house-rent and taxes high; our neighbors daily breaking; their furniture at vendue at every corner." [14]

At such a moment the people were in no humor to tolerate extrava-

gance on the part of the well-to-do; or even legitimate recreation.
When it was announced that a play would be presented in May, 1766,
at the Chapel Street Theatre, there was great indignation. Was it
proper, they said, to waste money in this way, "when great numbers of
poor people can scarce find means of subsistence." Threats of violence
kept many timid souls at home, but when the doors opened there were
enough ticket holders who had decided to risk it to make a fair house.
They had taken their seats and the play had begun, when a mob,
which had gathered outside, burst the doors open and surged in. There
was a wild scramble on the part of the audience to escape, some even
jumping out of the windows, leaving hats and "other parts of dress"
behind. Several were badly hurt; one boy had his skull fractured. The
mob then proceeded to wreck the theatre "both inside and out," and
carrying the pieces in triumph to the Common several blocks away,
made a bonfire of them.[15]

Moved by the distress of the poor, and alarmed at the growing
scarcity of manufactured goods, some of the leading citizens of the city
organized the Society for Promoting Arts.[16] If the restrictions upon our
trade make it impossible for us to purchase from Great Britain, they
said, it becomes necessary for us to supply ourselves. Let unemployed
sailors, clerks, dock workers, instead of walking the streets, take up the
loom or the needle, to turn out the cloth and the clothing which have
become so scarce and dear.

The activities of the society were varied. They lent money to those
who wished to purchase looms for the weaving of linen; they offered
gold medals for the erection of flax mills; they gave premiums for the
best work. They founded two schools for spinning, one in the barracks
near the new jail and the other at the Fresh Water, providing each
pupil with a wheel, a chair and reels. When country people complained that they had to stroll through the streets in order to sell their
linen and woolen yarn and cloth, the society opened a market for them
in the Exchange at the foot of Broad Street.

At first these efforts gave every promise of success. "You can scarce
believe how it cheered us in our distress," wrote one worker.[17] The
rich set the fashion of wearing clothes made of local cloth, and even
the Governor made a point of appearing in public in homespun.[18] "A
young lady in town" wrote a friend in the country, with calm disre-
gard of the latter's feelings, that the women of New York City were
"resolved to resign the charms of dress and let a horrid homespun cov-

ering (which can become none but a country wench) take the place of the rich brocade and graceful satin." [19]

In every home the housewife and her daughters sat long hours at the spinning wheel; the farmers doubled and tripled their crops of flax; mutton found no purchasers in the market since sheep were needed to meet the demand for wool; "sassafras, balm and sage" were used as substitutes for tea; the wearing of mourning at funerals was greatly restricted in order to save cloth.[20] The *Post Boy* announced with a note of triumph that weaving had been brought to "such perfection" that a piece of green linen made by John Hill had sold for eight shillings per yard.[21] Obadiah Wells opened a linen factory in Mulberry Street, "near Fresh Water," and advertised for "a large quantity of good well drest spinning flax." [22]

Then came disappointment. "This country is not ripe for manufactures," Peter Hasenclevor wrote to Sir William Johnson. "Labor is too high—too much land to be settled." [23] Another writer pointed out that the lack of capital would make it impossible for New York City to switch its interest from commerce to industry. "Let people talk what they will—I assure you nothing can be carried into execution." [24] Colden reported to the Ministry: "What has been published of the manufactures lately set up are absolute falsehoods . . . All the wool in America is not sufficient to make stockings for the inhabitants, and severe weather in North America renders the production of wool in great quantities impracticable." [25]

So the people of New York, especially the lower classes, were in an ugly humor long before the news of the passage of the Stamp Act reached them. They would undoubtedly have resisted the collection of the tax under any circumstances, but their anger against the assault upon American liberty was intensified by their empty stomachs and bitterly cold houses. The riot of November first, especially the sacking of Vauxhall, was as much a protest against poverty and suffering as against taxation by Parliament.

The fury of the mob, though more restrained than that of the rabble in Paris during the French Revolution, was a thing few dared face. James McEvers, who had been appointed stamp distributor, seeing that he was in for serious trouble, sent in his resignation to Colden. "I find it will be attended with the greatest risk to my person and future . . . to execute the office. If I had attempted it my house would have been pillaged, my person abused." [26] No doubt it was with a sigh of relief that, a few days later, he read an article in the *Mercury* which announced that he had cleared himself of "the imputation of joining in the design to enslave his country." But he must have smiled at the editor's further statement that his resignation had been voluntary and "not the effect of any menace or disturbance." [27]

The lieutenant governor, for his part, had visions of an armed mob's turning the guns of the Battery on Fort George, "so as to enfilade the whole," storming up to the bastions, swarming over the walls and setting fire to the Barracks and other buildings. So he had the little garrison working feverishly to prepare for the worst. The cannon at the Battery were spiked, firewood was used to construct merlons for the fort, the artillery was so placed as to rake Broadway, Stone Street, Bridge Street and Whitehall, all the gates were strengthened and some blocked up, the two frigates in the harbor were brought up and anchored at a point from which they could command the fort.[28] Nor were these precautions uncalled for. The mob was ready to respond to the command of their leaders, and at every street corner placards had been posted threatening that unless the stamps were surrendered the fort would be stormed.

Caught between his fear of the mob and his fear of the Ministry, the aged lieutenant governor was in an agony of uncertainty. Even when the Common Council opened a way out by offering to take charge of the stamps, he hesitated to accept. But at last, after consulting General Gage, he yielded, and a few minutes later carts loaded with seven boxes of stamps emerged from the fort and rattled off over the cobbles to the City Hall, accompanied by a crowd of 5,000 people.

A few days later the new Governor, Sir Henry Moore, arrived unexpectedly and coming ashore, went directly to the fort, where he was admitted at the wicket. After the Council had assembled and his commission had been read, Moore ordered the gates to be opened. This greatly alarmed Colden, for a crowd was by this time surging around the fort, and he had no desire to have the scene of November 1 reenacted with himself in person taking the role of his effigy. But Moore calmed him by assuring him that if there was any violence he would "share the same fate with him." [29]

So the gates were thrown open, an announcer called out that all were at liberty to enter, and the crowd pushed in. They offered no violence to the 160 redcoats who were drawn up in the court, and taking off their hats when the new Governor appeared, listened in silence to the reading of the commission. Sir Henry and all the Council, save Colden, whose distrust of the mob had not yet been dispelled, now made their way through cheering throngs to the City Hall, where the ceremonies were concluded. That evening the people expressed their appreciation of the trust which Moore had shown in them, with bon-fires and illuminations.[30]

But while they thus toasted Sir Henry, they in no way relaxed their vigilance to prevent his executing the Stamp Act. Though they made no attempt to break into the City Hall to gain possession of the stamps deposited there, any others which fell into their hands were promptly destroyed. When it was bruited about the city that a sloop was coming in from Egg Harbor with a package of stamps from the ship *Ellis,* which had been wrecked off the Jersey coast, a crowd assembled. They had no trouble in gaining possession of the "royal contraband," and carting it off in triumph to the Coffee House, "purified" it by fire.[31]

In the meanwhile conditions in the city were becoming intolerable. Governor Moore, despite his policy of non-resistance, was determined to prohibit all activities for which the stamps were required. "I have absolutely refused the holding of any courts," he wrote Secretary Conway, "and as no vessel will be suffered to go out of the harbour, all their commerce must be inevitably ruined if they persevere in their obstinacy." [32] But persevere they did. "The people of the province seem to have such an aversion to taking the stamp papers, that they will sooner die than take them," wrote a New Yorker. "Our port is shut up, no vessel cleared out, no law, and no money circulating." [33]

Had the resistance to the Stamp Act been but the spontaneous movement of an unorganized mob, it would in time have burnt itself out. But it acted under the orders of able leaders. Of these the most influential was Isaac Sears. A shipmaster of long experience, a small merchant and a privateer of the French and Indian War who had acquired a reputation for daring and skill, he was regarded as a hero by the sailors and artisans of the city water front. Sears was a man of considerable property and owned a brick house on Queen Street two doors from the house of Robert R. Livingston. King Sears, the Tories called him, because of the power he exercised through the populace. Working with him, and equally determined, was John Lamb, an ardent patriot and later a general in Washington's army. Lamb had an especial grievance against the British Ministry, since the enforcement of the Molasses Act and the Sugar Act had ruined his lucrative trade with the French and Spanish West Indies. But his denunciations of the Stamp Act in burning speeches and well-written broadsides show that his chief concern was for American liberty.[34]

In February, 1765, when Grenville proposed the Stamp Act in Parliament, Colonel Isaac Barré, in a retort to Charles Townshend, called the Americans "Sons of Liberty." Jared Ingersoll, who sat in the gallery during the debates, quoted Barré in an account which was published in the London newspapers. Thereafter the patriots were universally termed Sons of Liberty, in ridicule by the Tories, reverently by all friends of freedom. In the critical years from 1765 to 1775, this group exerted a powerful influence in the colonies, practically controlling the press, intimidating the public officials, inflicting severe punishment upon Tories, and organizing resistance to the encroachments of the reactionary British government.

Despite the great influence of Sears, Lamb, McDougall and other Sons of Liberty, more moderate men represented New York at the Stamp Act Congress, which had been called to voice the united opposition of the colonies to the assault of the British Ministry upon American rights. Robert R. Livingston, Mayor John Cruger, Philip Livingston and Leonard Lispenard, men of wealth all of them, had too much at stake in the existing social order to carry things to extremes. But when the other delegates arrived and the meetings began in the recently repaired City Hall on Wall Street at the head of Broad, the New Yorkers were second to none in the cause of freedom. Leonard Lispenard was active in the debates, while it was John Cruger who penned the address to the House of Commons, protesting against taxation by Parliament, insisting upon the right of Americans to trial by jury, and declaring that the Stamp Act tended to overthrow "the rights and liberties of the colonies."

But while Congress petitioned, the New Yorkers acted. The visiting delegates had hardly set their faces homeward when several hundred merchants gathered at Burns' City Arms tavern on Broadway to organize resistance to the Stamp Act. A representative group it was, for side by side with bewigged merchant princes—the Livingstons, Bayards, Morrises—were small traders, men whose mercantile interests were confined to a shop on Dock Street or a share in a trading sloop.

There was general agreement that English goods should be boycotted. Over two hundred of those present pledged themselves to make all future orders conditional upon the repeal of the Stamp Act and to cancel "by the very first conveyance" those already sent. The retailers, for their part, promised to buy no merchandise shipped from the mother country after January 1.

But some of the prominent merchants who were prompt in joining in the boycott, drew back when they were asked to serve on the Committee of Correspondence, designed to keep the patriots in touch with men of like mind in other colonies. They had too much to lose to put themselves in the spotlight and so incur the frowns of the ministry. Not until Sears, Lamb and three other Sons of Liberty volunteered could the committees be filled.

At three o'clock on the morning of April 26, 1766, the people of New York were awakened by the clanging of all the bells in the city. When they rushed out into the streets to learn the cause of the "hideous din," they were told that a packet boat from England had arrived with the news of the repeal of the Stamp Act. That evening, at dusk, when the captain came ashore a great crowd met him at the wharf, placed him in a chair and carried him through cheering throngs to the post office. But when the mail was opened and it was found that the repeal had not yet had its third reading, the bells were silenced and the people dispersed.[35]

Several weeks later newsboys were distributing through the streets a broadside entitled "Joy to America," announcing that copies of the *London Gazette* which had come by way of Boston had fully confirmed the glorious news of the repeal. A few days later the city "blended in one festival" the celebration of the King's birthday and the release from the Stamp Act. That evening every house was illuminated, and the booming of guns from the warships was echoed by those on shore. On the Common beer and grog were handed out to the crowd, while two barbecued oxen provided meat for all. Nearby, in the spacious hall of the City Arms, Governor Moore, with a number of military and civil officers, was feasted at the expense of the city. The Reverend Mr. Laidlie made a congratulatory address, after which toasts were drunk to the King, to Pitt "the guardian of America," and to other "never-to-be-forgotten friends at home and abroad." After each toast a cannon was fired and the crowd outside cheered.[36]

The hero of the hour was Pitt. He it was who had opposed the Stamp Act, had befriended America, had proved himself the great champion of constitutional government. When William Davis presented to the city a portrait of this statesman "sat in an elegant and genteel frame," the Council voted him the freedom of the corporation.[37] The Assembly followed suit by resolving to erect a statue to Pitt, for his "many eminent and essential services," especially in promoting the repeal of the Stamp Act. To show their loyalty to the mother country they voted also to set up in the city an equestrian statue of King George.

It would have been well had Grenville, Lord North and other reactionary ministers realized that the affection of the colonists for the mother country gave them their strongest hold upon America. New Yorkers, New Englanders, Virginians alike were proud of Great Britain, boasted of her power, of her riches, of the extent of her empire, read English books, wore English made clothes, built their homes in the English style. To snap this bond of affection in a vain attempt to strengthen the political bond was an act of folly. But George III was not satisfied with loyalty, he insisted upon obedience, and the results were disastrous.

With the repeal of the Stamp Act life in New York for awhile became more normal. The well-to-do, as in former days, amused themselves with dancing, feasting, music and the theatre. Every two weeks there was a "dancing assembly" in the long room of the City Tavern, while for those not yet acquainted with the minuet or the reel a Mr. Le Gry opened a school at the sign of the Roebuck, in Horse and Cart Street.[38] Despite a chronic dispute between the Sons of Liberty and the British garrison, the people were glad to listen to a benefit concert for the "Royal American Band of Music." The John Street Theatre was reopened by permission of the Governor for a performance of *The Stratagem,* to which was added "a dramatic satire called *Lethe.*" [39] The audience enjoyed the acting of the American Company, despite the crudeness of the playhouse and the protests that at a time when the poor were in distress money should not be wasted on theatrical performances.[40]

For those who demanded less sophisticated entertainment, there was bull baiting over in the Bowery Lane, not far from the De Lancey Arms Tavern; [41] or cock-fighting in one of the side alleys; or tennis at the Sign of the Hurlers; or racing on the New Market Course on Hempstead Plains. At the upper end of Broadway, north of Reade Street, a certain John Jones had opened a pleasure garden at Ranelagh, formerly the country estate of Anthony Rutgers, and here every Monday and Thursday evening crowds came to see the fireworks "played off," listen to a concert, and stroll through the garden walks.[42] Less exciting, but more useful, was the regular drill of the Hand in Hand Fire Company, when the buckets, bags, belts, handbarrows and other equipment were carefully inspected.[43]

New York in the decade preceding the Revolution was a Dutch town slowly changing into a provincial English city. Visitors who attended services in the New Dutch Church, on Nassau Street, heard one Sunday the Reverend Lambertas de Ronde preach in Dutch, the next the Reverend Archibald Laidlie preach in English. Those who went, basket in hand, to shop at the Fish Market on Dock Street, or the Old Slip Market, found it difficult to make purchases unless they understood Dutch. The New Jersey farmer who for the first time stepped ashore at Albany Pier was bewildered to discover that "Dutch houses, Dutch goods, Dutch manners, Dutch words, Dutch men and Dutch lassies were much in vogue." [44]

But when he strolled up Broad Street the signs of increasing English influence became apparent. Here and there, it is true, he saw houses whose stepped or Flemish or concave gable-ends fronting on the street, recessed windows, colored brickwork and glazed tiles betrayed their Dutch origin. But beside them were other structures, with gambrel roofs, regularly spaced windows and classical doors "after the London taste." Rising over the roofs in the distance was the tower and spire of St. Paul's suggestive of Wren and Gibbs, while straight ahead facing Broad was the City Hall.[45]

But the city was by no means entirely English and Dutch. It was prophetic of its future that the Irish were numerous enough to celebrate St. Patrick's Day with a "very elegant breakfast" at Hull's Tavern, and the Jews to have their own place of worship and their own cemetery. The Germans had no less than four churches, the old Lutheran on Broadway, the New Lutheran, the German Reformed and the Moravian meeting house, on Fair Street. The Scots, who on Sundays sat with sober faces in the Presbyterian Church, on Wall Street, once a year forgot their piety at the hilarious feast of the Sons of St. Andrew.[46] Among the crowds on the wharves, or at the market, or on the streets, Negroes were so numerous as to "hurt the eyes of Europeans," who were unaccustomed to slavery. In short, New York in 1766 was almost as cosmopolitan as it is today.

It was also then as now a city of striking contrasts. Up some back

Top: New Amsterdam as it appeared in 1640 while still under the Dutch Government. A. The Fort. B. Church of St. Nicholas. C. The Jail. D. Governor's House. E. The Gallows. F. The Pillory. G. West India Company's Stores. H. City Tavern.

Right: The Canal in Broad Street.

Beekman Mansion near Turtle Bay on the Banks of the East River. This house, because of its fine situation and extensive gardens, was a favorite residence during the Revolution of a number of British commanders, among them General Howe.

Burn's Coffee House on Broadway, Headquarters of the Sons of Liberty.

New York in 1766–1767. This map, drawn by Bernard Ratzer and
engraved by Thomas Kitchin, was considered "the most beautiful,
important and accurate early plan of New York."

Fulton Ferry in 1740.

The Merchants Coffee House at the Corner of Wall and Water Streets, a popular place of assembly for committees protesting the policy of the British Government. The Coffee House is the corner building to the right.

Burning Stamps in New York. Riots expressing strong resentment
to the Stamp Act were common throughout the colonies.

The TIMES are
Dreadful,
Dismal,
Doleful,
Dolorous, and
Dollar-LESS.

An Emblem of the Effects of the STAMP.
O! the fatal Stamp.

Adieu Adieu to the LIBERTY of the PRESS.

Thursday, *October* 31, 1765.   THE   NUMB. 1195.

PENNSYLVANIA JOURNAL;
AND
WEEKLY ADVERTISER.

EXPIRING: In Hopes of a Resurrection to LIFE again.

I AM sorry to be obliged to acquaint my Readers, that as The STAMP-ACT, is fear'd to be obligatory upon us after the First of November ensuing, (the fatal To-morrow) the Publisher of this Paper unable to bear the Burthen, has thought it expedient to STOP a while, in order to deliberate, whether any Methods can be found to elude the Chains forged for us, and escape the insupportable Slavery; which it is hoped, from the last Representations now made against that Act, may be effected. Mean while, I must earnestly Request every Individual of my Subscribers, many of whom have been long behind Hand, that they would immediately Discharge their respective Arrears, that I may be able, not only to support myself during the Interval, but be better prepared to proceed again with this Paper, whenever an opening for that Purpose appears, which I hope will be soon. WILLIAM BRADFORD.

Glorious News.

BOSTON, Friday 11 o'Clock, 16th *May* 1766.
THIS Instant arrived here the Brig Harrison, belonging to *John Hancock*, Esq; Captain *Shubael Coffin*, in 6 Weeks and 2 Days from LONDON, with important News, as follows.

From the LONDON GAZETTE.

Westminster, March 18th, 1766.

THIS day his Majesty came to the House of Peers, and being in his royal robes seated on the throne with the usual solemnity, Sir Francis Molineux, Gentleman Usher of the Black Rod, was sent with a Message from his Majesty to the House of Commons, commanding their attendance in the House of Peers. The Commons being come thither accordingly, his Majesty was pleased to give his royal assent to

An ACT to REPEAL an Act made in the last Session of Parliament, intituled, an Act for granting and applying certain Stamp-Duties and other Duties in the British Colonies and Plantations in America, towards further defraying the expences of defending, protecting and securing the same, and for amending such parts of the several Acts of Parliament relating to the trade and revenues of the said Colonies and Plantations, as direct the manner of determining and recovering the penalties and forfeitures therein mentioned.

Also ten public bills, and seventeen private ones.

Yesterday there was a meeting of the principal Merchants concerned in the American trade, at the King's Arms tavern in Cornhill, to consider of an Address to his Majesty on the beneficial Repeal of the late Stamp-Act.

Yesterday morning about eleven o'clock a great number of North American Merchants went in their coaches from the King's Arms tavern in Cornhill to the House of Peers, to pay their duty to his Majesty, and to express their satisfaction at his signing the Bill for Repealing the American Stamp-Act, there was upwards of fifty coaches in the procession.

Last night the said gentleman dispatched an express for Falmouth, with fifteen copies of the Act for repealing the Stamp-Act, to be forwarded immediately for New York.

Orders are given for several merchantmen in the river to proceed to sea immediately on their respective voyages to North America, some of whom have been cleared out since the first of November last.

Yesterday messengers were dispatched to Birmingham, Sheffield, Manchester, and all the great manufacturing towns in England, with an account of the final decision of an august assembly relating to the Stamp-Act.

Top: Newspaper Reaction to the Stamp Act.

Left: Announcement of the Repeal of the Stamp Act.

The Tontine Coffee House and the East End of Wall Street. The two figures in the left foreground are John Jay and Robert R. Livingston.

alley, or on Cliff Street, or on Hedge Street, or out on Warren Street were little wooden houses where lived the poor—day laborers, carters, carpenters, dockhands, widows. Down on Water Street were several tenement houses of only five or six rooms each into which were crowded two, three or even four families.[47] In such houses filth, the heat of summer, the bitter cold of winter, impure drinking water and only too often improper or inadequate food made life hard and the mortality rate high. In times when trade was dull and unemployment widespread, the sheriff made frequent visits to these "slum" sections to carry off to the New Gaol in the Common those who had fallen into debt.[48]

Yet a few blocks away were the houses of the rich, stately mansions which would have done credit to Bath or to Berkeley Square. The poor man whose work took him down to the foot of Broadway must have viewed with envy and perhaps resentment the fine group of residences facing the Bowling Green—the Kennedy, the John Watts, the Livingston, the Stevens, the Van Cortlandt houses. No. 1 Broadway, erected by Archibald Kennedy in 1760, was typical of the others. Its classical front entrance, Palladian window, ornate cornice, spacious rooms, grand staircase, elaborately decorated walls and ceilings, its great banqueting hall bespoke both good taste and opulence.

Even more pretentious was the mansion built in 1754 by the wealthy merchant William Walton, on St. George's Square, which at that time was "well out of town." It is described as a brick edifice, fifty feet in front and three stories high, built with Holland bricks relieved by brown stone water tables, lentils and jambs, with walls as substantial as many modern churches. The staircase of the great hall, with its mahogany handrails and banisters, the front doorway with pilasters and broken pediment, the balustraded roof covered with tiles, the costly interior paneling would not have been out of place in a palace.[49]

Out in the nearby countryside there was not less magnificence than in the city, for it was customary for the successful merchant or government official or land speculator to purchase a farm on lower Manhattan, erect a mansion, lay out an elaborate garden, and cultivate the fields. The Bowery Lane and the Greenwich Road, the two chief highways leading out of the city, were lined with handsome estates. One had hardly got beyond the Out Ward on the former when one passed the country place of James De Lancey. North of this was the De Peyster farm; further on, were the residences of Nicholas, Gerardus and Peter

Stuyvesant, each approached by a long, tree-lined lane; next were the Tiebout and the James Duane estates. After turning right into the Kingsbridge or Boston road, one passed the country estate of John Watts on the right and the Robert Murray place on the left.

A ride up the Greenwich road would have been equally interesting. One passed first Vauxhall, and then, on the banks of the North River, the residence of Mr. George Harrison, Surveyor of Customs; next a foundry; and then to the right, perched on a hill, the country mansion of the merchant and alderman, Leonard Lispenard.[50] A mile further on was the Captain John Jauncey house, next the delightful mansion of William Bayard, and lastly the country home of Oliver De Lancey, later burnt by the Revolutionists.[51]

We catch a glimpse of life on these charming Manhattan estates by a bread and butter letter of Governor John Wentworth of New Hampshire to William Bayard, dated July 3, 1767. "Pray make my compliments acceptable to good Mrs. Bayard and the two young ladies . . . I wish [I were with you on] your piazza at Greenwich, remarking the pleasant views over to Hoebrick, discovering new prospects, examining the varied improvements of Mrs. Bayard's parterre, or turning over the music while Miss Bayard['s] harpsichord and voice calls our pleased attention from delightful scenes to better harmony." [52]

For the De Lanceys, Bayards, De Peysters and others whose country estates were situated in southern Manhattan, to move out from the city in the spring was fairly easy, since it required only a ride of an hour or so in the family coach. But for Chief Justice Robert R. Livingston, whose manor house "Clermont" was some eighty miles up the Hudson, it was a major undertaking, the journey consuming several days whether he moved his numerous family and his long train of servants by land or by water.[53]

Most of the stately mansions, both in the city and the country, were built by the merchant aristocracy. This group was composed in part of families long distinguished in the history of the colony, in part of those who had risen from the lower ranks in recent years through successful business ventures or by smuggling during the French and Indian War. But though a Stuyvesant or a De Peyster might turn his nose up at some of the upstarts, the group was knit together, not only by like interests, but by intermarriage. And their influence was out of all proportion to their numbers.

Cadwallader Colden stated that their only aim in life was to get money, yet some of them spared enough time from their counting houses to take a leading part in city and provincial politics. The De Lanceys especially, with the backing of most of their fellow merchants, for many years directed the fortunes of the colony. A combination of astute leadership, power politics, and corrupt practices was the secret of their success. There were hundreds of voters—small shopkeepers, sea captains, cabinetmakers, carpenters—who looked to the De Lanceys or the Waltons or the Bayards for jobs or for patronage. If an artisan, at one of the *viva voce* elections, called out the name of a candidate opposed to the interests of the merchant group, the orders for silverware, or furniture, or wigs might come to a sudden end. In 1770 a law was proposed to introduce the secret ballot in order "to prevent men of property, power and tyrannical dispositions [from] . . . intimidating the electors from a free disposal of their votes," but unfortunately it failed of adoption.[54]

If the voter could not be intimidated, he might see the light if he were offered a bribe. One indignant citizen stated, in 1768, that at a certain dram shop "every freeholder or freeman, who was willing to part with his vote, might there meet with a purchaser." [55] "How often have the votes of the people been purchased . . . without the least endeavor to conceal the bribery?" exclaimed one editor. To hand out free drinks so as to get the voter drunk, he thought "a perillous invasion of our constitutional rights." [56]

When the British Ministry and Parliament made their assault upon the colonial Assemblies by levying taxes without their consent, the wealthy merchants were as deeply concerned as the man in the street. Since they had long controlled the New York Assembly, they could not wish to have its power sheared. But they feared mob rule, they did not want to surrender their leadership to what they termed "demagogues," they dreaded an internal social and political revolution. Above all they wished to avoid open hostilities with Great Britain, for they had visions of the royal frigates' blockading New York Harbor or chasing their merchantmen from the seas, or of the Ministry's excluding them from the ports of the mother country or of the British West Indies. In the end, when they had to choose between King and country, most of the large merchants, though as resentful as ever at the assault on American liberty, threw in their lot with the British.

The political supremacy of the merchants was strongly contested by a group led by great landed proprietors and able lawyers. This party drew to its standards those who wished to curb the King's prerogative, end corruption and favoritism in the government, and restrain the power of the Anglican Church. The dissenting congregations—Presbyterians, Dutch Reformed, German Reformed, Methodists, etc.— deeply resented the fact that they were taxed to support the Episcopal establishment. No doubt the Reverend Samuel Auchmuty, the rector of Trinity, was a very good man; but this was no reason why they should have to pay part of his salary. They resented, moreover, the control which the Anglicans exercised over the newly founded King's College, and the recent attempts to establish an American bishopric.

Led by a triumvirate of young lawyers—William Livingston, William Smith, Jr., and John Morin Scott—the party for years waged a war of pamphlets with the De Lanceys. It would seem that these young writers borrowed some of their ideas from the French intellectuals, but Colden placed the "blame" on Yale. "For some years past three popular lawyers educated in Connecticut, who have strongly imbibed the independent principles of that country, calumniate the administration in every exercise of the prerogative, and get the applause of the mob by propagating the doctrine that all authority is derived from the people." [57]

Livingston, who was the most active of the trio, was a man of wide learning, political acumen and keen insight into human nature. The biting sarcasm of his articles in the *Independent Reflector* made his opponents writhe.[58] The tall, slight, graceful lawyer, with his powdered wig, his velvet coat, embroidered ruffles, silk stockings and gold buckles, became the most talked of man in New York. The "razor blade," the ladies called him, perhaps because of his thin face and aquiline nose, perhaps because of the sharpness of his wit.

"Will," Lieutenant Governor James De Lancey is reported to have said to him upon meeting him in the street one day, "you would be the cleverest fellow in the world if you were only one of us."

"I will try to be a clever fellow and not be one of you," was the reply.[59]

In the elections of 1759 and of 1761 the Livingston party won the victory, and for several years were the controlling force in the colony. The lawyers "rule the House of Assembly," complained Colden. "Every man is afraid of offending them and is deterred from making any public opposition to their power and the daily increase of it." [60]

It was only in 1768 that the apprehension of all property holders at the growing power of the populace caused many of the Livingston party to shift over to the De Lanceys and once more gave the merchants control of the Assembly.

Like other American commercial cities New York possessed a vigorous and prosperous middle class, artisans, most of them. Colden thought that they constituted the strength of the province, but only too often were the dupes of the lawyers and merchants. Certainly the politician who hoped for success at the polls had to have their support, since they constituted the bulk of the voters. The man who wished to enjoy the suffrage had only to appear in court with proof that he owned an estate of 40 pounds, or that he plied one of a designated list of occupations. In October, 1765, no less than 216 men, most of them mechanics, or leather aprons as they were called, were accorded the franchise, while perhaps as many more were forced to wait another opportunity, the "Court being tired and not having time for it."

Despite this comparatively liberal policy, the bulk of the population, the freeholders of Liliput, as one writer called them, were denied the suffrage. Day laborers, sailors, dock workers, apprentices, servants, carters, they were the sansculottes of the American Revolution, the material from which Sears, McDougall and Lamb recruited their mobs. How clearly they understood the issues involved in the contention with the mother country is a matter of doubt, but they obviously enjoyed the power which it gave them. One suspects that they were more concerned with local social and political reforms than with the rights of a provincial legislature in which they were not represented. As the "rabble" streamed through the streets of New York during the Stamp Act riots, shouting for liberty, the bewigged aristocrats who looked from the windows of their mansions wondered whether the chief threat were not to their own privileges, wealth and power.

For this reason at least some of them, who had resented bitterly the Sugar Act and the Stamp Act, heaved a sigh of relief when in June, 1766, transports arrived bearing the 28th and 46th regiments of British regulars. As for Colden, his joy and relief were unfeigned. The populace would no longer dare defy the government, no longer dangle his effigy from a gallows and threaten to storm the fort. A proclamation declaring that disobedience to the laws would be treated as rebellion, he thought, would now bring the people to submission.[61]

When the British officers gave a "grand entertainment and ball," at the York Arms, it attracted "the most numerous and brilliant" assembly in the history of the city.[62]

But the "entertainment" accorded the rank and file by the Sons of Liberty and the lower classes was of an entirely different nature, marked as it was by abusive language and the hurling of brickbats. The people bitterly resented the presence of the troops. They are kept here, not to protect but to enslave us, they declared. They are the enemies of liberty, the hirelings of tyrants.

Perhaps it was the consciousness that they were unwelcome guests which prompted some of the soldiers to cut down the Liberty Pole on the Common. The pole, with "a large board fixed on it" bearing the inscription "George III, Pitt and Liberty," had been set up in May, 1766, as a part of the celebration of the repeal of the Stamp Act. To the Sons of Liberty it was a sacred symbol of their battle for American rights. So, when they woke up on the morning of August 11, to find it prostrate, and the word was passed around that some of the soldiers quartered in the barracks nearby were responsible, they were greatly enraged.[63]

Immediately they set to work to raise the pole again, while the "leather aprons," deserting their shops or laying aside their tools, poured out on the Common. Seeing a British drummer passing by, the crowd began to revile him and then to beat him. A corporal rushed up to his assistance, but both he and the drummer might have been seriously injured had not a body of soldiers emerged from the barracks. There ensued a brief battle, marked by bayonet thrusts on one side and volleys of oaths and brickbats on the other. And when, at the command of their officers, the redcoats retired to their barracks, the mob surrounded the building, shouting defiance and damning the soldiers with the choicest bits of billingsgate.[64]

This was the beginning of a feud which lasted for years. To cut down the Liberty Pole became for the soldiers a standing challenge; to protect it was for the Sons of Liberty a sacred duty. The second pole had been standing but a few weeks when it came down. The very next day a third took its place.[65] This one stood, its ensign flapping defiance across the Common to the barracks, until March, 1767, when it suffered the fate of its predecessors. That the fourth pole survived for several years was due to the fact that it was girded by iron bars held in place by metal hoops. In March, 1767, the soldiers tried to cut it down, then to undermine it, then to blow it up, but each effort failed.[66]

Thus matters stood until January, 1770, when the soldiers again tried to destroy the pole. They had sawed through the iron braces and bored a hole in the wood which they filled with powder, when some persons at Montagne's Tavern across Broadway from the Common discovered them. Thereupon, they left the pole and with swords drawn rushed in the tavern, beat the waiter, broke lamps and bowls, smashed the windows and drove the patrons pell mell out of the windows. A few days later another and more successful attempt was made. "Availing themselves of the dead hours of night," they brought the pole down, hacked it to pieces and left the fragments at the door of the tavern.[67]

The erection of the fifth pole was delayed for several weeks by the refusal of the city corporation to give permission for it to stand in the Common. Whereupon Isaac Sears purchased a small lot nearby, where, on February 6, 1770, the new pole was set up. It was 58 feet long, with a top mast of 22 feet, was cased in iron bars laid lengthwise and fastened with large flat rivets and iron hoops. When all was ready it was bedecked with flags and ribbons, and drawn by six horses from the shipyards to the Common, accompanied by several thousand persons. As it slid into the twelve-foot hole which had been dug for it, the band struck up "God Save the King," and the workmen proceeded to brace it with timbers, great staves and earth.[68] This time, the pole, with its gilt vane spelling out the word "Liberty," stood until October 28, 1776, when the British, after their capture of the city, removed it.[69]

In the meanwhile, serious trouble was brewing in England. When the Stamp Act was repealed Parliament made it clear that they relinquished none of their authority over the colonies, and George III and his Ministry were still harping upon "obedience" and "dutiful submission." There was no occasion for surprise, then, when in June and July, 1767, Parliament passed a series of repressive measures introduced by Charles Townshend, Chancellor of the Exchequer. A Board of Customs Commissioners was created to enforce the trade laws; duties were placed on paints, paper, glass and tea imported into the colonies; the Assembly of New York was denied its legislative function until it had complied with the Billeting Act.

The Billeting Act required the Assembly of each colony to provide quarters, food and drink for British troops stationed in its territory. Against this bill the New Yorkers demurred. They had already been at greater expense than any other colony in supplying the troops, they said. They were willing to assist the forces while on the march through the colony, but to assume responsibility for their expenses during a whole year would establish a ruinous precedent. When Moore reported this answer to the British government, Townshend, then at the height of his power, decided to make an example of the New Yorkers. So the Mutiny Act, requiring the Governor to veto all legislation until the Assembly complied fully with the Billeting Act, was pushed through Parliament.

Although in the election of 1768 the conservative De Lancey-merchant-Anglican party had gained control of the Assembly, there was no thought of submitting tamely to this act. As the members gathered in the City Hall there was much shaking of heads, many heated discussions by groups in the arcade or in the hallways. If a mere vote of Parliament can deprive the colony of representative government, we may as well go home and acknowledge ourselves slaves. So when they convened they stated their case in no uncertain terms. "This colony . . . enjoys an integral legislature of its own, in which the crown and the people of the colony are constitutionally represented . . . the power and authority of the said legislature cannot lawfully . . . be suspended, abridged, abrogated or annulled by any power . . . whatsoever." [70] Thereupon Governor Moore, in a message chiding them for calling the supremacy of Great Britain into question, dissolved the Assembly.[71]

An exciting election followed. When John Morin Scott, one of the Livingston-lawyer-dissenter candidates, was reported to have called the New York Germans firebrands, they all resolved to vote with firebrands in their hands—against him. When someone said that the Irish had come over "upon a bunch of straw," they began wearing straw in their hats. Sentiment was worked up against the lawyers in a series of broadsides. They had not joined in the resistance to the Stamp Act; it was wrong for the same persons to be makers and interpreters of the law; a mercantile city should be represented by merchants rather than lawyers.

In this way the De Lancey group beclouded the real issue and swept the election. Thus at the moment when a liberal Assembly was sorely needed to resist the continued encroachments of the British

Ministry, a group of conservatives, many of whom later became Tories, were placed in power. Though they soon earned the hatred of the patriots in other colonies and the scorn of their own constituents, it was impossible to get rid of them, since the governors were careful not to dissolve them. So they continued to misrepresent New York until forced out of power by the Revolution.

When they met on November 22, 1769, Colden, who upon the death of Governor Moore a few weeks before had again taken the reins of government, told them that the funds for the support of the garrison had been exhausted and asked for another appropriation. Had the Assembly lived up to its brave protest of December 31, 1767, it would have refused to give a penny until the Mutiny Act had been repealed. Instead, it voted 2,000 pounds.[72]

This craven action was received in the city of New York with incredulity. A huge gathering in the Common voiced its disapproval, while a volley of broadsides lashed the Assemblymen for their betrayal of the rights of the people. An anonymous writer in a broadside addressed to "the betrayed inhabitants" declared that the pusillanimous conduct of the Assembly at a time when the minions of despotism were laying every snare their wicked hearts could suggest to enslave a free people, made it obvious that they had gone over to the enemy. Since the troops had been sent to America to enforce the tyrannical decrees of the British Parliament, it was folly for a free people to grant them any supplies whatsoever.[73]

This so enraged the Assembly that they offered a reward of 100 pounds for the discovery of the author, and when the printer and his journeyman accused Alexander McDougall, that fiery Son of Liberty was lodged in jail, charged with publishing a libel against the government. "He is a person of some fortune and could easily have found the bail required of him," wrote Colden to Secretary Hillsborough, "but he chose to go to jail, and lies there imitating Mr. Wilkes in everything he can." [74]

In fact the Sons of Liberty openly proclaimed McDougall the "Wilkes of America." And since it was No. 45 of the *North Briton* in which Wilkes had criticised the British government, and for which he had been prosecuted, the number 45 became the symbol of this new struggle for freedom of speech. A "female friend of American liberty" called on McDougall in prison to present him with a fine saddle of venison marked with 45, forty-five Sons of Liberty marched to the jail to shake his hand, at the dinner in celebration of the repeal of the Stamp Act forty-five "loyal and patriotic toasts were drank." So constant was the stream of people who came to condole the prisoner and to ask his advice and directions, that the jail became the headquarters for the resistance movement in New York.[75] The governor and the Assembly, finding that they were making a hero of McDougall, heartily wished that they had ignored his broadside, and when the chief witness died, quietly let the case drop.

The resentment of the people at the Mutiny Act and the Assembly's submission was intensified by the renewal of the attempt of Parliament to tax the Americans. Wealthy merchants, shopkeepers, artisans, lawyers, lowly "leather aprons" alike resented the placing of duties on glass, painters' colors, lead, paper and tea, as a threat to American liberty. That the revenue from these levies was to be kept in America to support the provincial governments, so far from mollifying them, redoubled their opposition. If the governors could look to England for their salaries, rather than as heretofore to the Assemblies, their power would be vastly increased. In the tap rooms of the taverns, in the Merchants Coffee House, in the counting rooms, in the homes of rich and poor alike, angry men denounced this latest assault on their rights and vowed never to submit. We will buy not one crate of British goods, they said, until the Townshend Acts are repealed.

Even the Assembly plucked up courage enough to protest. An exact equality of constitutional rights should be maintained in every part of the empire, they declared, and therefore, just as it would be illegal to tax the people of Great Britain without the consent of their representatives in Parliament, so it was illegal to tax the Americans without the consent of their Assemblies.[76]

When word passed around that vessels from London had come in with English wares, a committee of merchants gave orders that every crate should be stored away unopened.[77] At the same time they issued an appeal to all patriotic citizens to hold the line. They hoped, they said, that all persons whatever, the ladies in particular, "whose conduct may have great influence," would treat those who for selfish reasons broke through the boycott, with the scorn they deserved, "let their station in life be what it will." [78]

But experience soon showed that it required something more than the scorn of the ladies to make certain dealers conform. Alexander Robertson, for smuggling British goods in by way of Philadelphia, was forced to make a public apology.[79] Thomas Richardson, another offender, was ordered to stand on a scaffold near the liberty pole, to ask pardon for his offense and promise for the future to keep his "contraband" under lock and key.[80]

The case of a certain Simon Cooley, "haberdasher, jeweller and silversmith," from London, aroused especial resentment. When it was first discovered that Cooley had imported English goods, he escaped censure by vowing that they had arrived long before the boycott started and by agreeing to put them in store. But later he plucked up courage to throw off the mask, bid defiance to the Sons of Liberty, openly sell his wares and send orders to England for more. Thereupon he was denounced in the press as "a vile ingrate," a knave, and a liar. Fearing violence to his person, he secured a file of soldiers to stand guard before his door, and refused to stir when summoned to answer for his conduct before a crowd of citizens in the Common. And when General Gage removed the guard and word came that a mob was moving on his house, he decided that it would be the part of prudence "to decamp to the fort." In the end he yielded, going with shaking knees to the Common, where he implored pardon and promised solemnly to store his goods.[81]

In the meanwhile, every packet which reached the city from England brought rumors that the Townshend Acts would soon be repealed. At the same time their English friends warned the patriots not to be caught off guard. "Don't give too much credit to men who would, if they dare, enslave both you and the people of England," wrote a Londoner. Stick to your guns until the revenue acts are repealed and all your grievances redressed. This is your opportunity to secure your liberty; seize it.[82]

Despite warnings of this kind, hopes were running high in New York until it became known early in 1770 that even though other duties should be removed, that on tea would certainly be retained.[83] So, when definite word arrived that the tea tax had been continued as a token of British sovereignty in the colonies, no one was surprised. But though Parliament thus served notice that it had by no means given up its efforts to force its will upon the Americans, the repeal of the Townshend Acts marked the beginning of a lull in the struggle. When, several years later, the smouldering fires of discontent burst into the flames of open resistance, the quarrel with the mother country assumed a new and more serious character which led straight to war.

CHAPTER II

REVOLUTION

WITH THE repeal of the Townshend Acts there ensued a welcome though deceptive lull in the struggle between the British government and the colonies. Many of the leading men of New York—wealthy merchants, the more ardent of the Anglicans, lawyers, office holders—were inclined to accept the apparent olive branch held out by the British government. Whenever two or more met the repeal of the Townshend Acts was the topic of conversation. Would it not be wise to respond to this important concession by withdrawing the boycott on all British goods save tea? Had not the interruption of commerce hurt New York as much as Great Britain? Would not its continuance mean ruin? Would this not be a good opportunity to put an end to the agitation of the Sons of Liberty and to the rule of the mob?

So it was decided to "take the sense of the city." A number of gentlemen went from house to house to ask, "Do you approve of a general importation of goods from Great Britain except tea, provided Boston and Philadelphia concur?" Had this been voted on at a mass meeting in the Common, there would have been a thunderous "No." But so afraid were the shopkeepers and artisans of offending the "great men" of the city that when the proposition was put to them individually they voted for it. "I am told that 1,800, among which are the principal inhabitants, declared for importation, about 300 were neutral or unwilling to declare their sentiments, and a few of any distinction declared in opposition to it," Colden wrote the Earl of Hillsborough.[1]

That Colden minimized the opposition is shown by the violent protests of the Sons of Liberty. The breaking of the non-importation agreement would be a base desertion of the other colonies, they declared, it would make New York infamous, it would be the means of enslaving the whole continent.

26

These sentiments were echoed throughout the colonies. "Can it be possible that men who have soared so high . . . should at once sink so low as to become the contempt and derision of every individual?" a Virginian wrote a friend in New York. "But I hope it is not possible that for a mess of pottage you should sell your invaluable liberties and entail the curse of slavery upon your descendants forever." [2] The people of Connecticut thought it astonishing that New Yorkers, who had been the first to sign the agreement, should now "flinch" and "turn back." [3] The merchants of Boston and Philadelphia "unanimously and absolutely" rejected the proposal, being "resolutely determined firmly to adhere to the non-importation agreement as it stands." [4]

But the New York merchants were neither to be shamed nor intimidated. Again they went through the farce of a referendum, this time as to whether they should renounce the boycott even though other cities demurred. And though a group of radicals followed the poll takers from door to door, "insulting and abusing" them, and urging the people to refuse to vote, 794 gave their voices for a resumption to trade. On the evening of the day this poll was taken, Sears and McDougall headed a protest procession, which marched through the principal streets, with bands blaring, colors flying, and with "Liberty" and "Non-importation" placards held aloft. When the magistrates tried to interfere they were set upon with sticks, clubs and stones and put to rout.[5]

A few weeks later the packet *Earl of Halifax* moved down the harbor and headed for Falmouth, taking with her orders for all kinds of merchandise save tea. A day or two earlier messengers had taken horse for Boston and Philadelphia to apprise the merchants of those cities of this action. As one of them was passing through Princeton, the students of the college seized his letter, and to the tolling of the bell in Nassau Hall, took it to the front campus, where the hangman burnt it as a warning "to all betrayers of their country." [6]

But though the letter went up in flames the news it contained was not long in reaching Philadelphia. "We cannot forbear telling you," the Quaker City merchants wrote to the New Yorkers, "however you may color your proceedings, we think you have in the day of trial deserted the cause of liberty and your country." [7] A few days later came another letter which must have made the New Yorkers wince. "The inhabitants of the city of Philadelphia present their compliments to the inhabitants of New York and beg they will send them their old Liberty Pole, as they imagine they can, by their late conduct, have no further use for it." [8]

But the die having been cast there was little that the patriots, either of other cities or of New York, could do about it. After all the British goods were desperately needed. So for some months things quieted down and the normal course of life was interrupted only by the arrival of a new governor, an occasional fire, the celebration of the King's birthday, reviews of the British garrison, horse races at Paulus Hook, and launchings at the Totten and Crossfield shipyards.

Early in June, 1770, the *Britannia* arrived with the long expected statues of George III and William Pitt. Permission was granted by the city to have the statue of the King set up in Bowling Green, and crowds gathered there daily as the workmen built the pedestal and lifted the gilt figures of horse and rider in place. It was said that the sculptor had taken as his model the statue of Marcus Aurelius in Rome.[9]

The unveiling took place on August 16, 1770. The members of the Provincial Council, Assemblymen, the city magistrates, the British officers, the clergy of various denominations and other prominent citizens gathered at the fort, to join Lieutenant Governor Colden in drinking the King's health, amid the firing of cannon and the strains of the military band. Then, forming in procession, the group crossed over to the green, where they made their way through the cheering crowd to circle the statue and then return to the fort.[10]

A few weeks later the figure of Pitt was "fixed on the pedestal erected for it" in Wall Street, "amid the acclamations" of a crowd which filled all the adjacent streets. The image was of white marble. It showed Pitt in a Roman toga, his left arm extended, in his right hand a partly unrolled scroll, bearing the inscription "Articuli Magna Charta Libertatum." [11]

People were still discussing the relative merits of the two statues and of the men they represented when interest was diverted by the arrival of the new governor, John, Earl of Dunmore. As he stepped ashore at the Whitehall Slip, Colden and the members of the Council shook hands with him, accompanied him to the fort and then to dinner at the Province Arms Tavern. The next day, after he had taken the oath of office, he went to the City Hall, where he appeared on the balcony as his commission was read.[12]

The New Yorkers were not long in discovering that this Scottish nobleman, who later as Revolutionary governor of Virginia won the detestation of the people of that province, was entirely unsuited for the post to which he had been appointed. "This poor creature exposes himself daily," wrote William Smith. "How can the dignity of government be maintained by so helpless a mortal, utterly ignorant of business of all kinds?" At the feast of the Sons of St. Andrew, Dunmore got drunk, and in the words of Colonel John Bradstreet, who was present, acted like "a damned fool." Not only was he noisy in giving the toasts, but "sank himself" so low with the vilest language that the entire company was abashed.[13] So when word came that Dunmore had been ordered to Virginia and that Governor William Tryon, of North Carolina, would succeed him in New York, there was general satisfaction.

Yet Tryon's arrival was attended with little ceremony. Dunmore and Oliver De Lancey went down to the Narrows to meet him and escorted him in an oyster boat to the landing. At the fort John Smith, brother of Judge William Smith, found "Dunmore walking the room and reading a newspaper and Tryon another," while Mrs. Tryon sat neglected on a sofa. The next day Tryon took the oath of office. At the reading of the commission there was no "signal of joy" and no huzzas until "the mayor ordered it." [14]

That evening at a farewell dinner for Dunmore, the retiring governor "took too cheerful a glass, and forced it upon the company." This seems to have unloosened his fists as well as his tongue, for he squared off, not only against Charles Ward Apthorpe, a member of the Council, but against Colonel Edmund Fanning, Tryon's secretary, who no doubt showed his resentment when Dunmore called Tryon a coward. My Lord was free in expressing his resentment at being transferred to Virginia. "Damn Virginia," he cried. "Why is it forced on me? I asked for New York. New York I love and they have robbed me of it." [15]

Reports of this debauch enlivened conversation in the drawing rooms of the rich, but the lower classes found excitement in events more spectacular if less scandalous. In March, 1770, fire broke out in a large wooden building on Ann Street, where the St John's Lodge of Masons held their meetings. The fire company appeared on the scene, armed with engines, ladders and buckets, but the narrowness of the streets and the distance from the rivers which made it difficult to bring water, for a time baffled their efforts. The fire "burnt with great fury, carrying everything before it," until at last when seventeen houses had been destroyed, it was brought under control.[16]

Less exciting, but equally spectacular, was the military review held on the Common, in December, 1772, before Governor Tryon, and "a splendid assembly of the principal ladies and gentlemen" of the city. The newly formed companies of militia were the object of especial interest, and won great applause by the "neatness of their uniforms," and the "regularity" and skill with which they went through the maneuvres. "After the review was concluded Governor Tryon tendered the officers a splendid entertainment." [17]

A few months later the governor again reviewed the militia as a part of the celebration of the King's birthday. That evening the city was illuminated, while from one of the bastions of the fort and from the Bowling Green "curious fireworks were played off." A great crowd looked on in wonder at the representation of an engagement between two ships, with furious broadsides and the final sinking of one of the vessels. Among the assemblage at the fort were many ladies who, the editor of the *Journal* was convinced, "must have been delightful to his Majesty himself had he been present," and convinced him that America vied with Great Britain "in the charms of beauty and female attractions." [18]

The people of New York learned with regret that General Gage was preparing to return to England, for he had won their gratitude by his tact and the reins which he put upon the garrison. On May 27, many of the merchants and others tendered him "an elegant entertainment" at Hull's Tavern. Among the guests was George Washington, who had come to New York to enter his stepson, John Park Custis, in King's College, and who no doubt seized the opportunity to exchange reminiscences with Gage of the terrible defeat inflicted on Braddock's army by the French and Indians eighteen years before. On the day of Gage's departure the chief military officers escorted him to Murray's Wharf at the foot of Wall Street, where a company of the Royal Artillery stood at attention. As his ship got under way the gunners discharged a farewell salute, which was echoed from the Battery as it passed out of East River into the harbor.[19]

The winter of 1772–1773 was bitterly cold, the ice in East River being so firm that many people walked over to Long Island and back, and in the humble homes of the poor the suffering was so great that

Governor Tryon ordered the distribution of 100 cords of firewood.[20] The coming of spring brought not only the relief of milder weather but the return of the American Company of Players, who in May presented *The Tempest* "to a numerous and brilliant audience with universal applause." [21] In September interest centered in the laying of the first stone of the new hospital on Broadway between Duane and Anthony Streets.[22] In July General Haldimand, who had succeeded Gage as commander of the garrison, reviewed the Welsh Fusileers "in the plain near the shipyards." The soldiers wore sprigs of oak leaves in their caps, an insigne the regiment had used at the battle of Minden, where they had distinguished themselves.[23]

In the meanwhile Tryon was making a good record as governor. Having got rid of Dunmore, the people were in the humor to give his successor every reasonable support. Tryon, for his part, wished only the good of the province and was wary of aligning himself with any faction. He refused to be "the dupe of the Assembly or Council," on the one hand, or "steer by the popular voice," on the other. Although he found this course difficult, since he had many "insolent requests" from various groups, he managed to avoid serious difficulties until the British Ministry, by one of its worst blunders, forced his hand.

On May 5, 1773, the King signed an act giving the East India Company a monopoly of the tea trade to the American colonies. The tea had first to come to Great Britain, where formerly it had paid a heavy duty, which, of course, was passed on to the consumers. But now this was rebated on that part of the crop shipped to America, so that despite the three pence to be paid on every pound when it arrived in the colonies, the price was reduced by one half. This, it was thought, would tempt the Americans to buy tea and so give tacit consent to the right of Parliament to tax them, would produce a revenue from which the salaries of the governors could be paid, would put an end to the smuggling of tea from Holland and relieve the East India Company of its financial difficulties.

The actual result was far different. The merchants, alarmed at the revival of the ancient principle of the monopoly and angered at the threat to their illegal trade, once more joined hands with the Sons of Liberty in violent protests and measures of resistance. "A new flame is apparently kindling in America," wrote William Smith in his *Diary*. "We have intelligence that the East India Company resolved to send tea to America to be sold, they paying the duty on importation . . .

That Mr. Pigon, of London, had then chartered a ship to carry 300 chests to Boston, 600 to New York and as many to Philadelphia . . . The fact is that ever since the duty of 3ᵈ a pound was laid . . . all tea had been smuggled from Holland . . . and now the Sons of Liberty and the Dutch smugglers set up the cry of liberty . . . virtue and vice being thus united I suppose we shall repeat all the confusions of 1765 and 1766 . . . Our domestic parties will probably die and be swallowed up in the general opposition to the Parliamentary project of raising the arm of government by revenue laws." [24]

A few days after Smith wrote these words, an excited group jammed into the State House in Philadelphia to protest against the Tea Act. The disposal of their own property was the inherent right of freemen, they declared, the use of the returns of the duty on tea for the support of government had a direct tendency to render Assemblies useless and introduce arbitrary rule and slavery, the attempt of the East India Company to send their tea to America was a violent attack upon the liberties of the people and whoever abetted them by unloading, receiving or selling the tea should be stigmatized as an enemy of his country.[25]

These sentiments were echoed in New York. On October 6, a folio leaflet was issued called "The Alarm," denouncing both the Ministry and the East India Company. When it was reported that a certain William Kelley, then in London, had encouraged the sending of tea to America, his effigy, suspended from a gallows with a tea canister before him, was drawn through the streets and then burnt in front of the coffee house.[26] On November 27 a broadside, signed "The Mohawks," declared that the Americans were "determined not to be enslaved by any power on earth," so that anyone who should offer his warehouse for the reception of tea, which they termed "the infernal chains," could expect an unwelcome visit from them.[27]

As the date for the expected arrival of the tea ship *Nancy* approached, there was a division of opinion as to whether she should be turned around and sent back with her cargo untouched, or whether the tea should be landed and stored. On December 17, the governor and Council met to debate the question, while several thousand people waited impatiently at the City Hall for their decision. Tryon sent them word that he favored storing the tea, which he proposed to do openly, and urged them not to disgrace the city by destroying it. To this proposal the assemblage made no reply, though the leading Sons of Liberty were confident that had a vote been taken, it would have been three to one against it. But they chose a new Committee of Correspondence to cooperate with the other colonies in resistance to the Tea Act.[28]

Such was the situation when Paul Revere came riding into town with the news of the Boston Tea Party, in which a number of men, disguised as Indians, had gone on board one of the tea ships and dumped the cargo overboard.[29] "The Boston news astonished the town," wrote William Smith. "Those who were for storing the tea now affect to change sentiments . . . [and] intreat the governor to change his resolutions for fear of the multitude." To persuade Tryon proved an easy matter. He prided himself on the good order preserved in the city during his administration, and he had no desire to have this record broken by a local tea party.[30]

In the meanwhile week after week passed and the anxious look-outs at Sandy Hook waited in vain for the *Nancy*. They learned later that the tea ship had been delayed by a succession of gales which had driven her temporarily from the coast, snapped her anchor chain, and sent her top mast and mizzen mast overboard. At that she had been lucky, the New Yorkers thought, since she had "on board something worse than a Jonah." [31]

By the time the ship limped up to Sandy Hook, Tryon had left on a visit to England, and Cadwallader Colden, now eighty-seven years old, once more assumed the reins of government. Colden, as an ardent loyalist, was most anxious to have the cargo safely landed, but the force at his command was entirely inadequate for its protection. When the master, Captain Lockyer, came up to the city in the pilot boat to take on supplies he was followed by a threatening throng of people who kept an eye on his every movement. So he was not a little relieved when the merchants to whom the tea had been consigned refused to receive it.[32]

At this moment word was received that the ship *London* was approaching the Hook, with eighteen boxes of tea on board. About four o'clock on the afternoon of April 22, the vessel came in and tied up at the wharf. Immediately a number of citizens went on board to question the captain, James Chambers, concerning the "contraband." Chambers at first denied that his cargo included tea, but when he learned that committees had been appointed to open every package, he confessed his "guilt." This news was passed on to "The Mohawks," who now prepared at an appointed hour in the night to dump the tea overboard.

But the New York Tea Party was destined to be more open than its famous Boston counterpart. At eight o'clock in the evening the crowd which filled the wharf became impatient, and a number of men, scorning disguise, went on board the *London*. Bringing up the boxes of tea, they broke them open and dumped their contents into the river. "Several persons of reputation" were stationed about the companionway and in the hold to see that no damage was done to the ship nor to her legitimate cargo, and no violence offered to Captain Chambers. Two hours later all was over and the crowd dispersed.[33]

The next day at eight in the morning all the church bells rang out, colors were run up by the vessels in the harbor and a large flag was hoisted on the liberty pole. An hour later the greatest crowd of people the city had ever known collected in lower Wall Street. At nine-fifteen, some of the leading patriots emerged from the Coffee House with Captain Lockyer, and the band struck up "God Save the King." There was a call for Captain Chambers. "Where is he? Captain Lockyer must not go until we find Captain Chambers to send him with the tea ship." But Chambers, deserting his own vessel, was already on his way to the Hook in a small boat, where he went aboard the *Nancy*, thankful to escape with a whole skin.[34]

In the meanwhile the crowd in Wall Street conducted Lockyer to Murray's wharf, where he went on board the pilot boat amid huzzas and the firing of cannon. Awaiting him at the Hook was not only his own ship, but a sloop with a Committee of Observation on board. A few days later, with the springing up of a favorable breeze, the *Nancy* weighed anchor and stood out to sea, the sloop at her heels. When they were three leagues off the Hook the Committee, judging that Lockyer and Chambers and the unwelcome cargo were well on their way to London, bade them good-bye, turned about and headed back to the city.[35]

Two weeks after these exciting events the ship *Samson,* from London, arrived with the alarming news of the passage of the Boston Port Bill. Parliament had decided to punish Boston for what they termed "the violent and outrageous proceedings" in that city, by closing the port to all commerce, until the people had compensated the owners of the tea they had destroyed and given promises of future good behavior. "We want language to express our abhorrence of this additional act of tyranny to America," wrote Isaac Sears.[36] Even the conservative William Smith was distressed and pessimistic of the future. "A general consternation and disgust works among the people . . . I fear we shall lose all that attachment we once had in so great a degree for the parent country." [37]

How greatly the Ministry and even the British public misjudged the spirit of America is shown by a letter from a Londoner to a friend in New York. "The present great topic and universal inquiry is, what will the Americans do now? 'Tis generally answered, they must submit. The Boston Port Bill will speedily and effectually execute itself. Taking away the trade ruins every man of property in the place. This idea will strike such a panic as must render it easy for Mr. Gage to obtain not only ample indemnification for the East India Company, but submission on the part of the Bostonians and acknowledgment of the Parliament's right to tax them. And should the port bill fail of effecting all this, a corps of reserve is at hand, a bill . . . new modelling their constitution and government which will put such a ruin in the Minister's hand as may enable him to pull them which way he pleases or tear their jaws." [38]

But the Bostonians had no idea of submitting. Three days after receiving word of the passage of the Port Bill, their Committee of Correspondence sounded the alarm bell with letters to the other colonies. "This attack, though made immediately upon us, is doubtless designed for every other colony who will not surrender their sacred rights and liberties into the hands of an infamous Ministry. Their grand object is to divide the colonies. Now therefore is the time when all should be united . . . The single question then is whether you consider Boston as now suffering in the common cause." [39]

The response of Sears, McDougall, Lamb and other ardent Sons of Liberty was immediate. The people of New York, even "many timid and selfish persons" who had taken little interest heretofore in the controversy with Great Britain, now expressed the greatest indignation at "the shocking and detestable act of Parliament," they wrote the Boston Committee. They were in favor of calling a Continental Congress; they demanded a general boycott, not only of British, but of West Indian goods; they were "stimulating" the merchants of New York to call a meeting to draw up measures of resistance.[40]

But a surprise was in store for the radical leaders. Heretofore the

wealthy merchants, even those who bitterly resented the encroachments of the British Ministry, had taken little part in the movement
of resistance. When Sears or Lamb called a meeting of the citizens,
the De Lanceys, Van Cortlandts, DePeysters and others of like stamp
staid at home. Now, however, they decided to join the stream of revolution in order to direct it into safer channels. There must be no
more rioting, no violence, no dictatorship by Sears and McDougall,
the so-called Jack Cades of New York.[41]

Realizing that the first move of the conservatives would be the
demand for a new and more representative Committee of Correspondence, the radicals tried to forestall them by themselves nominat-
ing a group of twenty-five. So, a few days later when the merchants
met at the Queen's Head Tavern, at Broad and Dock Streets, many
Sons of Liberty were on hand to urge their candidates. This so swelled
the numbers that the reception room would not hold them all, and
they were forced to move over to the nearby Royal Exchange.

Here the conservatives won the first test of strength by electing
Isaac Low chairman. They then carried one resolution after another
—that a new Committee of Correspondence should be nominated at
once, that it should consist of fifty members rather than twenty-five,
that the list should be submitted to a meeting of the citizens three days
later. After this they nominated a compromise committee, in which
they included all save two of the list presented by the Sons of Liberty,
together with twenty-seven others.[42]

On May 19, the list was presented to "a great concourse" of people
at the coffee house. An interesting assemblage it was. Young Gouverneur Morris, who stood in the balcony looking out over the crowd,
noted that on the right "were ranged all the people of property, with
some few dependents," on the left "all the tradesmen, etc., who thought
it worth while to leave daily labor for the good of the country." It
was a critical moment, Morris thought, a moment which might decide
whether the future government "should be founded on aristocratic or
democratic principles." [43]

Low made an address pleading for unity. "It is but charitable to
suppose we all mean the same thing and that the only difference
amongst us is, or at least ought to be, the mode of effecting it. I mean
the preservation of our just rights and liberties . . . We ought therefore, gentlemen, to banish from our hearts all little party distinctions,
feuds and animosities, for to our unanimity and virtue we must at

last recur for our safety." Pleased with the thought that the great and wealthy men of the city were now openly joining hands with them in the defence of liberty, many of the "leather aprons" voted with the conservatives, and the fifty men nominated by the meeting at the Exchange were elected.[44] With the consent of both parties Francis Lewis was added so that the committee as finally constituted numbered fifty-one.

The conservatives exulted. "The power over our crowd is no longer in the hands of Sears, Lamb and such unimportant persons, who have for six years past been the demagogues of a very turbulent faction in the city," wrote the Tory editor James Rivington to a friend in Boston.[45] Another conservative declared that "in spite of all that could be done by the old committee, which consisted of eight or ten flaming patriots without property or anything else but impudence, a new committee was chosen consisting of fifty men, most of them men of sense, coolness and property." [46]

That the Tories were over optimistic soon became apparent. As the British Ministry forced the issue with one repressive act after another—the Massachusetts Government Act by which the people of that colony were stripped of many of their most cherished rights, an act enabling royal officers when brought into any colonial court to transfer their cases to Great Britain, a new Quartering Act—the conservatives on the Committee of Fifty-One were borne along by the current of revolution. It was an exaggeration for William Smith to say that the Liberty Boys were driving before them those who "came in to repress their zeal," [47] since the committee undoubtedly added to the revolutionary movement in New York an element of moderation lacking in some of the other colonies, but the conservatives discovered that resistance to the British Ministry was inevitable, so that they must either take the lead in it or turn it over to Sears, Lamb and McDougall.

On the day the Boston Port Bill went into effect the New York populace, to the anger and alarm of many committee members, staged a demonstration in the best traditions of the Stamp Act riots. The crowd carried through the principal streets a gallows from which hung the effigies of Lord North, Governor Hutchinson of Massachusetts, hated because of his support of the coercive measure, and Solicitor-General Wedderburn, who had so grossly insulted Benjamin Franklin before a committee of the Privy Council. With the three figures was another, representing Satan, to which was attached the words: "Devil do thy office. With tartarean sulphur destroy these pests of mankind." The procession headed for the Merchants Coffee House, where the torch was applied and all the figures went up in flames.[48]

This demonstration served only to steel the determination of the Committee of Fifty-One. On May 23, they had written the Bostonians, refusing to comply with their plea that they commit New York to a general boycott of British goods. Instead they suggested the calling of "a Congress of deputies from the colonies," to which all important questions should be submitted. With this the Boston committee had to be content, though they thought that the New Yorkers had deserted them in the hour of distress.

Now followed a long and bitter struggle over the naming of representatives to the Continental Congress. It is probable that the Committee of Fifty-one would have refused to make any nominations at all, or at best would have selected a group of conservatives who would have been a hindrance rather than a help to Congress, had not the radicals outmaneuvered them. Organizing a rival body to represent the populace, which they called the Committee of Mechanics, they threatened to use it to put forward a list of nominations of their own and submit it to a referendum in the Common. This left the Committee of Fifty-one the alternative of acting at once or having New York represented by a group of radicals.[49]

They stalled for a few more days, and then yielded so far as to name a group of five moderates—John Jay, Isaac Low, James Duane, John Alsop and Philip Livingston. But they demurred when McDougall moved that they submit the list to the Mechanics. Instead they directed the Chairman to issue a notice inviting the inhabitants of the city and county to meet at the City Hall to pass on them.[50]

John Jay, a tall, graceful young man, with aquiline nose, arched eyebrows and long chin, bookish and pious and steeped in the law, shared the merchants' fear of the mob. He was for resistance without going to extremes. In this he was seconded by James Duane, whom John Adams thought very sensible and very artful, with "a sly, surveying eye, a little squint-eyed." Isaac Low, despite his great wealth and his elegant mansion on Dock Street, was loud in proclaiming his attachment to the cause of liberty, but there were many who doubted his sincerity. John Alsop, a merchant of good heart, was thought unequal in point of ability to the responsibility placed upon him. Philip

Livingston, Adams found a great, rough man "who blustered away," protesting against Ministerial oppression, but predicting that if England should turn the colonies adrift they would fall victims to anarchy and "the levelling spirit." But his kind heart was attested by his philanthropy, and his patriotism by the fact that he signed the Declaration of Independence.[51]

The radicals, angered at the omission from the list of nominees of any of their number, withdrew from the Committee of Fifty-one and then called a meeting of the Committee of Mechanics. There it was resolved that since the Committee of Fifty-one had refused the Mechanics representation in their body, had not consulted them, nor asked their approval of the list of nominees, they would put forward candidates of their own. But they showed a spirit of moderation by accepting three of the original nominees—Low, Jay and Livingston— and contenting themselves with substituting Alexander McDougall and Leonard Lispenard for Duane and Alsop.[52] They then issued a call for a meeting in the Common, "where every friend to the true interests of this distressed country" was asked to attend.

Though many thought that their action tended to cast odium upon the Committee of Fifty-one by taking the leadership in the resistance movement out of their hands, a large crowd assembled on July 6. With McDougall in the chair, they agreed unanimously upon several "spirited resolves," denouncing the Boston Port Bill as "unconstitutional," declaring that an attack on one colony was an attack on all, urging non-intercourse with Great Britain as "the salvation of North America and her liberties," and asking for a subscription to relieve the distress of the poor of Boston.[53]

The next day the Committee of Fifty-one met and, after criticising the proceedings in the Common as apt to "create groundless jealousies and suspicions," drew up what William Smith called some pusillanimous resolves of their own. But when they were presented to a mass meeting on July 19 John Morin Scott derided them in a fiery speech and "to the confusion of the committee," they were rejected.[54]

In the meanwhile many of the ardent patriots, fearing that a contested election, with perhaps two sets of delegates claiming to represent New York in Congress, would do great harm, brought pressure to bear on the Committee of Mechanics to withdraw their nominations of McDougall and Lispenard. Thereupon the Mechanics asked all the candidates whether they would promise to use their utmost

endeavors to have Congress proclaim a boycott on all imports from
Great Britain, and when Livingston, Low, Alsop and Jay answered
in the affirmative, acquiesced in the original nominations of the Committee of Fifty-one. With but one list before them, the voters, many
of them with serious misgivings, gave their unanimous consent.[55]

Had the delegates had any doubt as to the hopes reposed in them,
it must have been dispelled by the ovation accorded them on September 1, when Low, Duane, Alsop and Livingston left for Philadelphia.[56] As they came out of the Merchants Coffee House a "number
of respectable inhabitants" escorted them to the Royal Exchange with
"colors flying" and "music playing." There Duane, "in a very affectionate and moving" address, promised that nothing in their power
should be wanting to relieve the "once happy but now aggrieved
country." [57]

Four days later the New Yorkers took their seats beside their colleagues from the other colonies in charming Carpenters' Hall,[58] and
the Continental Congress began its session. A body of moderates it
was, wishing to defend American rights, but recoiling at the thought
of war. Many of the members no doubt agreed with Isaac Low when
he pleaded for justice to the mother country and denounced those
who aimed at independence. But to stay the hands of the extremists,
they were forced to enter a protest against the oppressive measures of
Parliament and the Ministry and to back it up with an agreement to
end trade with Great Britain and the British West Indies.

Against cutting off the West India trade Low protested. Could the
Americans live without rum, sugar and molasses, he asked. If the
West Indian market for fish were sacrificed, would it not "throw a
multitude of families" in the New England fishing towns "into the
arms of famine?" [59] But he pleaded in vain. Congress drew up an
Association binding themselves and the American people to import
after December 1 no more goods from Great Britain nor, with some
exceptions, from the British West Indies, and after September 15,
1775, if their grievances had not been redressed, to extend the prohibi-
tion to exports. They also sent addresses to the King, to the people of
Great Britain, and to the people of all the British colonies. The opposition of the people of Massachusetts to "the late Acts of Parliament"
was endorsed, and the support of all America promised to prevent their
execution.[60]

While Congress thus petitioned and threatened "peaceful coercion," the people prepared for war. The King, once considered the friend and father of his people, was now denounced as their betrayer and oppressor. "It is astonishing to observe to what a pass the populace are arrived," wrote William Smith. "Instead of that respect they formerly had for the King, you now hear the very lowest orders call him a knave or a fool." [61]

John Thurman warned a London friend that "free men are not to be governed by power and force." There was yet time to call back America's love, but should Great Britain drive her into rebellion it would be easier to conquer France than to subdue her. "There is not a man born in America who does not understand the use of firearms and that well," he added. "It is almost the first thing they purchase to take to all the new settlements, and in the cities you can scarcely find a lad of twelve years old that does not go agunning." How ready the people were to use their arms was shown when, upon a false rumor that a skirmish had occurred in Massachusetts between redcoats and patriots, every Son of Liberty took down his flintlock, and with muttered oaths and dark brows, cleaned the barrel and rammed down the charge of ball and powder.[62] "We hear of nothing but extravagances," General Gage wrote Dartmouth, "of military preparations . . . in which the whole country seems to be united." [63] A gentleman upon arriving in London from New York reported that "he saw nothing but rubbing up arms, enlisting, exercising and every other preparation denoting a vigorous resolution in the people to defend themselves against all oppressors to the very last." [64]

The patriots, fearing that their supply of arms and ammunition was inadequate, sent to Holland and even to Great Britain for more. One shipment of ten chests of arms, three boxes of lead and one barrel of gunpowder consigned at London as hardware upon reaching New York was transferred to a vessel bound for Rhode Island. When Andrew Elliot, collector of the port, discovered them and placed them on board a man-of-war, the "Mohawks" denounced him as an enemy of the liberties of America. "From you we shall demand these arms whenever they are wanted, which it is probable will be soon. You will, therefore, if you have the least regard to the safety of yourself or of your servants who seized them, be careful to prevent their being sent away." [65]

As the crisis in the struggle between the British Ministry and the colonies drew near, the middle course followed by the Committee of Fifty-one became increasingly difficult. Congress had taken its stand, and Americans everywhere had either to endorse what they had done or place themselves in the ranks of the "Loyalists." Since the old committee was obviously unsuited to enforce the Association, they themselves proposed that another body be formed to take over its powers.[66] So, after a conference with the Mechanics, and after a mass meeting of "leather aprons," a new committee, consisting of sixty members, was elected.[67] This body, though still representing all shades of opinion, was distinctly more radical than its predecessor and gradually pushed aside the Assembly as the real governing power in the city and colony.

Their first task was to enforce the Association. The people were overwhelmingly in favor of the boycott, and the merchants, though they viewed their idle vessels and empty warehouses with sour faces, realized the futility of resistance. A subcommittee was appointed "to observe the conduct" of all vessels arriving after February 1, 1775, having on board any goods "not allowed to be imported by the Association." [68]

The very next day the ship *James* came in from Glasgow with a cargo of coal and dry goods. As she neared the city some "ministerial tools" with "a few vagrants" assembled on the wharf to unload the "contraband," but they were dispersed by a crowd of indignant patriots. Thereupon the captain backed off and anchored four miles down the harbor. A week later, after he had taken aboard some armed men from the cruiser *Kingfisher,* he ventured to approach again. The alarm was sounded and in a few minutes angry men began to assemble in the streets. The captain of the *James,* who was in the city at the time, was taken from his lodgings, conducted through the streets to the wharf, put on board a boat and rowed out to his ship. On February 11 the *James* got under sail, and, accompanied by two committee members in a small boat, headed for the ocean. Two hours later she was out of sight.[69] "I was greatly chagrined that a ship which arrived here from Glasgow should be sent away with her cargo in compliance with the orders of Congress," Colden wrote Gage. "None of the consignees had resolution enough to demand their goods, so that government had no opportunity to interfere." [70]

Nor were subsequent events more consoling to the aged lieutenant governor. Hardly had the *James* gone than the *Beulah* arrived at the watering place about three leagues from the city. When committee members went out to watch her, the captain promised them that as soon as he had secured supplies and a new bowsprit, he would turn about and head back. A few days later, she too had disappeared over the horizon.[71] In short, there was no avoiding the vigilance of the Committee and the force of the mob. "Several ships have arrived within this fortnight from England and two or three from Scotland," wrote a New Yorker to a friend in England, "all of them are obliged to depart without unloading a single article." [72]

When Gage, finding that he could not secure supplies in New England for his troops nor workmen to construct their winter barracks, sent to New York for aid, the patriots there did their best to thwart him. Not one carpenter, not one bricklayer, not one painter would go.[73] The merchants, "to their immortal honor," refused to let Gage use their vessels. And when the General sent British transports, the local pilots were warned not to bring them up to the city.[74] Ralph Thurman, Robert Harding, William Ustick, and Henry Ustick, who had agreed to supply boards and nails for the barracks, spades for entrenching, straw for the horses and provisions for the troops, were pleaded with and threatened. Some of the patriots had a conference with the two Usticks at the widow Van de Water's house, but found them "so infatuated with the hope of gain that no impression could be made on their minds of the cruelty or injustice of their act." [75]

With Harding and Thurman the Sons of Liberty took more severe methods. Notices were published summoning the people to meet at the liberty pole on the afternoon of April 15. Thereupon Mayor Hicks arrested Isaac Sears and Marinus Willett for disturbing the peace. Willett gave bail, but Sears, probably hoping to become like McDougall another Wilkes, refused. As the magistrates were conducting him to the jail, the crowd espied them and rushing across the Common rescued the prisoner. They then marched to Harding's house, only to find that he had fled. Thurman was not so lucky, and it might have gone hard with him had not "the magistrates and others repressed the fury of the multitude." A few days later when the Council met to discuss means for preserving order, the mayor confessed that he was helpless, while Leonard Lispenard reported that the militia were all Liberty Boys.[76]

While thus doing their best to embarrass Gage, the New Yorkers were equally active in bringing relief to the distressed people of Boston. At the meeting in the Common of July 6, 1774, a subscription list had been started, and before the end of the year vessels were on their way for New England laden with flour, pork, and butter.[77] A cargo of 376 barrels of rice, contributed by the people of South Carolina, was sold in New York and the proceeds amounting to 1,200 pounds sent to "the sufferers of Massachusetts Bay." [78]

Had an election for a new Assembly been held at this juncture there is little doubt that the patriots would have won a majority of the seats. But Colden had no intention of dismissing the old conservative House which he had inherited from the election of 1769. So, in January, 1775, when he called them together, he looked down into the faces of James De Lancey, James Jauncey, John Cruger and others who a few months later definitely aligned themselves with the British against their country. Many of them had long since forfeited the esteem of their constituents, wrote a disgusted New Yorker to a Bostonian; many were hoping for favors from the Crown. "In short, Sir, no virtuous nor spirited act could be expected from a House which had . . . provided support six years for troops kept here for the express purpose of enslaving America. But although these miscreants are the legal representatives of the people, yet I can assure you they are not the true representatives." [79]

Colden opened the session with an address in which he pleaded for the reestablishment of harmony between Great Britain and the colonies, and the House made a "dutiful" reply "which gave him great satisfaction." Then ensued a bitter conflict over a resolution to approve the proceedings of Congress, with the patriot group using what Colden described as "every machination that restless spirits could devise." So when the Tories won the victory, though by the close vote of 11 to 10, "Old Silver Locks" was overjoyed, crying out, "Lord, now let they servant depart in peace." [80]

With several late arrivals adding to the strength of the Tory majority, there was now "no chance of the Assembly's aiding or abetting the Congress." By a vote of 15 to 9 they refused to thank the New York delegates "for their faithful and judicious discharge of the trust reposed in them by the good people of the colony." [81] A few days later they voted down a resolution to thank the merchants and people of New York City "for their repeated, disinterested, public spirited and patriotic conduct" in adhering to the Association.[82] On February 23, 1775, they refused by a vote of 17 to 9 to appoint delegates to the Second Continental Congress.

The resistance of the Assembly to the revolutionary movement was hailed by the Tories both in the colonies and in England. "The friends of government plume themselves on this victory," wrote a New Yorker to a Bostonian, "and are open-mouthed about the proceedings of Congress, and no one dares, among gentlemen, to support them." [83] General Gage was delighted. "The conduct of your Assembly gives fresh spirits to the Loyalists in this province," he wrote from Boston. "I sincerely pray that New York may continue to . . . merit the distinction of the Loyal Province." [84] The Philadelphia Tories reported that the New York Assembly was "revered by all sensible men" for "making a stand against lawless usurpers of power." [85] And from England came word that "the behavior of the New Yorkers had raised the drooping spirits of the Ministry," and steeled them against any compromise. [86]

On the other hand, the friends of liberty were scathing in their denunciations of the Assembly. "With what contempt ought the base majority . . . to be held," wrote a Londoner. He trusted that they had been tarred and feathered, as they so richly deserved. [87] Another Englishman expressed the hope that the province would "soon disperse these treacherous Tories," who dared "negatively to encourage the system of despotism." [88] The New York patriots, angered and humiliated, protested that the Assembly by no means represented the sentiments of the people of the province. "But they are unhappily in the hands of dependent placemen, contractors, informers . . . and other the veriest reptiles on earth. This therefore is the only colony on which the British junto must rely to enslave America." [89]

But as events hastened on to the inevitable crisis, the people more and more ignored the reactionary Assembly and looked to the Committee of Sixty as the real government. In the taprooms of the taverns, on street corners, in the shops of the small merchants, down on the wharves, wherever men came together, the action of the Assembly in refusing to name delegates to the second Continental Congress was bitterly denounced. "Are we to permit this handful of Tories to prevent New York from joining with the other colonies in the common cause?" it was asked. "Are we to sit idly by while they betray American liberty and give the British Ministry the impression that this province will submit to anything they do?"

The answer was not long in coming. The Committee of Sixty, on March 1, suggested that the voters meet to decide upon a method of electing delegates and proposed the calling of a Provincial Convention for that purpose.[90] This greatly alarmed the conservatives. At a meeting at "the widow De La Montagnie's," on Broadway south of Warren, voicing the fear that a Provincial Convention might supersede the Assembly, they planned a campaign of resistance.

Three days later New York resounded to the noise of the contending parties as the leaders on each side marshalled their forces. At nine o'clock the "friends of freedom" assembled at the liberty pole, under "a union flag with a red field," and at eleven marched to the Exchange with bands playing. Soon after the opposing group arrived. When it was noted that "among them were some officers of the army and navy, several of His Majesty's Council, . . . together with officers of the customs and other dependents on the court," it seemed for a moment that some violence would be offered them. But order was quickly restored.

Thereupon the chairman put the questions: Whether there should be a Provincial Convention? Immediately a roar of "ayes" came from the Sons of Liberty, followed by a vigorous, if weaker, cry of "nay" from the conservatives. The meeting next voted to empower the Committee of Sixty to name the delegates to the Convention and then adjourned, the "friends of freedom" celebrating their victory by parading through the streets back to the liberty pole, their standards waving in triumph.[91]

It was a determined body of men who assembled at the Exchange on April 20, 1775, to carry out the people's mandate to select the New York delegates to Congress. They sincerely wished and hoped for reconciliation with the British government, but not by submission, not by yielding the English heritage of liberty. Among them were some who were destined to play important roles in the Revolution and in the creation of the nation—John Jay, Philip Schuyler, George Clinton and others. After some deliberation they named twelve men to represent the colony at Philadelphia—the astute James Duane, the youthful John Jay, Philip Schuyler, a violent champion of popular rights, George Clinton, later governor of New York, Philip Livingston, the wealthy John Alsop, the urbane Francis Lewis, Simon Boernum, William Floyd, Henry Wisner, Lewis Morris, Robert R. Livingston.[92]

The Tories stood by helplessly as the Provincial Convention thus took this first step in making itself the real government of the province. "It is not in the power of government to prevent such measures,"

Colden wrote Dartmouth. "They are supported by individuals in their private characters and do not come within the energy of the law." [93]

"Old Silver Locks" was helpless, also, to suppress new outbreaks of violence. William Cunningham, who had made himself obnoxious as a Tory, was taken to the liberty pole by a mob of 200 men, forced to his knees and commanded to damn King George. When he exclaimed instead "God bless King George," the crowd tore his clothes from his back and "dragged him through the green." A certain John Hill received like treatment.[94] That Cunningham, at least, deserved his punishment we may infer from his cruelty to American prisoners a few months later when he became Provost Marshal after the British took possession of New York City.

Despite mobbings such as this, it is noteworthy that the patriots would do nothing to violate the liberty of the press. They were sorely tempted to put an end to James Rivington's "lying" *New York Gazetteer,* but when they recalled the victory the colonists had won for freedom of speech in the famous Zenger trial four decades earlier, they stayed their hands. But they did not stay their tongues. Not only in the city, but in New Jersey, Connecticut, Rhode Island, Rivington was denounced as a traitor to America.

The Whigs of Newport assailed his "love of self" and his "domineering spirit," which impelled him to fill his "dirty *Gazetteer*" with every falsehood which his wicked imagination . . . could suggest . . . to spread jealousies, fear, discord, and disunion through this country." They recommended that every person who took the paper should at once cancel his subscription.[95] Mr. Rivington had appealed to the principle of the freedom of the press, but "should a press disgorge calumny and falsehood with impunity?" asked a Connecticut patriot. Must the people in their hour of peril put up with this invidious spy who had converted his press into an "engine of tyranny"? [96] But put up with him they did until after the outbreak of war.

And now with the colonies on the brink of revolution, there were last minute efforts for compromise both in Great Britain and America. "There are everywhere many people who are seriously alarmed," Colden wrote to Dartmouth. "They . . . would rejoice in any prudent plan for restoring harmony and security." [97] But his suggestion that Parliament "lay aside" the right of taxing the Americans, in return for a promise that the colonial Assemblies guarantee grants sufficient to pay the governor's salary and other governmental expenses, merely begged the question. The Assemblies would never have surrendered the gains of a century by striking off the financial chains with which they had bound the governors.

But when John Thurman pleaded with Great Britain to make peace if it could be done "without degrading herself below the dignity of a superior," there were many on both sides of the water to second him. In Parliament Edmund Burke also demanded peace, but peace through reconciliation. Even Dartmouth wished for a compromise. "The idea of union upon some general constitutional plan is certainly very just," he wrote Colden, "and I have no doubt of its being yet attainable through some channel of mutual consideration and discussion."

In keeping with this view the Commons, on March 3, handed the colonies a last-minute olive branch by offering not to tax them, in return for a pledge from the various Assemblies to contribute "their proportion for the common defence" and engage to make provision also for the support of the provincial governments. This proposal reached America too late to receive serious consideration, but it would probably have been rejected under any circumstances. It would have been hard to convince the Americans that taxation by duress differed in any essential point from taxation without representation.

The colonists had hoped for greater concessions, since news came with every packet of the widespread opposition in Great Britain to the Ministry's policy. Benjamin Franklin wrote that the clamor of the people in favor of America was great, that five or six hundred merchants in Bristol had petitioned for the repeal of the oppressive acts and that similar petitions were being drawn up all over Great Britain.[98] The Americans heard that when the Commons opened the debate in February, 1775, "the avenues leading to the House were so extremely crowded that there was not room for the members to pass" until orders were issued for the lobby to be cleared. One writer reported that the people were so incensed against Lord North that it was feared violence might be offered him. North himself belittled the danger, however, declaring that the people would content themselves with mere clamor, or perhaps "the breaking of his coach door, or some such trifle."

On the floor of the Commons Edmund Burke asked whether fighting a people was the best way of gaining them. He thought that force was not only "an odious but a feeble instrument for preserving a people so numerous, so active, so growing, so spirited" in a profitable and subordinate connection with Great Britain. Charles Fox gave it as his conviction that the coercive measures would bring "defeat on one side of the water and ruin and punishment on the other." And everywhere in England cartoons were circulated lampooning Grenville, North and Townshend and depicting the sufferings of America. The press of the smaller cities was almost unanimously pro-American.[99]

The English liberals in their letters to the Americans denounced the Ministry and the King in language which might have come from the mouth of a Tom Paine or an Isaac Sears. George III was determined to be as absolute as the French King, they said, and with the most obstinate head and bad heart he had set himself against the people, discarding men of veracity from high office and substituting "the most abandoned villains on earth." Two millions of pounds sterling had been squandered in bribery and corruption, so that now there were 285 members of Parliament who were all paid with the people's money to vote whatever North proposed. But the Americans had only to be firm. "If you hold out a few months England will rise and do you justice, as well as relieve themselves from those accursed tyrants who want to corrupt you and deprive you of both liberty and property." [100]

The Americans held out, but the English did not rise. With the beginning of hostilities sentiment in favor of America gradually grew weaker. "I am persuaded the body of the British people are our friends," wrote Franklin, in October, 1775, "but they are changeable, and may soon be our enemies." When the colonies declared their independence the English people turned against them still more; when they committed the unpardonable sin of allying themselves with France, even their most ardent friends no longer defended them.

And in the colonies, as war became inevitable, every man had to make his choice between King and country. A hard decision it was for many, as they weighed loyalty, patriotism, love of liberty, religion, self-interest one against the other. Some there were who went down on their knees to ask divine guidance. Others were deeply influenced by the advice freely given in the sermons of the clergy. But when they went to Trinity church Dr. Auchmuty argued that God was on the side of the King; if they attended services at the North Dutch Church or the Scotch Presbyterian Church, the Reverend John H. Livingston and Dr. John Mason were sure He favored the defenders of American liberty.

It is not difficult to follow the reasoning of such a man as John Watts, as he paced the floor of his handsome residence on Broadway, or strolled through the garden walks of Rose Hill, his country estate on the East River. As an American he resented the encroachments of the British Ministry and Parliament—the Sugar Act, the Stamp Act, the Townshend Acts and the others. He seconded the protests of the Assembly against them all. But to protest was one thing, to rebel was another. His ties to the British government were strong, for he was a member of the Council, his son Stephen was an officer in the army, and his son-in-law was Sir John Johnson, son of Sir William Johnson, the distinguished Indian agent. With the old New York aristocracy he was affiliated through his marriage with Ann De Lancey, daughter of Stephen De Lancey. To turn his back on his King and his own family, however right the cause, was too much to expect. So he aligned himself with the Tories, and in 1775 left for London never to return.

For John Cruger the decision must have been harder. Cruger had been a leader in resisting the encroachments of the Ministry both in the Stamp Act Congress and in the New York Assembly. But he recoiled at the thought of war. War meant ruin. Would not Bristol and the ports of the British West Indies to which his firm had traded for many years be closed to him? Would not the British cruisers chase his ships from the seas or perhaps send some of them to the bottom? Might not the royal navy come into the East River and seize or destroy his warehouses on Cruger's Wharf? So, in 1775 we find him refusing to sign the Association, voting in the Assembly against approving the proceedings of Congress and finally retiring to private life at Kinderhook, when the British occupied New York City.

When the hour of decision came for Elias Desbrosses, the prosperous merchant, real estate owner and confectioner who specialized in candy dogs, hawks, owls, lambs and swans, he quietly joined the ranks of the Tories. Desbrosses, despite his Huguenot descent, was an ardent Anglican, a warden of Trinity and a generous contributor to the parish charity school. To him rebellion against the King meant rebellion against the head of the Church. He might risk his property and his business for liberty's sake; he would not imperil his soul.

As for the De Lancey family, many considerations led them to remain loyal to the Crown. They had enjoyed great privileges under the old regime—political power, wealth, social prestige; it was only human that they should wish to perpetuate them. They dreaded the mob, and hated the "upstart demagogues" who were elbowing them out of the political leadership of the province; their business interests were injured by the boycotts; as orthodox Anglicans they wished to maintain the privileged position of their Church. Though they criticised the policies of the reactionary Ministry and used all their influence in Great Britain to combat them, they demurred at open resistance. So James De Lancey sold his stable of fine race horses and set sail for England; his uncle Oliver remained to welcome the British forces and to raise a body of Loyalists to defend Long Island against the revolutionists; Oliver De Lancey, Jr., fought with the British and succeeded Major André as Sir Henry Clinton's adjutant-general; another James De Lancey won the title of the "Outlaw of the Bronx" through the activities of his so-called cowboys in raiding the farms of Westchester to supply the British army with cattle.

But not all the New York aristocrats became Tories. Most of the Livingstons, Morrises, and other wealthy and influential families risked their all in the cause of liberty. Lewis Morris, the third Lord of the Manor of Morrisania, choking down his dread of democracy, signed the Declaration of Independence and later served as a general in the militia. His brother Gouverneur Morris, who took no pains to conceal his dislike of Sears, Lamb and McDougall, when the news of the fight at Lexington reached him, went over heart and soul to the revolutionary cause. Philip Livingston, reared in almost princely surroundings, a large ship owner and merchant, who had one fine residence in the city and another on Brooklyn Heights, threw in his lot with the patriots. William Livingston, after broadcasting his patriotism by naming his new estate at Elizabeth "Liberty Hall," became a revolutionary leader and governor of his adopted state.

In recent years scholars have re-examined the causes of the American Revolution and have given us some new interpretations which would have startled George Washington or Thomas Jefferson. And though these scholars have thrown welcome light on many points, their labors have resulted chiefly in obscuring the obvious. The Americans rebelled against Great Britain because they insisted upon governing themselves, as for decades they had done, while George III and his Ministers tried to govern them from London. If one goes through the private correspondence of Liberty Boys and Tories alike, if one will read the newspapers of the time, the diaries, the petitions to the King, the minutes of the Committees of Correspondence one will find the word "liberty" on almost every page.

Those who try to make the events leading up to the Revolution fit the theory of economic determinism forget that the Southern tobacco planters, when they broke with Britain, risked the market upon which their entire prosperity was founded; that the merchants of the coastal cities, who were the chief sufferers from the enforcement of the Molasses Act and the Sugar Act, despite their early protests, fought the final breach with all their might. When the colonists placed themselves outside the British Empire they were sacrificing far more in an economic sense than they gained, and they all knew it. In other words, the Americans rebelled in spite of the economic situation, not because of it.

It is as enlightening as it is pathetic to find the New York Assembly, Tories and patriots alike, a few weeks before the battle of Lexington petitioning the King for their liberty. They thought themselves equally entitled with their fellow subjects in Britain to their birthright of freedom. They thought it essential to liberty that no taxes be imposed on them without their own consent.

But it was now too late for protests. On April 18, General Gage sat down at his headquarters in Boston and wrote an order to Lieutenant-Colonel Smith. "Having received intelligence that a quantity of ammunition, provision, artillery, tents and small arms have been collected at Concord for the avowed purpose of raising and supplying a rebellion against His Majesty, you will march with the corps of grenadiers and light infantry . . . with the utmost expedition and secrecy to Concord where you will seize and destroy . . . all military stores whatever." The next day Smith's force clashed with the Massachusetts militia at Lexington and the Revolutionary War had begun.

CHAPTER III

NEW YORK DIGS IN

THE QUIET of Sunday morning, April 23, 1775, was broken by the sound of hoof beats as a dispatch rider galloped at top speed along the Bowery, past the windmill, the tanyards and the Common, into Broadway. Here he reined in his horse to announce to groups of startled churchgoers that the war had begun, that the redcoats had fired on the patriots at Lexington, that the Americans had resisted and that a number on both sides had been killed. To those who were incredulous, he showed dispatches confirming the alarming news, signed by committee members in Massachusetts and Connecticut.

In a few minutes the city was in an uproar. Excited men and women rushed into the streets to join the throngs there, to ask for the latest details and to express their indignation.[1] So at last the Ministry had thrown off the mask! At the very moment when they were pretending to send out feelers for reconciliation, they had revealed their real intent, which was to govern by force of arms.[2] But they would discover that Americans everywhere, like the heroes of Lexington, would fight for their liberty.

The wildest rumors were "invented, believed, denied, discredited." [3] Sears, Lamb and others started a parade through the principal streets "with drums beating and colors flying." [4] As they passed, angry men stepped out of their houses, rifle in hand, to join them. Later in the day the mob converged on one of the wharves to which two sloops laden with provisions for the troops at Boston were tied up, and removed their cargoes. With the coming of evening a great throng assembled before the City Hall, demanding the key to the armory room. When this was refused them, they broke open the door and carried off 522 muskets, together with hundreds of bayonets and cartridge boxes filled with "ball cartridges." They next seized the public powder house, near Freshwater, helped themselves to part of the store of powder and left fifty men to guard the rest.[5]

53

The excitement and confusion in the city are reflected in the terse entries which Judge William Smith made in his *Diary*. "The taverns filled with politicians at night. Little business done in the day. Few jurors and witnesses attend the courts. Armed parties summon the town publicly to come and take arms and learn the manual exercise . . . Consternation in the faces of the principal inhabitants . . . Sears . . . with 360 armed men waited on Eliot the collector and got the keys of the Custom House to shut up the port." [6]

It was a time of triumph for the radical leaders. Now that it was clear that America must resist in arms or be enslaved, there could be no more half-way measures, no more "loyal petitions," no opposition to the Continental Congress. Lexington put them in the saddle over night, to ride the horse of liberty whither they would.

But the conservatives were in despair. They had either to turn about and join their former opponents, or face the wrath of the populace. There were open threats of tarring and feathering, and even of hanging. "The merchants are . . . so humbled as only to sigh or complain in whispers," states William Smith. "They now dread Sears' train of armed men." [7] "It is no time now to dally or to be merely neutral," the radicals declared, "he that is not for us is against us." [8] A shotgun marriage is seldom permanent, and of the scores of Tories who joined the throngs daily parading through the streets and shouted for liberty with the best of them, many recanted as soon as the redcoats set foot on New York soil. But for the moment their apparent defection gave to the revolutionary movement an aspect of unanimity. [9]

Some, however, took refuge in flight. John Watts, Colonel Roger Morris, Colonel John Maunsell, Isaac Wilkins and others arranged their affairs in desperate haste to catch the packet for England sailing May 4. [10] Morris, formerly an officer in the British Army who had won the hand and fortune of Mary Philipse, the beautiful "Captain Polly," deserted 51,000 fertile acres in Duchess County and a mansion on Stone Street. Wilkins was marked for vengeance because in the Assembly he had denounced the patriots as parricides and inveighed against what he called the "ill-judged, tyrannical and destructive measures of Congress." [11]

Watts was "hurt exceedingly" by a published letter, denouncing him, together with Colden, James De Lancey, President Myles Cooper of King's College, Henry White and the publisher James Rivington, for having encouraged the British Ministry to persist in their assaults on American liberty. They were responsible for the failure of the attempts at reconciliation, they had unsheathed the sword of Britain against the bosom of their country, they had brought on all the miseries of civil war with towns in flames, butchered fathers and weeping widows and children. "Go now," the letter concluded, "fly for your lives, or anticipate your doom by becoming your own executioners." [12]

The anger against the "odious six" was so great that for a time they were in imminent danger. Rivington, after a narrow escape from a mob, took refuge on the British warship *Kingfisher*, from which retreat he made a public apology and asked forgiveness. De Lancey saved himself by going among the crowd and protesting his innocence. Watts and White drew up and published affidavits denying the charges.

President Cooper, whose pamphlet *The American Querist* had been publicly burned by the Sons of Liberty, and who had taken revenge by referring to them as "sons of licentiousness, faction and confusion," was one of "the most thoroughly hated men in America." He could not have been greatly surprised, then, when one of his former students rushed in to his apartment in the college to warn him that a mob was approaching. Springing out of bed, the president grabbed a few clothes, climbed the back fence and hid in a house on the bank of the North River. The following night he joined Rivington aboard the *Kingfisher,* and a few days later sailed for England.[13]

Colden, too, fled, but not so far. However great his fear of the mob, he did not want to desert his government entirely. So he retired to Spring Hill, his country estate on Long Island, to exercise from that comparatively safe retreat what powers were left him. "When Congresses and Committees had taken the entire direction of government it was extremely disagreeable to me to remain a spectator of the proceedings and confusions in town which I had it not in my power to prevent," he explained.[14]

It was more than a year after Lexington that the colonies declared their independence; but independence in all save theory began with the outbreak of hostilities. The Americans might insist that George III was still their King, they might speak of Gage's men as the Ministerial troops rather than the British army, but they could not fight Great Britain and at the same time be subject to her. So the royal governors, if they were fortunate enough to escape arrest, found their authority ignored, while the old Assemblies gave way to revolutionary bodies.

A century and a half before the American Revolution, the Pilgrims, in the little *Mayflower,* when they found themselves in strange waters outside the jurisdiction of the London Company and so without legal authorization for their settlement, drew up their famous Compact. By it they constituted themselves a body politic and pledged themselves to establish a government, to which they were to give "all due submission and obedience." It is improbable that many in New York had ever heard of the Mayflower Compact, but now, when the people of the city found themselves adrift in a sea of uncertainty, they took similar action.

On Saturday, April 29, a crowd of from six to seven thousand persons assembled on "the plains," where Isaac Low addressed them. Since the British Ministry had pursued a systematic plan to enslave America, it was necessary for all to unite in resisting them. To this end he asked them to sign an Association, which he proceeded to read. "We . . . do in the most solemn manner resolve never to become slaves, and do associate under all the ties of religion, honor and love to our country to adopt . . . whatsoever measures may be recommended by the Continental Congress or resolved upon by our Provincial Convention for the purpose of preserving our constitution." [15] When he had finished, the great Assemblage voiced its approval by loud huzzas. The document was then spread out on a table and Low signed it, followed by Judge Robert R. Livingston, Peter R. Livingston, and scores of others. Later copies were posted in the various voting places, so that every citizen, Colden alone excepted, might have the opportunity of affixing his signature.[16]

In the meanwhile, the work of organizing a new government was pushed rapidly. Since the Provincial Convention and the Committee of Sixty had proved their efficiency, it was decided to use them as models for new and more powerful bodies. On April 26, the Committee of Sixty decided to withdraw in favor of a Committee of One Hundred, nominations for which they submitted to the voters. And despite the violent protests of Isaac Sears, who objected to some of the more conservative nominees, the entire list was carried. The next day the new committee met at the Exchange and began its career as the revolutionary government of the city.

Three weeks later delegates to the Provincial Congress made their way to the city from Westchester, Orange, Ulster, Kings, Albany, Richmond and other counties, to join the local delegates at the Exchange. Here, as the exciting history of the early months of the Revolution unfolded itself and the old Assembly sank into impotence, they gradually assumed the character of a State legislature. And though many of them ardently hoped for reconciliation and opposed extreme measures, from the first they were dominated by Sears, McDougall, Scott and their fellow radicals.[17]

And now the streets of the city resounded to the tramp of soldiers, the rattle of drums and the sharp commands of drill sergeants. Both the Committee of One Hundred and the Provincial Congress urged all citizens to procure guns, powder and ball and "to perfect themselves in the military art." "In every corner of the town you see parties drilling and learning their exercise," Major Isaac Hamilton, who commanded the local British garrison, wrote in alarm to General Gage.[18] The carpenter laid aside his saw, the butcher his knife, the clerk his account book to don his uniform, seize his rifle and join his company, and he who refused to do so, though he might plead that his business made it impossible, was "looked on in a contemptible light." Even some of the Royal Irish regiment, tempted by the offers of a handful of half-joes, discarded their red uniforms to join the Americans.

As the men marched and drilled it was noted that many wore the uniform of the provincial militia, while others had to content themselves with their everyday clothes. But when the companies were organized as the First Provincial Regiment, with Alexander McDougall as its colonel, a distinct uniform was adopted. With their blue coats faced with red, white linen stocks, waistcoats and breeches of Russian drilling, woollen home-knit stockings, low shoes, felt hat with low crown and wide brim cocked up, the men made a picturesque and martial appearance. The company of artillery which served under Captain John Lamb had a like uniform, save that the facings were buff. Colonel John Lasher's battalion of Minute Men wore gray.

But to put uniforms on the men's backs was easier than to put arms and powder in their hands. True, there were many fowling pieces in the colony, and many muskets, bayonets and accoutrements belonging to the city and kept in the City Hall, but these were entirely inadequate for a war, even a short war. Soon the company and regimental commanders were making urgent requests of the Provincial Congress for cannon, powder, balls, ramrods, canteens, case shot and petards.

When it was noted that the five companies of British troops stationed in the barracks in the Common were guarding stores of arms and accoutrements, some of the revolutionary officers pointed out that it would be an easy matter to capture the entire outfit, imprison the men and distribute the arms. But the Provincial Congress vetoed this proposal. New York was not yet at war with Great Britain, there was still hope for reconciliation, it would be most unwise to force matters by some rash act of hostility.

A few days later Major Hamilton, finding that his force was melting away through desertions, decided to put them on board the warship *Asia,* which had arrived a few days before from Boston and was lying in the East River. Before starting he had received assurances from the Committee of One Hundred that the men would not be molested. But he had failed to reckon with the populace. As soon as the British emerged from their barracks a crowd assembled around them urging them to desert and carrying off in triumph a few who did so. When the men had reached the dock, at the foot of Broad Street, and the arms and ammunition carts in the rear were near the Exchange, several citizens stepped out from the crowd, and, seizing the reins of the horses, turned the carts out of the line and rifled them at their leisure.[19] A few minutes later the troops were rowed out to the *Asia* amid the hisses of the people. The Provincial Congress promptly ordered every person who had "any of the said arms" to return them immediately, but few seem to have heeded.

The very next night a party of men made a raid on a royal magazine on Turtle Bay, at what is now the foot of East Forty-eighth Street opposite the southern tip of Blackwell's Island. Francis Stephens, the keeper, at once notified the Provincial Congress, who sent several of their members to the spot to see that the plundered arms and ammunition were restored, but they were too late to prevent the removal of several boxes of saltpetre.

Sears and Lamb, determined not to let the British retain what was left of the munitions, wrote to friends in Stamford, Connecticut, urging them to send down a vessel to take them off. Accordingly a sloop sailed into Turtle Bay on the night of June 11, from which a band of armed men landed and took possession of the storehouses and made prisoners of the guard. It so happened, however, that one sentinel escaped, and hastening to the city, notified Stephens. Stephens, in turn, gave the word to Captain Vandeput of the *Asia* and Captain Montague of the *Kingfisher*. The two warships at once hoisted sail, but before they reached Turtle Bay the Connecticut men had "got clear off with their plunder." Stephens reported ruefully to General Gage that they had taken fifty or more boxes of case shot and various other stores.[20]

But it soon became evident that the Americans could not arm themselves adequately merely by raiding British stores, so they concentrated their efforts on importing guns and ammunition from abroad, and on setting up foundries and powder mills of their own. The Provincial Congress was greatly encouraged when Robert Livingston reported that he was starting a powder mill and that he had secured 180 pounds of saltpetre from Philadelphia.[21]

So great was the need for gunsmiths that a committee was appointed to write to Great Britain promising to pay the passage of any who would come to New York. In every local smithy the sparks were flying day and night as the workers turned out the needed gun-barrels, bayonets and ramrods.[22] And great was the anger of the patriots when it was discovered that the British were trying to induce the gunsmiths either to leave for England, or, if they remained in America, neither to work themselves nor instruct others in their craft.

The artillery companies cast longing eyes on the cannon at the Battery. But for the moment they left them undisturbed, since the Provincial Congress did not wish to aggravate the already tense situation, by interfering with Crown property. On the other hand, the hundred or more pieces of ship cannon belonging to the merchants which were stored on the docks, it was thought prudent to move out of range of the *Asia* and *Kingfisher*. Even though some of them, which had seen service on the privateers of the French and Indian War, were out of date and in poor condition, the Americans could not afford to overlook them. So for several days gangs of men, working under Isaac Sears, loaded them upon carts and hauled them out of the city and over the Manhattan roads to Kingsbridge, fourteen miles away.[23] Here some were mounted behind hastily constructed works to protect the approaches from Connecticut and upper New York.[24]

The calling of the Provincial Congress, the organizing, arming and drilling of military companies, the violence used against Cooper and Rivington, did much to erase the reputation for Toryism which the Assembly had won for the province and city. Yet some of the Connecticut patriots were so doubtful of the cooperation of the New Yorkers that they sent a warning that they were prepared to invade Manhattan and force them into line.

Had the members of the Wethersfield committee who wrote this letter been at Kingsbridge two weeks later to witness the reception of the New England delegates to Congress, they would have been convinced of the patriotism of the New Yorkers. A number of the most prominent came out to meet the delegation and to accompany them down the island. About three miles from the city the New Englanders found the "grenadier company," the militia, many gentlemen on horseback or in carriages and "many thousands of persons on foot," waiting to receive them.

As they passed along the road, amid a great cloud of dust, men, women, and children pressed forward to cheer them and wave to them. Some of the younger men twice stopped John Hancock's carriage, which led the procession, and would have unhitched the horses to draw it with their hands had he permitted them. So they entered the city, and passing through the principal streets "amidst the acclamation of thousands," halted at Fraunces Tavern where they spent the night.[25] "This is a sad mortification to the Tories," Hancock wrote Miss Dorothy Quincy. "Things look well here."

They looked still better on June 25, when George Washington arrived on his way to Cambridge to take command of the American army. Several members of the Provincial Congress met him at Newark and escorted him to the North River, where boats were waiting to ferry his party over to the Manhattan side, not far from the Lispenard estate. Awaiting him was a great crowd of people who gave repeated huzzas as Washington, a commanding figure with his blue suit and purple sash, stepped ashore. After he had had luncheon at Lispenard's mansion, he was conducted to the city, the militia companies in the lead, followed by the members of the Provincial Congress, two members of the Continental Congress, a company of Philadelphia horse and a vast crowd of citizens. The procession made its way to Hull's Tavern, amid the ringing of church bells and the cheering of the throngs which lined the streets and looked down from windows and roof tops.[26]

While the city was thus giving Washington an uproarious welcome, Governor Tryon, whom the British Ministry had sent back to his post, had arrived in the harbor and was waiting to land. Some of the Council members and others who still hoped for a reconciliation, had planned a demonstration and were chagrined when Washington "stole the show." But in the evening, when the patriots had exhausted themselves with marching and shouting, the governor stepped ashore at the foot of Broad Street. Here he was received by a group of Councillors, judges, Assemblymen, Anglican ministers, the mayor and others, who escorted him to his lodgings. There was some shouting, William Smith tells us, "a proof that the populace esteem the man, tho' they at this instant hate his commission and would certainly have insulted any other in that station." [27]

But Tryon discovered immediately that he was only the shadow of a governor. America was at war with Great Britain, and the people, while in theory acknowledging the authority of the King's representative, in fact paid little attention to it. Preparation for defence was the business of the day, and for that "all good men" took their orders from the Continental Congress, the Provincial Congress and the Committee of Safety.

New York was vulnerable to attack from two widely separated points, from Canada by way of the Richelieu River and Lake Champlain, and from Boston or Halifax by sea to New York Bay. There was great rejoicing, then, when word was received that the gateway from the north had been closed. Ethan Allen, with his Green Mountain Boys, had surprised the small garrisons at Ticonderoga and Crown Point, and had taken more than 300 cannon and other sorely needed supplies.

But the probability of an attack by sea continued to worry the patriots. On June 14 a ship's captain, just in from Cork, reported that when he had sailed four regiments of redcoats were preparing to leave for New York.[28] Realizing that the local companies were inadequate to repel such a force, the Provincial Congress sent a messenger post haste to General David Wooster, requesting him to reinforce them with the Connecticut troops under his command at Greenwich, Stamford and elsewhere. Should the British occupy Manhattan and the Hudson River, they pointed out, the New Englanders would be cut off from their friends in the other colonies. So, a few days later, the Connecticut men came marching over the Post Road to Kingsbridge and down the

Bloomingdale road to the Herring farm, near what is now Washington Square, where they encamped.[29]

Whatever comfort these troops gave the people of the city was more than offset by the presence in the East River of the British warships *Asia* and *Kingfisher,* with their frowning guns pointing out over Whitehall and the Exchange. It was Colden who had sent to Admiral Graves for these vessels, in the hope that they might protect the persons and property of "his Majesty's loyal subjects." But to the patriots they constituted an entering wedge for the British invasion. Moreover they were a constant threat to the city itself, since they might, if their commanders saw fit, let loose with a destructive bombardment.

But neither Captain Vandeput of the *Asia* nor Colden wanted to injure the place. Not only were many of the residences and warehouses owned by Loyalists, but the city could, and probably would, be made the chief base for the British army in its approaching invasion of America. It gave access to the Hudson River, it was convenient for an invasion either of New England or New Jersey, its harbor could float the entire British fleet.

So there resulted a kind of stalemate, in which the warships refrained from acts of hostility, while the Provincial Congress actually agreed to permit provisioners to supply them with "small necessaries." When they learned that one of the boats of the *Asia* had been seized by a mob and burned, they actually promised to replace it. The carpenters had made considerable progress in building this "indemnification" boat, when "some disorderly persons" one night sawed it to pieces.[30] A few weeks later a small sloop, which had come down the North River "to carry two women on board" a British transport, on her way back was captured, hauled on shore and dragged to the Common, where it was burnt.[31]

And the Provincial Congress, after long deliberation, so far overcame their fear of the *Asia* as to order the removal of some of the King's guns from the Battery. On the night of August 23 a large group of men, working under the protection of Captain Lamb's artillery and a detachment of light infantry, began to carry off some of the ninepounders. But they kept a sharp eye on a barge full of armed men from the *Asia* which was hovering off shore. Suddenly there came across the water the sharp report of a musket. Not knowing that this was merely a signal, and thinking they had been fired upon, the Americans discharged a volley at the barge, killing one man.

Right: Philip Livingston.

Below: Method of Choosing Delegates from New York for the First Continental Congress.

ADVERTISEMENT.

THE Committee of Correspondence in New-York, having on Monday Night laſt proceeded to the Nomination of five Perſons to go as Delegates for the ſaid City and County, on the propoſed General Congreſs at Philadelphia, on the 1ſt of September next; the five following Perſons were nominated for that Purpoſe,

Philip Livingſton,
James Duane,
John Alſop,
John Jay,
Iſaac Low.

The Inhabitants, therefore, of this City and County, are requeſted to meet at the City-Hall, on THURSDAY next, at 12 o'Clock, in order to approve of the ſaid five Perſons as Delegates, *or to chooſe ſuch other in their Stead, as to their Wiſdom ſhall ſeem meet.*

By Order of the Committee,

ISAAC LOW, CHAIRMAN.

TUESDAY, 5th July, 1774.

Cadwallader Colden, Lieutenant Governor of the Province of New York.

A NEW METHOD OF MACARONY MAKING AS PRACTISED AT BOSTON

For the Custom House officer's landing the Tea
They Tarr'd him and feather'd him just as you see
And they Drench'd him so well both behind and before
That he begg'd for God's sake they wou'd drench him no more.

Rough Treatment of a Loyalist. John Malcomb, a collector of the British tea tax in Boston, is being tarred and feathered and forced to drink the health of the royal family in scalding tea. (In the 18th century a "Macarony" was one of a class of traveled young men affecting foreign ways.)

Southwest View of Fort George with the City of New York, 1778.

Fraunces Tavern at the Corner of Broad and Pearl Streets, famous gathering place of American Patriots in the eighteenth century. It is now owned by the Sons of the Revolution.

Washington Taking Command of the Army. By decision of the Second Continental Congress, Washington was nominated Commander-in-chief of the Continental Army. He took command on July 3, 1775, at Cambridge Common. Artemas Ward, leader of the minute-men who fought at Bunker Hill, greeted him and transferred command to him.

The Capture of Fort Ticonderoga by Ethan Allen and His Green
Mountain Boys.

Marinus Willett Preventing the Removal of Arms by the British. This incident occurred when the British

This provoked a few scattered shots from the *Asia*, followed by a discharge of musketry and several broadsides of nine-, eighteen- and twenty-four-pounders. Instantly the city was in an uproar. Amid the rattle of drums, the shouts of workmen and soldiers and the crash of falling cannon balls, half-dressed women and children fled through the streets. With the coming of daylight it was found that several houses near the fort had been damaged, that one eighteen-pounder had gone through the roof of Fraunces Tavern, that another had hit a house nearby, and that several men had been wounded. The net gain for the patriots was twenty-one nine-pounders, which they dragged up Broadway and ranged triumphantly under the liberty pole.[32]

Thereafter the fear that the British might destroy the city hung over the people like a nightmare. As early as April 29, many panic-stricken persons fled, and during the next few weeks family after family followed. The day after the bombardment the streets were filled with carts, some laden with men, women and children, others with household goods, all heading for the open country. "The moving out of town continues and the city looks in some streets as if the plague had been in it, so many houses being shut up," the Moravian minister Gustavus Shewkirk wrote in his *Diary*, on August 28.[33] Two weeks after the bombardment "at least one third of the citizens" had gone.[34] Some of the refugees found lodgings with relatives, but others lived in "tents and huts" until they could erect better houses. Uncomfortable as they were in these crude shelters, they did not lack for food, since the "back settlers" supplied them "in great plenty." [35]

Not all of the fugitives were fleeing the British guns, for some left to escape persecution at the hands of Sears and his followers. "People who did not chuse to submit to their insolent demands have been obliged to quit town with their families to escape the insolent treatment they are threatened with," Major Isaac Hamilton wrote General Gage.[36] All who were suspected of aiding the British were arrested and sent to Connecticut, perhaps to the dreaded Simsbury mines. A Mr. Moran, who Sears had reason to believe was taking a verbal message to Sir Guy Carleton in Canada, was arrested by twenty armed men and hustled off to Hartford.[37] One Angus McDonald was brought before the Provincial Congress for enlisting men to serve under Gage, and was immediately imprisoned at General Wooster's camp at Greenwich.[38]

With such examples before them the Tories, if they remained in the city, kept a discreet silence. "I am determined not to transgress," wrote one to a friend in Boston, "and not to do anything that may cause banishment or . . . being sent to the mines of Simsbury, which are punishments daily inflicted." [39] Less severe but more humiliating was the treatment accorded a youth at Kinderhook. At a quilting party, where he was the only male present, he regaled the girls with a bitter attack on Congress. Thereupon they seized him, stripped him to the waist, gave him a coating of molasses and then added a layer of down from the tops of flags growing in the meadow.[40]

Such incidents caused Governor Tryon great uneasiness. What if the irresponsible Sears should seize him? What if he should suffer by "the insolence of the armed mob"? On July 7 he wrote to Dartmouth asking permission to return to England. But before receiving a reply, hearing that the Continental Congress had advised the local govern-ments to arrest all persons hostile to the liberties of America, he thought it prudent to flee to the protection of the British warships. So, on October 19 he gathered up his effects and, together with Attorney General Kempe and others, rowed out to the Halifax packet the *Duchess of Gordon,* which for the time being became the floating capitol of provincial New York.[41]

It was as well that he fled, for a few weeks later Sears did lead an expedition from Connecticut to the city with the avowed purpose of suppressing Tory activity. With about 100 horsemen he crossed into East Chester, where they entered the house of Judge Jonathan Fowles, put him under arrest and confiscated his sword, guns, and pistols. They then proceeded to Westchester to seize the Reverend Samuel Seabury and Nathaniel Underhill. Seabury complained afterwards that they rifled his desk, thrust a bayonet through his daughter's cap and cut to pieces the quilt in a frame upon which she was working.[42]

The raiders then mounted their horses and rode down to New York City, which they entered about noon on November 23, and "with bayonets fixed" clattered over the pavements to the printing office of James Rivington, at the foot of Wall Street. Placing a guard at the door, they crowded in, destroyed the press and carried off his type. They then "wheeled to the left," and in perfect order rode out of town to the tune of "Yankee Doodle" and amid the cheers of the crowd.[43]

But though the people thus shouted their approval, the Provincial Congress considered the raid a serious infringement by one colony upon the rights of another. If New York Tories were to be arrested or New York newspapers suppressed, it should be done by the New York authorities, not by raiders from Connecticut. So emphatic were they in their protest that Governor Trumbull, after some hesitation, released Seabury, Fowler and Underhill. But Rivington never got his type back, and his *Gazetteer* ceased to appear on the tables of the coffee houses and taverns.[44]

It served him right, the patriots said, for this was no time for scruples in dealing with the "enemies of freedom." There was good reason to think that some were corresponding with General Gage to keep him informed of the military plans of the Americans. In fact a week previous to the raid on Rivington's press, Governor Tryon, from his safe retreat aboard the *Duchess of Gordon,* had given Gage an accurate report of the intended attack on Canada. "The New York troops under command of Colonel McDougall ordered to march immediately for Ticonderoga," he wrote. "When joined by 1,000 riflemen will amount to at least 3,000. There to be joined by 4,000 New England forces to rendezvous at Crown Point; from thence to proceed to Montreal and Quebec even if over ice."[45]

For weeks the city was busy with the preparations for the campaign —the gathering of stores, drilling on the Common, the shipping of beef up the Hudson. On August 8 Lieutenant Colonel Rudolphus Ritzema, with four companies of the First New York Regiment, climbed aboard waiting sloops and set sail up the Hudson. Other detachments followed—Colonel James Clinton's Third Regiment in their gray coats faced with green; Colonel Holmes' men in dark brown faced with scarlet; Captain John Lamb's company of artillery; General David Wooster with his Connecticut men.[46]

Awaiting them at Ticonderoga was their commander, General Philip Schuyler. A tall, slight man, with florid face, keen dark eyes, prominent nose, brown hair, he radiated energy and confidence. But he was deeply disappointed when the New York detachments marched into camp. Many of the men were ill; many had deserted. The others were poorly equipped for an expedition in the north, where ice and snow might overtake them, some lacking tents, others shoes, stockings and underwear. One detachment had to be kept penned up on the boats until supplies arrived. "Give us guns, blankets, tents, etc., and we will fight the Devil," they promised, "but don't keep us here in market-boats like a parcel of sheep or calves." [47]

The Connecticut troops, under their praying officers and their pious chaplains, thought the New Yorkers a wicked, blasphemous lot. "I don't see how any of us can expect the blessing of God when his holy name is so often profaned," one of them remarked sorrowfully.[48] But when it came to drinking rum, to support them in the long marches in the soaking rains through forests and marshes, the Yankees were the full equal of the New Yorkers.

As the weeks passed news gradually filtered back to anxious wives and parents that the army had at last been set in motion, had ferried down Lake Champlain and the Richelieu River and were investing the fort at St. John's. Then came the discouraging news that Schuyler had joined the ranks of the sick, and had been forced to relinquish his command. But there was consolation in the fact that his successor was the gallant and able young Richard Montgomery.[49]

The capture of St. John's, which came only after a very stubborn defense, the irrepressible Lamb thought a "fatal stab at the hellish machinations of the foes of freedom." But the chief task still lay ahead, and the difficulties were many, for the men had to make their way through swamps and mires "mid-leg deep," before emerging on the bank of the St. Lawrence. There was compensation, however, when they reached Montreal and the small British garrison promptly surrendered.[50]

The anxious people of New York were still exulting at this important success, when word came that Montgomery had placed his men on board a flotilla captured from the enemy, had joined Arnold's New Englanders at Point au Tremble and had begun the siege of Quebec. It seemed certain that this great stronghold would be taken, Canada linked with the revolting colonies and the northern approach to New York closed to the British.[51]

Then, in January, 1776, came bad news. A Canadian named Antill, who was deeply attached to the American cause, driving his sleigh at breakneck speed over the icy roads, brought letters from Arnold and others to say that the assault on Quebec had failed. Despite the gallantry of the troops, who stormed up to and over some of the principal fortifications of the city, they were thrown back with heavy losses; the brave Montgomery had been killed, Arnold wounded in the leg, Captain Lamb had been shot down and later found by the British unconscious and weak from loss of blood.[52] The Canadian expedition had failed.

Back in New York, though the troops were thus openly at war with the King's forces, the people continued, at least in theory, to recognize the royal authority. They had taken up arms, not from a desire for independence, they assured Tryon, but solely because of the attempts to enslave them.[53]

When on December 4, Oliver De Lancey, William Smith, Cruger, Apthorp and others rowed out to the *Duchess of Gordon* for a meeting of the Council, one wonders whether they realized how farcical it was for them to pretend to govern a colony on whose soil they dared not assemble. As they sat in the cabin their impotence was emphasized by the governor's proposal to remove all records of land grants from the city to one of the British vessels. This, he thought, would so alarm property owners, by throwing all into confusion, that it would be "a mortgage for their return to their ancient union with Great Britain." [54] Smith protested against this slap on the wrist, since it might involve the Council members in suits for damages, but Tryon insisted.

Of more significance, though equally futile, were the efforts of the old government—Tryon, the Council, and the Assembly—to bring about a belated reconciliation. Two weeks after the news of the battle of Lexington reached New York, fourteen members of the Assembly wrote General Gage begging him to call a halt to hostilities, reiterated their loyalty and their affection for Great Britain and, though "tenacious of their rights and liberties," ardently desired an adjustment of all differences.[55]

Their plea was seconded by Tryon in his letters to Dartmouth. Would it not be the part of wisdom "to hold forth some further conciliatory measures?" he asked. "The terror of being taxed without their own cooperation once removed . . . the contest would . . . cease." Why, then, should the Ministry not give them the assurances they asked for and end the unhappy conflict? [56]

But the Ministry at this time were in no humor for compromise. When the Continental Congress sent Richard Penn to England with a petition to the King which was so moderate in tone that it became known as the Olive Branch, it met with an icy reception. Dartmouth kept Penn waiting for weeks before he would receive him and then told him there would be no answer. "The King and his Cabinet are determined to listen to nothing from the illegal Congress," said Suffolk. Although Dartmouth was careful to let it be known that he was prepared to treat with each colony separately, the snubbing of the Olive

Branch seemed to many Americans to slam shut the door of reconciliation.

Yet the Loyalists refused to relinquish hope. Surely there must be some way of settling the dispute short of military conquest by the British forces on the one hand, or of the independence of the colonies on the other. In the homes of the wealthy or around the tables of the Merchants Coffee House, serious faced men advanced plans of compromise and argued over this point and that. William Smith thought Parliament ought to pass a resolution, declaring that the contribution of the colonies to the defence of the empire should be voluntary, not forced. "Give them a constitutional security against arbitrary levies, that is to say, covenant that they shall be Englishmen, and the advocates of independency will be found such an inconsiderable handful . . . that they may be left to the correction of the rest of their own countrymen." [57]

Hope that the Ministry might assent to a settlement along these lines grew stronger with the arrival of young Lord Drummond to sound out sentiment in America. In an interview with certain members of the Continental Congress, he denied that he had any official proposal to make, but he drew out a paper which he said Lord North had given him, and after cautioning secrecy, read it aloud. The colonies must pledge themselves to supply a revenue for imperial purposes, and in return Great Britain would renounce her claim to the right to tax. There might be some difficulty over the quartering of troops, as the prerogative of the Crown was concerned in that matter, but Massachusetts would undoubtedly have her old charter restored. [58]

But the Americans placed little confidence in such underground approaches. If the Ministry really wished for reconciliation, why did they not come out openly with their proposals? And whereas assurances of concessions were vague and unofficial, the evidence that the Ministry was straining every nerve to force obedience by military and naval might was obvious to all. "The preparations making against your poor devoted country are amazing," a Londoner wrote a friend in New York. "The Ministry are determined to persevere," stated another correspondent. "There will be a considerable army in America, from 30,000 to 50,000 men; it is expected some foreign troops will be taken in pay." [59]

To New Yorkers this was of especial concern since it was generally understood that it would be upon their city that the gathering clouds would burst. The reasons were obvious. The possession of New York would give the British an excellent base for operations either to the south or the north; its harbor was unsurpassed; it was the gateway to the Hudson and the Hudson was the gateway to Canada. Washington saw clearly what was coming, Congress saw it, the friends of America in England saw it. "I feel for you and my other New York friends," wrote one, "for I expect your city will be laid in ashes." [60]

There were many in New York who agreed with him. The presence in their harbor of the two warships was proof enough of their helplessness. Resistance to an invading fleet, if there was to be resistance, could be made only from land batteries, and what hope was there for the city itself in a battle between batteries and ships of the line? Would not their homes come tumbling upon their heads? Would not men, women, and children fall by the hundreds before the murderous British fire?

Their fears were redoubled when General Lee with the vanguard of the American army entered the city, and on the same day the British warship *Mercury,* with General Clinton aboard, sailed into the harbor. They were right in conjecturing that Washington had decided to defend the place and that Lee had been selected as the man best fitted for the task. A local troop of light horse and a number of the "principal inhabitants" went out to meet the general and escort him to his lodgings at Mrs. Montagne's Tavern. They saw a man "plain in his person to a degree of ugliness," whose ungainliness was accentuated by the gout which was so painful that he had to be carried in a litter.[61] Lee had had long military experience and would have been invaluable to the American cause, had not his egotism, his crabbed disposition and his jealousy of Washington lowered his efficiency and culminated in open insubordination.

While Lee's horsemen were clattering over the Manhattan roads on their way to the city, they met scores of refugees, hastening north, with their families and what household goods they could take with them. These poor people, upon hearing of Clinton's arrival, had expected at any moment to see a fleet of ships of the line, frigates and transports sailing up the harbor. "I assure you that when Mr. Clinton arrived I fully expected that hostilities would immediately have commenced and the scene which would then have ensued was sufficient even in idea to shock my humanity," wrote Congressman Andrew Allen, who happened to be in the city at the time. Even when Clinton sent a message giving his word of honor not to land a man, the panicky flight continued.[62]

"Clinton came into our harbor," wrote one eyewitness, "away flew the women, children, goods and chattels." [63] Many families crossed over to Long Island and New Jersey, trying desperately to steer clear of the cakes of ice which imperilled their little boats.[64] Though every wagon, every cart, every horse that could be found was pressed into service, much had to be left behind. Many of the refugees did not know where they were going, or where they would find shelter. The Committee of Safety broadcast a message to the neighboring counties urging "all among whom such poor may come" to provide them "with habitations and other necessaries of life." [65] Some of the wealthy were more fortunate. "I have taken a house for my family at a place called Paramus," wrote Frederick Rhinelander. "The speaker has desired me to get a place for him in the same neighborhood." [66]

Lee's first step upon taking command in the city intensified the fears of the people. Despite the raid of the previous August a number of cannon and large quantities of stores remained at the Battery and in the yards at the water's edge, under the very muzzles of the guns of the warships. Tryon and Captain Parker, of the *Phoenix,* had "threatened perdition to the town" if these were removed, but Lee decided to take the risk. All day long, on February 11, "men and boys of all ages worked with the greatest zeal and pleasure," loading wagons and dragging the guns through the streets to the Common.[67] Though it was confidently expected that at any moment the warships would open upon the town, the hours passed without any signs of hostility, and when night fell not a gun had been fired.

Parker spread the report that he had saved the city to spite Lee and his New England troops, who manifestly wanted its destruction because it was a nest of Tories.[68] But to Tryon he gave another explanation. He could not concentrate his fire on the Battery and Fort George, because of the ice in the rivers and harbor. To fire at random on the city would not have prevented the removal of the guns and the stores, and would have entailed great losses upon "many friends of government." Moreover, the preservation of the town as a base for the King's army seemed of the utmost importance.[69]

But the people, not knowing what Parker would do, fled in increasing numbers. The entire city was in an uproar, as the rumbling of carts over the pavements mingled with the shouts of the men who were drawing the cannon.[70] Occasionally a touch of comedy relieved the otherwise tragic scene. When one fugitive was moving his household goods, "something broke by accident." Whereupon the poor fellow, who stuttered badly, exclaimed, "Da-da-damn Lord North! Da-da-damn Lord North!" [71] It was Sunday, but the churches were almost empty. In some there were no services; in others the few who attended had difficulty in hearing the preacher's voice over the din from without.[72] Especially tragic was the plight of the poor, "many of whom could scarcely pay their ferriage," and had no idea of where they would find shelter from the bitter cold.

For a few days New York seemed nearly deserted. In street after street most of the houses were empty, the doors locked, the shutters closed. But the place soon woke to new life as regiments from neighboring colonies marched in to reenforce Lee's little army. On February 7, William Alexander, Lord Stirling, had ferried over from New Jersey with 1,000 men. A few days earlier Colonel David Waterbury had marched in with 600 New Englanders. "Troops are daily coming in," wrote Frederick Rhinelander on February 23, "they break open and quarter themselves in any houses they find shut up." [73]

Quartering in fact now became a major problem. Waterbury's regiment had taken over the upper barracks on the Common, and Stirling's men were placed in the lower barracks, but other troops as they arrived had to be lodged in private houses. The Provincial Congress appointed John Van Cortlandt, Isaac Roosevelt and Captain Henry Rutgers a committee "to examine the lists of empty houses . . . and to ascertain such as they may think proper for the use of the troops." [74]

These gentlemen were instructed to select only such houses as were "least liable to be injured by the troops," but necessity knows no laws and soon some of the stately mansions of the rich, especially of rich Tories, were swarming with the rough soldiery. Men who a few months before had been farm hands or carters or sawyers, now made themselves at home in the paneled rooms of the Kennedy House and the Jonathan Mallet House. "Oh, the houses in New York, if you could but see the insides of them, occupied by the dirtiest people on the continent!" wrote one observer. "If the owners ever get possession again, I am sure they must be years in cleaning them." [75]

In the meanwhile General Lee was conferring with a committee of

Congress to "devise the best ways" for the defense of the city. Putting his finger upon the one almost insuperable difficulty, Lee pointed out that with the Narrows presenting an open gateway to the harbor and with Manhattan surrounded by navigable water, it would be hard to hold the place against an assault by a combined land and naval force. He might with reason have gone a step further and, arguing that it was impossible, advised its evacuation. To scatter the American forces from Kingsbridge to Flatlands, with a great river intervening, was to invite disaster. However serious would be the loss of New York, the loss of the American army would be more so.

A century earlier almost to a day, another band of American patriots had burned the capital of Virginia when they found that they could not defend it against the fleet under the command of the British governor, Sir William Berkeley.[76] And news had come but a few weeks ago that the Virginians of 1776, no whit less determined than those of 1676, had laid Norfolk in ashes to prevent Lord Dunmore from using it as a base of operations.[77] Had Washington, Lee and Congress applied the torch to New York the course of the Revolution might have been different.

But they drew back from such drastic action. Lee was confident that even though the redcoats should effect a landing under the guns of the warships, he could prevent their taking possession of the town. New York could not be converted into a tenable fortification, he thought, but it could be made a most advantageous field of battle, so advantageous that it would cost the enemy thousands of men to take it. "The streets must be traversed and barricaded, so as to prevent their coming on our flanks, three redoubts thrown up on the three eminences Judge Jones, Bayard's Hill, and either Lispenards or Haldermans house on Hudsons River. But these measures are not to be confined to the town, the whole island is to be redoubted . . . quite to King's Bridge." [78]

So now New York and Manhattan became a beehive of activity, as workmen dug trenches, cut down trees, erected redoubts, dragged cannon from this point to that. In the city itself barricades were thrown across Broad, Cortland, Wall, Crown and other streets; batteries were placed "near the air-furnace" at the foot of what is now Harrison Street, on Reed Street overlooking the Hudson; behind Trinity Church; at the old Battery and Fort George; on the Whitehall Dock; on Bayard's Hill and elsewhere.[79] In an incredibly short time the city took on the appearance of a fortress, so that one would hardly recognize it as the peaceful, mercantile town of former days.

"It would make you sorry to see the place so changed," wrote a New Yorker. "The old fort walls are demolished in part, though that is an advantage to the Broadway, as it opens the view there greatly; there is a battery carried across the street. . . . You remember Bayard's Mount covered with cedars; it commanded a prospect exceedingly extensive; the top of it so cut away that there is room enough now for a house and garden." When the Connecticut soldiers began cutting down a beautiful wood Oliver De Lancey had been nursing for forty years, he tried to stop them by explaining that a third part of it belonged to the Earl of Abingdon, a champion of the American cause, who had married his granddaughter. "Well," said one of the men, pausing in his work, "if he be such a great liberty-boy, and so great a friend of our country, he will be quite happy that his wood was so happy for our use." With that he resumed his chopping.[80]

"You may recollect a sweet situation at Horne's Hook that Jacob Walton purchased, built an elegant house, and greatly and beautifully improved the place," wrote one observer. "He was obliged to quit the place, the troops took possession and fortified there. When Mrs. Walton received the order to go out of her house, she burst into tears, for she was fixed to her heart's desire. By what uncertain a tenure do we hold the good and desirable possessions of this world?" [81]

On February 11, it was noted that the *Mercury*, together with a transport, the decks of the latter crowded with redcoats, were hoisting sail. A few minutes later anxious watchers in the town saw them drop down the harbor and proceed out to sea. Six days later the *Phoenix*, the *Asia* and the *Duchess of Gordon*, with two prizes, also got under way. But the elation of the people at the prospect of getting rid of these unwelcome guests was turned to apprehension when the *Asia* ran aground off the foot of Broad Street. And when Lee's men began dragging cannon out on the docks with the obvious intention of firing on her, there was another precipitous flight from that part of the town. But before a shot could be fired the tide rose, the crew of the *Asia* managed to get her afloat, and the little flotilla moved away.[82]

But joy was premature, for, instead of going out to sea, the vessels anchored off Bedloe's Island. From this position Tryon continued to communicate with the Tories and to forward information to the Ministry. On March 16, he addressed a letter to the people of New York urging them to return to their allegiance. "A door is still open to such honest, but deluded people, as shall avail themselves of the justice and benevolence which the supreme Legislature has held out to them of being restored to the King's grace and peace." [83] He urged the Tories to stand firm, promising them speedy support. But this the patriots greeted with ridicule. "It is generally a matter of laughter and surprise that he could do anything so weak and ill-judged," it was stated. "The friends to liberty hung him in effigy and printed a dying speech for him." [84] William Smith was shocked at the governor's action, which threw the Tories into consternation at being thus "held up to the wrath of the populace." [85]

It troubled the Tories, too, that Tryon's ill-judged action threatened to snap completely the already attenuated connection between the province and the old government. The governor was their chief link with the Ministry, their chief hope for reconciliation. When Tryon was accused of purchasing a boat to forage for provisions for the British army at Boston, the Tories entered a heated denial. "Yet such was the malignity of the times that the scandal was propagated," wrote William Smith. "No measures were taken to make the Governor's innocence known to the town." [86]

Even the Provincial Congress, refusing to acknowledge that America and Great Britain were at war, were outraged when General Lee issued orders that all communication with the British ships be cut off and that any persons supplying them with provisions would be severely punished. A committee was appointed to interview Lee and ask his reasons for ignoring their "resolves" in this matter. They had been informed, they said, that sentries near the wharves had fired at boats entering and leaving the docks and slips, whereby the persons on board were in danger of losing their lives.[87] But Lee, and later Putnam and Washington, pointed out that the warships were a menace to the city and to all America, and that the best way to get them out of the harbor was to cut off their supplies of food and water. They had information that sundry base and wicked persons, under the pretense of coming to the city markets, had supplied the ships with both provisions and information. This, they added, must stop.[88]

Hearing that the British were using Bedloe's Island, which since has become famous as the site of the Statue of Liberty, for a base of supplies and a Tory refuge, Lee decided to attack it. So, on April 2, he sent 400 men in seven periaguas to the island. Unheedful of the fire of the *Asia*, which lay nearby, they burnt the hospital and made off with a large number of white shirts, some "great coats," scores of entrenching tools and "an abundance of poultry of all sorts." [89]

Five days later two British vessels, the *Savage* and the pilot boat *James,* taking advantage of a thick fog, sent two boats ashore on Staten Island to take in water. While the men were at work, the crews of the *Savage,* noting a body of American riflemen approaching, opened a brisk fire and signaled the boats to return. In the melee which ensued one boat succeeded in getting away, but the other, with thirteen men, was captured.[90] Governor Tryon, who witnessed the affair from the deck of the *Duchess of Gordon* "by the help of a spy glass," wrote to Lord Germain gloomily: "All communication between the ships and the shore is now cut off. Even the element of water is denied us, which cannot probably henceforth be procured but under the fire of his Majesty's ships." [91]

A few days later the little fleet moved down the harbor and through the Narrows. When Washington arrived in the city on April 13, he reported that the *Asia* and some of the other vessels were at Sandy Hook, and that the rest had "gone to sea." [92]

The departure of the British marks the end of the transition from provincial control in New York City to the control of the Revolutionary Provincial Congress, the Committee of Safety and the Continental Congress. In July, 1776, when the colonies declared their independence, New York had been free of the last vestige of British control for several months. The change had been gradual, beginning with the organization of the Sons of Liberty and culminating in the flight of the governor, the failure of the Council to meet and the collapse of the Assembly. The next period, a period covering a few months only, was marked by the occupation of the city by Washington's army, by military preparations and by conquest by the British.

CHAPTER IV

THE REDCOATS TAKE OVER

THE YEAR 1776 was marked by a succession of revolutionary changes for the city of New York. When it opened, despite the flight of so many families, the place was essentially the old Dutch-English trading town which it had been for a century. Some of the residential streets were almost deserted, it is true, but down at the wharves there was still activity, with the farmers' boats coming and going, and here and there a merchant vessel loading or unloading, while on Whitehall or Broad Street the stores were open as usual. Three months later the approach of hostilities had driven off all except a fraction of the citizens, and left the town but a hollow shell.

Then, in the course of a few weeks, with the coming of thousands of American troops, it awoke to new life, a life which contrasted strangely with that of the old days, a life marked by the marching of soldiers, the sound of drums, the rattle of munition carts over the cobbled streets, the commands of officers, the waving of flags, the flash of bayonets. For a few months New York was the military capital of America.

With the invasion of the British army and navy under Sir William Howe and his brother, Lord Richard Howe, with the Battle of Long Island, the invasion of Manhattan, the retreat to Harlem Heights and then to White Plains, the loss of Fort Washington and Fort Lee, New York City once more experienced a sudden transformation. Gone were the soldiers from New England or New Jersey or Pennsylvania, save the poor fellows who were confined in the prisons, and in their places were the British and Hessians. And this time the change was more lasting, for the city was destined to remain in British hands, as their chief base and port of entry, for the remainder of the war. More than seven years were to elapse before Sir Guy Carleton put the last of his redcoats on board transports, and sailing out past Sandy Hook, left New York to Washington and the Americans.

Yet the city, under Howe and Clinton and Carleton, was not destined to be so exclusively military as under Washington. After its capture, it began to fill up with Tories, not only New York Tories, but Tories from other parts of the country, from New Jersey, Connecticut, Philadelphia, Norfolk. Under the British regime civil life was resumed; the taverns were opened; merchants chatted as of old over the tables of the coffee houses; the slips, the streets, the stores teemed with activity; but the population, despite the appearance here and there of a familiar face, was a new, a strange population, a population which looked hopefully eastward across the Atlantic and prayed for King George and for the success of his armies.

But as yet this was in the future. For the moment all eyes were turned upon the concentration of the American forces in the city. When, in March, 1776, Washington sent word that Howe was evacuating Boston, it was the general opinion that he would head at once for New York. Nor was apprehension lessened by his voyage to Halifax, for it was obvious that he went there to await reinforcements and to make final preparations for an irresistible assault on the lower Hudson region.

To ward off the blow Washington hastened every available man to the city. From Boston he wrote Congress on March 13 that he was sending General Israel Putnam with the advance guard, and would follow himself with the remainder of the army at the earliest possible moment.[1] On March 27 a regiment of riflemen 1,000 strong arrived and three days later General William Heath, whose brigade of New Englanders had marched to Norwich and there embarked on transports, sailed into Turtle Bay.

The few remaining inhabitants, who paused in their work to wave welcome to the New Englanders when they entered the city, noted with interest their varied and picturesque uniforms. In Colonel Charles Webb's Connecticut regiment, one company wore blue coats, buckskin breeches, white stockings and half boots; another green shortcoats with brass buttons and black velvet jackets and breeches; another blue coats and small castor hats set off by a black band and a silver buckle; another brown coats and jackets. In Colonel William Bond's Massachusetts regiment the company uniforms also varied, despite the fact that all wore blue coats. Captain Daniel Egery's company wore blue jackets, striped waistcoats and round hats; Captain Nathaniel Fuller's men gray surtouts, green coats and small-brimmed hats.[2]

"Picture to yourself the once flourishing city evacuated by most of

its members, especially the fair," Major Nicholas Fish wrote Richard
Varick on April 9. "Business of every kind stagnated . . . We have
Generals Putnam, Sullivan, Heath, Thompson and Lord Stirling
among us, with I believe about 14,000 troops; fresh arrivals from
Cambridge daily." [3] The next day twenty-three transports came in
through Hell Gate to put ashore Sullivan's brigade of six regiments.
On the 13th Washington arrived with Adjutant General Horatio
Gates "and several other gentlemen of distinction." [4] A few days later
General Nathanael Greene, who had embarked at New London, sailed
down East River and landed his entire brigade.

In the meanwhile Washington was sending out urgent appeals to
all the neighboring provinces for the militia. In June they began to
arrive—Pennsylvanians, some in hunting shirts and leggings suggestive
of the frontier, some in green coats, some with yellow striped jackets
and trousers; regiment after regiment of Connecticut men, some in
brown coats, some in blue, others in white hunting shirts; regiments
from Rhode Island, from upper New York, from New Jersey. As they
came ashore from ferryboats and transports, the onlookers pronounced
them "hearty fellows," quite capable of holding their own with the
King's regulars or his hired German troops.[5] They did not stop to consider that the militia, however effective they might be in the type of
warfare they were accustomed to, were not trained to meet disciplined
troops in the open and knew nothing about defending prepared works
against a landing under the protection of frigates. In the difficult task
of defending New York the militia were to prove a liability rather than
an asset.

There was some apprehension that among such a mixed assemblage there would be some who would get drunk, or commit robberies,
or offer insults to civilians. Colonel Thomas Mifflin, the quartermaster
general, limited the number of inns and dramshops which were licensed
to sell strong liquors and confined the men to their barracks and
quarters after the sounding of the tattoo. But they seem to have behaved
well, and we may discount the statement of a Tory who called them
"filthy and unruly." "The behavior of the New England soldiers is
decent and their civility to the inhabitants very commendable," stated
the *New York Packet*. "They attend prayers with the chaplain evening and morning regularly, in which their officers set the example.
On the Lord's Day they attend public worship twice." [6]

Living conditions for the men were not easy. "We are quartered in a good house," the youthful chaplain Philip Vickers Fithian wrote his wife, "but it is totally empty. . . . I sleep with Mr. Holmes; he has two blankets and a pillow; these we spread down and cover us with one; but the hard floor and rough blankets, believe me, they are not pleasant." [7]

It would have been impossible to find even such crude accommodations as these in the crowded city, had not regiment after regiment moved out to man the various fortifications that ringed the harbor, East River and the Hudson—Governor's Island, Red Hook, Paulus Hook, Kip's Bay, Horne's Hook, Kingsbridge, Harlem Heights, Buchanan's Island, [8] Montressor's Island, [9] etc. And fortunate indeed was the soldier who had in these posts a house to shelter him from the cold or the rain. At Red Hook Fithian's regiment was quartered in one house and a barn, "so that many chose rather to sleep in their blankets on the ground, than with the throng." [10] Later they were supplied with tents, but these proved poor protection from the cold and wet. "Our tent living is not very pleasant," wrote Fithian. "Many heavy showers today, and every shower wets us. . . . We shall be cold next month. But we must grow inured to these necessary hardships." [11]

But Fithian did not become inured to hardships, for two weeks later he suffered an attack of dysentery. On October 4 his friend, the Rev. William Hollingshead, "found him lying upon a thin bed raised from the floor only by a little straw covered with a blanket or two; with no other shelter from the inclemency of the season than a small marquee." His only nurse was "an unknowing country lad," while his physician was "an unskilful quack of a surgeon's mate." Four days later he expired.[12]

Fithian's case was typical. Hardship, exposure, unwholesome food, bad drinking water, improper sanitary arrangements, insufficient hospitals, a dearth of physicians, the general ignorance of the nature of diseases and the proper treatments, sent hundreds of poor fellows to the grave. In the defense of New York sickness cost Washington more men than British bullets. "Putrid disorders, the smallpox in particular, have carried off great numbers," one observer stated. "When I left the city there were 6,000 in their hospitals." [13]

When the spectre of smallpox made its appearance, the Provincial Congress suggested that the ill men be isolated on Montressor's Island and placed under the care of Dr. Malachi Treat. Washington gave orders for a careful examination of every man in the army, so that anyone showing the symptoms of the dreaded disease would be taken out of the ranks immediately, and the soldier who had himself inoculated was to be cashiered as an enemy of his country, for it was thought that this, so far from checking the infection, would spread it.[14]

Fithian, before he himself was laid low, was indefatigable in visiting the sick. "I walked to the hospitals of three regiments," he wrote in his *Journal,* on July 26. "A sight that forces compassion . . . These brave youths, when brought to the necessity of changing their time of rest . . . changing wholly their diet, and in this uncommon heat and drouth, when no vegetables can be procured, sicken. . . . In every apartment are many in the dysentery. Many have putrid fevers." [15] When the men lived in the open they were assailed by "camp fever," or what is now called typhus; when they remained in town they succumbed to dysentery or possibly typhoid fever. Dr. Solomon Drowne said that duty alone made him continue his work in that "shocking place. . . . The air of the whole city seems infected." [16]

The hospitals were filled to overflowing. Unfortunately the New York Hospital, which had been partly restored after its destruction by fire in February 1775, was converted into barracks for the troops. So King's College was taken over for the reception of the sick, its students forced to leave, and the books and scientific apparatus deposited in the City Hall.[17] In August, 1776, when additional space was urgently needed, the Provincial Convention authorized Washington to use as hospitals the Apthorpe, Oliver De Lancey and Robert Bayard Houses at Bloomingdale; the William Bayard House at Greenwich; the John Watts House near Kip's Bay, the William McAdams House "near the old glass house"; the Nicholas Stuyvesant and the Peter Stuyvesant Houses.[18] It was thought especially appropriate that the mansions of the Tories be made to serve the cause of liberty to compensate for the defection of their owners.

But there were other and more violent ways of making the Loyalists suffer. On the evening of June 10, Pastor Shewkirk was greatly shocked to see several men in the hands of a mob who "carried and hauled" them through the streets with candles in their hands, which they were forced to hold aloft on pain of having them pushed in their faces. Two days later, he tells us, the scene was far worse, for "several, and among them gentlemen, were carried on rails, some stripped naked and dreadfully abused." [19] At every corner the names of the victims were proclaimed by a cryer, the crowd gave three huzzas and the procession moved on.[20] Among those who suffered this humiliating penalty, "till now peculiar to the humane republicans of New England," were Donald McLean; Fueter, the silversmith; an apothecary named Queen; Lessly the barber; and a Mr. Rapalje. Theophilus Hardenbrook, architect and builder, "was taken from his house by a desperate mob, who tore all his clothes from his body, rode him round the city in a cart, pelted and beat him with sticks in so cruel and barbarous a manner that he . . . very nearly had lost his life." [21]

The harsh treatment of the Loyalists was inspired as much by fear as by resentment. It was certain that the British were receiving accurate reports of the number of troops in the city and the location of the batteries, and who but the Tories could have sent it? In Westchester a certain Joshua Barns was caught red-handed, trying to enlist men for Tryon's service "who were to be called the Governor's Life Guards." [22] Sloops filled with provisions were slipping out of creeks and coves under cover of darkness to provision the British fleet at the Narrows. Everyone knew that there were hundreds in the city who waited only for an opportunity to join the enemy. And though few were so daring as to drink openly to the success of the King's army and fleet, as did a certain John Lewis, no doubt many did so in the privacy of their homes.[23]

The Provincial Congress appealed to the people to restrain their resentment against the Tories, promising that the civil and military authorities would deal with them effectively. So a net was spread throughout the city and province. "The persons of the mayors of the cities of York and Albany, judges, Councillors, magistrates and the principal gentlemen of the country, that are not in rebellion, [are] seized and secured; even down to the meanest planters persecuted and tyrannized over." [24] When Washington sent a regiment into Queens to break up a nest of Tories there, many "hid themselves in swamps, in woods, in barns, in holes, in hollow trees, in cornfields and among the marshes." John Harris Cruger, of the Council, and Jacob Walton, a member of the Assembly, hid in the barn of an old Quaker; the aristocratic Augustus Van Cortlandt took refuge in a cow house; Theophilus Hardenbrook, after his beating by the mob, concealed himself "in the woods, houses and barns about Bloomingdale." Whenever a Tory was discovered and dragged out of his hiding place, he was marched off to New York City, "insulted and abused upon the road," and then sent to Connecticut.[25]

That these measures were justified became obvious to all when news spread like wildfire throughout the city that the authorities had uncovered a Tory plot to blow up the powder magazine, spike the cannon and turn the place over to the British. Amid the greatest excitement, David Matthews, the Mayor; "a short thick" gunsmith "with a white coat," named Gilbert Forbes; Thomas Hickey, one of Washington's bodyguard; William Green, a drummer; and James Johnson, a fifer, were taken into custody. As a committee of the Provincial Congress prepared to examine the accused, the most exaggerated reports were spread and eagerly listened to—the conspirators had intended to murder Washington and Putnam, they planned to burn the city, the whole thing had been concocted by Governor Tryon.[26]

Although at the trial no evidence was produced against Matthews, he was deported, as a dangerous Tory, to Litchfield, from which place he made his escape to the British some months later. Forbes and Green saved their necks by telling all they knew of the plot, but Hickey, who refused to talk, was sentenced to death. On June 28 he was led out to a field near the Bowery Lane, and there hanged "in the presence of near 20,000 spectators." [27]

And now the hitherto banned word "independence" made its appearance in conversation, the newspapers and public addresses. The Americans took up arms, not to secure independence, but to preserve their liberty. "Till my arrival here, I acknowledge I was ignorant enough to imagine that the Colonists had renounced their Sovereign and were actually contending for absolute independence," wrote one of Gage's officers from Boston in July, 1775. "But I am now convinced that they desire nothing more than peace, liberty, and safety." [28] Washington was opposed to independence, Jefferson was opposed to independence, Congress opposed independence. Franklin declared in March, 1775, that he had never heard an American, "drunk or sober," express a desire for separation.

In New York City it was not only the De Lanceys, Van Cortlandts and other aristocrats who dreaded independence, but many of the most ardent Sons of Liberty as well. Whenever the matter was discussed, in committee meetings, at social gatherings, in taprooms, the dangers of a complete separation from England were pointed out. The colonies needed the protection of the royal army and navy; they were too weak in numbers, too divided to stand alone; they would be ruined if England closed British ports and the ports of her West Indian islands to their tobacco, naval stores, grain, fish and furs; they were tied to Great Britain by blood, by language, institutions, religion.

But now sentiment began to change. The ten years of conflict with the British Ministry gradually wore away much of the old affection. Gage's attack at Lexington and Concord came as a shock to all Americans. When this was followed by preparations to force obedience at the bayonet's point, by the hiring of troops from the petty German princes, by the inciting of Indians to raid the back settlements, by the snubbing of the Olive Branch, the old loyalty gave way to resentment and hatred.

But in the end the Americans declared independence because they found it necessary to do so in order to win their battle for liberty. To drive the British armies from American soil and British fleets from American waters the aid of the King of France was of first importance. But Louis XVI had no intention of entering the lists as the champion of the rights of peoples. Only if the Americans meant to break up the British Empire and thus weaken his traditional enemy, was he interested. In effect Vergennes, the French Minister of Foreign Affairs, said to Franklin, "If you want our aid, declare yourselves. We might join if you are fighting for independence; we will not sacrifice one French soldier to uphold what you term the traditional liberties of Englishmen."

Such was the situation when a pamphlet entitled *Common Sense*, by an anonymous writer,[29] made its appearance in the New York bookstores. When it was learned that this little volume gave a striking presentation of America's case against England and that it pointed out that independence was already in fact accomplished, there was a general rush to secure copies. In every household it was read, discussed, lauded or denounced. *Common Sense* had a profound effect in hastening independence, not so much because it won people over to it, but because it put into words what they were thinking and confirmed them in an opinion already formed.

While the New Yorkers were still talking about the pamphlet, word came that the Virginia Convention, meeting in the Capitol at Williamsburg, by a unanimous vote, had instructed their delegates in the Continental Congress to propose a declaration of independence. This made it necessary for each colony to take a definite stand for or against separation. The New Yorkers were divided, the mass of the people favoring immediate action, while the conservatives took refuge in delay. On

May 29, the Committee of Mechanics addressed the Provincial Congress to urge them to instruct the New York delegates at Philadelphia to vote for independence.[30] When the Congress side-stepped the issue by declaring that they had no authority to give such instructions, the Committee of Safety called upon the voters to invest them with it or "to elect by ballot others in their stead." [31]

But while New York hesitated the Continental Congress acted. On June 8, Richard Henry Lee, in accordance with his instructions, submitted resolutions declaring the colonies "free and independent States" and absolving them from all political connection with Great Britain. On July 2, after three weeks of debate, the resolutions were carried, with nine States voting in the affirmative, two States opposing, the Delaware delegation tied and the New Yorkers not voting. On July 4, 1776, the Declaration of Independence, drawn up by a committee headed by Thomas Jefferson, was read and agreed to. Five days later the newly elected Provincial Congress of New York, meeting at White Plains, instructed their delegates at Philadelphia to give a belated assent.[32]

On the evening of the same day each brigade of Washington's army was drawn up to listen to the reading of the Declaration. The troops in the city were formed in a hollow square on the Common, with Washington and other officers on horseback in the center. Amid deep silence one of the aides, in a clear voice, read the document, which was greeted with three cheers.[33]

The troops had long viewed the gilt statue of George III in the Bowling Green with resentment, declaring that none but the New York Tories would have so honored the man who had tried to enslave the Americans and had brought so many misfortunes upon them. So, on the evening of July 9, after the reading of the Declaration, a large group, in company with many civilians, marched to the Green and entered through the gates of the iron fence. While some clambered up the white marble pedestal and on to the horse to fasten ropes to the figure, scores of others grabbed the other ends and at a given signal pulled it over. As horse and rider came crashing to the ground, the mob vented their fury by cutting off the King's head, clipping the laurels from around the brow and mutilating the nose.[34] A procession was then formed to carry the trunk through the principal streets, with fifes playing and drums beating the "Rogues March." [35]

The head was later taken to a tavern at Kingsbridge. When word of its presence reached the British military engineer Captain John Montressor, he sent a party in through the American lines who made off with it and buried it. After Kingsbridge fell to the British, Montressor dug it up and sent it to Lord Townshend.[36] A year later Thomas Hutchinson wrote in his diary: "Lady Townshend asked me if I had a mind to see an instance of American loyalty, and going to the sopha, uncovered a large gilt head, which at once appeared to be that of the King." [37]

The body and the horse were cut into fragments and carted off by Colonel Hugh Hughes to be cast into bullets. At Litchfield, Connecticut, "a shed was erected in an apple orchard, where Governor Oliver Wolcott chopped a part of it up with a wood axe, and the girls had a frolic in running the bullets and making them into cartridges." Another part of the statue, comprising the saddle and saddle cloth, was taken to Norwalk, and later, during a Tory raid, hidden in a swamp. Four other pieces, among them the tail of the horse, were plowed up on a Connecticut farm in 1871, and later purchased by the New York Historical Society.[38]

The importance of the destruction of the statue is the light it throws on the change in sentiment which one decade had brought about. For a century and a half the King had been revered as the father and protector of all his people, the people of America not less than the people of England. The colonists celebrated his birthday, drank to his health, included him in their prayers. If danger threatened, if misfortune struck, if their rights were infringed upon, it was to him they appealed. He symbolized, too, their union with Great Britain, so that their loyalty and affection for his person was expressive also of their loyalty and affection for the mother country. But now love had given way to resentment and hatred. As the dismembered statue of the King lay on the turf of the Bowling Green, there were those who realized that George III could never really reign again in America. His armies might conquer the country, the old governments might be reestablished, but his place in the hearts of the people had been lost forever. As one spectator, to whom the sight recalled the fallen angel Lucifer, exclaimed in Milton's words, "If thou beest he; but O, how fallen! how changed!"

Although it is probable that every inhabitant remaining in the city had become acquainted with the Declaration of Independence as soon as it was read to the soldiers, a great crowd assembled at noon on

July 18, before the City Hall for its "publication" to the civilians. As before there was perfect order during the reading, but at its conclusion several men rushed into the building to seize a painting of the King's arms which hung in the hall, and throw it out of the window to the throng beneath. There it was "seized, and torn, and stamped, and at last burned with unparalleled rage." After this the crowd smashed the stone in the front façade of the building in which the King's arms had been chiseled, "amidst the acclamations of the throng." [39]

In the Anglican churches the ministers themselves removed the King's arms, not because they wished to do so, but to prevent the mob from defacing the buildings.[40] For the Episcopal clergy it was a time of anxiety and sorrow. Associated in the minds of the people with the effort to establish an American bishopric, suspected of Tory sympathies, regarded by many as parasites, since they were supported in part by taxation, they were threatened and abused. Some went into hiding to await the arrival of the British. One Sunday, when Mr. Inglis was holding services, a company of about one hundred American soldiers marched into the church, "with drums beating and fifes playing, their guns loaded and bayonets fixed, as if going into battle. The congregation was thrown into the utmost terror and several women fainted." But after standing some minutes in the aisle, they took seats at the sexton's request, and the services continued.[41]

It had been hinted to Mr. Inglis several times that it might be wise to omit the usual prayers for the King, but he had steadily refused until independence was declared. Then, rather than comply, he decided to close the churches. To have prayed for him would have been rash "to the last degree," he stated afterward. "The inevitable consequence would have been a demolition of the churches and the destruction of all who frequented them. The whole rebel force was collected here and the violent partisans from all parts of the continent." Even the closing of the churches "was attended with great hazard, for it was declaring in the strongest manner our disapprobation of independency and that under the eye of Washington and his army." [42]

Early on the morning of June 29, watchers in the city, seeing a slim column of smoke rise on Staten Island, hastened to Washington's headquarters with word that the British fleet from Halifax had been sighted. Later in the day an officer, who had been on the lookout, arrived to verify the signal and to add that forty-five ships had arrived at Sandy Hook. As the day wore on other vessels, transports most of them, their decks covered with redcoats, kept coming in "like the swarm of locusts escaped from the bottomless pit," until more than a hundred were assembled in the shadow of the Atlantic Highlands.[43]

To the calm, dignified man who had risked his all in the cause of liberty by taking command of the American army, it seemed that for his country the hour of fate had arrived. "The time is now near at hand which must probably determine whether Americans are to be slaves or freemen," he told his men in an address issued from headquarters. "The fate of unborn millions will now depend, (under God) on the courage and conduct of this army. . . . We have therefore resolved to conquer or die."

At the very moment when the soldiers were reading this appeal, word came that the British fleet was moving north as though headed for New York Harbor or the Hudson. Instantly the city was all activity.

At three o'clock on the afternoon of July 12, the boom of six or more guns sounded an alarm, and the American troops rushed to their posts. A few minutes later the *Phoenix,* a 44-gun frigate, the *Rose,* carrying twenty-eight guns, the schooner *Trial,* and two tenders, got under sail and headed up the harbor. As they approached the mouth of the Hudson, the batteries on Red Hook, Governors Island, lower Manhattan and Paulus Hook opened on them with every gun. The frigates returned the fire, doing little damage to the American works, but injuring several nearby houses. "This affair caused a great fright in the city," says Pastor Shewkirk. "The smoke of the firing drew over like a cloud, and the air was filled with the smell of powder . . . Women and children and some with their bundles came from the lower forts and walked to the Bowery which was lined with people." [44] The throng gazed expectantly at the battle, hoping to see the invading fleet sunk or at least badly damaged by the fire which was concentrated on it. They were greatly disappointed, then, when with a strong, southerly wind and an incoming tide to aid them, the vessels sailed triumphantly past the batteries almost unscathed and proceeded up the river. One tar, to show his contempt for American marksmanship, climbed to the top gallant yard of the *Phoenix* and sat there throughout the engagement.

This demonstration of the inability of the Americans to hold the entrance to the North River foreshadowed the defeat of Washington's army. If the enemy's warships could ascend and descend this great waterway at will, they might flank all the elaborately prepared positions and trap the men stationed on Manhattan. And though Washington as yet had no idea of abandoning New York without a struggle, events proved that it would have been wise had he done so the moment the *Phoenix* and the *Rose* sailed unscathed up the river, their guns blazing and their pennants waving defiance.

The city was still in a state of excitement over this incident, when, shortly after six in the evening the breeze wafted the sound of firing up from the Narrows. It was occasioned by the arrival of the warship *Eagle* with Admiral Lord Howe, it was learned later. "Nothing could exceed the joy that appeared throughout the fleet and army upon our arrival," stated Ambrose Serle, the Admiral's secretary. "We were saluted by all the ships of war in the harbor, by the cheers of the sailors all along the ships and by those of the soldiers on the shore. A finer scene could not be exhibited, both of country, ships and men." [45]

There followed frequent meetings aboard the *Eagle,* marked by elaborate dinners and long discussions of the military and naval situation, while leaders and men alike awaited impatiently the arrival of two additional fleets. The first of these, bringing General Henry Clinton, Lord Cornwallis and eight regiments of veterans from an unsuccessful campaign in South Carolina, hove in sight on August 1. Eleven days later the second, comprising no less than 107 vessels, with General Philip von Heister and a large body of Hessians, also came in. "This morning, as soon as it was light, we were gladdened with the sight of the grand fleet in the offing," wrote Serle on August 12. "The joy of the navy and army was almost like that of a victory . . . So large a fleet made a fine appearance upon entering the harbor, with the sails crowded, colors flying, guns saluting and the soldiers . . . continually shouting." [46] In the city, where "the tops of the houses were covered with gazers" and all the wharves "lined with spectators," there was wonder, mingled with apprehension, as "ship after ship came floating up." [47]

In the meanwhile the Americans were preparing to make things uncomfortable for the *Phoenix* and the *Rose,* which for five weeks had been anchored up the North River. On the night of August 18, a sloop and a schooner, laden with combustibles, bore down on the British squadron. The schooner headed for the *Phoenix* and tried to grapple her, as the fire, leaping upward, began to crackle in the frigate's rigging. "But the wind not proving sufficient" to bring the fireboat "close along side or drive the flames immediately on board," the *Phoenix* after much difficulty succeeded in getting clear. But one of the tenders caught and burnt to the water's edge.[48]

This narrow escape convinced the captains of the *Phoenix* and *Rose* that to remain longer so far from the main fleet would be imprudent. So the next day, taking advantage of a favorable breeze and a driving rain, they went down the river as every battery on each bank blazed away at them. A number of galleys, each fitted with one 32-pounder, followed the squadron, "playing smartly" upon them until they had got out in the harbor. Thousands of spectators in the city watched the engagement, from windows and housetops, risking death from the balls of the frigates. A few were wounded but none killed. One family "experienced a kind preservation." "A 9-pounder came through the old German church in the Broadway, into the house they lived in . . . and into the room where they slept. But they were up and out of the room. The ball came through the window . . . went through the opposite wall near the head of the bedstead, crossed the staircase to another room." [49]

General Washington, faced by the most formidable force ever seen in America, had to reckon also with the Tory "Fifth Column." He was determined, therefore, to prevent their joining the royal army, supplying the British with provisions or giving information to the two Howes. So he posted troops along the shores of Long Island and New Jersey, patrolled nearby water with armed whale boats, pettiaugers and other small vessels, and seized or destroyed all the canoes, hay boats, bateaux and floats that could be found.[50]

Yet numbers of Tories succeeded in slipping past the guards and going out to the fleet. A few days before the arrival of the Halifax fleet, Oliver De Lancey, Major Bayard and Charles Ward Apthorpe, taking advantage of a dark night, escaped from Apthorpe's Bloomingdale mansion, and, crowding into a canoe, paddled down the Hudson out into the harbor and through the Narrows, where they climbed aboard the *Asia*.[51] Others followed. On July 26 a number of sloops, filled with Tories from New Jersey, succeeded in joining the fleet.[52] In some cases the Tories, in their eagerness to escape the revenge of their countrymen, took serious risks. When two young men paddled out to the *Phoenix* and *Rose* on the night of August 19, their canoe overturned, throwing one of them into the water where he perished.[53]

Now followed long conferences between the British officers and the leading Tories. On July 17, Governor Tryon, Oliver De Lancey, Major Bayard and others dined with Admiral Lord Howe on board the *Eagle*. There was much talk over the table of the persecution of the Loyalists, the probability that the people would revolt against the arbitrary conduct of Congress and the ardent desire of thousands to aid the British army and navy.[54] At other meetings at General Howe's headquarters on land, the Tories, with a map of the region spread out before them, pointed out the location of Washington's batteries and the disposition of his troops.

The two Howes were deeply troubled to learn that the colonies had declared independence, though they did not go so far as Serle, who thought that "a more impudent, false, and atrocious proclamation was never fabricated by the hands of man." [55]

But Admiral Howe had brought instructions for himself and his brother to propose reconciliation upon what Lord Germain considered most liberal terms, terms which Congress itself had suggested in the Olive Branch petition. As a sincere friend of the Americans, Howe had hoped that he could reach a satisfactory agreement with them which would return the old happy relationship of mother country and colonies, and make further bloodshed unnecessary. But the Declaration of Independence at once dashed his hopes. If the colonies insisted on independence, then the sword would have to decide.

None the less, the Howes thought that it was their duty to let the Americans know that the Ministry was ready to compromise. On July 14, two American officers, Colonel Samuel B. Webb and Colonel Reed, seeing a small boat approaching the Battery with a flag of truce, went out to meet it. Thereupon a British naval officer handed them a letter from Admiral Howe addressed to George Washington, Esq. Webb and Reed drew themselves up stiffly and returned the letter, declaring that it would not be received until addressed to General George Washington.[56] Congress heartily approved of this stand, and it was only by sending Lieutenant Colonel Paterson for a conference with the American officers, that Lord Howe could apprise them of his powers to negotiate.

Paterson met General Washington and his staff at Colonel Henry Knox's quarters on July 18. "After the usual compliments," in which the British officer addressed Washington as "your Excellency," he produced Lord Howe's letter. When Washington noted that the title of general was still omitted he "declined the letter." So the missive lay unopened on the table while Colonel Paterson proceeded to inform the Americans that the King, out of his "goodness and benevolence," had appointed Lord Howe and General Howe his commissioners to accommodate the unhappy dispute. They had great powers, he added, and were sincerely hopeful of success. General Washington replied that it was understood that the Howes were empowered only to grant pardons, and that those who had committed no crime needed no pardon. He pointed out, also, that he was not authorized to treat with the commissioners and referred them to Congress. Thereupon, Paterson bowed himself out, and after expressing his appreciation at not being blindfolded on passing the American batteries, returned to the fleet.[57]

There was now nothing left for the Howes to do but proceed with the war. At dawn on August 22, Colonel Hand's riflemen, who were posted near Denyee's Ferry at the Narrows, saw the *Phoenix,* the *Rose,* the *Greyhound* and other warships move into Gravesend Bay close to the shore. Behind them, from the Staten Island side, followed a flotilla of flatboats, bateaux, and galleys, each crowded with redcoats. As they approached, Hand's little band, eyeing the frigates' long rows of guns pointing out over the beach, decided that resistance would be useless, and beat a hasty retreat. So the boats ran in to shore, where the men jumped into the surf and waded to the beach—four battalions of light infantry, the light dragoons, and Colonel von Donop's Hessian grenadiers and jägers. This done, back went the flotilla to Staten Island. The next trip brought over 5,000 more troops and the next an equal number. As evening fell on that eventful day, 15,000 British and Germans were encamped near the ferry or on the road from New Utrecht to Flatlands.

In preparation for the defence of Long Island, the Americans had taken what seemed to be an exceedingly strong position. Stretching from near Gowanus Bay northeast lay the thickly wooded Guana Heights,[58] which were almost impassable save where cut by four roads —the Narrows Road near the shore, the Flatbush-Brooklyn Road, the Flatbush-Bedford Road and, far out to the east, the Jamaica-Bedford Road. Had all of these passes been strongly garrisoned, General Howe might well have been balked in his attempt to reach the left bank of the East River. But the American commanders contented themselves with posting Lord Stirling at the Narrows Road, and General Sullivan at the passes leading to Brooklyn and Bedford, leaving the Jamaica Road almost completely undefended.

It would have been only common prudence for General Israel Putnam, who had just taken command to post in this gap the regiments Washington was hastening over to reinforce him. But Putnam was unacquainted with the topography of the region and, though a brave, stubborn fighter, was a very poor tactician. "Dashing along on horseback at fine speed, his uniform consisting of a soiled shirt, over which he wore a sleeveless waistcoat," he issued "orders right and left" without "any well defined purpose." [59]

On August 23, Howe feinted at the Flatbush and Bedford Passes, with De Heister's Hessian division. But it was a feint only, and when they encountered sharp resistance from Sullivan's men, they retired. The next day Fithian, who left his regiment to visit the scene of this encounter, gives us a picture of what was going on within the American lines just prior to the decisive battle. "Some of the men were in companies sitting under the shady trees and conversing about the occurrences of the day—who were killed, or wounded, or taken prisoners . . . Others were preparing their victuals and eating. Many were lying on the sides of the hills opposite the enemy and securely sleeping, while others, as it comes in turn, were standing among whistling bullets, on the other side of the hills, taking trees for their security and shooting when they can." [60]

Little did these poor fellows realize what the British had in store for them. At nine o'clock on the night of August 26, General Howe dispatched a column of 10,000 men under General Henry Clinton and Lord Cornwallis from Flatlands, with orders to surprise the undefended Jamaica Pass and then swing west so as to get in the rear of the main American positions. Led by three Tories, the light dragoons, regiment after regiment of infantry, four battalions of grenadiers, a regiment of Highlanders and fourteen pieces of artillery moved on in the dark past the quaint houses and waving fields of the Dutch farmers. Arriving at the pass early in the morning, Clinton captured five American lookouts, and then after his men had filed through, halted for breakfast. [61]

As this threatening cloud hung over the left flank and rear of the American line, De Heister at the Flatbush Pass and General James Grant on the Narrows Road, advanced to attack Sullivan and Stirling and pin them to their positions. The result was disastrous. An American scout far out to the left, while watching the sun rise "red and angry," was amazed to see a long column of British, like a red ribbon on the horizon, advancing down the Bedford Road. As the news spread along the heights to one post after another, the American line began to fold back to avoid capture. Soon 2,000 men "were hurrying through the woods, down the slopes and across the fields, some singly, some in groups, some keeping together in companies, some in battalions, all aiming" to reach the forts and redoubts which protected the American camp at Brooklyn.[62]

This uncovered Stirling's flank and left him exposed, not only to Grant's attack from the south, but to a crushing blow by Cornwallis in his rear. Between him and the camp was Gowanus Creek, two large mill ponds and a wide expanse of marsh. It seemed that nothing could prevent the destruction or capture of the entire brigade. But Stirling acted with promptness and heroism. With a handful of men he advanced to attack Cornwallis and for half an hour kept up a stubborn fight, while the rest of his men plunged into the swamps.[63]

Fithian thus describes this part of the battle: "They [Stirling's men] stood formed in a large body, on a good eminence, in our plain view, but where we could give them no relief! On three sides of them were the enemy, on the other side was a broad marsh and creek. There the brave men stood for more than four hours. They found their enemies surrounding them more. At last they divided; placed a body to attack the enemy while a part crossed over the water. Here was a desperate fire. But it was the best they could do. The officers swam their horses over; the men some swam and some passed in boats, but many stood behind, among them Lord Stirling." [64]

The defeat on Long Island was a telling blow to the American cause. Stirling, Sullivan, and other high officers were taken; hundreds of the men had been killed, other hundreds captured; discouragement spread through the army. The only consolation was that Howe had not turned his victorious regiments against the American camp, swept over the redoubts and destroyed Putnam's entire army. In fact the grenadiers and the 33rd Regiment had pursued some of the fleeing Americans up to their very redoubts, in defiance of the blast they received from small arms and cannon.[65] But Howe ordered them back, not wishing to lose men in a frontal assault when it seemed certain that the camp would be taken "at a very cheap rate by regular approaches." So his men retired, leaving the wounded to limp, crying with pain, into the American redoubts.[66]

For several days the armies faced each other across the line from Gowanus Creek to Wallabout Bay. But the position of the Americans was perilous in the extreme. With a vastly superior force facing them, with a great river at their backs, with Lord Howe's frigates threatening to cut off their retreat, disaster seemed imminent. So Washington had no alternative save to abandon his positions and attempt to ferry the troops over to New York. On the night of August 29, the men shouldered their luggage in the midst of a drenching rain and waded through ankle-deep mud to the water's edge. There they found a "Dunkirk fleet" awaiting them—rowboats, flatboats, whaleboats, large dugout canoes, sloops—and climbing in shoved out into the inky darkness of the river. As day broke the last boats were leaving the Long Island side, and a few minutes later the entire force was assembled on Manhattan.[67]

A discouraged, weary, bedraggled group of men they were. "The merry tones of drums and fifes had ceased," said Pastor Shewkirk. "It seemed a general damp had spread, and the sight of the scattered people up and down the streets was indeed moving. Many looked sickly, emaciated, cast down; the wet clothes, tents—as many as they had brought away—and other things were lying about before the houses and in the streets . . . in general everything seemed to be in confusion. Many, as it is reported for certain, went away to their respective homes." [68]

No doubt their great leader was also deeply discouraged. The retreat from Brooklyn made necessary the evacuation of Red Hook and Governor's Island, and opened the East River to the enemy's warships. This, in turn, exposed all Manhattan to attack from the east, so that New York City was in danger of being cut off and its garrison captured. How imminent was this peril was amply demonstrated on the night of September 3, when the *Rose*, accompanied by twenty flatboats, went up the East River unmindful of the fire from the batteries at Corlear's Hook.

But Washington was not the man to hesitate in the face of danger. Calling a council of war at his headquarters at Richmond Hall, the beautiful Abraham Mortier mansion,[69] he outlined his plans for the defence of Manhattan. Five thousand men under Putnam were to remain in the city and 9,000 at or near Kingsbridge, under General William Heath, while the remainder under General Joseph Spencer were to be distributed at Harlem Heights, Kip's Bay, Turtle Bay,

Israel Putnam.   Sir William Howe.

The British Fleet at Anchor in the Narrows between Long Island
and Staten Island on July 12, 1776.

The Reading of the Declaration of Independence to the Troops
in New York. Each brigade in Washington's army assembled on
the Common, now City Hall Park, for the reading. Old St. Paul's
appears in the background.

American Troops and Civilians Tearing down the Gilt Statue of
George III on Bowling Green. The rioting occurred on the evening
of the day of the reading of the Declaration of Independence.

The Retreat from Long Island. Washington himself took charge of the evacuation which has often been hailed as one of the most masterful operations of the war.

The Capture of Nathaniel Woodhull near Jamaica, Long Island, on August 28, 1776. This well-trained American general was practically defenseless when surprised by a detachment of seven hundred men.

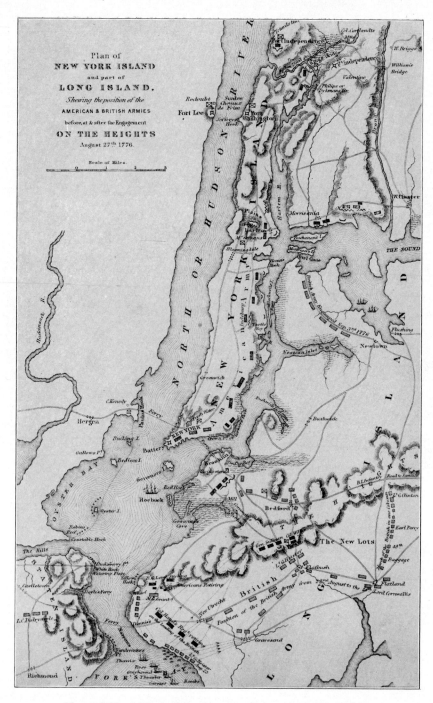

Plan of New York Island and a Part of Long Island.

Mrs. Murray Entertaining General Howe and British Officers while
General Putnam Escaped.

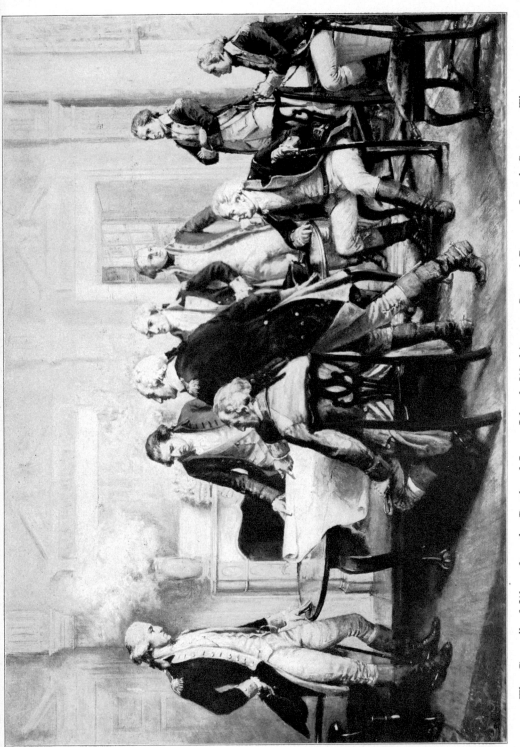

The Council of War after the Battle of Long Island. Washington, Samuel Parsons, Joseph Spencer, Thomas Mifflin, John Morin Scott, Alexander McDougall, Israel Putnam, Peleg Wadsworth, and John Fellows

Horne's Hook and other intermediate points. The advice of some officers that the city be evacuated without delay was overruled.[70]

The Americans had not long to wait before the effectiveness of their defences was put to the test. On the afternoon of September 14, the frigates *Phoenix, Roebuck, Orpheus* and *Carrysfort* moved into the East River, and, despite the fire of the American batteries, arrived safely above Bushwick where they joined the *Rose*.[71] In the meanwhile General Howe had collected a formidable force of light infantry and Hessian grenadiers and chasseurs at Newtown Creek, under the command of General Clinton, ready for the assault on Manhattan.

The next morning at seven the men clambered aboard a fleet of small boats, which a few hours later moved down the creek and out into East River. They saw a magnificent scene—"The hills, the woods, the river, the town, the ships and the pillars of smoke, all heightened by a most clear and delightful morning, furnished the finest landscape that either art and nature combined could draw or imagination conceive." [72] Across the river, lying close in to Kip's Bay, were the five frigates. After the small boats had rowed over to take their place behind the warships, Admiral Hotham gave the signal and the guns opened upon the American positions. "So terrible and so incessant a roar of guns few even in the army and navy had ever heard before." [73] Under cover of this barrage the troop boats headed for the Manhattan shore. The flash of the guns, the deafening noise, the pall of smoke which hung over the river, the splash of oars in the water, the brilliant red uniforms, were "altogether grand and noble." In a few minutes the boats grounded and the men leapt ashore, the light infantry and some of the grenadiers on the rocky hill to the right of the bay, and the rest of the grenadiers on the low promontory to the left.[74]

They met with no opposition, for the Americans, when the grapeshot from the frigates began to spatter around them, had given way and retreated rapidly through the woods towards the Post Road. Thereupon the British formed in line on the shore and the drums beat the signal to advance. "The horror and fright of the few inhabitants of the first house we came to were shocking," states Colonel Archibald Robinson.[75] In high good humor at this easy victory, Clinton pushed on toward the Robert Murray estate on the Inclenburg Heights.[76]

As the first sound of the firing reached the ears of General Washington at the Charles Ward Apthorpe house in Bloomingdale three miles away, he sent orders for Parsons' and Fellows' brigades to hasten up to the point of danger, and then, mounting his horse, gal·loped down the Bloomingdale Road to take personal command. When he arrived at the Murray farm he found the militia fleeing before the British van, throwing aside arms, knapsacks, hats and even coats in their haste to get away. Ignoring them, he tried to form the rein-forcements in line. "Take to the walls!" he shouted. "Take to the corn-field!" Some of Parsons' men obeyed, but in "a confused and dis-ordered manner." Then panic seized them, too, and they broke and fled.[77] Washington, Putnam and Mifflin tried desperately to rally them, even laying the cane on the backs of some of the fugitives, but in vain. All was "fright, disgrace, and confusion." "Are these the men with which I am to defend America?" Washington is said to have ex-claimed, dashing his hat to the ground. So outraged was he that he would have remained on the field to be captured, had not an aide seized the rein of his horse and turned him back.[78]

The disaster of Kip's Bay put the 3,500 men left in the toe of Man-hattan in a cul-de-sac. All the British had to do was to pull the cord by crossing the island and they were lost. But, if we may believe Dr. James Thacher, Clinton and the other commanding officers lingered at the Murray House, where the charming Quakeress, "Mrs. Murray, treated them with cake and wine," while the light infantry and Hessians rested on their arms. Governor Tryon, who was with the group, as he sipped his wine could not help twitting the good lady over her "American friends." [79]

In the meanwhile, when Putnam saw that nothing could stem the flight of Parsons' and Fellows' men, putting spurs to his horse, he galloped down the Bowery Lane to warn and if possible save the New York garrison. Fortunately, the sick, wounded, and large quantities of stores and munitions had been removed after the Battle of Long Island, and even the bells had been taken down from the church towers and carted off. But for Silliman's brigade and Colonel Knox's artillery, who were still at the Bayard Hill Fort, the only hope was instant flight.

When Putnam rushed up to give the warning, Knox thought escape impossible, and advised fighting it out. But young Aaron Burr, Put-nam's aide, convinced him that he could lead them to safety, and the column was put in motion through the woods and across the fields of lower Manhattan. It was "insupportably hot," but there was no rest for the sweltering men. The officers urged them on, riding here and there along the column, gathering up stragglers, giving encouragement, keeping a sharp watch for the enemy. At one place they encountered a small party of British, but Silliman detached 300 men to beat them off while the main column hastened on. At last, as night fell, the exhausted men marched into the American works at Harlem, amid the cheers of their comrades, after one of the most remarkable retreats in American military history.[80]

The last hours of the revolutionary regime in the city were marked by confusion and lawlessness. A few of Knox's men, who had been left behind when Putnam's march began, fled up the left bank of the Hudson to the "Glass House," where they found a number of boats in which, under cover of night, they escaped to New Jersey.[81] The Committee of Safety fled. With the removal of the guard at the storehouses, certain persons broke in and made off with all the provisions they could carry. And for hours the ferryboats to Paulus Hook kept crossing and recrossing to take off the last refugees, leaving only a small group of Loyalists to welcome the British.[82]

A joyous welcome it was. One woman entered the fort, pulled down the American flag, trampled it under foot and then raised the King's colors. When a group of officers from the fleet rowed ashore, the people, women as well as men, lifted them to their shoulders and carried them through the streets. A party of marines who followed were received with shouts of joy. At noon on the following day a body of redcoats marched into town and formed in two lines on Broadway. In the crowd which went out to greet them, "joy and gladness seemed to appear in all countenances, and persons who had been strangers . . . were now very sociable together." For the Tories it was the hour of deliverance.[83]

And so ended the period of American military occupation of the city of New York. For the remainder of the war it was to be the chief center of British military and naval activity and a haven of refuge for the Tories. Seldom in history has a city been so completely transformed in so short a period, for the change was not merely one of military power but of civilian population as well. It was as though at a theatrical performance, one set of actors should leave the stage, and without changing the scenery, another entirely different set should come on to begin another play. Twice during the remainder of the war, with the presence of French fleets in American waters, Washington entertained hopes of recapturing the city, but each time the opportunity was missed. And so New York, with a small area of surrounding country, remained a Loyalist fortress in a hostile country.

CHAPTER V

THE TORY HAVEN

WHEN THE British took possession of New York City they found it
a very different place from the busy, cosmopolitan, pleasant town
which it had been a few years before, with its parks, shaded streets,
Georgian mansions, churches, public buildings, wharves, warehouses.
Many of the trees had been cut down, barricades obstructed some of
the streets, most of the people had fled. "There were not 3,000 left
when the King's troops took possession," it was stated, "and of these
above half are Dutch and German traders . . . the rest, composed of
aged, sick and such persons as refused to enter into the measures
of the Congress." [1]

Major General James Robertson, who was placed in command
in the city, found many and perplexing problems. Should civil government be restored, or the city left under the control of a military
governor? How was he to find quarters for the troops, houses for the
refugees, warehouses for military stores, prisons for the thousands of
captured revolutionists? How provide food, clothing, fuel for soldiers
and citizens? What buildings should be set aside as hospitals? What
measures should be taken to revive the shattered trade of the city?
Should the schools and the college be reopened?

While General Robertson was considering these problems, they
were made far more difficult by the great fire of September 21, 1776.
With the arrival of the British fleets and the landing of Howe's army
on Long Island, there had been a heated debate in the American
camp over the advisability of destroying the city. General Nathanael
Greene had urged it strongly. "I would burn the city and suburbs,"
he said, "and that for the following reasons: If the enemy gets possession of the city, we can never recover the possession without a superior naval force to theirs; it will deprive the enemy of an opportunity of
barracking their whole army together . . . It will deprive them of a

general market . . . Two-thirds of the property of the city of New York and the suburbs belongs to the Tories. We have no very great reason to run any considerable risk for its defence." [2]

In the British camp it was reported that the New Englanders were insisting upon setting the town on fire, but that the New York and New Jersey troops opposed so drastic a move. It was even said that the argument had culminated in a pitched battle in which many had lost their lives. "We have a fine view of New York," wrote a British officer from Long Island, "which we expect soon to see in flames." [3]

Washington left the decision to Congress. "If we should be obliged to abandon the town, ought it to stand as winter-quarters of the enemy?" he asked. Congress hastened back orders that the city be spared, observing sagely that they were confident that the Americans would "recover the same." [4] Washington was not the man to disobey orders. But when he replied that he would do all in his power to prevent the burning of the city, it is obvious that he thought it might be done surreptitiously, despite his positive orders.[5]

The British had been in possession of New York less than a week, when, in the early hours of September 21, a fire broke out in a small wooden house on a wharf near the Whitehall Slip. It was a clear night, with the wind blowing briskly from the south, and the flames almost instantly spread to nearby buildings. Had it been in times of peace every church bell in the city would in a few minutes have been clanging, but now there were no bells, for the American troops had carted them all away for conversion into cannon. The fire companies were disorganized and undermanned, the engines and pumps out of order, many of the houses were of wood and nearly all covered with cedar shingles.

As women and children rushed out of the burning houses, and the men tried to work the engines and to form bucket lines, the flames swept on. They leaped Dock Street, Bridge Street, Stone Street, Marketfield Street, and Beaver Street. It was an awe-inspiring sight as they engulfed alike the lowly wooden houses of the poor and the mansions of the rich, the quaint Dutch houses, some of them perhaps built in the days of Peter Stuyvesant, and the more pretentious buildings of the Georgian period. "Several women and children perished in the fire. Their shrieks, joined to the roaring of the flames, the crash of falling houses and the widespread ruin . . . formed a scene of horror grand beyond description, and which was still heightened by the darkness of the night." [6]

When watchers on the *Eagle* informed Admiral Howe that the city was on fire he ordered a number of officers and sailors to hasten ashore to offer their aid. At the same time General Howe sent two regiments from his camp north of the city, so that seamen and soldiers united in battling the conflagration. It was due to their efforts, especially "in pulling down such wooden buildings as would conduct the fire," that "the whole city was not consumed." [7]

In the excitement and horror of the conflagration, sailors, soldiers and citizens alike dealt summarily with persons suspected of spreading the fire. So many and so detailed had been the rumors that the Americans had planned to burn the city that now, when it was actually in flames, the enraged mob made every effort to find the incendiaries. And it was to be expected that any man whose conduct brought him under suspicion should be punished on the spot, without a chance to prove his innocence. A carpenter named Wright White, a "violent Loyalist," seems to have chosen the wrong night for a drunken spree, which led him into interfering with the work of fighting the fire, for the crowd seized him, placed a rope around his neck and hanged him to a tavern signpost.[8] One unfortunate man who, it was said, was caught with a bundle of "matches" dipped in "melted rosin and brimstone" was tossed into the roaring flames, where he perished. Another was bayonetted and hung up by his feet. It was only when General Robertson issued strict orders against violence of this kind that the lynchings came to an end. At one place the general in person rescued two suspects from the "enraged populace," just as they were preparing to "consign them to the flames." [9]

At about two o'clock in the morning the wind veered from the southwest to the southeast, which drove the fire away from the main part of the city and confined it to the comparatively small strip of land between Broadway and the North River. But here the destruction was very great. The flames moved across Broadway to a group of buildings on Beaver Lane,[10] and from that point turned northwest to Rector Street. Directly in their path lay venerated Trinity Church. As the crowd looked on, powerless to prevent, "flakes of the fire," borne by the wind, began to fall on the south side of the roof. A few minutes later the building was a roaring furnace. "The steeple, which was 140 feet high, the upper part of wood, and placed on an elevated situation, resembled a vast pyramid of fire and exhibited a most grand and awful spectacle." [11]

The church yard seems to have checked the progress of the flames up the west side of Broadway, so that the buildings directly north of Trinity were saved, but there was consternation when the fire moved up Lumber Street to Partition Street,[12] where it threatened St. Paul's Chapel. Immediately a number of persons armed with buckets rushed to the roof, where the low lines and protecting balustrades gave them a safe footing, and extinguished each spark as it fell. "Thus happily was this beautiful church saved from the destruction of this dreadful fire." [13] But to the west of St. Paul's the flames reached Barclay Street, where the college grounds and a number of vacant lots at last checked their progress.

Parson Shewkirk gives us a vivid account of his experiences on the night of the fire. In its early stages, while alone in the Moravian chapel on Fair Street, on looking out of the window he "saw the whole air red." When he went into the street and noted that the blaze was in the south end of the town, he started down Broadway to join the fire fighters. On the way he met "Sister Sykes," one of his congregation, carrying her child in one arm and a large bundle in the other. After conducting her to his residence, he returned with several buckets, but so fierce was the conflagration that "all what was done was of but little effect. If one was in one street and looked about it broke out already again in another." With the coming of daylight, when the fire was threatening St. Paul's, Shewkirk was alarmed to note that a house on the corner of Fair Street [14] on the east side of Broadway, not far from his meetinghouse, had caught. Hastening with ladders and buckets to the threatened spot, with the aid of his congregation, he at last checked the flames.[15]

The fire was a major disaster for the British and the Tories. "Our distresses were great before, but this calamity has increased them tenfold," wrote one New Yorker. "Thousands are hereby reduced to beggary." [16] When at last the flames were subdued, no less than 493 houses had been destroyed, and a path of desolation a mile long had been driven through the heart of the city. The problem of finding proper quarters for the soldiers, warehouses for military supplies, hospitals for the sick and wounded, houses for the returning Loyalists, was made doubly difficult.

The origin of the fire remains to this day a matter of doubt. Gen-

eral Howe reported to Lord Germain that "a number of wretches"
set the town on fire "in several places with matches and combustibles"
and that "many were detected in the fact." [17] Shewkirk thought there
were great reasons to suspect that some wicked incendiaries had a
hand in this dreadful fire,[18] while the *New York Mercury* declared
that "this atrocious deed" was not less villainous than the Gunpowder
Plot.[19] On the other hand, the *Pennsylvania Journal* denounced these
reports as "scandalous" and ascribed the start of the fire to some of
Lord Howe's seamen, who had gone ashore for a frolic and "care-
lessly set a house on fire on Whitehall Slip." [20] It is significant that of
the scores arrested as incendiaries, none seem to have been found
guilty. Shewkirk says that about 200 were taken up, but that "on
examination the most men were as fast discharged." [21] The lynching
of several unfortunate persons is insufficient evidence that they started
or were spreading the flames. That the British themselves in time
came to question the incendiary origin of the fire is shown by Sir
Guy Carleton's action in October, 1783, in appointing a committee
of three officers to enquire into the matter "to ascertain whether the
same was accidental or the effect of design." [22] Certainly the evidence
of incendiarism laid before this committee is unconvincing.

Amid the excitement and bitterness which attended the fire the
people of the city seem to have ignored another tragedy which occurred
the next morning a few miles north of the city—the execution of a
young American spy. If they knew of it they probably dismissed it with
a shrug of the shoulder. Perhaps he had had a hand in starting the fire.
In any event he must have known, when he came within the British
lines, that the penalty of detection was death.

In the general orders for September 22, 1776, is the following
terse entry: "A spy from the enemy (by his own full confession) apprehended last night, was this day executed at 11 o'clock in front of
the Artillery Park." [23] When Nathan Hale was led out to meet his
doom, the British officers and men saw a handsome youth, with fair
skin, flaxen hair, blue eyes, not tall but very erect, his face sedate, his
body agile. As he looked around he could see not one face "that spoke
either respect or compassion," and "everything that was said or done to
him was adapted to make him feel that he was considered as a traitor
and a rebel." As he was about to be turned off he called out: "I am so
satisfied with the cause in which I have engaged, that my only regret
is that I have not more lives to offer in its service." [24]

Even before this sad event the Tories had begun to flock back to the city. They found it "a most dirty, desolate and wretched place." The Reverend Charles Inglis, who arrived the day after the British took possession, says it presented "a most melancholy appearance, being deserted and pillaged." His own loss he estimated at £200.[25] Up at Horne's Hook, when the widow of the Reverend John Ogilvie returned with "a numerous family of children" to the mansion of her father, Nathaniel Marston, a wounded British officer, who had taken refuge there, was deeply moved at "seeing mother and children, grandfather and grandchildren, etc., down to the black children of the slaves, hugging and kissing each other." [26]

Every day swelled the number of the returning Loyalists; the roads were crowded, the ferries busy. One large group, among them several officials and men of wealth, who had taken refuge on the *Brune,* a frigate lying in the harbor, now came ashore. Henry White, of the Council, came back; Hugh Gaine came back and resumed the publication of *The New York Gazette,* at his shop in Hanover Square; some of Shewkirk's flock came back, "though they met with many difficulties in their removal." [27] By the end of February, 1777, the population of the city had mounted to 11,000.[28]

Over on Long Island hundreds of fugitives, returning to their quaint Dutch villages, found their "dwellings empty, furniture smashed, not a window left whole and their cattle gone forever." Gradually, as the British armies advanced, not only the city of New York, but the surrounding country became the center of Tory America. Within its borders every citizen who wished to escape suspicion had to wear on his hat a red ribbon, the insignia of loyalty to the King.[29]

The joy of the Loyalists was dampened, not only by the fire and the ruinous condition of what escaped the flames, but at the appointment of General Robertson as Commandant. This man, "near eighty years of age, sickly, infirm and paralytic," bore an unsavory reputation. For years he had been barrack-master in the colonies, which office, if we may believe the Tory historian Thomas Jones, he managed "so well" that in a few years it made him a rich man. Thus "so far from having any interest, popularity or influence in the colony, he was universally despised and execrated." [30] In his new post he might have retrieved his reputation had he conducted himself with probity and dignity, but, on the contrary, he exposed himself to ridicule by "smelling after every giddy girl that will let him come nigh her." [31] That such a man should be selected to rule over New York at this critical juncture the Tories thought a calamity.

None the less, Robertson went to work to bring order to the ruined city with a vigor that is surprising in one so old. His first act was to put an end to disorders by the British troops. Jones tells us that when they entered the city, "the soldiers broke open the City Hall and plundered it of the college library, its mathematical and philosophical apparatus and a number of valuable pictures which had been removed there . . . This was done with impunity and the books publicly hawked about the town for sale by private soldiers . . . I saw in a public house upon Long Island nearly 40 books bound and lettered, in which were affixed the arms of Joseph Murray, Esq., under pawn from one dram to three drams each." [32]

Having stopped this kind of disorder and having stationed a guard over the military stores left by Washington's men, Robertson turned to the problem of assigning quarters to the soldiers. Already some of them had been forcing themselves on the citizens. When a company of officers came to the house of Parson Shewkirk "some talked but of some rooms; others said they must have the whole house and the chapel too. One, a cornet of the Light Horse, marked one room for himself; desired [me] to clear it this afternoon and let him have a table and a couple of chairs, and he would willingly pay for it." But when the Moravian pastor reported the matter to Robertson, the general said "he had given them no orders." [33]

To the householders who had joined the revolutionary movement, there was no leniency. Officials went from door to door and marked "all the houses which were inhabited and deserted by the rebels" with the letters G.R., as a sign that they had been confiscated and dedicated to the King's service. Colonel Henry Rutgers, when he returned to the city at the end of the Revolution, preserved the G.R. on his door for a half a century, as a distinguished badge of his patriotism. [34]

The housing problem was complicated by the necessity of finding living quarters for the hundreds of women and children who accompanied the British forces. In modern warfare it has been found best, when an expedition is sent overseas, to leave the families of the soldiers at home. Not so, however, with the British army of occupation in New York. In March, 1779, the number of wives of British soldiers who had to be fed and housed was 1,550 and of their children 968. These families were crowded into the less pretentious houses in all parts of the city, and at any time the children might have been seen playing in the streets or the back lots, the wives gossiping with each other, perhaps in a Welsh accent, perhaps with the Highland burr.[35]

A stroll up Queen Street will give us an idea of the housing situation.[36] Isaac Sears' brick house, No. 49, was occupied by Hessian officers; No. 66, owned by Widow Thorne, housed the servants of Colonel Clark of the 7th Regiment; No. 71, a frame house owned by Adolphus Degrove, was filled with soldiers' wives; No. 84 was used as a guardhouse; No. 86, owned by Evert Byvanck, was crowded with soldiers; Nos. 131, 132, 133 and 134 were all given over to soldiers' wives; officers of the 45th Regiment lived in No. 138; Captain Thomalson was in No. 146, a large brick house owned by Captain Codrvis; a Mr. Shimier lived in Isaac Roosevelt's[37] six-room brick house at No. 150.

Many of the warehouses along the waterfront of East River were reserved for the vast quantities of stores needed for the King's army and navy. At any time during the period of the British occupation one could have seen dock workers bringing ammunition, firearms, boxes of clothing, barrels of food, pipes of wines, etc., into the Henry Kip, James Wright, John De Peyster and Gilbert Giles warehouses on Water Street, or the Evert Byvanck and James Pearson warehouses on Dock Street.[38]

The large numbers of sick and wounded sent back from the front made it necessary for Dr. Booth, Superintendent of Hospitals, to press into service every available building. King's College was filled to overflowing; the Baptist Meetinghouse on Gold Street, Montagne's tavern, the Lutheran Church at the corner of William and Frankfort Streets were filled with beds and still there was not enough room.[39] So the doctors took over Isaac Sears' house, No. 123 George Street, and Cornelius Bogart's house, No. 94 George Street, as hospitals for the Hessians, and No. 12 Vandewater Street, owned by a Mr. Midwinter and Dirk Amerman's house, No. 5 Vandewater Street, for the Waldeckers.[40]

Most of the larger buildings were reserved for prisons. As week after week hundreds of crestfallen Americans were marched into the city, not only the New Gaol, but the sugar refineries and some of the churches were filled to overflowing. Hundreds more were confined on board prison ships. Jabez Fitch, who was captured at the Battle of Long Island, tells us that he was sent in a "flat bottomed boat" down to the British fleet and, in company with about 400 others, put on board the *Pacific*. Here his "lodging was no other than a great gun or a quilt of rigging." [41] Later other British vessels—the *Whitby,* the *Good Hope,* the *Scorpion,* the *Jersey*—were converted into prison ships into which great numbers of unfortunate Americans were crowded.

But this by no means relieved the congestion of the city. After the surrender of Fort Washington, 800 prisoners "were stowed away into a house called New Bridewell, a cold, open home, the windows not glazed"; [42] while others were sent to the John Van Cortlandt sugar refinery, a bleak, five-story, stone building in the northwest corner of Trinity churchyard. The small windows of the John Livingston refinery, which prevented a proper circulation of air in the heat of summer, together with the gloomy cellar which did service as a dungeon, made that building a place of torture for the prisoners. [43] And hardly more fortunate were the 800 men who were put in the North Dutch Church on William Street, between Fair [44] and Ann. On December 18, Fitch, who was then on parole, went down to this church to visit "the poor prisoners," whom he found "in a very miserable condition," four of them lying dead in the yard and several others dying in the house." [45] In addition to the North Dutch Church, the Presbyterian churches, the French Church, the Baptist meeting-house and the Quaker meetinghouse were utilized either permanently or for various emergencies as they arose.

The Moravians, despite their loyalty to the King, narrowly escaped having their chapel taken. In the forenoon of November 18, four men came to examine this building and Pastor Shewkirk showed them about. That afternoon, looking out of the window, he saw the street full of people. "The sergeant of the guard came to the door and asked whether this was the Moravian meeting? He was ordered to bring these 400 prisoners here . . . By and by the mayor . . . and another man came in and looked at the chapel and said it was too small . . . The prisoners, with their guard stood about half an hour in the street before our door and many spectators." At last, to Shewkirk's great relief, the prisoners were marched away to the nearby North Dutch Church. [46]

In taking over so many church buildings as prisons or as hospitals, the military authorities made exceptions of St. Paul's and St. George's. It was only just, they argued, that the dissenting congregations should suffer for their support of the "rebellion" and that the Anglicans be rewarded for their loyalty. So, a few days after the evacuation of the city by the American troops, services were held in St. Paul's by Lord Howe's chaplain.[47] Later St. George's also was reopened, and the people, many of them newcomers who had been driven from their homes in New England or New Jersey, began to attend in large numbers.

The Anglican rector, the Reverend Samuel Auchmuty, when he heard that the British had entered New York, made his way through the American lines and after a journey on foot of a week, in which he often had to hide during the day in the woods and travel by night, arrived in the city. Here he viewed with sorrow the ruins of Trinity Church, of the rectory where he had lived for so many years and of the Charity School. "Upon searching the rubbish of his late venerable church and his large, elegant house, he could find only a very few trifles of litter of no value, except the church plate and his own." He estimated his personal loss at £2,000 sterling, and the loss by his church at ten times that amount. His wife and daughters were still in the hands of the revolutionists, he complained; his health was broken.[48] He died March 4, 1777, at the age of fifty-six, and two days later his body was interred in the chancel of St. Paul's.[49]

For the Anglican clergy of Connecticut, New Jersey and upper New York, whose principles of loyalty to the King had marked them for persecution, the city became a place of refuge. Isaac Browne, the aging rector of the Newark Church, leaving his wife and family to the mercy of the revolutionists, escaped across the river. His property was at once confiscated, and his wife sent after him "without so much as a bed to lay on." [50] From Westchester came Samuel Seabury, the many recent indignities inflicted on him by Captain Sears and his Connecticut men still fresh in his memory; from Poughkeepsie, the Reverend Mr. Beardsly; from Salem, New York, the Reverend Mr. Townsend; from Phillipse Manor, the Reverend Mr. Sayre; from Perth Amboy, the Reverend Mr. Preston; from Trenton, the Reverend Mr. Panton; from Massachusetts, the Reverend Mr. Winslow and the Reverend Mr. Walton.

Safe within the British lines these gentlemen could now have prayed for the King or dwelt on the enormity of rebellion in perfect safety, had they had congregations before whom to pray or to preach. But Charles Inglis, who had succeeded Mr. Auchmuty as rector of

Trinity, with his assistant, the Reverend Benjamin Moore, sufficed to serve both St. Paul's and St. George's, so it became necessary to provide for the reverend refugees elsewhere. Mr. Beardsly was made chaplain of a battalion of provincials, Mr. Preston chaplain of the 46th British regiment, Mr. Panton of General Browne's brigade, Mr. Winslow of General Skinner's brigade, Mr. Walton of the man-of-war *Centurion*.[51]

But all hardships were borne patiently, willingly, for the refugees were confident that the royal army and navy would soon annihilate Washington's forces and restore the King's authority. Then they would regain possession of their property, would be restored to their former positions of dignity and power, would be avenged for all the indignities which had been heaped upon them. So it was with smiling faces that they greeted each victory of General Howe's forces, and watched the expanding circle of conquered territory. As neighbor greeted neighbor on the street, the query was: "Have you heard of the capture of Paulus Hook?" or, "Is it true that the rebels have evacuated Manhattan?" or, "Can Washington continue in the field after his defeat at White Plains?" or "Will not Philadelphia soon fall before the royal arms?"

The efforts of the Americans to destroy the British fleet, or even to impede its progress up the Hudson, were greeted with ridicule. On September 15, four fire-vessels moved against a small squadron in the North River, but were easily eluded when the British ships moved their positions.[52] The Americans had gone to great trouble and expense to throw a *chevaux-de-frise* across the river from Fort Washington on the Manhattan side to Fort Lee on the Palisades, which they hoped would effectually close the river. But it proved to be no serious obstacle to the enemy. "On the morning of October 8, the *Roebuck* and the *Phoenix,* with three or four tenders, headed up the river. As the batteries of the two forts played upon them, the American generals waited expectantly for them to run afoul of the obstructions. "But to our surprise and mortification," wrote Washington, "they ran through without the least difficulty." [53]

In August, when the British fleet was lying above the Narrows off Staten Island, an attempt had been made with a primitive submarine to blow up one of the vessels, and now the experiment was repeated against a frigate off Bloomingdale. The machine, a crude one-man affair, shaped somewhat like a clam, was the invention of

David Bushnell of Saybrook. It was propelled by paddles, revolving upon a front axletree and turned with a crank, which made possible a speed of three miles an hour. Two forcing pumps, by which water could be admitted or expelled, enabled the navigator to rise or sink at pleasure. The torpedo, which contained 130 pounds of powder, together with a clock and a gun lock, was to be fastened to the bottom of the ship picked for destruction by means of a sharp iron screw.

In the first attempt, the navigator, one Ezra Lee, got under one of the warships, but found it impossible to attach the torpedo, the submarine rebounding from the bottom with each turn of the screw. On the return trip he narrowly escaped capture, and the torpedo, which he detached in self-defense, exploded in the water with tremendous violence. In the second trial, with the frigate *Eagle* the intended victim, he planned to fasten the powder to the rudder. But when the watch discovered him he submerged, and after a vain attempt to get under the vessel, reluctantly headed for shore.[54] It was only after the lapse of nearly a century and a half, when the science of engineering had made revolutionary advances, that the submarine was to become a major factor in naval warfare.

Though the New York Tories could congratulate each other over these failures which made it clear that there was no force in America capable of standing before the British on the water, news filtered down to the city of an engagement in upper Manhattan which indicated that on land they were not to have things all their own way.

The American army was posted on Harlem Heights, where they busied themselves making a double line of entrenchments extending from the Harlem River to the Hudson. Facing them across an open plain, and partly hidden by dense woods, was Howe's formidable army. Before dawn on September 16, Washington sent a small detachment under Lieutenant Colonel Thomas Knowlton to reconnoiter Howe's left flank. Knowlton had led his men over a depression known as the Hollow Way and up the woody heights beyond, when he ran into a superior force of the enemy, and was forced to retire. The British followed, and coming out in the open "sounded their bugles in the most insulting manner, as usual after a fox-chase." This was too much for Washington. Planning a trap for the overconfident enemy, he made a feigned attack in front, while a large party under Knowlton and Major Andrew Leitch swung around to the east to take them in the rear. Thereupon the enemy retreated, firing as they went. Both sides now poured in reinforcements, Putnam, Greene and George Clinton hurrying their men to the point of action, while the British grenadiers, a regiment of foot and a detachment of Hessians came up on the run "without a halt to draw breath." After a sharp engagement of two hours, the British began to give way, closely pursued by the triumphant Americans. But now Washington, not wishing to bring on a general engagement, gave the order for his men to retire.[55]

Although the Battle of Harlem resulted in no change in position for either army and although the number of killed and wounded was inconsiderable, it was for the Americans an important victory. It proved to them and to the enemy that they could stand up to trained regulars and even put them to rout. "You can hardly conceive the change it has made in our army," wrote Colonel Joseph Reed to his wife. "The men have recovered their spirits and feel a confidence which before they had quite lost." [56]

But to the Tory refugees, as they joyfully turned their faces toward New York City, the affair seemed unimportant, a temporary pause in the conquest of Manhattan. Nor did the events of the next two months give them reason to change this opinion.

For several weeks the British sat facing the strong American position on Harlem Heights, while General Howe pondered his next move. A frontal attack would be costly, possibly disastrous. With undisputed possession of the North and East Rivers, was there any reason why he should not land the bulk of his army in the rear of the Americans and leave them the alternative of retreating or being surrounded?

On October 12, several thousand redcoats went aboard flatboats in the East River, and, moving through Hell Gate, landed on Throg's Neck. Here they were joined by General von Heister's men, who had marched up from Jamaica to Whitestone and crossed over to the opposite shore. To Howe it seemed that all that was now needed to close the trap on Washington was a quick march over Fordham Heights to Kingsbridge. But this was not to be. When he had advanced several hundred yards he found himself confronted by a creek and a marsh cutting across the Neck, from the opposite side of which a group of hidden riflemen opened fire. This gave Washington six precious days in which to make a counter move.

It was a grave group of men who gathered at General Charles Lee's headquarters, with Washington presiding, while around him

Head Qrs. New york Island, Septr. 22: 1776

Parole London

Count: Great Britain

the 2d. & 6th. Brigades & 3d Battn. of Light Infantry & Artilery as orderd for to day are to March to Morr. at 9 oClock under the Command of L Genl. & Percy

the Packet for Europe will be Ready to Sail Tuesday the 24th. Inst.

A Spy from the Enemy (by his own full Confession) Apprehended Last night, was this day Executed at 11 oClock: in front of the Artilery Park.

Memmorandum

QMrs. to take Particular Care that the Necessary Houses are frequently Changd

Field offr. for Pt. this Evening Lcolo Howe
In Waiting Lolo: Hyde

A Page from a Manuscript Orderly Book Kept by an Officer of British Fort Guards in New York City, September, 1776. The record shows the execution of a spy, Nathan Hale.

British Warships Forcing an Entrance to the Hudson River, October 9, 1776. Forts Washington and Lee appear on either side of the river. The ships are the *Roebuck*, the *Tartar*, and the *Phoenix*.

The Ruins of Trinity Church after the Great Fire of September 21, 1776.

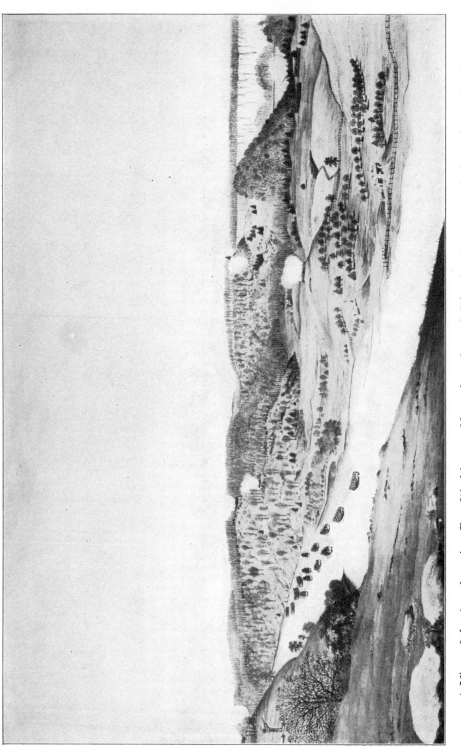

A View of the Attack against Fort Washington, November 16, 1776. The drawing was made from the east bank of the Harlem River from what is now the campus of New York University. The Morris Mansion at the top of the hill at the left was Washington's Headquarters during the Battle of Harlem.

Landing of the British Forces in New Jersey on November 20, 1776, under the Command of the Rt. Hon. Lieut. Gen. Earl Cornwallis.

Washington's Troops Disembarking on the New Jersey Shore of
the Delaware River above Trenton.

The Americans Surprising the Hessians at Trenton.

The Retreat through New Jersey.

were grouped Lee, Putnam, Heath, Stirling, McDougall, Lincoln, George Clinton, Knox and others. After Washington had asked them whether it was possible to hold their position on Harlem Heights in view of the threat to their communications, a long debate followed. In the end all save Clinton agreed that they must retreat immediately or face annihilation or capture. But, since Congress had ordered them to obstruct the navigation of the Hudson at "whatever expense," they decided to leave a strong force to hold Fort Washington.[57]

The next day the movement northward began, the long line of men, guns and wagons streaming over the Harlem River and up the right bank of the Bronx in the direction of White Plains. In the meanwhile Howe had made use of his fleet of flatboats to shift his army from Throg's Neck to Pell's Neck and was also moving northward on another road a few miles to the east. Should he succeed in heading off Washington, he might force him against the Hudson, bring up the fleet to prevent escape to the west bank and compel him to surrender at discretion. Fortunately, the American van, led by Stirling, won the race to White Plains and gave to Washington the choice of positions.

The British army advanced to the attack on October 22. To the Americans, who from their elevated situation had an excellent view of the enemy, the spectacle was "truly magnificent." "A bright autumnal sun shed its full lustre on the polished arms, and the rich array of dress and military equipage gave an imposing grandeur to the scene." [58] Howe centered his attack on Chatterton's Hill on which rested the right of Washington's line and which was the key to his position. A bitterly contested engagement followed, in which McDougall's New Yorkers, the Third New York regiment, Haslett's Marylanders, and Webb's Connecticut men, together with about 600 militia, twice repulsed the enemy and gave way only when threatened by overwhelming numbers. Technically a victory for the British, the battle was chiefly important in demonstrating to Howe that to oust the Americans from easily defended positions was a costly and perhaps futile business. So, when Washington retired across the Croton River to the heights of North Castle, the British thought it prudent to leave him in peace.

For six days the two armies remained inactive. "In the night time the British lighted up a vast number of fires, the weather growing pretty cold," wrote Heath in his *Memoirs*: "These fires . . . seemed

to the eye to mix with the stars and to be of different magnitudes." [59]
But though Howe would not attack, he did a great deal of thinking.
Had not the Americans, by dividing their forces into three separate
bodies—the main army at North Castle, the strong detachment at
Fort Washington and the garrison at Fort Lee—made a serious blun-
der? If he could not crush Washington, he could turn on Fort Washington in overwhelming numbers, cut off all avenues of escape and
force its surrender.

His first step was to send General Wilhelm von Knyphausen, with
a division of Hessians, to seize Kingsbridge. Next Percy brought up
a part of his forces to Harlem Plains, while Lord Cornwallis closed
in on the east bank of the Harlem River. Howe himself, leaving
Washington helpless to aid the threatened garrison, moved down
from the north. The situation for the Americans was hopeless. On
November 16 the British launched simultaneous attacks on the American outposts, and after some severe fighting drove all the defenders
into the fort. Here the 2,800 men were so crowded together in a
restricted space devoid of bomb-proofs and casements that a bombardment would have resulted in slaughter. There was nothing left
for Colonel Robert Magaw, the commanding officer, but to surrender.[60]

The news of Howe's successes brought joy to New York City.
With all Manhattan cleared of the rebel forces, with Washington's
battered army driven into the Westchester hills, with New Jersey open
to invasion, the city would have a much needed living space. "Now
one may hope that the communication with the Jerseys will be
opened, as also with the places up East River, so that the inhabitants
may come to the city and provisions be brought in, especially wood,
which is not to be had and is extremely dear," wrote Shewkirk.[61]
And as the long lines of crestfallen prisoners from Fort Washington
were marched through the streets on their way to the sugar-houses
and churches, the people who lined the streets looked on exultantly.
At last these miscreants were receiving their just rewards for rebelling
against their King and for their cruelty to their fellow subjects.

Even better news was to follow. When Washington found that
Howe was withdrawing his forces from his position in front of North
Castle, he concluded that it was his intention to invade New Jersey.
So, leaving General Heath with 3,000 men at Peekskill, and General
Charles Lee with 7,500 in Westchester, he crossed the Hudson with

the "southern troops," 5,000 in number, and took post at Hackensack. It was agreed that if Howe moved into New Jersey, Lee was to follow immediately. So, when Sir William did send over 6,000 men under Cornwallis, forcing Nathanael Greene to abandon Fort Lee with such precipitation as to leave his artillery, tents, blankets and provisions, and even the kettles boiling over the fires, Washington sent word to Lee to bring his men to the west side of the Hudson. But Lee, whose overweening ambition made him hope for Washington's defeat so that he could succeed him as commander-in-chief, refused to budge. "There is a time when we must commit treason against the laws of the State for the salvation of the State," he wrote Governor Bowdoin of Massachusetts. "The present crisis demands this brave, virtuous kind of treason." [62]

Thus deserted by his second in command, Washington's only hope was to withdraw his dispirited, dwindling force behind the Delaware. Assembling his shattered regiments, he pushed on in the chilling, gloomy rains of early winter, over the soggy roads to Newark. Here he halted for a few days in the hope that the New Jersey militia would flock in to join in the defense of their State. When the farmers showed no inclination to leave their comfortable firesides, he continued to New Brunswick, and thence through Princeton to Trenton. At that place he had assembled a fleet of Durham boats, those picturesque merchant vessels of the upper Delaware, so that after a delaying action against Howe's vanguard, he crossed over and posted his men on the right bank of the river.[63]

As reports of Howe's conquest of New Jersey, of Washington's narrow escape from capture or destruction, of the disintegration of his army, of the reluctance of the militia to come to his aid filtered back to New York, the Tories were confident that the end was at hand. Ambrose Serle thought that the heart of the rebellion had been broken and that a vigorous exertion of force would shortly reduce the country to subjection, "if not to reason." Every intercepted letter showed that the American leaders were in despair. "We all think our cause is nearly ruined," Putnam confessed.[64]

The New Jersey Tories rejoiced that they could now return to their homes. Word came to them that not only many of their friends, who had submitted to the revolutionary regime to protect their families and their prosperity, were now joyfully renewing their allegiance, but that there was a general rush to take the oath of loyalty.[65] Some of the most ardent formed themselves into associations to join the British as fighters, and General Howe gave Cortlandt Skinner a commission to raise five battalions of 500 privates each. In addition, a loyal militia, whose chief purpose seems to have been to take revenge on their "rebel" neighbors, were provided with arms and ammunition from the royal magazines.[66]

From the beginning, the sympathies of the people of New Jersey had been divided. The region between the Passaic and the Raritan, settled largely by New Englanders, attached to their civil liberties and under the influence of the Presbyterian clergy, were ardent revolutionists. Only in Newark and Elizabeth were there an appreciable number of Tories, "all members of the established Church." And the revolutionists, with all "their attachment to democracy and independence," if we may believe the British spy Peter Dubois, would not be able to put any formidable force in the field. Somerset, Dubois declared, was foremost in disloyalty, but in Sussex, Middlesex, Monmouth and Hunterdon the Tories had a majority. As for south Jersey, it abounded in Quakers, of whose attachment to the British government there could be no doubt.[67]

Just what proportion of the population was Tory it is now impossible to say, but all contemporary reports agree that the loyal group was large and active. But the British army, in its passage through the State, seemed determined to render the King's cause unpopular, to turn every Loyalist into a rebel, and to create a lasting detestation for Great Britain and the men who represented her in America. The soldiers, British and Hessians alike, acted on the principle that to plunder the defenseless inhabitants was one of their emoluments, a legitimate part of the game of war. If the man whose farm happened to be along the line of march was fortunate enough to escape being robbed by the regular troops, he was certain to be stripped of his all by the camp followers who trailed along behind—women, officers' servants, drummers, Negro workers.

"I have seen soldiers loaded with household utensils which they have taken for the wanton pleasure of spoil and which they have thrown aside an hour afterwards," Major André reported to General Clinton. Often the owner was a "harmless peasant, a decrepit father of a family, a widow or some other person as little an object of severity." "But when the property is plundered of a man who is conducting us, fighting with us or complying with what is by the general's proclamation the price of protection, what can be said to vindicate a conduct so atrocious which involves our friends in ruin and falsifies the word of the general?" [68]

The evidence of Captain Patrick Ferguson of the British army is equally damaging. It filled his breast with horror and detestation, he said, to behold "the ravages everywhere wantonly committed, without regard to sex or age, friend or traitor and the consequent alienation of every thinking mind from the royal cause . . . Most of the houses are thoroughly and indiscriminately plundered, the beds cut up, the furniture and windows broke to pieces, the men rob'd of their watches, shoe buckles and money, whilst their wives and daughters have their pockets and clothes torn from their bodies, and the father or husband who does not survey all this with a placid countenance is beat or branded with the name of traitor and rebel . . . Every man, however attached to the King and constitution, must lose all these impressions in the . . . misery heaped upon every person, loyal or rebel, that has the misfortune to be within reach of our ravages." [69]

The first fruit of this brutality was the determined assumption by the Americans of the offensive, an offensive in which farmers and artisans, as well as regulars and militiamen, assailed the enemy with furious determination. And they assailed them in the manner which many decades of experience had shown to be, under conditions existing in America, the most effective. A century earlier Nathaniel Bacon, the leader in the rebellion against the government of Sir William Berkeley, when he heard that a British army was on the way to the Chesapeake to restore Virginia to its obedience to the King, had calmly outlined his plan of defense. "Are we not acquainted with the country, so that we can lay ambuscades? Can we not hide behind trees to render their discipline of no avail? Are we not as good or better shots than they?" [70] It is improbable that many of the New Jersey farmers or the leaders of the militia, or even General Horatio Gates or General Heath or General Alexander McDougall or the other commanders of detached units of the American army in New Jersey, had ever heard of Nathaniel Bacon. Yet in the offensive campaign which they now opened they adhered closely to his formula.

Entrenched in the Highlands where Howe did not dare to attack them, they sent out parties to make lightning raids on isolated camps, to cut off detached groups, intercept post riders, capture baggage trains, drive off cattle. Whenever the British moved along a road, they had to keep a sharp lookout to right and left for the sharp-shooters concealed behind rock fences or trees or bushes. General Howe himself narrowly escaped death at the hands of the guerrillas. When he was riding back to New York after his occupation of Trenton, his guard discovered a group of farmers armed with muskets lying in wait for him in a ditch. The soldiers were for hanging them on the spot, but Howe, realizing that this might lead to reprisals, gave orders that they be treated as prisoners of war.

Garrisoned in a string of posts from Hackensack to Burlington—Paulus Hook, Newark, Elizabeth, New Brunswick, Princeton, Trenton, Bordentown—the British were at a loss how to meet this kind of warfare. To them it seemed unfair, counter to all the rules of the game. But gradually it dawned upon their leaders, first upon Howe, and later upon Clinton, that it was to be an important, if indeed not a decisive, factor in the war. They might conquer a province with a force of 5,000 men but it would require 10,000 to hold it. Again and again they were to write to the British government for reinforcements, pointing out that without far more men than were ever placed at their disposal, they saw no hope of garrisoning the vast reaches of America.[71]

In this view Washington did much to confirm them by his surprise attack on the Hessian garrison of Trenton on the morning of December 26, 1776. Gathering a fleet of Durham boats at McKonkey's Ferry, the Americans, perhaps 2,400 strong, crossed the Delaware in the face of a bitter wind, battling the swift current and the floating cakes of ice. Once on the left bank they descended on the unsuspecting Hessians, killed or wounded 106 and captured over 900. Colonel Johann Gottlieb Rall, their commander, was fatally wounded.[72]

The significance of the Battle of Trenton was not lost on the New York Tories. Tryon declared that it gave him "more real chagrin than any other circumstance of the war." Some criticized Howe for scattering his forces in small detachments which could be "insulted" and destroyed. Moreover, it was added, why did he assign the most dangerous post of all to a garrison of foreigners, under a noisy drunkard who could not speak English? [73]

Over in London one observer published an article explaining the military significance of the topography and the huge spaces of America. "The small scale of our maps deceived us; and as the word 'America' takes up no more room than the word 'Yorkshire' we seem to think the territories they represent are much the same bigness, though Charleston is as far from Boston as London from Venice. Braddock might tell the difficulties of this loose, rugged country, were he living . . . We have undertaken a war against farmers and farmhouses, scattered through a wild waste of continent, and shall soon hear of our general being obliged to garrison woods, to scale mountains, to wait for boats and pontoons at rivers, and to have his convoys and escorts as large as armies. These, and a thousand such difficulties, will rise on us at the next stage of the war." [74]

As the Battle of Trenton changed the strategy of the war, so the Battle of Princeton revived the waning spirits of the revolutionists and proved to all that in Washington they had a leader who was not only patient, resolute and persevering, but capable of brilliant strategy. The news from Trenton had brought Lord Cornwallis hastening down from the north with 8,000 veterans. Late on the afternoon of January 2, 1777, when he reached the town, he found Washington's forces drawn up on the left bank of the Assunpinck Creek. Cornwallis delayed his attack, since his men were weary and he was expecting reinforcements. But with dawn the next day he discovered that Washington had eluded him. Moving off silently in the night, the Americans had marched twelve miles over back roads to Princeton, where they attacked and scattered three British regiments under Colonel Charles Mawhood. Cornwallis came back, his men "running, puffing, blowing and swearing," but they were too late to prevent the destruction of Cornwallis' reinforcements, the cutting of his line of communications and the junction of Washington with the American forces in northern New Jersey.[75]

In the meanwhile the two Howes, while holding out the sword in one hand, had been offering the olive branch with the other. Having picked up General Sullivan in a cornfield at the Battle of Long Island, they convinced him that King George was ready not only to forgive and forget, but to grant all that the Americans had ever asked of him. So Sullivan went to Philadelphia to break this news to Congress, and Congress, though some of the members suspected "an ambuscade," delegated Benjamin Franklin, John Adams and John Rutledge to see what the British commissioners had to propose.

At Perth Amboy they found a barge awaiting them, in which they passed over to Staten Island. Here, at the Billopp house, a plain old building at Tottenville, now known as the Conference House, they sat down with Lord Howe to partake of "good claret, good bread, cold ham, tongues and mutton," while exchanging views on the possibility of reconciliation.

Howe began by stating that he had long believed that the differences between England and the colonies could be ironed out to the satisfaction of both. He had come to America prepared to use the petition of Congress to the King as a basis of settlement, but on his arrival he had been surprised to find that the Americans had changed their ground by issuing a Declaration of Independence. "That act, gentlemen, if it cannot be got over, precludes all treaty-making." He explained, also, that he could negotiate with them in their private characters only, and not as representatives of Congress, which body the King did not recognize.

"Your Lordship may consider me in what light you please . . . except that of a British subject," replied Adams surlily.

"It is desirable to put a stop to these ruinous extremities, as well for the sake of our country as yours," continued Howe. "The question is: Is there no way of turning back this step of independency, and thus opening the door to a full discussion?"

To this Franklin replied that since the drawing up of the petition of Congress to the King, the situation had greatly altered. "Forces have been sent out, and towns have been burnt. We cannot expect happiness under the domination of Great Britain. All former attachments are obliterated."

Adams pointed out that Congress, in declaring independence, had acted under instructions from the individual States. "It is not in our power, therefore, my Lord, to treat otherwise than as independent States."

"I can answer for South Carolina," broke in Rutledge. "With regard to the people consenting to come again under the English government, it is impossible . . . They would not, even if Congress should desire it."

Disappointed and undoubtedly saddened at this impasse, Lord Howe replied: "If such are your sentiments, gentlemen, I can only lament that it is not in my power to bring about the accommodation I wish . . . I am sorry, gentlemen, that you have had the trouble of coming so far to so little purpose." So, accompanying the commissioners to the shore, he saw them aboard their barge and bade them farewell.

To the Tories this was a bitter disappointment. A reasonable agreement would have brought the restoration of their confiscated estates, the reestablishment of civil government, the freeing of the avenues of trade, a return to their positions of influence in the colonial councils, assemblies and courts, and not least, a guarantee of self-government in provincial affairs. But now all they could look forward to was a British victory or utter ruin.

Should Great Britain ever have to acknowledge American Independence and withdraw her forces, the Tories knew that for them there would be no mercy.

And that things might eventually come to this dire extremity some now began to think possible. Suppose the French, who had long nursed the hope of revenge for their defeat in the Seven Years War, should decide to come to the aid of the Americans! It was known that Benjamin Franklin, Silas Deane and Arthur Lee had gone over to Europe with instructions from Congress to propose a treaty of amity and commerce; if they should succeed, if Louis XVI should give active support to the rebels, war between Great Britain and France would be inevitable. Then, with French fleets contesting with the British admirals the control of American waters, with French gold bolstering the weak American finances, with French troops fighting side by side with Washington's soldiers, it might be impossible ever to reestablish the authority of the King.[76]

Yet most of the Tories, even the far-seeing William Smith, convinced themselves that this was merely a passing nightmare, that France would not dare go to war, and that even if she should, British might on land would force the Americans to seek terms. So they went about their daily tasks, seeking by business activity, or by sports, or by the theatre, or by military parades, or by social functions, to divert their minds from the possibility of disaster.[77]

Holidays connected with the royal family were celebrated with more than usual zeal. On the anniversary of the King's accession to the throne "the flagships hoisted the royal standard, and all the ships in the harbor gave a salute of twenty-one guns each." The roar of the cannon was answered from the shore with loud huzzas. That evening glasses clinked as many loyal toasts were drunk at a banquet given by Admiral Howe and Admiral Shuldham.[78]

Since George III was born in June and his consort in May, it was customary to celebrate the queen's birthday four months ahead of time. So, on January 18, 1777, the "guns, as usual" were fired at Fort George; in the evening a "very splendid exhibition of fireworks" was "played off at Whitehall." Lord Howe invested his brother Sir William, with the Order of the Bath, and Sir William, not to be outdone, "gave an elegant ball and supper," which was opened "by Miss Clark and his excellency, Governor Tryon." [79]

When Jabez Fitch heard of this extravagant affair, he could not refrain from asking whether it would not have been more humane had the people who were dancing and feasting given a thought to the starving American prisoners in the jails and sugar-houses and donated "at least a part of this extraordinary expense to their relief." [80] He might have added that if resentment against the Americans precluded such an act, there were many poor Loyalists in the city who would have welcomed a few viands from the overflowing tables. The presence of the army within the restricted limits of the military lines, the influx of Tories from the surrounding regions, the partial cutting off of the flow of meat, vegetables and grain from Connecticut, upper New York and New Jersey had produced a serious food shortage. It is true that when the wife of a laborer, or of a shopkeeper, or of a refugee whose property had been confiscated by the revolutionists, went to the Fly Market or Peck's Slip Market, they found there beef, fish and grain in comparative abundance, but at such prices as few could afford to pay. It was stated that the "markets were raised 800 per cent for the necessaries of life," so "that a man even of small fortune could hardly afford" to buy provisions. [81]

General Robertson made the experiment, tried with such doubtful success in present times, of putting a ceiling on prices. Since so many complaints that bread was "extravagantly high" had reached him, he said, he had decided to fix the price of a loaf made of the finest flour and weighing three pounds and four ounces at fourteen coppers. Those who charged more were to be arrested, and "the bread in their possession . . . given to the poor." [82] To what extent this order was obeyed we do not know, but there is reason to believe there were many under the counter sales to those who had the money. There were hundreds of poor persons who were glad to get the less palatable, but cheaper, ship bread which Francis Marschalk offered for sale at his store on Broad Street, opposite the post office. [83]

But though life for many was hard, it gradually assumed a more normal aspect. Taverns and coffeehouses were reopened, where the hosts did a thriving business with British and Hessian officers; coopers, coachmakers, cobblers, carpenters, bricklayers, blacksmiths resumed their occupations; the shops on Water Street, William Street, at the Fly Market and on Broadway, once more displayed for sale goods imported from Great Britain or the West Indies; ferryboats crossed regularly to Long Island; a music school was opened on Maiden Lane; the street lights were put in order and kept burning throughout the night; [84] John Ramage fitted out a studio in William Street, where he painted the portraits of "all the military heroes or beaux of the garrison, and all the belles of the place." [85]

On John Street workmen were busily employed refitting the theatre in preparation for amateur plays in which "gentlemen of the army and navy" were to be the actors. The scenery, painted by Captain De Lancey, was said to have such merit that it would not have disgraced a theatre under the management of a Garrick. The season was opened on January 25, 1777, with "the celebrated burlesque entertainment of Tom Thumb." The prologue, the product of the "infant muse" of one of the officers, was so "replete with true poetic genius," that it won great applause from the audience which filled the house. The receipts of their first season of theatrical performances were donated to the widows and orphans of soldiers and sailors who had lost their lives in the war. [86]

Despite the diversion of the theatre, life seemed dull for the officers left on garrison duty, and every unusual event was eagerly discussed, if not always welcomed. The British had been in possession of the city but a few days when the Hon. J. Talmash, brother of the Earl of Dysert and commander of the *Zebra,* fought a duel with Captain Pennington, of the guards, in an upper room of Hull's Tavern. Talmash received a wound "of which he expired immediately," but Pennington, though "wounded in seven different parts," came through with his life. [87]

The New Yorkers must have been shocked by this fatal affair. True there were a few old men who could remember the duel in 1715 in which Thomas Dongan killed Dr. John Livingston, but to most of the people, even the Tory aristocracy; such affairs of honor were almost unknown. Unfortunately, however, instead of condemning the officers for their folly, the Americans caught the infection, so that in the years following the Revolution some of the most prominent men in the country lost their lives in duels. Had Aaron Burr and Alexander Hamilton realized, when they faced each other at Weehawken, that they were aping the men who had sought to conquer their country, Hamilton might not have been lost to the nation.

It was with intense satisfaction that the Tories, when they strolled down to Whitehall or Fort George to look out over the harbor, noted the great fleet lying at anchor there. These vessels were the "wooden walls of Athens," their defence against the American privateers, the carriers which brought them the food and manufactured goods essential to their existence. When a frigate moved into the harbor, followed by several prizes—a tobacco ship which had been heading for France, a Philadelphia brig caught on its way to the West Indies, perhaps a "rebel" privateer—there were smiles of satisfaction. On February 25, 1777, alone, five vessels, taken off the capes of the Delaware and Chesapeake Bays, came in,[88] to add to the "immense" number of prizes at anchor in the North River on Upper New York Bay.[89]

The death of Cadwallader Colden at his estate in Flushing would have excited great interest, had it not occurred on the day of the great fire. A distinguished scientist, several times acting governor, an ardent Anglican, his passing at the age of eighty-nine snapped an important link with former days.

For Colden, the chief executive, the Tories had had respect, for Tryon real affection, but for Dunmore only contempt. They were by no means pleased, therefore, when Dunmore took a house on Broadway as his residence for the winter. The presence of this Scottish earl among them was a reminder not only of his undignified conduct when Governor of New York, but of his failure in Virginia—his flight from Williamsburg, his futile efforts to organize a slave insurrection, his defeat at the Battle of Long Bridge, the evacuation of Norfolk.

More welcome was General Charles Lee, whom a detachment of thirty British light dragoons under Lieutenant Colonel Harcourt had captured in a house near Basking Ridge, some distance outside the American lines. Tories and soldiers alike rejoiced when the egotistic general was brought over from New Jersey and confined in the City Hall. "Victoria!" exulted one of General Howe's adjutants. "We have got our hands on General Lee, the only rebel general we had to fear." [90] But it was the Americans who profited from the capture, not the British, for the troops Lee had been holding back now marched without delay to join the main army, making it possible for Washington to regain all New Jersey save Perth Amboy and New Brunswick. Yet Washington would have been greatly worried had he known that in New York Lee was fraternizing with the British officers and had submitted to the two Howes "a plan for the easy subjugation of the colonies." It was only later, at Monmouth Court House, that Washington became aware of Lee's true character, and only after the lapse of three-quarters of a century that the discovery of "Mr. Lee's Plan" gave conclusive evidence of his treason.[91]

The news that a new constitution for the State of New York had been adopted by the convention at Kingston was received in the city with ridicule. A pitiful commonwealth this, the Tories said, a rump nation, a fragment, embracing only the counties of Albany, Ulster and Duchess, with parts of Westchester, Orange and Tryon. Repudiated by Manhattan, Long Island and Staten Island, cut off from their outlet to the sea, threatened from the north by the King's army in Canada and from the west by the Indians, this "ape of a nation" would be a universal laughing-stock.

The constitution, drafted by the youthful John Jay, with the help of the even more youthful Gouverneur Morris and Robert R. Livingston, was not the radical document which Sears, McDougall, and the leather-aprons had hoped for, and Tryon, William Smith, John Watts and other conservatives had feared. The suffrage, though considerably widened, still excluded large masses of the people— day laborers, apprentices, small tenants. There was no bill of rights, the colonial quit rent system was continued, the large proprietors were permitted to retain their holdings. On the other hand, the right to trial by jury was to "remain inviolate," there was to be no interference with "the free exercise and enjoyment of religious profession and worship," while bills of attainder, though permitted during the Revolution, were forbidden after its conclusion.

With the drawing up of this document many ardent patriots believed that the movement for which they had risked their all had failed of one of its main objectives. Washington's armies might be victorious, independence might be won, but the aristocracy which had dominated the colonial government would still be in the saddle; there would be freedom, but no democracy. But in this they were mistaken. The old aristocracy had in fact committed suicide by siding with the royal cause. Their rich estates, which in some cases embraced thousands of acres, were confiscated, they had become outcasts, destined, with the evacuation of New York City by the British forces, to become exiles. Try as they would, Jay and his colleagues in drafting the new constitution could not place the patriot rump of the old ruling group in the position of power once held by the De Lanceys and the Livingstons.

Nor could they prevent the trend of the times from setting in toward democracy. This must have become evident to them at the first state election, in which the aristocratic Philip Schuyler was defeated for governor by George Clinton, the friend of the tenant farmer and the mechanic. A lawyer, a keen politician, an able administrator, an ardent patriot, Clinton was destined to be reelected six times. Schuyler, though disappointed at his own defeat thought that Clinton was "virtuous and a lover of his country," though "his family connections" did not entitle him to so "distinguished a preeminence." But Schuyler and the other conservatives soon came to the realization that in the new commonwealth it was to be popular appeal rather than the support of the aristocracy which was to carry elections.

By the end of the first half-year of British occupation, life in New York City had assumed the pattern it was to follow for the remainder of the war. The dearness of food, the inadequate supply of fuel, the eager desire to have news from the front, the return of the sick and wounded, the uneasiness over the international situation, the absence of civil government, the growing importance of privateering, the squalor of the group of shanties and tents known as canvas town amid the blackened ruins left by the fire, the well-to-do families now forced to live on charity—all these things were to mark Tory New York until the day when Sir Guy Carleton, with the last of the British garrison, sailed through the Narrows and out into the Atlantic.

It was not a normal New York, this New York of the two Howes, of Sir Henry Clinton, of Sir Guy Carleton, of General James Robertson, of Oliver De Lancey, of Governor Tryon, of Judge William Smith, but a strange, tense, fearful New York. It had ceased to be a part of America; its people, exiles from their home communities many of them, were no longer Americans. A nest of traitors, the revolutionists called the place, a leprosy colony. But to the Loyalists themselves it was the chief outpost of British authority in the colonies, an oasis in the vast desert of Revolutionary America.

CHAPTER VI

FRANCE TURNS THE SCALES

AS THE spring of 1777 wore on the murmurings against Sir William Howe began again. The refugees, many of them crowded into inadequate quarters, hungry and cold, waited impatiently for the British to take the field and crush Washington's army, so that they could return to their homes. And though they dared not speak openly against the man upon whom they were dependent for their bread and butter, they loosened their tongues in the privacy of their families, or whispered to each other when they were sure there were no eavesdroppers to report their words to headquarters.

It is well known, they said, that Howe has at his command 23,000 of the best troops in the world, 14,000 of them in New Jersey. It is also well known that Washington has only 8,000 Continentals and a body of undisciplined militia whose numbers vary from day to day. His men are poorly armed, they are suffering from a shortage of provisions, hundreds are sick, their pay is overdue, many are deserting. Can there be any doubt that a vigorous offensive would drive him out of New Jersey and perhaps even Pennsylvania? The truth is that Howe is reluctant to exchange the pleasures of life in the city for the hardships of a campaign. So, while he is "feasting, gunning, banqueting, and in the arms of Mrs. Loring," his mistress, the war is at a standstill.[1]

Nor were the British officers and men less disgusted as the army remained inactive throughout the winter and much of the spring in its cramped position along the lower Raritan. For the troops it was a time of suffering and hardship, since it was difficult to find living quarters in the embers of burnt farmhouses or the desolated buildings of Perth Amboy. When foraging parties went out from New Brunswick they were sure to run into ambushes; provision boats on their way up the Raritan were fired upon by sharpshooters posted on the south bank. In time the lack of proper food began to tell on the troops and many succumbed to scurvy. To make matters worse, the Americans kept frayed nerves on edge by threatening constantly to surprise this post or that as a few weeks before they had surprised Trenton.

In the meanwhile Howe, though keeping his own counsel, was laying his plans. His chief hope had been to overwhelm Washington by mere force of numbers, for in addition to the 23,000 men at his disposal Lord Germain had promised large reinforcements. But these were long delayed, and when at last they arrived they proved to be few in numbers. At one time Howe had definitely decided to open a winter offensive, but was deterred by the New Jersey weather and New Jersey mud. "My expectations of a move in the winter against the enemy . . . have been frustrated by a deep fall of snow which rendered the country impassable," he wrote Lord Germain, "and since the breaking up of winter, the depth of roads forced me to relinquish the idea." [2] In the meanwhile other plans were being formulated which made the proposed campaign a secondary consideration.

At the very outset of the Revolution the British had dallied with the possibility of an invasion of New York from Canada by an advance up the Richelieu River and Lake Champlain. Dartmouth had suggested it, Howe had suggested it, Carleton drew up a detailed plan and sent it to England in care of General Burgoyne. In February, 1777, Burgoyne submitted his own ideas to Germain. The main British army was to move south by the Lake Champlain route; St. Leger with 1,600 men, was to advance from Oswego; while Howe was to come up the Hudson, the three forces meeting at Albany. Thus would New England be severed from the other States, as Lincoln eighty-six years later severed Arkansas, Louisiana and Texas from the rest of the Confederacy by gaining control of the Mississippi. Burgoyne's plan was approved by Lord Germain, and King George, after going over it with attention, took a pen and wrote his endorsement on it. Burgoyne himself was selected to head the main British army.

But while Germain and the King were poring over the map with Burgoyne and cautioning him "never to lose sight of his intended junction with Howe, as his principal object," Howe himself was beginning to turn his eyes in an entirely different direction. In December, 1776, he had written Germain that he hoped not only to send 10,000 men up the Hudson to Albany, but to keep 10,000 in New Jersey to threaten Philadelphia, which he would "propose to attack in the autumn." Later, when disappointed in the number of expected reinforcements, he decided to relinquish the plan for opening the Hudson, and to concentrate on conquering Pennsylvania. Possibly he thought Burgoyne strong enough to take care of himself; possibly he was influenced by Charles Lee, who assured him that Pennsylvania was the key to the situation and that by its conquest "the whole machine" would be unhinged and "a period put to the war." Lee it was, also, who was largely responsible for Howe's belief that the Pennsylvania Tories would rise up to welcome him. "I flatter myself and have reason to expect the friends in that part of the country will be found so numerous and so ready to give every aid . . . that it will prove no difficult task to reduce the more rebellious parts of the province."

Thus did Howe and the British Ministry work at cross purposes. As soon as Germain had given his approval to the triple campaign in the north, he should have insisted that Howe carry out his part of the plan. It would serve no useful purpose for Burgoyne and St. Leger to reach Albany, if the Hudson below that point continued in the hands of the Americans. As for the capture of Philadelphia, so far from its ending the war, it would mean merely that the British would have to garrison another city and so divide their forces. Yet Germain permitted Howe to go ahead, though he must have realized that it unhinged the whole northern campaign.[3]

Had this confusion of strategy been known to the New York Tories it would have thrown them into despair. But Howe kept his own counsel and they could only speculate as to what he had in mind. As late as May 1777, William Smith took it "for granted that the main object of the British general is to penetrate the New England colonies."[4] But, as month after month elapsed, and Howe made no move, the Loyalists began to wonder whether he had any plans at all.

They were elated, then, when on June 9, he bade good-bye to his pleasures in the city and went over to Perth Amboy to take personal command of the army. For several weeks there had been signs of activity in the British camp. At New Brunswick and Perth Amboy the troops left their cramped quarters and marched out to the lovely countryside; boat after boat, filled with women and children moved down the Raritan; transports at the mouth of the river began to take on baggage and light equipment. Obviously Howe was preparing for some important move, no one knew what.

Sir William himself had decided to make one attempt to lure Washington into a general engagement, failing which he would start immediately for Philadelphia. He had pondered long over the alternative of advancing overland or going around by sea. The former was more direct, it would enable him to conquer large areas of New Jersey and Pennsylvania, it would be an encouragement to the Tories to rise in his behalf. But it entailed the crossing of the Delaware with Washington hanging on his flank and rear, and this Howe did not relish. To approach Philadelphia by way of the Delaware or the Chesapeake, though it would necessitate the complete abandonment of New Jersey, was far safer. So, like McClellan many years after in a similar situation while contemplating an attack on Richmond, Howe decided on the sea route.

While he was laying these plans Washington was on the alert to divine and thwart them. Since it at first appeared that the main British effort was to be made in New Jersey, he moved his army from Morristown to a very strong position behind the First Watchung Mountain, where he could obstruct any advance toward the Delaware, or move quickly north in case Howe embarked his army for an assault on the Hudson River forts. Sullivan, with 1,600 men, he ordered to move from Princeton to Rocky Hill, where he could fall back on the Sourland Mountains. In northern New Jersey the militia began to gather, eager to avenge themselves for the plundering and burning in which the redcoats had indulged on their march through the State in the previous autumn.

For several days the British army remained motionless, while Washington's lookouts on the Watchung Mountains viewed the impressive array. "I believe that no more select corps can exist than the one General Howe has here," wrote one observer. "All the Hessians and veteran English officers say that they have never seen such a corps—meaning in quality of course. Of the Englishmen, the grenadiers, light infantry and light dragoons, and of the Hessians, the grenadiers and Jägers are the elite of the corps. Every fellow serves with joy, and everyone would rather cut loose today than tomorrow." [5]

On the night of June 13, Howe did "cut loose," not to attack Washington's main army, but to surprise and cut off Sullivan's isolated division. When Sullivan got word of what was intended and slipped off to Flemington, the British swept off to the right and took a position between Somerset Court House and Middlebush. Here they lingered for four or five days waiting for Washington to attack them. This the American general was too wise to do. But the militia hovered around the British like a swarm of mosquitoes, annoying them unceasingly. A shot from out the darkness and a sentinel would fall; scouts were greeted by a deadly fire from behind barns; patrols had to run the gauntlet of hidden riflemen.

Tired of losing valuable time and valuable lives, Howe hit on a ruse to draw Washington out of his position. On July 19, the British began a retreat, abandoning New Brunswick and marching down the Raritan under a pall of smoke from burning farmhouses. At Perth Amboy regiment after regiment passed over to Staten Island and some actually went on board the waiting transports.[6]

The temptation for the Americans to attack while the embarkation was under way was almost irresistible, and Washington's officers urged him not to let the opportunity escape. But the general was suspicious; the invitation to attack was too obvious.[7] None the less, he was at last persuaded to come down from the hills and send Lord Stirling forward towards Metuchen to be prepared should a favorable opportunity to strike present itself. When Howe received word of this move, he must have rubbed his hands in glee, for it was just what he had hoped for. Late on the afternoon of June 23, 1777, the vessels returned to Perth Amboy, the men were debarked and before dawn the next morning sent forward in two columns to envelop and destroy Stirling's detachment.[8]

But Washington was not caught napping. The pickets sounded the alarm, Stirling hastened back to join the main body of the army, the whole retreated to the almost impregnable passes of the Watchung Mountains, and when Howe closed his trap by uniting his columns, he was chagrined to learn that the intended prey had eluded him. All he had to show for his maneuvre was three small brass French cannon and a few prisoners, while his own men had suffered severely from the galling fire of snipers.

Having failed a second time to draw Washington into battle, Howe realized that he had nothing to gain by remaining in New Jersey. So he brought his army back to Perth Amboy, whence they were ferried over to Staten Island. With a few of his officers, the British general waited until the last of the men had left, and then himself went aboard a waiting boat to join them. The next day, with his suite, he returned to New York.[9]

His reception there was cool. The New Jersey Tories, who saw all their hopes dashed, could regard the evacuation of their State only as a calamity. What excuse was there for this humiliating retreat in the face of an inferior enemy? they asked. Why had Howe opened the campaign if he had no intention of fighting? Could it be that Washington had outgeneraled him? Nor were the British officers less chagrined than the Loyalists. Some "complained loudly, and perhaps . . . indiscreetly," stated one. "The infection of discontent from this period has spread amongst us. I can scarce hear a man speak on that subject but in passion or despair." [10]

Yet they were in part consoled by the preparations for another expedition, directed against what, they did not know. Did Howe intend to attack Boston, or would he move up the Hudson, or would he head for the Delaware or the Chesapeake? The preparations were obvious to all, for regiment after regiment left their posts on Staten Island to go aboard the waiting transports, and small boats were kept busy plying between the city and the fleet with stores and baggage. William Eddis, who came in through the Narrows while all this was going on, thus describes the scene: "My mind was forcibly struck with the splendid appearance of a numerous and formidable equipment. A grand fleet, attended with innumerable transports, arranged in their several divisions, lay at anchor off Staten Island. The island itself was covered with troops ready for embarkation, and every appearance indicated an expedition of the most decisive consequence." [11]

Another interested spectator was Sir Henry Clinton, who arrived with a convoy from England on July 7. This man, who was to be the virtual dictator of New York City for four years, knew the place well, for he had resided there as a child when his father, Admiral George Clinton, was governor. A brave and capable soldier, the younger Clinton had won distinction under Prince Ferdinand in the Seven Years' War, at the Battle of Bunker Hill and at the Battle of Long Island. But he was egotistic, intolerant of the views of others, a poor administrator, immoral in his private life. To serve under him was hard, to cooperate with him impossible. He quarreled with Sir William Howe, he quarreled with Admiral Arbuthnot, he quarreled bitterly with Lord Cornwallis, he quarreled with his cousin and benefactor the Duke of Newcastle. The Tories hated and feared him. Thomas Jones says they found him "haughty, morose, churlish, stupid and scarcely to be spoken with." [12] The only person who seems to have had for him a real affection was his aide-de-camp, the unfortunate Major André.

Soon after Clinton had disembarked, Howe called him into consultation to get his opinion upon the Philadelphia campaign. Clinton opposed it. Had it been started months earlier it "might have been of infinite consequence," he said, but now it was too late. "The only thing therefore in my opinion left for us now in the middle of July is to cooperate in force with the northern army, not by a junction with it, (for that I can never advise) but that sort of communication which will give us possession of Hudson's River . . . I fear when our operations have finished near Philadelphia, it will be too late to look towards the northwards." [13] This advice was so "coldly received" that it stopped Clinton's mouth and Howe went ahead with his plans.

He had now gone too far to turn back, he told Clinton, he still considered Philadelphia rather than Albany the key to the American position, and Germain had given his full approval. So, placing Clinton in command of New York during his absence, he went aboard the fleet and gave the order to sail. On July 23, the armada of over two hundred vessels tacked back and forth across the bay, rounded Sandy Hook and, forming a long procession of white sails, headed southeast. [14]

With the departure of the fleet New York settled down to a monotonous, fearful, uncomfortable summer. Meat and vegetables, though to be found in the markets, sold at excessive prices. The weather was oppressive, sickness widespread, and the poor suffered severely. Shewkirk reported that the mortality was heavy, so that "on many evenings seven or eight were buried, and on one in particular seventeen." The men of the garrison, most of them unused to the New York summer, were so seriously affected that at one time no less than 1,094 were sick. [15]

Could the people have lived on rum and molasses, there would have been no hunger, for vessels were constantly coming in from the West Indies laden with these commodities. But what they wanted was bread and meat, so when the local markets had been glutted and the kegs began to pile up in the warehouses, the temptation to dispose of them to the Revolutionists for food was too great to be resisted. It was so easy for smugglers to slip across the Sound or Kill van Kull on dark nights, their little boats laden down with West Indian goods to be bartered off in some secluded cove for beef or flour. Howe tried to put a stop to this traffic before his departure by ordering that no local craft should take on more "rum, spirits, sugar or molasses than a barrel each," nor "any other kind of merchandize more than may be judged sufficient for the use of one family." [16] Yet the profits were so great that the dealers were willing to take the risk of detection and punishment, and so smuggling continued throughout the war.[17]

On September 24, the people of the city were elated at the report that a large fleet was coming in through the Narrows with 3,000 troops from England and several distinguished passengers—Major General Robertson, Major General Wilson, Major General Pattison, the Marquis of Lindsay and the publisher James Rivington. The last named was welcomed like a victor from the field of battle, rather than the notorious propagandist he was, returning with a new set of type and a fat subsidy from the royal government. In the evening the "King's Head Tavern was elegantly illuminated to testify the joy the true Sons of Freedom had on the arrival of Mr. Rivington from England," stated *The New York Mercury.* "Liberty he always firmly adhered to, licentiousness from his soul he ever detested." A few days later, when it was noised about town that Rivington's new paper, *The New York Gazette,* had appeared, the interest was so great that everyone rushed out into the street to secure copies, clerks, artisans, soldiers and merchants alike turning aside from their tasks to read it. [18] In December, Rivington changed the name of his paper to *The Royal Gazette.*

So the old falsehoods, misrepresentations, twisting of facts began all over again with a brazenness which would have won the admiration of Goebbels himself. Robert Morris had left Congress in disgust after having made a motion for "rescinding independency"; Washington had been made Lord Protector; Great Britain had signed a treaty with Russia under which 36,000 Cossacks had been taken into the British service. How much of this the Tories swallowed it is impossible to determine, but it excited the ridicule of the Americans. One editor observed that the printer of *The London Gazette* had been thought the greatest liar on earth, but Rivington had far exceeded him.

But the chief interest of all Loyalists and British alike was in the progress of the two armies, the one operating in northern New York, and the other in the south. And as news arrived of successes or defeats there was alternate elation and gloom. Burgoyne, it became known, had arrived in Canada in May, and was preparing for his descent on

Albany. With him were three British brigades and three Hessian brigades, totalling 7,213 men rank and file, together with 250 Canadians and 400 Indians, equipped with 38 pieces of light artillery and 10 pieces of siege artillery. On Lake Ontario, under Colonel St. Leger, were 900 Indians and 700 whites, ready to move up the Oswego River, Lake Oneida and the Mohawk River.

At first nothing but favorable reports reached New York of the northern campaign. On June 27, Burgoyne had landed unopposed at Crown Point. A few days later he had seized Mount Hope and Mount Defiance, commanding the American position at Ticonderoga, and had forced General St. Clair to abandon not only that important post but Fort Independence on the east shore of Lake Champlain as well. In their retreat the American rear guard had been attacked and completely shattered by General Fraser's brigade, reinforced by a body of Hessians under Baron von Riedesel. Elated by his easy success, Burgoyne had proceeded through the wilderness to the upper Hudson and had taken possession of Fort Edward. Albany was now but forty-five miles away and it seemed that nothing could prevent him from completing his part of the campaign.

The Loyalists were still rejoicing over these successes, when equally favorable reports of Howe's movements began to arrive. His fleet had arrived off Cape May on July 31, and after lingering there a few days had put to sea again. Later word came that it had been sighted rounding Cape Charles and heading northward up the Chesapeake bay. On August 24, it had arrived at Head of Elk, about forty-five miles southwest of Philadelphia, and the troops had begun going ashore.

When the British fleet left Sandy Hook and disappeared over the horizon, Washington could only guess its destination. It might have headed for Boston; it might be on its way south for an attack on Charleston. But when he found that it was in the Chesapeake, he collected his scattered divisions and marched south through Philadelphia, with colors flying and drums beating, as the crowds cheered and waved their welcome. The two armies met at Chad's Ford, on the Brandywine ten miles northwest of Wilmington, where a decisive engagement followed. Howe repeated his maneuvre of the Battle of Long Island, by feinting at the American position, while sending his main force under Lord Cornwallis on a wide flanking movement to strike it in the rear. Caught in this encircling stratagem, the Americans, despite heroic fighting, were forced from the field.

Washington was so far from being discouraged by this reverse that he was planning to attack Howe at Warwick Tavern, about twenty miles west of Philadelphia, when a violent rain storm, which continued for the greater part of two days, ruined all his ammunition and the greater part of Howe's. Taking advantage of Washington's temporary helplessness, the British general forced him to move up the Schuylkill, and then, without opposition, turned face about and marched into Philadelphia.

But the enthusiasm of the New Yorkers was chilled when rumors reached them that things were not going so well as at first with the British armies in the north. St. Leger had advanced to the upper Mohawk, where he invested Fort Schuyler, the site of Rome, but had been forced to turn aside to meet General Herkimer, who had gone to its relief with 800 frontiersmen. The Indians, under their famous leader, Brant, ambushed the Americans at Oriskany and would have wiped them out but for the most gallant resistance. Herkimer, though mortally wounded at the first fire, ordered his men to prop him up against a tree, lit his pipe and directed the battle for eight hours. In the end the garrison of the fort sallied out, captured the British camp and put the enemy to rout. Yet so heavy had been the American loss that they were forced to retire to Fort Dayton and to send to General Schuyler for aid. When Benedict Arnold, whom Schuyler hastened forward with 800 men, contrived to send pretended deserters into the British camp with exaggerated statements of his strength, the Indians took alarm and sneaked off into the forest. The next day St. Leger retreated hastily to Oswego, thus ending his campaign in failure.

With Howe in Philadelphia, two hundred and fifty miles away, and with St. Leger driven back to Lake Ontario, Burgoyne was left alone to face accumulating difficulties. Before the middle of August it had become apparent that he could not supply his army adequately from his base at Montreal over the hundred and eighty-five miles of land and water passage, and would be forced to look for food in the neighboring countryside. So, on August 14, he sent a foraging party of 600 men under Lieutenant Colonel Baume up the Hoosick River in the direction of Bennington, where he found a superior body of New England militia under General John Stark. Baume sent back for reinforcements and began to entrench, but the New England farmers, armed only with guns and cartridge boxes, closed in on him and inflicted a crushing defeat. When a force under Lieutenant

John Jay as he appeared when he was Chief Justice.

The Battle of Princeton. The battle revived the spirits of the Revolutionists and proved the mettle of their general.

Interview between Admiral Lord Howe and American Commissioners, near Tottenville, Staten Island, September 11, 1776.

Herkimer Directing the Battle of Oriskany.

The Battle of Bennington. The American forces led by General Stark repelling the British forces led by Colonel Baume.

View of the West Bank of the Hudson River three miles above Still Water, upon which the army under the command of General Burgoyne took post on September 20, 1777. The drawing shows General Frazer's funeral procession in progress on the hill on the right.

The Surrender of Burgoyne at Saratoga. Burgoyne turned over his sword to General Gates, who gave it back to him immediately.

Battle of the Brandywine.

Colonel Breyman came to his assistance, they too were routed. Of the 1,300 men who comprised Baume's and Breyman's forces, 207 were killed, many wounded and between 600 and 700 captured.

Burgoyne was chagrined at this unexpected disaster. Severe as was his loss in men, the failure to supply his needs from the neighboring farms was even more serious, since it forced him to resume the arduous task of moving provisions through the wilderness from Lake George. In the meanwhile, the clouds which were gathering became more threatening. Arnold returned from the Mohawk to swell the American forces; Stark's victorious New Englanders marched in to offer their services; reinforcements of Continentals were hastening up. On August 19, when General Horatio Gates superseded Schuyler in command, the Americans already outnumbered the British.

Planting himself in a strong position on Bemis Heights, directly in the path of Burgoyne's advance, Gates waited for the British to attack. On September 19, the Americans saw the redcoats approaching in three columns along three widely separated roads. Gates was in favor of remaining behind his redoubts, but Arnold, gaining a reluctant consent to go out to meet the advance guard of the British right, launched a furious attack. The fighting continued at close quarters for four hours, with American marksmanship matched against European discipline and European bayonets. The British held their ground, but at a loss in men they could ill afford. One of their regiments came out with only 60 men and five officers.

Burgoyne's unexpected reverses caused serious alarm at New York. It had been confidently expected that he would be in Albany by August 22, and here he was at Saratoga, a good forty miles away. On September 10, Clinton sent him a letter in cipher, explaining that his own force was inadequate for a major move to assist him, yet promising a diversion by attacking the Highlands forts on the Hudson. "But ever jealous of my flanks, if they make a move in force on either of them, I must return to save this important post." [19] When Burgoyne got his message, he and his officers bent over it in puzzled anxiety, for they had lost the key, and it was only after hours of work that they deciphered enough to understand that Clinton planned a move up the Hudson. "An attack, or even the menace of an attack on Fort Montgomery will be of use," Burgoyne replied hopefully, "and I will follow them close. Do it, my friend, directly."

Clinton waited until a fleet arrived from England with "a reinforcement of 1,700 recruits for the British, Hessians and artillery," and then, on October 3, started up the Hudson with a force of about 3,000 men. When he arrived at Verplanck's Point, he found awaiting him a Captain Campbell whom Burgoyne had sent forward to inform him as to his situation. It was a momentous meeting, there on the bosom of the river almost within the shadow of the Highlands, as the dust covered messenger explained how critical was Burgoyne's plight. His whole army did not exceed 5,000 men, he said, while the enemy, who were within a mile and a half of him, numbered between 12,000 and 14,000, with an additional body hovering in his rear. He wished to know as soon as possible whether Clinton would open communication with Albany.[20]

Burgoyne's dilemma did not swerve Clinton from his original plan of storming the forts, destroying the boom and chain across the river, sinking hostile war vessels, burning stores and then returning with his entire force to New York. He had received no orders from Howe to relieve the northern army, he wrote Burgoyne, and it was out of the question for him to penetrate to Albany with the small force at his command.[21]

But no one could have acted with more vigor and astuteness than Clinton in carrying out the attack on the Highlands forts. Since his main assault was to be directed against Fort Clinton and Fort Montgomery, on the right bank, he duped General Putnam, who was in command, into bringing most of his men to the left bank, by landing part of his army at Verplanck's Point, a few miles below Fort Independence. Then, early on the morning of October 6, he crossed over to Stony Point, and moved rapidly around Dunderberg Mountain to attack Fort Clinton from the south and Fort Montgomery from the west.

The Americans, reinforced by local militia, made a determined but futile resistance, and as the sun was sinking over the western heights, were forced to give up both forts. Thereupon Clinton destroyed the boom and chain, and sending the ships up the river to open fire on Fort Constitution while Tryon with his Tory troops assailed it by land, forced Putnam to abandon it too.

Clinton was elated. "*Nous y voici,* and nothing now between us and Gates," he wrote Burgoyne, concealing the letter in a hollow silver bullet. But it was the Americans, not Burgoyne who were destined to read this missive. When the messenger was captured the silver bullet might have escaped attention had he not been seen to swallow it. An emetic did the rest.

Burgoyne's messengers were more successful in eluding the Americans. On October 9, a Captain Scott arrived with word that Burgoyne could hold out only a few days longer, and that if communications were not opened between the two armies immediately, "he should make good his retreat to Canada before the ice sets in." At last aroused to the fact that a major disaster was imminent, Clinton, despite his fears for the safety of New York City, decided to go to the rescue. Sending word to Burgoyne that if he would "push for Albany," he would do all in his power to help, he hastened back down the river to prepare for the expedition.

When persistent rumors filtered into New York that disaster threatened the northern army, the Tories, at first incredulous and then dismayed, looked at the *Royal Gazette* to give them the real situation. But the *Gazette* was silent. "Since no accounts, properly authenticated, of the situation of the northern army, have yet been brought here, we will insert none of the reports that have been circulated." [22] But the American papers which were smuggled into the city, glorying in the humiliation of a great British army, heralded every item which came to their attention. Could it be true, the New Yorkers asked each other, that Burgoyne was in serious trouble? If so, why did not Clinton go to his relief? They had been greatly relieved when Sir Henry led the expedition of October 3 up the Hudson, and elated at the news that he had taken the Highlands forts and cleared the river. The excitement and anticipation increased when Clinton returned, gathered a large flotilla of small vessels, piled them high with provisions, embarked two battalions of Anspach troops and the British 45th Regiment, and headed up stream. At last, men told each other, a force large enough to give effective aid to Burgoyne is on its way.

In the meanwhile Sir James Wallace having proved that the fleet could pass the *chevaux-de-frise* at Nicoll's Point, Clinton ordered General Vaughan, with a force of 1,700 men, "to proceed up the Hudson's river to feel for General Burgoyne, to assist his operations and even to join him if that general required it." On October 16, Vaughan landed a force at Kingston, and after overcoming some resistance by the local militia, put the village to the flames. He was forced to do this, he reported to Clinton, because the citizens "fired from the houses on his troops." Only one house, the Van Steenbergh House, and one barn were left standing. "Destroying defenseless houses and villages cannot in the least contribute to the conquest of America," General Gates wrote Clinton bitterly. "You have destroyed by fire the beautiful town of Kingston in Esopus, and the buildings of those who could never have injured you, viz. the helpless widow." [23]

But Vaughan was destined to do no further damage on the upper Hudson. While the ruins of Kingston were still smoking, a message came to Clinton from Howe which put an end to the expedition. Unless Clinton was on the eve of accomplishing some major stroke, it stated, he must return to New York at once.[24] Clinton, who seems to have been under the impression that he was walking a tightrope over a precipice, was nothing loath. "Since he could hear nothing from Burgoyne," he stated, "and did not have any hope of effecting anything material, he returned to New York and left him to his fate." [25]

And Burgoyne's fate was hard. As the net about him was drawn closer and closer, he decided upon one more desperate attempt to cut his way through. On October 7, leaving the greater part of his force in their works along Mill creek, he led 1,500 regulars in an assault on the American left. But Arnold fell upon him furiously, drove him back and then, bringing up reinforcements, hurled them at the British redoubts. After prolonged fighting, in which Arnold was wounded, the Americans stormed over the so-called Horseshoe Works, a key position on the British right, and uncovered their entire line. That night Burgoyne withdrew his shattered forces to previously prepared works overlooking the Hudson.

The next day the British started their long-delayed retreat. But they got only to Saratoga, five miles to the north, when they discovered that they were surrounded. After some hesitation and some haggling over terms, Burgoyne surrendered. On October 17, 5,763 officers and men marched out of their camp and laid down their arms. In silence the Americans eyed their conquered foes—the British, deeply dejected, the dust which covered their white breeches and leggings detracting from their soldierly appearance; the Germans, weighted down by their cumbersome equipment, their uniforms in tatters; a group of slovenly women. Burgoyne's men, on their part, noted with interest the Americans, clothed in homespun, most of them, their tall, sinuous figures denoting strength and endurance. Before an open tent Burgoyne met Gates and handed him his sword, which the American general immediately returned.[26] "I pity poor Burgoyne," General William Phillips wrote General Clinton. "Your movement was too late and we had no alternative but to capitulate or starve . . . I must not enter on the subject, or I shall grow wild." [27]

A few days later passers-by on what is now Park Row were startled to hear the prisoners in the New Gaol give three hearty cheers. The jailer, too, heard them, and, "alarmed with such an uproar," rushed up to the second floor to find out what it was about. When the prisoners told him that they had received word that Burgoyne had surrendered with his entire army, he declared the report a "damned Yankee lie." The jailer did not know that word of the disaster had been smuggled in in a large loaf of bread, but he soon had it confirmed from official sources. After that his treatment of the prisoners was noticeably better.[28]

Though the Tories had had word of Burgoyne's difficulties, his surrender came to them as a severe shock. Fed on Rivington's lies, taught to believe that the American cause was on the verge of collapse, regarding Gates's army as an undisciplined mob, it was unbelievable that a powerful force of British and Hessian regulars, under an experienced and capable leader, should be forced to lay down their arms.

The disaster, the Tories told each other, was the result of inexcusable muddling. Why did Howe sail off on his expedition against Philadelphia, when every man he had was needed for cooperation with the northern army? Why did Clinton delay his push up the Hudson until it was too late? Why had not the government at home sent over reinforcements sufficient for the extensive operations which they had sanctioned? And the consequences of this piece of stupidity were already only too obvious. The Revolutionists, elated at their success, would redouble their efforts; the hope of opening the Hudson and isolating New England would have to be abandoned; France, always eager to weaken Great Britain, might now come to the assistance of the Americans; Gates's victorious army might swoop down on New York City and storm over its defenses; the militia were flocking in to reinforce Putnam.

"The provincials are grown so mighty upon this business, that their army has increased amazingly," stated one British officer. "They are said to have about 12,000 men encamped and quartered in the villages within a few miles of King's Bridge." [29] "We are all hurry and confusion and hardly know what to do," wrote a New Yorker. "We have 17,000 military and inhabitants in the city, but a great number of them are not to be depended upon. The ships are stationed to cover as much of the city as they can, but when the frost sets in they will be of little service as they will be easily burnt by the provincials." [30] The fear for the safety of the city was intensified when Clinton, in obedience to General Howe's orders, embarked several thousand troops and sent them off to aid in clearing away the American defenses on the Delaware.

Late in November the city was thrown into turmoil by the arrest of "one Mott and his wife in the Bowery," together with a "shoemaker, a saddler and a milkman," on the charge of plotting to deliver the city to the enemy. They had notified "the rebel commander," so it was said, "that on a certain night, on his making an assault on the place, they would set the city on fire in several different parts, in order to throw the whole into confusion, and make it the more easy conquest." [31]

The Americans did all in their power to increase the alarm. Raiding parties on dark nights descended on outlying posts, captured the defenders, and made off with munitions, food and cattle. One detachment crossed over to Staten Island, routed a party of provincials and, at the approach of reinforcements, retreated under cover of a battery at Elizabeth Town Point.[32] "How to account for all these matters and the poor outlook to defend what we have is difficult," wrote Shewkirk in his *Diary*.[33]

And now the bitterness which the war had aroused on both sides, especially between the Tories and Revolutionists, led to a series of raids, marked by plundering and burning. In November, when a party of Tories during a raid up the Hudson, set fire to a group of houses at Tarrytown, General Samuel H. Parsons wrote General Tryon a letter of protest. There could be no justification for such wanton destruction of property and for "stripping women and children of necessary apparel to cover them from the severity of a cold night." To this Tryon replied: "As much as I abhor any principle of inhumanity or ungenerous conduct, I should, were I in more authority, burn every committeeman's house within my reach, as I deem those agents the wicked instruments of the continued calamities of this country." [34]

Realizing that protests were futile, the Revolutionists retaliated by sending a small detachment of troops across the Hudson on a dark night to Bloomingdale to destroy the beautiful house of Oliver De Lancey. According to the *New York Mercury,* they "robbed and plundered his house of the most valuable furniture and money, set the house on fire before Mrs. De Lancey, her two daughters and two other young ladies could remove out of it, which was effected through the flames, in only their bed dresses." [35]

As the winter of 1777–1778 approached, with the end of the war not in sight, with the King's forces cooped up in a few coastal cities, with food and fuel scarce, the spirits of the Tories sank to a low ebb. The bitter weather which brought such hardship to Washington's ragged army at Valley Forge brought suffering, also, to hundreds of destitute refugees in New York City. As early as September "the streets were daily filled with poor begging from house to house," and the situation steadily grew worse.[36] Forced to flee from their homes with no more than the clothes which covered them and unable to find employment in the crowded city, many of the refugees, persons of large estates some of them, were "in a perishing condition and without any funds for their support." [37]

Their distress was increased by the exorbitant price asked by the farmers of Long Island and Staten Island for food and firewood. A poor widow or refugee housewife had every reason to be bitter when she found the markets stored with meat, flour, Indian corn and vegetables, priced far beyond her means. Clinton thought the whole thing wrong. Why should the people of the city "be left at the mercy of the farmers?" He wished to be fair to all groups, but the rise in the price of farm produce had vastly exceeded those of the articles which the farmer stood in need of. So he took it upon himself to fix the price of a bushel of wheat at twelve shillings, of a bushel of rye or of Indian corn at five shillings, of a hundred pounds of wheat flour at thirty-five shillings, of a hundred pounds of meal at seventeen shillings.[38]

These regulations would probably have discouraged the production of foodstuffs and aggravated the very evils they were intended to correct, had not a flourishing black market grown up. "It is reported by people who left New York about ten days ago that provisions . . . were very scarce," stated the *Journal* from its safe retreat at Poughkeepsie, "and, though prices are limited by martial law, yet the sellers usually found means to obtain more." [39]

In November, when the first chilly winds swept down on the city, Major General Jones took measures to regulate the price of fuel. It had been reported to him "that the boatmen and others who bring firewood to this city exact the most exorbitant prices." He gave orders, therefore, that "no more than five pounds currency shall be demanded for a cord of walnut wood," and "four pounds a cord for every other wood." If the farmers, on their part, refused to let the boatmen have their wood "at a reasonable price," it would be confiscated and they punished.[40]

But these regulations were of no help to those poor families who were penniless and so could not purchase at any price. The widespread distress was in part relieved by private acts of charity or when those who were comparatively well-off shared their food and clothing with distressed relatives or friends. John C. Knapp, who made a gift to forty poor widows of "forty weight of fresh beef and a half peck loaf each," on Christmas Eve, was no doubt emulated by others on a more modest scale.[41]

But charity of this kind was sporadic and inadequate, and the need for some organized relief continued urgent. So, on December 27, 1777, General Robertson appointed a group of prominent citizens, among them Elias Desbrosses, Isaac Low, Peter Stuyvesant and John Dyckman, to solicit donations for the poor.[42] It was a hard-hearted person, indeed, who tightened his purse-strings, when one of these gentlemen knocked at his door. In fact, so many merchants, shopkeepers, army and naval officers, artisans and others gave liberally that the *Royal Gazette* could announce: "To every benevolent mind it must afford unspeakable pleasure when they are informed that many hundred families have been relieved by this well-timed generosity." [43]

Encouraged though they were by the response to their appeals, the solicitors of these donations realized that there should be some permanent body to look after the poor with an adequate source of income at their disposal. So, with the approval of the military authorities, they united themselves with the magistrates of police to form a vestry, known as the "Mayor, Vestry and Overseers of the Poor." To this body was committed not only the almshouse and the care of the poor, but the task of looking after the pumps and city lights and of cleaning the streets.

Their first step was to suggest to Clinton that the old taxes known as poor rates be revived. When the general vetoed this proposal, they made another which proved more acceptable. Great numbers of people, they pointed out, had "got possession of houses" belonging to rebels, "to which they had no sort of title" and for which they paid no rent. Why not make these persons "pay half a year's rent to the Over-

seers of the poor"? To this Clinton not only agreed, but added the fees
from licenses and excise, and fines for breach of order. Six months
later the vestry was able to report that "many hundred lives were
saved by this judicious, benevolent regulation." [44]

Mingled with the poverty and suffering which marked the long
winter months, was much gaiety and extravagance. The young British
officers, who sought relief from the tedium of garrison duty, welcomed
invitations to dinner or tea at the homes of the well-to-do Tories, and
in turn took their daughters to Mrs. Treville's assemblies at the London Coffee House on Broad Street, where the hostess supplied "music,
fire and candles." [45]

Early in January, 1778, the "Theatre Royal in John Street" was
opened by "a society of gentlemen of the army and navy," and tickets
put on sale at "Mr. Rivington's, Mr. Hugh Gaine's, Mills's and Hick's
printing-house, at both Coffee Houses and at Marshal's tavern, opposite the theatre." The spending of money on theatrical performances
while so many loyal families were in want would have aroused much
opposition had it not been announced that the proceeds would be used
for "the widows and orphans of those who have lost their lives in his
Majesty's service." [46] The final seal of approval was put on the project
when Sir Henry Clinton not only gave it his blessing, but himself purchased a box for the season for fifty guineas. How substantial was the
relief afforded the poor is indicated by the fact that the receipts on
the first night alone amounted to over £260.[47]

But amid the gaiety of social life, while handsome men and charming young women were going through the stately steps of the minuet,
or while British officers were performing *Othello* or *The West Indian*,
a pall of fear hung over the city. Over their tankards in the taverns or
their cups in the coffeehouses, men asked each other what were the
chances that France would enter the war. It was well known that popular sentiment in France was overwhelmingly sympathetic with the
Revolutionists, that the followers of Voltaire applauded them as
champions of religious freedom and the followers of Rousseau as the
defenders of political equality, that hundreds of French officers had
offered to serve in the American army. It was known, also, that several
American envoys were in Paris and that King Louis had been induced
by their blandishments to send over large quantities of arms and
munitions which had been of great assistance to Washington.

Word came that Benjamin Franklin, one of the envoys, had become the lion of the brilliant society of Paris. His unpowdered gray hair, his fur cap, his plain clothes, his dignity, his tact, the wisdom of his conversation had won all hearts. The great of Paris sought his company; his head appeared on snuff-boxes and medallions. What all this would lead to the Tories did not know, but they were aware that Franklin's outward simplicity concealed great shrewdness, and his presence in France boded no good. Rivington's way of calming these fears was to publish a report that this "chief prop of rebellion" had been desperately wounded by a secret enemy, and that there was no prospect of his recovery.[48]

But even as the New Yorkers were reading this interesting news item, Franklin was bringing his mission to a successful conclusion. France had long been looking for an opportunity to tear up the humiliating Treaty of Paris, and Vergennes, King Louis's minister of foreign affairs, had been an interested spectator of the long quarrel between the colonists and the British government. But before he would commit himself in the matter of assisting the Americans, he insisted on knowing whether they were fighting merely for the restoration of their rights or for independence. If the former was all they had in view, he would advise his king not to send them a single louis d'or, not risk a single French soldier to aid them. But if they intended to weaken France's traditional enemy by breaking up the British Empire, it was obviously to her interest to second their effort, perhaps even by forming an alliance with them.

Yet even after the Declaration of Independence France hesitated. If she entered the war and later the Revolution should collapse, she would be left to face alone the might of Britain. But when, on December 3, 1777, the news of Burgoyne's surrender reached Paris, it seemed to Vergennes that the knell of British greatness had sounded. Two weeks later he informed the American envoys that the king had decided to become their ally, and, on February 6, France signed two treaties with the United States, one of amity and commerce, and one of alliance. On May 4, France and Great Britain were at war.

In the meanwhile, the British Ministry, sensing what was in the wind, had been making every effort to bring about a reconciliation with the colonies. On February 17, Lord North rose to propose two bills which conceded everything the Americans had asked short of independence. The act regulating the Massachusetts charter must go, the tea duty must go, Parliament, though retaining the right to regulate commerce, must promise to levy no taxes on the colonies for the sake of revenue. Commissioners were to be sent to America with full powers to put a stop to hostilities, grant pardons and suspend all acts of Parliament relating to the colonies since 1763. Such a complete renunciation of all the Ministry had contended for amazed the King's friends in the Commons, and when Lord North had finished "dejection and fear overclouded the whole assembly." [49]

But with war with France imminent the only hope of keeping the empire intact seemed to lie in coming to terms with the Americans, and Parliament gave a reluctant consent. So Lord Carlisle, who had once denounced the Revolutionists as traitors and rebels; William Eden, formerly under-secretary to Lord Suffolk, notorious for his advocacy of using Indians in the war; and George Johnstone, a former governor of Florida, were appointed commissioners, and sent across the Atlantic to wean the Americans from the French alliance and bring them back into the empire.

It would be difficult to exaggerate the dismay of the Tories when these events became known in New York. "We are all here in the greatest consternation at the pacific measures the Ministry seem disposed to take with the Americans," wrote one lady. "By all accounts a French war is inevitable, which is an alarming circumstance. Lord North appears, by his speech, to be frightened out of his wits. I am most wretched that I cannot get away." [50]

The Loyalists wondered whether Lord North, in making such sweeping concessions, had given thought to the situation in which they placed "the friends of government in America." If the colonies returned to their allegiance, not as chastened rebels, but as triumphant defenders of American rights, it would be the Washingtons, the Livingstons, the Franklins who would occupy the high places, not those who had risked their all for the King. In the America of the future, even though their confiscated estates were returned to them, even though they should be compensated out of the royal treasury for their sufferings and losses, the Loyalists would be little better than outcasts in their own land.

Yet there were those who argued that peace, even on the terms Lord North proposed, would be better than the defeat of the British armies and navy and the recognition of American independence which would follow. And with France girding herself for the struggle, defeat seemed far from unlikely. If the Revolutionists, by their own efforts

alone, had for two years held off the disciplined British armies, backed
by the Tories and aided by the supremacy of Britain on the sea, what
hope was there for ultimate victory, now that England's ancient enemy
had thrown her weight into the conflict? Soon the warships which
should have been blockading the coast of America, would be busy
fighting the French in European or West Indian waters; soon the troops
which were so desperately needed to reinforce Howe and Clinton
would be diverted to other parts of the world. The time might come
when a French fleet would blockade New York itself, while French
troops, joined to Washington's Continentals, stormed over the city's
land defences.

It became the policy of the Tory press, therefore, to represent in
the strongest terms the perils to America of the French alliance.
"Surely we have reason to distrust the restless and enterprising spirit
of France, and of those other commercial powers who are said to
favor the project of American independency," said Rivington in the
Royal Gazette. "And if the French King has agreed to such a treaty
as this . . . we must be madly credulous indeed, if we believe it to
proceed from any other motives than, at all points, to prevent our en-
joying now the benefits of a happy reconciliation, and with a view,
when the times will bear it, to bring us into such a state of domestic
and foreign dependence as must make us forever repent our folly in
not having embraced our opportunity of securing . . . religious freedom, peace and safety . . . with our mother country." [51]

But Rivington pleaded in vain. Hoping to win popular approval
for the plan of reconciliation before the news of the French alliance
reached America, Lord Germain rushed copies of the North bills to
America, with instructions that they be immediately given all the pub-
licity possible. They must have come over on a very fast vessel, since
four weeks after their introduction in Parliament the people of New
York were reading them in a broadside signed by General Tryon.
Tryon, in accordance with his instructions, spread this paper throughout New Jersey and elsewhere, no doubt using his network of spies
to place it where it would be most effective. He is said, also, to have
sent a copy to Governor Livingston, who promptly returned it "with
the greatest contempt possible." [52]

"The enemy, after the flogging of Burgoyne, have resumed their
old trick of sham-treaty," wrote one ardent patriot. "General Tryon
has introduced into New Jersey a ridiculous publication under the title

of 'Draught of a bill for declaring the intentions of the Parliament'
. . . Surely the Ministry might have found a more proper person for
that purpose than the most obnoxious of all obnoxious animals by his
professed declarations in the pleasure he takes in burning, kidnapping
and every species of desolation. And offering pardon, too—consummate impudence. Who wants and will stoop to accept of a pardon for
defending his country?" [53]

By the time the three commissioners reached America the dice
had been loaded against them. Arriving off the New Jersey coast early
in June, they entered the Delaware Bay and pushed up toward Philadelphia, expressing their wonder as they proceeded at the vast scale
of the country. But they were even more amazed by a message from
General Howe, which reached them on shipboard off New Castle, informing them that he had received orders to evacuate Philadelphia
immediately. It seems that the Ministry, having received word that
a large French fleet had been ordered to American waters, had decided that it would be prudent to concentrate the British forces in
New York, rather than have them divided in several garrisons and
so liable to destruction in detail. [54]

The commissioners were furious. Why had Lord North sent them
on this fool's errand without uttering one syllable about the orders to
Howe? "All agree that those orders tended to defeat all the objects
of the conciliation," wrote Eden, "that the people of England were
left to flatter themselves with the hope that their interests would be
promoted by the commission, when thirteen days previous to the date
of it, the Secretary of State for the Colonies . . . had secretly sent instructions to the Commander-in-Chief which obliged him to demonstrate to all America that the pressure of the King's naval forces was
immediately to be withdrawn from the coasts, that the British troops
were from that hour to act and be considered a retiring army." [55]

Prepared for failure though they were, the commissioners lost no
time in making their appeal to Congress. "At the same time that we
assure you of our most earnest desire to re-establish, on the basis of
equal freedom and mutual safety, the tranquillity of this once happy
empire," they reported, "you will observe that we are vested with
powers equal to the purpose, and such as are even unprecedented in
the annals of our history." [56]

To this Congress, by unanimous voice, answered that they would
be glad to consider a treaty of peace and commerce not inconsistent

"with treaties already subsisting," but only after an explicit acknowl-
edgement of independence or the withdrawal of British armies and
fleets from America. [57] A stunning rebuff this, and the commissioners,
after one more futile attempt to win over Congress, gave up in despair.

In the meanwhile there had been a change of commanders for the
British forces in America. Realizing that he would be criticised in
Great Britain for the disaster at Saratoga, and irritated that the Ministry had repeatedly ignored his advice, Sir William Howe had asked to
be relieved. Nothing loath, the King sent for him to return to England and put Clinton in his place. On May 8, Clinton arrived at
Philadelphia and sixteen days later Howe stepped aboard the *Androm-
eda* to bid farewell to the land which had been the scene of his
triumphs and his no less numerous failures.

Clinton waved him off with mingled feelings. Proud of his military
record, under ordinary circumstances he would have been elated at his
appointment. But it came at a most discouraging time. He had little
hope of success, he said, since it seemed to be the opinion of the Ministry that America might become a secondary objective in the war. He
wondered whether the person who had framed his instructions requiring him to evacuate Philadelphia had foreseen all the consequences
—that it would force him to give up all pretense of continuing the
offensive and even eventually to retire to Halifax. "My fate is hard,"
he added; "forced to an apparent retreat with such an army is mortifying."

The instruction to move his army by sea, Clinton decided to ignore.
In the absence of sufficient convoys, should a French fleet appear to
intercept them, all would be lost; the admiral had told him that the
troops could not be taken on board nearer than New Castle forty miles
down the river; the number of transports was inadequate; if the fleet
should be detained by contrary winds "Mr. Washington" might seize
the opportunity to make "a decisive push at New York." So, embarking the baggage and great quantities of stores, together with
several thousand Tories on such transports as were available, he sent
them down the Delaware and around to New York, while he, with
his army, crossed over into New Jersey and headed for Sandy Hook.[58]

If the order to evacuate Philadelphia angered the commissioners
and provoked Clinton, to the Pennsylvania Tories it brought despair.
The previous winter had been one of gaiety and social activity, for the
capture of the "rebel capital" had been celebrated with a series of

banquets, balls and receptions. The Quaker city had long ago thrown off much of its austerity, and the British officers, with their handsome uniforms, found a ready welcome in the stately Georgian houses of the Loyalists. There was some lifting of eyebrows when Sir William Howe appeared at a dance or a reception with the notorious Mrs. Loring on his arm, but the hostesses, learning that to omit this lady from the list of their invitations meant that they must omit Sir William also, were forced to accept her, though with ill-disguised distaste.

The gay season ended with a brilliant farewell festival for General Howe called the Meschianza. It began with a regatta, in which galleys "dressed in colors" and filled with officers and ladies, were rowed down the river amid the crash of guns on the warships and the strains of "God Save the King." This was followed by a tournament "according to the customs of ancient chivalry," in which knights dressed, one group in white silk, another in black, and mounted on richly caparisoned horses, vied with each other on the field of honor. When a herald had proclaimed that the "Ladies of the Blended Rose" were supreme in "wit, beauty and every accomplishment," and the Knights of the Burning Mountain had entered their dissent, the two parties began the joust. That evening the festivities ended with a ball, fireworks and a sumptuous midnight supper.[59]

The smiling faces of those who took part in the Meschianza concealed many a sad heart, for within the next few days the leading Loyalists were busy with their preparations to leave the city, and carriages and carts hurried over the streets on their way to the transports. There were many tragic scenes as relatives embraced each other or aged men and women turned for a last glimpse of homes they were destined never to see again. But better exile than to remain to suffer the penalty of their opposition to the Revolution and their defiance of Congress. A few days later the King's commissioners from the deck of their vessel off Reedy Island looked out on a great fleet, many of the vessels crowded with "ruined families," waiting for the order to sail. "Near 5,000 of the Philadelphia inhabitants are attending us to New York," Eden wrote Alexander Wedderburn.[60]

In the meanwhile, Clinton was hastening across New Jersey with his splendidly equipped army of 15,000 men. When they had reached Monmouth Court House, and were filing along the road to Middletown, Washington, who had swept around in a wide arc from Valley Forge to intercept them, sent General Charles Lee forward to the attack. Lee disobeyed his orders, making a mere pretense of an advance, and then, to the astonishment of his own officers, ordered a retreat. The British pursued him and were thrown back only when Washington came galloping up at the head of the main body. The opportunity for the Americans to strike a decisive blow was lost and Clinton reached Sandy Hook in safety, whence his troops were ferried up to New York on Lord Howe's transports.

And so ended in failure for the British the first period of the war, the period of the offensive in the north. There were to be no more campaigns to open the Hudson, no more attacks on Philadelphia. Henceforth the main British effort was to be directed against the south. New York City became a mere outpost of British power, a base where the fleet could put in for refitting or to escape the enemy and from which expeditions could be sent out against Virginia or the Carolinas or the West Indies. For five more years it continued to be the chief, almost the only, haven for the Tories in the north, five years of hoping or despairing, of forced gaiety, of hardship and suffering, of whispered criticisms, of jealousies, of bloody raids into New Jersey and Connecticut, of military government marked by corruption and inefficiency, to end finally in defeat and exile.

CHAPTER VII

CORRUPTION AND CRUELTY

IN THE autumn of 1776, when Sir William Howe's victorious red-coats took possession of New York and the Loyalists came flocking back, it was taken for granted that civil government would be re-established as soon as the military situation permitted. And as the sound of cannonading grew fainter and fainter while the battle front receded up Manhattan and then into Westchester, the day when the Assembly would be summoned to meet, when the courts of law would be reopened and power restored to the civil magistrates seemed to be at hand. Yet months and months went by and nothing was done.

"Is it possible," men asked each other, "that our loyalty and all our sacrifices are to be requited by the taking away of our most precious rights? Must we resign ourselves to the jurisdiction of a military dictatorship, submit our vital interests to the findings of military courts, obey the commands of military officials?" In the winter of 1776–77 many of the inhabitants of New York City, New York County, Long Island and Staten Island signed a petition asking "to be restored to the King's peace," which General De Lancey, Justice Horsmanden, William Axtell and other prominent citizens presented to Admiral Howe. Howe received them with his usual courtesy, prom-ised to consult his brother, Sir William, and then give his answer.

But no reply was ever received. Neither of the Howe brothers was inordinately fond of power, neither desired the thankless task of rul-ing the reconquered parts of New York, but they were fighting a bit-terly contested war which called for many prompt decisions. If certain of these decisions should run afoul of the provincial laws, the Council or even the Assembly might have to be consulted, and then disaster might overtake the British cause while the legislators were hesitating or debating. The suppression of representative government, of the right to jury trial, of the *habeas corpus*, might be unpalatable to the

151

people, but it was better than hampering the army and navy. So representative government, jury trial, the *habeas corpus* and other cherished rights had to wait.

Having reached this decision, the two brothers looked around for some legal grounds on which to base their action. It was the turncoat, Joseph Galloway, who, according to Judge Jones, gave it to them. In 1775 Parliament had passed an act to prohibit trade with the colonies with the hope that economic strangulation would hasten their conquest. The act contained not one word about suspending civil government. Yet when Galloway advanced this interpretation Lord Howe, General Howe, General Robertson, Mayor Matthews, the quartermasters and barrack-masters seized upon it eagerly; the two Howes because it gave them greater freedom in prosecuting the war, the others apparently from selfish motives since it left their hands untied to plunder the people and raid the British Treasury.[1]

But had Galloway never advanced his theory, the Howe brothers undoubtedly would have continued to rule New York. As early as September 24, 1776, they had taken it upon themselves to reappoint William Tryon to the governorship, with instructions to keep "the executive powers of civil government dormant." And dormant they remained until Tryon was replaced by General James Robertson in the spring of 1780. And though Robertson took a more active part in the government of Loyalist New York than his predecessor, this was because of his military rank, not his civil office.

Robertson, as we have seen, had already won the hostility of the Tories as commandant of New York City by his avarice, love of power and his foolish pursuit of young girls. From February 17 to September 27, 1777, while Robertson was in England, Major General Pigot served as commandant, and on May 4, 1778, the office was taken over by Major General Valentine Jones. On July 5, 1779, Jones was replaced by General James Pattison, while on August 13, 1780, the command fell to Brigadier General Birch, who held it until the British evacuated the city.[2]

These men seem to have performed reasonably well a difficult task, the task of directing the affairs of a city overcrowded with refugees, swarming with soldiers, some of them foreigners who could not speak English, in constant fear of attack by the Revolutionists and the French, often threatened by shortages of food and fuel, suffering from fatal epidemics. Now we find them fixing the rates for ferriage, now issuing orders against throwing refuse in the streets, now regulating the police, now setting a ceiling on the price of wood or of bread. But despotic power is dangerous even in the hands of the wisest and most upright, and the commandants were none too wise and at times not above selfish or corrupt motives.

Pattison especially laid himself open to criticism. According to William Smith he was hot-headed, vain and weak, so that it was rare for a day to pass in which he did not offend someone. Especially blameworthy, he said, was Pattison's treatment of a certain Doctor Baily. This gentleman happened to be passing when a Negro driver threw a drunken soldier off his cart. Seeing the wheel run over his breast he stopped his chaise, got out, gave first aid, took him to a nearby house and then notified the hospital. For his pains the doctor was arrested, refused access to the commandant, lodged in a jail and released only late that night. So enraged was he at this injustice that he was determined to get out of New York rather than remain under military government.[3]

Not less flagrant was the injustice done to one Hicks, who, to please the husband of the notorious Mrs. Loring, and "without the shadow of reason," was ejected from a house he had leased from John Peter De Lancey, to make room for a certain Roubalet. When Hicks had appealed in vain to General Clinton and General Robertson for justice, he set sail for London to enter suit in the English courts. Had he not died on the way over, says the historian Jones, "Westminster Hall would have rung and resounded with the illegal, the arbitrary, the despotic, cruel and unrighteous act." [4]

Even more unpopular than the dictatorship of the commandant was what the Loyalists called the "arbitrary, illegal, unconstitutional Court of Police." At its head was the Superintendent General of Police, Andrew Elliot, who was assisted by Mayor David Matthews and Police Magistrate Peter Dubois. Elliot, according to Judge Jones, was wholly unacquainted with the law, educated as a merchant, of very trifling abilities. Matthews, who had been forced to flee from the city in 1776 for his part in the plot to murder Washington, Jones denounced as a very poor lawyer, "abandoned and dissipated, indigent, extravagant and luxurious, over head and ears in debt." [5] But he made such good use of his office, Jones adds, that before the end of the war he had become wealthy, "lived in the style of a gentleman, gave what the military called 'damned good dinners.'" His colleague in power, Peter

Dubois, denounced him "as a profligate and villian." [6] What Matthews thought of Dubois, we do not know. To this trio was entrusted the suppression of vice, the support of the poor, the control of police, the regulation of the markets and ferries, etc.[7]

To the Loyalists it seemed a hard case that they were subject to the jurisdiction of this Court of Police without the benefit of a jury. The right to trial by a jury of their peers was a fundamental right of Englishmen; the Howe brothers, no matter what the exigencies of the military situation, had no right to deprive them of it. Moreover, the new court lacked power to decide complaints which had arisen prior to May 1, 1777, and debts contracted before that date could not be collected. Nor did their jurisdiction extend to the military, so that though citizens might be "plundered, robbed, pillaged, beaten, abused, insulted, kicked" by the soldiers, they could get no redress. Equally unfortunate was the fact that no power was vested in this body to try capital offenders. As a result murderers, pirates and robbers must either be tried by court-martial, remain indefinitely in prison without trial, or be turned loose upon the public. Since, however, there was good reason to doubt the power of courts-martial to sit in cases involving offenses against citizens, capital crimes were often left unpunished.

When a Hempstead miller named Amberman applied to a Major Stockton for payment of a debt, the latter, in company with a Major Crew, went to the mill to chastise him for the "insult." While Crew was applying the horsewhip, Stockton, apparently losing control of himself, drew his sword and ran the miller through. Stockton was tried for murder and convicted, but the sentence was never carried out, and within a few weeks he was walking the streets a free man.[8]

With such a lesson before them it is not difficult to understand the reluctance of the local merchants to press their claims for the payment of debts. Thomas Lynch stated in April 1783, that no less than £5,000 was owing him by "the gentlemen of the army," very little of which he ever expected to collect, since some were dead and others had been sent "to various parts of the world." [9]

Another incident which aroused the indignation of the Tories occurred in the spring of 1781. Three privates of De Lancey's Brigade broke into the house of Parmenas Jackson, a Quaker living near Jerusalem, in Queens County, murdered him in cold blood and made off with £1,200 in cash. The men were identified, tried by court-martial, found guilty and sentenced to be hanged. Yet they were not

executed. After remaining in jail about three months, and upon paying some trifling fees, they were all discharged.[10]

Equally important in impressing the people with a sense of insecurity was the case of a poor farmer named Jacobus Cropsey, who
came to Sir Guy Carleton in August, 1782, with a bitter complaint
against certain soldiers of the British Legion who had been billeted
upon him. They had abused his family, he said, and wantonly
"killed his most valuable horse and wounded two others with their
swords." They also had "cruelly and maliciously" pulled up his corn
by the root, "not to mention the stealing of poultry and other matters
not avoidable." The records, unfortunately, leave us in the dark as
to what compensation, if any, Jacobus received for these outrages.[11]

In November, 1778, when Carlisle and Eden were leaving for
England after their unsuccessful attempt to win the colonists back to
their allegiance, the Tories appealed to them to use their influence
in England to free them from military government. They were weary
of that "sanguinary system," they declared, under which so many
had lost life, liberty and property. Carlisle and Eden replied that the
great object of the war was "the reestablishment of the civil constitution," but they obviously thought that so long as the war was in
progress the "great object" would have to wait.[12]

Hope was revived in 1779, when it became known that the King
had appointed General Robertson governor of New York. Surely this
presaged the revival of civil government, men argued, since there
could be no purpose in naming one who already held an important
post to an office which carried with it neither honor nor power. And
as the military government daily grew more odious, the people looked
forward eagerly to Robertson's arrival.[13]

Nor had the general been back more than a month before he
issued a proclamation, stating that it was the King's wish, by the
revival of the civil authority, to prove to all that it was not his design
to govern America by military law. So, Robertson continued, "I shall,
as speedily as the public exigencies will permit, give order for the
opening of the courts of judicature and convening the Assembly."
Until he met the people in General Assembly, he pledged himself
that the suggestions that Great Britain intended to impair their rights
and privileges were entirely false.[14]

This announcement the people received with joy. Now there
would be an end to the insolence of the soldiery, now murder would

receive its just penalty, now officials would be responsible to the electorate for their actions, now there would be a means of ending corruption and graft. Anxiously they awaited the call for the election of an Assembly. But week after week passed and they waited in vain. In July the people of Kings County drew up an address to Governor Robertson reminding him of his promise. "It is with real pleasure we receive . . . the intimation of his Majesty's wish for the revival of the civil authority," they told him, "and we persuade ourselves so much benevolence will draw forth every exertion to enable your excellency to restore to the people of this colony the tranquillity they lately enjoyed." [15] Gradually came the bitter realization that something or someone had acted to block the King's good intentions, and that the restoration of civil government had been indefinitely postponed.

Had they been able to look into the Headquarters Papers they would have discovered, what some no doubt suspected, that it was Sir Henry Clinton who had defeated their hopes. When Robertson called upon him to discuss the matter, Clinton told him plainly that this was not the time for restoring civil government. But he expressed a desire that the people should enjoy all the benefits of self-government, even though self-government itself was nonexistent. "For this purpose I am to desire you will take upon you the direction of the police of the province; that you take care that justice be administered . . .; that no person be deprived of his property, but all be protected against every injury or insult." [16]

But the leading Loyalists, far from satisfied, continued to urge Clinton to restore at least some of the features of civil government. In November, 1781, Judge William Smith wrote him, pointing out that the rule of the military was keeping many persons from going over to the royal cause. It seemed inadvisable to him to revive the judicial and executive branches of the civil government, but he urged Clinton to call the Assembly at once. Such a measure could not result in harm, since if the legislators refused to work in harmony with the general-in-chief, he could at once dissolve them. And it would greatly hearten the Loyalists, at the moment when they were so discouraged at the recent surrender of Lord Cornwallis. [17]

But Clinton remained obdurate. In January, 1782, he wrote a fellow officer: "You may perhaps hear me abused for withholding my consent to the revival of civil government . . . Experience has proved that in all countries where the operations of war existed, the martial law has always been found to be better adapted to the exigencies of such a state . . . It will be unnecessary to describe the bad consequences which may result from the admission of civil jurisdiction in our continual state of warfare . . . After weighing the . . . disappointments it might throw in the way of our military proceedings, I have never to this instant seen a moment proper for its renewal." [18]

In 1782, with the appointment of Sir Guy Carleton as general-in-chief of the British forces in America, hope stirred once more. Carleton was a man of humane instincts, a friend of the Loyalists, an advocate of civil liberty. Had the British cause at the time not been in so desperate a plight, he probably would have been persuaded to call the Assembly.

As it was, he took Judge William Smith aside one evening before dinner at his headquarters, and after expressing his dislike of trials of citizens by court-martial, or by "sash and gorget" as he called it, asked what he thought the proper remedy. When Smith suggested that he establish a judicial commission to act as a court, he readily agreed and appointed Governor Robertson to preside over it. How necessary a service this body performed in curbing crime we may infer from the trial of John Clarke, James Wigmore and Joseph Royns for piracy, in June, 1782. Clarke they found guilty and sentenced to be hanged on June 28. Wigmore, though also guilty, they recommended for pardon. Royns they acquitted.[19]

One has only to read the Headquarters Papers, now in the archives of Colonial Williamsburg, to realize that Carleton was not a man who grasped after power. He was too modest, too sympathetic with the sufferings of others, too willing to accept advice, too anxious to cooperate with his fellow officers rather than dictate to them.

Not so Sir Henry Clinton. Possessed of a swollen ego, he revelled in being the dictator of New York. It was a satisfaction to him to have the guards at headquarters click their heels and salute as he entered and left; he enjoyed having the leading Loyalists come to him to ask for places to live, or for permission to draw rations, or for appointments in the provincial regiments, or for jobs in the supply service, or for licenses to become merchants; he felt a thrill of satisfaction when General Robertson, or General James Pattison, or Mayor David Matthews, or Lieutenant Governor Andrew Elliot referred to his opinion in governing New York; he asked for no advice in planning his campaigns and did not welcome it when volunteered; he gloried in being the one great luminary in the social life of the city, without whom no celebration, no dinner, no parade, no ball was a success. Whatever excuse he made for not reestablishing civil government, one suspects that his reluctance to part with power was not the least of his motives.

It is Clinton, therefore, who must take the major share of the blame for the inefficiency and corruption which marked the administration of both civil and military affairs so long as he was General-in-Chief, and was so important a factor in the failure of Great Britain to conquer the colonies. The appointments, in most cases, were Clinton's own. He had authority over judges, commissaries, and quartermasters, and if they defrauded the Loyalists, or looted the British Treasury, or starved the American prisoners, the blame was chiefly his. He should have seen to it that none but just and honest men were appointed to office, he should have audited their accounts, he should have dismissed or even imprisoned those detected in frauds. Under his administration "the unfortunate inhabitant was at the mercy of a soldier for what should be taken and of a commissary for what should be paid or restored." [20] Even the gentle Shewkirk pointed the accusing finger at Clinton when he wrote that "the general language of even the common soldiers is that the war might and would have been" waged successfully had it not been for those whose only ambition was "to fill their purses." [21]

If the host of commissaries, deputy commissaries, barrack-masters, quartermasters, deputy quartermasters, were guilty of a fraction of the frauds of which they were accused, the whole service must have been honeycombed with corruption. The testimony comes from many sources. Judge William Smith thought that Great Britain should recall all her generals, because they were the "plants of corruption." [22] Kemble denounced Admiral James Gambier as "a money getting, pompous fool," and blamed the shortage of provisions in the fleet to the schemes he used "to fill his pocket." [23] The staunch Tory, William Axtel, a member of the Council, spoke of "a parcel of rascals within these lines, who have been making thousands since the commencement of the troubles." [24]

We are indebted to Judge Thomas Jones, who was a personal witness of what was going on, for detailed accounts of many of the most flagrant frauds. In August, 1776, he tells us, the quartermaster appealed to the farmers of Long Island to supply the army with horses and wagons, and it was their prompt compliance which made it possible for General Howe to conduct his rapid marches in West-chester and New Jersey. When the campaign was over and the farm-ers demanded their property, many found that their wagons had been ruined or destroyed, and their horses killed or stolen. Yet the quarter-master refused to recompense them unless they could produce the drivers to swear to the loss. Since many drivers had deserted or been killed, scores of owners were defrauded. When they came in to the quartermaster's office demanding their money, some found it im-possible to get in, others were put off with promises, others were "cursed and damned," still others thrown out. None the less, the loss was duly charged to the King's account, and the quartermaster pocketed the money. "Had the King, the nation, or the country benefited by the transaction, the people would have been satisfied," says Jones. "But when they knew that their property was unjustly with-holden from them, in order to fill the purse of a greedy, peculating quartermaster, it is no wonder they complained." [25]

When the campaign of 1777 was opened, the quartermaster, be-cause of the unsavory reputation he had earned the year before, had to exercise the greatest cunning to victimize the farmers a second time. So he asked the justices of the various towns to call the people to-gether, and to promise them that this time all trouble would be fore-stalled by making entries in a book of the horses and wagons taken, together with their value, their owners and the time they were in service. Again the wagons proved indispensable, accompanying the army in New Jersey, thence by sea to Elk Creek, then to Philadelphia and finally on the retreat to New York. But when the farmers asked for the return of their property, they were stupified to have the quartermaster say that he had purchased them all, and at a valua-tion set when they entered the service. "This made a great noise, much clamour, some threats, and universal uneasiness." It availed nothing. When the owners refused to accept the sums offered, as most of them did, they got nothing.

Since the quartermaster had no receipts, he was forced into an-other fraud before he could charge the Treasury for what he had stolen. Upon paying the drivers, most of them former slaves who could not read, he inserted in their receipts the valuation of the horses and wagons to make it appear that the owners had been paid in full. When Sir Guy Carleton's accountant several years later went over this rascal's vouchers, he was not a little puzzled to find many of them signed with the marks, Cato, Caesar, Scipio, Pompey, Jack, Quash, Cuffee, etc. Even though Judge Jones's estimate of £150,000 as the profits of this transaction may be too high, it is obvious that for the quartermaster, employment in the King's service was highly profitable.[26] He now resigned, returned to England, where he "lived in the style of a prince."

In 1779 his successor, after having enjoyed the office about a year, also sailed for England a rich man. In 1780 a third and in 1781 a fourth quartermaster made off with rich spoils. "Thus went the money of John Bull." [27]

The barrack-masters were not one whit behind the quarter-masters in making hay while the sun shone. As Washington's troops retreated from Long Island to Manhattan and from Manhattan to White Plains in 1776, these officials took possession in the King's name of all the abandoned houses, whether the property of Loyalists or Revolutionists, together with King's College, the three Dutch churches, two Quaker meetinghouses, two Presbyterian churches, two large breweries, besides other buildings on Staten Island, Long Island and elsewhere. "Though the Crown was regularly charged for the hire of them in all the barrack-masters' accounts . . . the proprietors never got a cent. The whole was pocketed by the barrack-masters." [28]

Not less reprehensible was the firewood graft. The barrack-masters took over for the King's service vast tracts of woodland on Staten Island, Long Island, Westchester and elsewhere, some of it belonging to the Loyalists, some to the "rebels," and cut down the trees to supply the army with fuel. Although the owners were paid nothing, or at best but little, the barrack-masters charged the Treasury the full value of every tree that was felled. In this way they defrauded both the Loyalists and the government.[29]

The injustice done the Tory farmers at Bergen Neck, on the New Jersey side of North River near Paulus Hook, was notorious. The barrack-master sent there a number of so-called refugees, "whites and Negroes," to cut wood for the King's magazine. Despite the violent protests of the owners, within a few months they left nothing of the woods which had blanketed the region but bare stumps. When the outraged farmers laid their complaints before the quartermaster, and begged him to consider how cruel it was to bring ruin to widows and orphans, they met only with rebuffs and insults. One of them, a certain John Van Boskerke, it is true, "upon repeated and various complaints," received some compensation for 750 cords taken from his property, but only at half the rate fixed by the military authorities.[30]

Not content with fleecing the owners of woodlands, the barrack-masters still further enriched themselves by paying low wages to the choppers, wood-pilers and cartmen, while charging the military chest for much higher wages. The workmen, many of them Germans who knew little English, others Negroes and Indians who could not read, made their marks on any receipt which was placed in front of them. "By this contrivance the nation was cheated out of amazing sums." [31]

Equally dishonest was the practice of the barrack-masters of buying wood from the farmers of Long Island and Staten Island by a cord set at four cartman's loads, and delivering to the army a "cord" of no more than three loads. The cartmen called the fourth load, which was withheld yet charged to the chest, the barrack-master's cord." [32] And when the citizens of the city were short of fuel in the bitter winter of 1779–1780, these crooks supplied their needs from the army woodpile at five or six times what they paid for it. "I spent my winter in 1780 in New York," says Judge Jones, "had my wood from the wood yards and paid £4 for oak and £5 10s. for nut, and for a cord received three cart-man's loads only." [33]

"No wonder the former commanding generals connived at this piece of wickedness," the judge adds sourly, "when it is a well-known fact that the mistresses, the little misses, and dulcineas of Clinton, Robertson and Birch were all supplied with large quantities of wood, by their orders, out of the wood yards in New York, and were regaling themselves in routs, dinners, little concerts and small parties over good, warm, comfortable fires . . . while the poor soldiers . . . were, with their wives and children, perishing in their barracks in the severity of winter." [34]

When to the ill-gotten gains of the quartermasters and barrack-masters are added the great sums stolen by the commissary of artillery, the commissary of cattle, the commissary of forage, the commissaries of prisoners and others, the whole amounted to a staggering sum. In fact a sum so large that many of the Loyalists believed that had it gone to the purposes for which it was intended, the King's forces would have won the war. It was with intense bitterness that they complained that the cause for which they had sacrificed so much, and upon which their all was staked, had been sacrificed to the avarice of a group of unprincipled officials.

And though, when Sir Guy Carleton arrived to take command in April 1782, it was too late to retrieve the British cause, the Loyalists were elated when he cleaned out the entire group of leeches. "It is said that a couple of hundred of deputy commissioners in different departments have been or will be dismissed," wrote Shewkirk. "We rejoice that the chain of enormous, iniquitous practices will be at last broken! They must have ended in misery to the nation had they continued much longer." [35]

Judge Jones records his deep satisfaction. Sir Guy, he tells us, opened a vigorous offensive against corruption in the service, and "in a short time broke, discharged, dismissed, and cashiered such a number of supernumerary barrack-masters, land commissaries, cattle feeders, hay collectors, hay inspectors, hay weighers, wood inspectors, timber commissaries, board inspectors, refugee examiners, refugee provision providers, and refugee ration deliverers, commissaries of American, of French, of Dutch, of Spanish prisoners, naval commissaries and military commissaries, with such a train of clerks, deputy clerks . . . as saved the nation in the course of one year only, about two million sterling." [36] Thus did Carleton deliver a counter-offensive at what John Weatherhead called a "golden war against the Treasury of Great Britain." [37]

But Sir Guy was not content with cleaning the Augean Stable, he took steps to see that it remained clean. "He means that all the accounts . . . of the different departments shall be regularly examined into, for the mutual satisfaction both of the public and themselves," one official was informed. "And it is with this view he has desired you to prepare a detailed account of the money which has come into your hands, together with the expenditures and all the vouchers." [38]

These accounts and vouchers were subjected to a thorough examination by Major Drummond, the commissary of accounts, and then passed on to the Board of Public Accounts. The working members of this body were Drummond, Henry White and the prominent business man Hugh Wallace, with all British general and field officers of the line having a seat whenever they wished to attend, and Carleton, or in his absence, General Robertson presiding. [39] By the time the accounts of commissaries, quartermasters, deputies and others had run this gauntlet, one may be reasonably sure that all or most of the graft had been squeezed out.

But Carleton could not bring back to life the American prisoners whom the cupidity and cruelty of the commissaries had sent to an untimely grave. Judge Jones, who certainly was not partial to the "rebels," tells us that the notorious Joshua Loring, after selling his wife to Sir William Howe in exchange for the office of commissary of prisoners, "by appropriating to his own use nearly two-thirds of the rations allowed to the prisoners, . . . actually starved to death about 300 of the poor wretches before an exchange took place . . . And hundreds that were alive at the time were so emaciated and enfeebled for want of provisions, that numbers died upon the road on their way home, and many lived but a few days after reaching their habitations." [40]

Loring's brutality was more than matched by that of the provost-marshal, William Cunningham. This man in his dying confession in 1791, is quoted as saying: "I shudder at the murders I have been accessory to, both with and without orders from government, especially while in New York, during which time there were more than 2,000 prisoners starved in the different churches, by stopping their rations, which I sold." [41] When Elias Boudinot, on behalf of Congress, visited the provost prison, he found nearly "thirty officers from Colonel downward in close confinement," who complained that "they had received the most cruel treatment," being on the most trifling occurrences "locked in the dungeon" for long periods. When Boudinot reproached Cunningham for this, he "with great insolence answered that every word was true," and "swore that he was as absolute there as General Howe was at the head of his army." [42]

Some writers have questioned the accuracy of the reports of brutality in the British prisons, but the evidence is overwhelming. Numbers of officers and men alike, who escaped or were exchanged, stated that they had been half-starved, exposed to the bitter cold of winter without adequate clothing or fuel, given foul water to drink, refused medical care, crowded into cramped quarters.

William Darlington, who was confined in the New Bridewell, says the rations for three days were a half pound of biscuit, half a pound of pork, a half pint of peas, half a gill of rice and half an ounce of butter. Two days a week they were defrauded even of this. "They had no straw or hay to lie on and no fuel but one cart-load per week for eight hundred men." "At nine of the clock at evening the Hessian guards would come in and put out the fires and lay on the poor prisoners with heavy clubs for sitting around the fire." The water was very bad, the bread "beyond all comparison bad," so that "they began to die like rotten sheep with cold, hunger and dirt." [43]

Oliver Woodruff, another American prisoner in the New Bridewell, said: "We never drew as much provision for three days' allowance as a man could eat at a common meal. I was there three months during that inclement season, and never saw any fire except what was in the lamps of the city. There was not a pane of glass in the windows, and nothing to keep out the cold except the iron grates." [44]

When Boudinot visited the prisoners in the French church, they told him that they were so crowded there that it was impossible for all to lie down at once. From October 15 to January 1 "they never received a stick of wood, and that for the most part they eat their pork raw when the pews and door and window facings failed them for fuel." [45]

This cruel treatment took a heavy toll in sickness and death. When Jabez Fitch, himself a prisoner but on parole, visited the prisoners in one of the Dutch churches on November 28, 1776, he "went into the burying ground and see four of the prisoners buried in one grave." [46]

Ashbel Green, who later became president of Princeton, states that when some of the prisoners who had been exchanged were left at his father's door, they were half dead with starvation and "putrid fever," and covered with filth and vermin. Despite the loving care which they received at the Green home, many of them died. Two of those who recovered remained with their benefactors for three months.[47]

The provost-marshal took the ground that it was not the responsibility of the British to clothe the prisoners, so that in time they were mere walking bundles of rags. "Many of them are such ragamuffins as you never saw in your life," reported a British officer. "I cannot give you a better idea of them than by putting you in mind of Falstaff's recruits, or poor Tom in King Lear; and yet they had strained every nerve to cover their nakedness by dismantling all the beds, and tearing down the tapestry, hangings, and window-curtains." [48]

When reports of the conditions in the British prisons reached General Washington, he appointed Elias Boudinot commissary-general with orders to look after the welfare of American prisoners. Accordingly Boudinot, securing permission from General Howe to inspect the prisons in New York, sailed to Staten Island in his sloop and thence to the city. General Robertson and Commissary Loring received him with civility, and a British officer accompanied him to the prisons. The wretched captives, overjoyed to see him, poured out the story of their sufferings. Prior to Burgoyne's surrender, they said, "their treatment had been cruel beyond measure," but since that happy event the fact that so many British soldiers were now in American hands, had made the jailors more lenient.[49]

When Boudinot placed the facts before the British authorities, they at once agreed to "measures for alleviating the miseries of war." But, very wisely not trusting too much these promises, he himself alleviated some of the worst miseries before he took his leave. With $26,-666.66 which he borrowed on his own credit, he "furnished 300 officers with a handsome suit of clothes each and 1,100 men with a plain suit, found them blankets, shirts, etc. and added to their provisions . . . a full half ration of bread and beef per day for upwards of 15 months." [50]

Thereafter the complaints of brutal treatment came chiefly from the naval prisoners. With the outbreak of war, many American merchants, selecting their fastest vessels, had equipped them with guns, and sent them out to prey on British commerce. Some of these privateers brought in handsome prizes which enriched the owners and filled the pockets of the sailors with pistolas and sovereigns. But in the end they were apt to be caught in the British drag-net of frigates, taken to the nearest British port, and the crew put in prison. In the course of the conflict thousands of these unfortunate men were brought to New York and incarcerated in one of the prison ships in Wallabout Bay.

Conditions aboard these old hulks were deplorable. Congress was informed that the prisoners were subjected to "every species of insult, outrage and cruelty," both officers and men being thrown into the hold and there deprived of fuel and the common necessaries of life. There was constant complaint of overcrowding, one of the prisoners, George Batterman, declaring that 1,100 men were jammed together below decks on the *Jersey* alone. The mortality was appalling. "Our ship's company is reduced to a small number by death and entering into the service," wrote one prisoner. "We bury 6, 7, 8, 9, 10 and 11 men a day; we have 200 more sick and falling sick every day; the sickness is yellow fever, small-pox, and in short everything else that can be mentioned . . . Our morning's salutation is, 'Rebels! turn out your dead!'" [51] It must have taken heroic determination to resist the temptation, daily put before them, of escaping from *Hell* as they called the *Jersey,* by taking service in the British navy, and we are not surprised to learn that many did so.[52]

"If you were to rake the infernal regions, I doubt whether you could find such another set of demons as the officers and men who had charge of the old *Jersey* prison ship," wrote Captain Alexander Coffin, Jr., an American naval officer who had been a prisoner there. "On my arrival . . . I found there about eleven hundred prisoners; many of them had been there from three to six months, but few lived over that time if they did not get away by some means or other. They were generally in the most deplorable situation, mere walking skeletons, without money, and scarcely clothes to cover their nakedness, and overrun with lice from head to foot. The provisions . . . was not more than four or five ounces of meat, and about as much bread, all condemned provisions from their ships of war, which no doubt were supplied with new in their stead and the new in all probability charged by the commissaries to the *Jersey* . . . There never were provisions served out to the prisoners that would have been eatable by men that were not literally in a starving situation. The water that we were forced to use was carried from this city and I positively assert that I never, after having followed the sea thirty years, had on board of any ship, water so bad . . . There were hogs kept in pens on the gun-deck by the officers . . .; I have seen the prisoners watch an opportunity and with a tin pot steal the bran from the hogs' trough and go into the galley and when they could get an opportunity, boil it on the fire and eat it . . . How many hundreds of my brave and intrepid brother seamen and countrymen I have seen in all the bloom of health brought on board that ship, and in a few days numbered with the dead." [53]

Five months later, when Captain Coffin was again placed aboard the *Jersey,* he found that the greater number of his former fellow prisoners "had taken up their abode under the surface of the hill," where their bodies were mouldering to dust. Since the *Jersey* was so crowded, he was transferred to the *John,* where the treatment was even worse. The *John,* which was a merchant vessel, had no port-holes, so that at night when the hatches were closed, the air was so

Old Jail in New York which was used during the American Revolution.

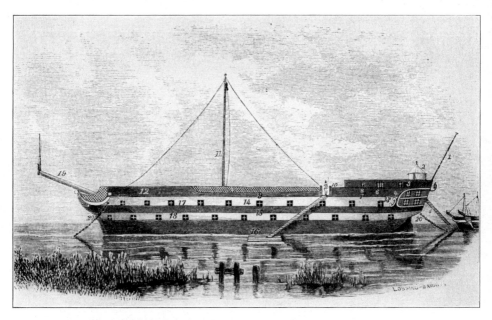

The *Jersey* Prison Ship Moored at Wallabout, Long Island. Conditions on the vessel were so bad that the daily mortality rate was appalling.

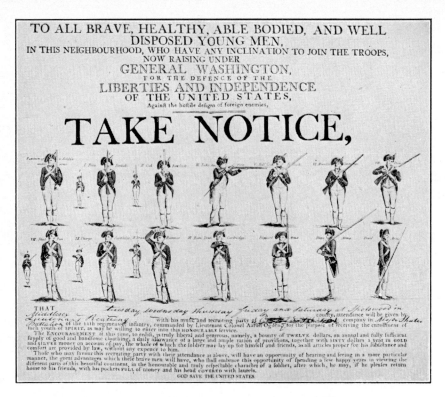

A Recruiting Poster. The poster reads in part: "The encouragement at this time to enlist, is truly liberal and generous, namely a bounty of twelve dollars, an annual and fully sufficient supply of good and handsome cloathing, a daily allowance of a large and ample ration of provisions, together with sixty dollars a year in Gold and Silver money on account of pay, the whole of which the soldier may lay up for himself and friends, as all articles proper for his subsistance and comfort are provided by law, without any expence to him. . . . Those . . . who shall embrace this opportunity of spending a few happy years in viewing the different parts of this beautiful continent, in the honorable and truly respectable character of a soldier, after which, he may, if he pleases return home to his friends, with his pockets full of money and his head covered with laurels."

PROSPECT HILL.	BUNKER's HILL.
I. Seven Dollars a Month.	I. Three Pence a Day.
II. Fresh Provisions, and in Plenty.	II. Rotten Salt Pork.
III. Health.	III. The Scurvy.
IV. Freedom, Ease, Affluence and a good Farm.	IV. Slavery, Beggary and Want.

Handbill sent among the British troops on Bunker Hill.

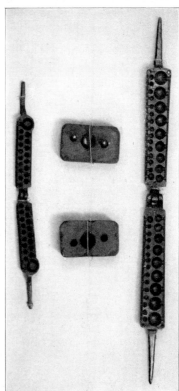

Revolutionary Drum and Bullet Molds.

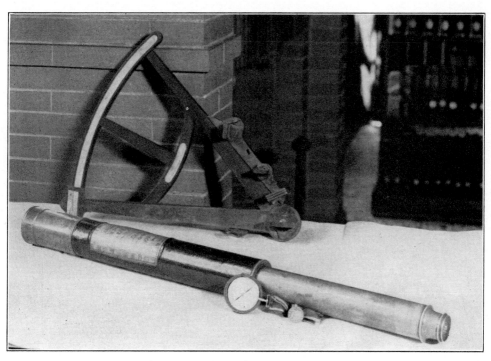

Commodore Edward Preble's Glass, Quadrant, and Compass.

In COUNCIL of SAFETY,

PHILADELPHIA, *December 8*, 1776.

SIR,

THERE is certain intelligence of General Howe's army being yesterday on its march from Brunfwick to Princetown, which puts it beyond a doubt that he intends for this city.—This glorious opportunity of fignalizing himfelf in defence of our country, and fecuring the Rights of America forever, will be feized by every man who has a fpark of patriotic fire in his bofom. We entreat you to march the Militia under your command with all poffible expedition to this city, and bring with you as many waggons as you can poffibly procure, which you are hereby authorized to imprefs, if they cannot be had otherwife—Delay not a moment, it may be fatal and fubject you and all you hold moft dear to the ruffian hands of the enemy, whofe cruelties are without diftinction and unequalled.

By Order of the Council,

DAVID RITTENHOUSE, Vice-Prefident.

To the COLONELS *or* COMMANDING
OFFICERS *of the refpective* Battalions *of*
this STATE.

TWO O'CLOCK, P. M.

THE Enemy are at Trenton, and all the City Militia are marched to meet them.

Broadside Urging Pennsylvania Militia to Come to Defense of
Philadelphia Against General Howe's Army.

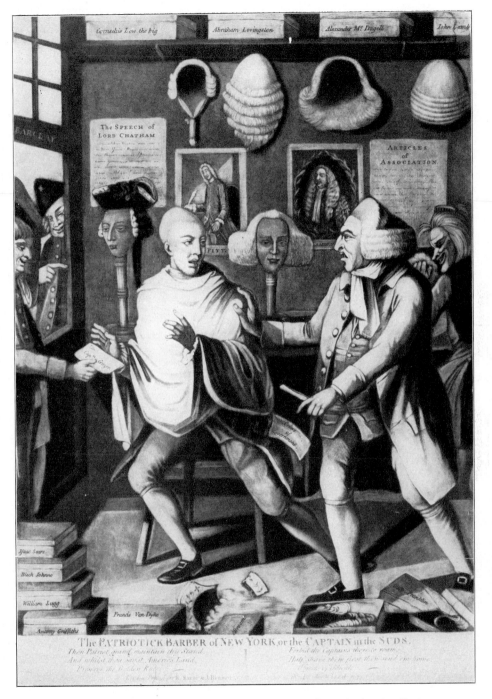

The Patriotick Barber of New York, or the Captain in the Suds. The Patriot Barber is sending his Loyalist customer home only half-shaved, to be the laughingstock of the neighborhood. This cartoon is representative of a considerable number of political cartoons and satirical prints issued in England during the American Revolution,

Bulls Head Tavern in the Bowery, between Bayard and Pump Streets, now Canal Street, New York, 1783.

Broad Street, New York. This print is the only contemporary view of the upper end of Broad Street in the eighteenth century. The steeple on the left is that of St. Paul's, and the cupola of the First Presbyterian Church may be seen above the gable of the tall building on the West Side of Broad Street.

New York from Brooklyn Heights, August 6, 1778.

foul that it "was enough to destroy men of the most healthy and robust constitutions. Almost, and in fact I may safely say, every morning a large boat from each of the hospital ships went loaded with dead bodies, which were all tumbled together into a hole dug for the purpose, on the hill where the national navy-yard now is." [54]

The sufferings of Captain Coffin and his fellow prisoners have been vividly described by the poet of the Revolution, Philip Freneau:

"The various horrors of these hulks to tell,
These Prison Ships where pain and horror dwell,
Where death in tenfold vengeance holds his reign,
And injur'd ghosts, yet unaveng'd complain;

. . . . .

"Hail, dark abode! what can with thee compare—
Heat, sickness, famine, death, and stagnant air—
Pandora's box, from whence all mischief flew,
Here real found, torments mankind anew!—

. . . . .

"Three hundred wretches here; denied all light,
In crowded mansions pass the infernal night,
Some for a bed their tatter'd vestments join,
And some on chests, and some on floors recline;
Shut from the blessings of the evening air,
Pensive we lay with mingled corpses there,
Meagre and wan, and scorched with heat below,
We loom'd like ghosts, ere death had made us so—" [55]

Despite the overwhelming evidence of the cruelty to Americans on the prison ships, the Loyalists in New York and to some extent even the Revolutionists were deceived into thinking that conditions were not so bad as had been represented. The *Royal Gazette* in February, 1781, published the report of a board of enquiry, consisting of Captain George Dawson, of the *Iris;* Captain Rupert George, of the *Avenger;* Captain Battersby, of the 19th Regiment of foot; and Ensign DeChambault, of the 24th Regiment of foot. When these officers came aboard the *Jersey,* the prisoners were ordered on deck and various ones picked out for questioning. As they stood there, ragged and cowed, they assured the board that "they have never been and are not now crowded in the prison ship"; that "their situation was made at all times as comfortable as possible and that they were in no instance oppressed or ill treated"; that their weekly allowance of food was sixty-five ounces of bread, forty-three ounces of beef, twenty-two ounces of pork, eight ounces of butter, one and a fifth pints of peas and two pints of oatmeal, which was always issued to them without "drawback or deduction"; that the prevailing sickness among them was no more than the consequence of a lack of sufficient clothing and of their own uncleanliness. So the officers, in their fine uniforms, turning their backs on the poor ragged prisoners, rowed away and reported that all was as it should be on the prison ships. Apparently none of them had taken the trouble to enquire what would happen to any prisoner who failed to give the answer expected of him.

Since Congress and General Washington were not convinced by this farce, David Sproat, the British commissary-general for naval prisoners, in June 1782, decided to enact another. So, when twelve masters and one surgeon of American vessels came into his clutches, he secured paroles for them and then asked them to appoint six of their number to inspect the prison ships. They visited the ships and then put their names to a report stating that the prisoners were treated with every consideration, given good and plentiful food and made as comfortable as possible.

A few weeks later an American sea captain who happened to be at Bracket's Tavern, Boston, overheard two gentlemen discussing the treatment of naval prisoners. Since he himself had more than once been confined in the prison ships at New York, and had "suffered everything but death," he at once pricked up his ears. One of the gentlemen expressed gratification that the treatment of the prisoners was so greatly bettered as to warrant the report which the shipmasters had signed. But his companion replied that "he could satisfy him in regard to that matter," that he had conversed with several of the men who had put their names to the paper and they had told him that Sproat had given them the option of signing, and going home to their wives and families on parole, or of refusing and joining the other prisoners. They had not even read the paper. "He asked one of them why he did not contradict it since it had appeared in the public papers, and was false; he said he dare not at present for fear of being recalled and sent on board the prison ship and there end his days; but as soon as he was exchanged he would do it." [56]

The capture of Burgoyne's army at Saratoga proved a godsend to the American prisoners, not only because of the better treatment it brought them, but because it gave Washington a reserve of British prisoners from which to effect exchanges. So, now, from time to time, the welcome announcement came to some despairing man in the Livingston Sugarhouse or the Provost Jail that his exchange had been effected and that he was at liberty to go home.

But for the men on the prison ships, deliverance was rare, since the Americans made far fewer captures on the sea than the British. Even if we accept Sproat's statement that he exchanged no less than 3,000 men during his first year as commissary-general, there were other thousands left to hope and pray that their turn would come before death overtook them. Their situation became almost hopeless in January, 1781, when Congress issued orders that no British sea officer or seaman be exchanged until the enemy returned to America such naval prisoners as were confined in Great Britain. Later, when this was done,[57] a new difficulty arose because Congress refused to exchange soldiers for sailors.

Most of the American naval prisoners had been privateers whose return would not greatly strengthen the American cause, and to send back to the British lines a well-trained grenadier or a Hessian Jäger for one of these tars seemed to Washington a very bad bargain. But the poor fellows on the prison ships, seeing no reason why they should be discriminated against, sent out an appeal to their fellow countrymen. "What is to be done?" they asked. "Are we to lie here and share the fate of our unhappy brothers who are dying daily?" [58]

With the arrival in New York of the humane Carleton, hope sprang anew in the breasts of the prisoners. Nor were these hopes entirely disappointed, for Sir Guy let it be known that all who suffered would be the especial objects of his care. And though men confined in prison ships were not under his jurisdiction, he took it upon himself to visit them, made an effort to learn the truth regarding their treatment and took steps to better their situation. It was due to his efforts that permission was granted the prisoners to go ashore on Blackwell's Island during the heat of the summer.[59] The following winter, finding some of them almost naked, he threw them into "an extacy" by presenting them each with a new suit of clothing.

The naval prisoners, we are told, "wish'd themselves under the general and not the admiral." [60]

It was on Sunday, April 6, 1783, that Captain John Beazley, of the *Ampheon,* came aboard the prison ships one by one, accompanied by Commissary General Sproat. When the prisoners had been lined up on deck, wondering what the turn of fate now had in store for them, Captain Beazley read them King George's proclamation of the cessation of hostilities, and told them that in a few days they would be freed. One can imagine with what transports of joy the men listened to this announcement; how it thrilled them to realize that they were to be reunited with the wives and children they had despaired of ever seeing again. Three days later they were transferred to six vessels in Wallabout Bay, which took them to the ports nearest their homes.

One is inclined to ask why the Loyalists in New York did little or nothing to alleviate the sufferings of the prisoners. Even though those in the ships in Wallabout Bay were not under their immediate observation, they could not have been entirely ignorant of what was going on there. And for all who passed one of the sugar houses or the Provost Jail or any other of the prisons in the city, the plight of the inmates must have been obvious. A few boxes of cast-off clothes, a few gifts of meat or bread, an occasional load of firewood, would have saved hundreds of lives. But such gifts were few indeed.

This apparent heartlessness is explained in part by the denials of the provost-general and his commissaries of harsh and inhumane treatment. The *Royal Gazette* actually boasted of "the wonted benevolence which distinguishes the British from all other nations,"[61] which was in marked contrast to the severity shown by the Americans to the British who fell into their hands. Moreover, the Loyalists, many of whom had suffered humiliation and loss of property at the hands of the Revolutionists, agreed heartily with Dr. Samuel Johnson that they richly deserved any penalty short of hanging. So the people of the city went about their daily tasks, giving little heed to the bitter suffering within the walls of those grim prisons in their midst.

Though there could be no compensation for those who lost their lives in the British prisons, there was very real compensation for the country as a whole, for the cause for which they gave their lives, since the corruption which permeated the military administration, and was in such large measure responsible for the mistreatment of prisoners, was an important factor in the failure of the British to win the war. "It may be presumed," says Judge Jones, "that the commissaries of every kind, barrack-masters, quartermasters, engineers, etc., within the British lines at New York during a seven years' war, did not cost less than five millions of money." When to this is added the activities of similar "blood-sucking harpies" elsewhere, they swallowed up not less than "twenty millions sterling of the money raised by Great Britain for the support of the American war." [62] Even though this estimate may be far too large, had the money stolen by corrupt officials been put into additional warships with which to combat d'Estaing or de Grasse, or additional regiments to throw against Washington, the outcome of the war might have been different.

CHAPTER VIII

THE PLOT FAILS

EARLY IN the summer of 1778 rumors that a great French fleet of warships and transports filled with troops was assembling at Toulon in preparation for an expedition across the Atlantic struck terror into the hearts of the Loyalists. That New York, which every one knew to be the citadel of British power in America, would be their objective, there could be little doubt. Should the Comte d'Estaing, who commanded the armada, blockade the harbor, while 4,000 French troops landed to cooperate with Washington, Lord Howe and Sir Henry Clinton would be caught like rats in a trap. Nor was it beyond the realm of possibility that the French ships might force their way into the lower bay, and after sinking or capturing Howe's fleet, move up to bombard the city.

These fears were intensified when Clinton evacuated Philadelphia and, sending the Pennsylvania Loyalists by sea to New York, brought his army by forced marches across New Jersey to Sandy Hook. It was as clear as day that the British had abandoned the offensive, and it remained to be seen whether they could hold what they had. And the Loyalists watched with concern as regiment after regiment took up new posts on Long Island or upper Manhattan, as though in preparation for an expected assault.

On July 8, as Clinton's outlooks, no doubt stationed on the Atlantic Highlands, anxiously scanned the horizon, the French warships came into view—twelve great ships of the line, five frigates and innumerable supply vessels and transports. On they came until they arrived just off Sandy Hook, where they furled sails and anchored in plain view of the British fleet in Sandy Hook Bay. Howe had his ships drawn up in two lines just inside the Hook, the *Vigilant* guarding the channel off Coney Island and two armed galleys and a battery on the New Jersey shore the channel south of the shoals. To

172

prevent a landing on the Atlantic side, General O'Hara was posted with strong detachments along the beach.

Thus prepared for a desperate resistance, the British waited for d'Estaing to force his way into the Lower Bay. Howe had only nine ships of the line, and 534 guns to the French admiral's 834. But he had the more advantageous position, since, if the French vessels passed the bar one by one, the leaders in turn would receive the concentrated fire of the entire British fleet, until all had been sunk or disabled.[1] But day after day passed and still the French did not move. D'Estaing may have been discouraged by the strength of the British defenses, he may have feared that Admiral Byron, who he knew was on the way to America, might arrive to take him in the rear. Colonel Pluyette, who has made a careful study of d'Estaing's operations in America, says that he could not find a pilot who would conduct his fleet over the bar. The pilots insisted that it was impossible for the larger ships to get in, and in spite of d'Estaing's threats and pleadings and offers of huge rewards, they remained obdurate.

But though the French failed to enter the bay, they established a complete blockade. One unsuspecting merchant vessel after another sailed up, only to find themselves in the hands of the enemy, while the British and the Loyalists were in the greatest apprehension lest the fleet from Cork, upon which the army was dependent for its supplies, would also be taken. "I tremble for the Cork fleet," wrote Eden. To the Loyalists it seemed clear that if the French admiral should hold his position, a few weeks would find New York in the grip of a famine. "Nothing but rice, instead of bread or flour, has been dealt out to the soldiery," stated one observer. "A loaf of bread that used to cost 4d. now sells in the city for a dollar. In short, it appears to me not at all impossible that if they should be thus kept hemmed in on the sea and land side, they will be reduced to the necessity of surrendering the city in less than a month." [2]

"By a person who came out of New York . . . we are informed the Tories were in the greatest consternation," said the *Pennsylvania Packet*. "Their insolence had quite vanished. And now they begin to send toast and butter to the prisoners by way of making fair weather for themselves against our army takes possession of that city, which time is near at hand." [3] "Every countenance in New York friendly to the British cause was appalled," it was stated. "The merchants were solicitous to turn their goods into money at any rate, or to conceal them, or to exchange them for the least bulky and most portable articles." On all sides it was freely acknowledged that the tables were turned and the Loyalists put on the defensive.[4]

The only hope, the Tories thought, was that Byron would come in with the Spithead fleet. "If Byron arrives before the monseers depart, I hope that Messrs. d'Estaing and Bougainville will shortly afterwards dine with us as prisoners of war," said Eden. "If he should not arrive and if we cannot beat them . . . I must in some capacity dine with them, for I shall not have means of dining elsewhere."[5]

Two days after Eden wrote these words, the news was flashed back to the city that the French had hoisted sail and were heading out to sea. The Loyalists rejoiced. So, after all, New York would not fall into the hands of the hated French and the even more hated rebels.

At the time they did not know that they had escaped famine only because of one of those almost unbelievable blunders for which the British Ministry became famous. Had they not sent the Cork fleet to Philadelphia two months after they had ordered the evacuation of that place, instead of to New York as they should have done, it would almost certainly have fallen into d'Estaing's clutches. As it was, it had a narrow escape, for it had ascended the Delaware River as far as Reedy Island and had waited there three days before the commanding officer discovered his mistake and beat a hasty retreat back down the river. Because of this delay, when the fleet reached New York the French had left, and the British army, which had on hand provisions for five weeks only, was saved.

But Clinton had little time to give either to rejoicing at this narrow escape or to wondering at the stupidity of the Ministry, for word came to him that the British garrison of 3,000 men at Newport under General Pigot was in imminent peril. The New England militia were flocking in to reinforce General Sullivan at Providence, and Lafayette, followed by Nathanael Greene, was hastening east with detachments from Washington's army. If d'Estaing had left New York with the purpose of closing in on Newport from the sea, Pigot would be completely cut off. So Clinton and Lord Howe resolved to hasten to his relief.

They were greatly heartened when some of the ships of Admiral Byron's fleet, which had been scattered by a storm, one by one began to come in. Late in July the *Cornwall*, of seventy-four guns, arrived, followed by the *Centurion* and the *Raisonable*. A few days of feverish preparation followed, after which Howe signaled the fleet to weigh anchor, and as one ship after another got under sail, headed for Rhode Island.[6]

It was with mingled hope and fear that the Loyalists bade good-bye to the fleet. If Lord Howe succeeded in defeating d'Estaing, all would be well, at least for the moment; but if the French should triumph, New York would be lost, and with it the British cause in America.

For ten days the city waited before the British fleet was sighted off the Hook. The hearts of the watchers sank when they noted not only that Lord Howe did not bring back as the fruits of victory a single French vessel, but that many of his own ships were missing, that others seemed badly battered, and one, the *Apollo*, was entirely dismasted. But when some of the men came ashore they were relieved to hear that it was not the French, but a terrific storm which had caused the damage.

It seems that d'Estaing, upon arriving off Narragansett Bay, had sailed in boldly past the Newport batteries, and would have taken several frigates had Pigot not burned them. For the moment the British force appeared to be doomed. But before the French troops could be landed, the masts of Howe's ships appeared in the distance, and d'Estaing decided to go out and fight. Sullivan pleaded with him to leave his troops behind, but he refused to do so, though they would have been safer on land than in the midst of a naval battle.

For two days the fleets had maneuvred off Block Island without coming to grips, when a furious gale swept down upon them and scattered the ships as though Boreas was offended that men should seek to kill each other. The subsiding of the wind found the vessels dispersed along the Atlantic coast from New York to Cape Henlopen, most of them with torn rigging and broken masts and yards. "Had we been in action when the gale came on us . . . one half of both fleets at least would have gone to the bottom," one of Howe's officers wrote to Eden. "This might have answered well enough to save Rhode Island, . . . but it would have been poor sport to us in the water."[7]

Now began a race between the two admirals to collect their ships, repair the damage and put to sea again. D'Estaing got away first and headed for Rhode Island, but still in such bad shape that when Howe followed, he thought it prudent to continue to Boston for refitting. The British fleet, which now had a decided superiority in ships, after missing the French at Newport by twelve hours, spread every sail in the hope of overtaking them. Failing in this, they turned back to New York.

The Tories, who had set high hopes on a naval victory, were dejected at this new failure and critical of Lord Howe. "The return of our fleet to this port without M. d'Estaing in his custody is a very sensible disappointment to us," wrote Eden, while Sir Charles Blagden thought it another example of "the fiddle-fuddle preciseness or designed backwardness" which had all along characterized the movements of the British.[8]

There was still hope of a major victory, however, since there was every prospect that Sullivan could be overwhelmed by superior forces now that the French had left him in the lurch. So Clinton embarked 4,000 men on transports and set sail for Rhode Island. But he was delayed a full week by unfavorable winds, Sullivan extricated his men by a skillful retreat and once more the British had missed what all agreed "would have been a great stroke."[9]

After returning to New York, Clinton, deciding upon still another move before the season ended, dispatched General Grey to break up several nests of privateers in eastern New England. Grey did a thorough job. At Fairhaven he not only destroyed seventy sail of shipping, together with wharves, stores, warehouses and ropewalks, but set the torch to dwellings and churches. He then proceeded to Martha's Vineyard, Nantucket and Block Island, and turned all the Loyalists in those places into ardent Revolutionists by plundering their houses and robbing them of their cattle, horses, sheep and hogs.[10]

This served to alleviate the shortage of food in New York, but it by no means raised the drooping spirits of the Loyalists. "Thus ended a campaign, if it deserves the appellation, without anything capital being done, or even attempted," wrote Isaac Ogden to Joseph Galloway. "How will the historian gain credit who shall relate that at least 24,000 of the best troops in the world were shut up within their lines by 15,000 at the most of poor wretches, who were illy paid, badly fed, and worse clothed, and scarce at best deserved the name of soldiers?"[11]

The bitterness of the Tories was intensified by the rumor that the British Ministry had ordered the evacuation of New York in order to concentrate all available forces in the West Indies. The American newspapers played up this report to the full,[12] and not even Clinton was in a position to deny it. All he could say was that he had received no such orders. And when he sent a detachment up the Hudson to divert the northern militia from joining Sullivan in an expedition against the Iroquois, he thought that it would also serve notice that New York was "not to be immediately abandoned by the King's troops." [13]

More important than this move was the arrival of reinforcements totalling 3,800 men. But great was the alarm when it was discovered that half of them were ill and that they were rapidly infecting the other troops. "This made us wretched indeed," wrote Clinton, "and threw 9,000 into hospitals." Later, when 4,000 men embarked on an expedition to Jamaica to defend that island against an assault by d'Estaing, the old reports of the evacuation of New York once more gained currency. It was only when the Loyalists observed that no steps were being taken to move the hospitals, stores and prisoners, that they were finally convinced that Great Britain had no intention of deserting them.

From that dreadful night in September, 1776, when so much of New York went up in flames, the British and the Loyalists were fearful that another fire might lay in ashes all that remained, for such a disaster would bring suffering upon soldiers and citizens alike. "There are no doubt at this time a number of bad, disaffected people who have come in and reside in the city, who have no property there and are more to be dreaded than the enemy without," T. Bache wrote to General Clinton. "Some of them may be so hardened in iniquity as to attempt the destruction of its remains, and that at a time when the loyal inhabitants may be called out in its defence." [14]

General Robertson, too, thought that "the rebels, not satisfied with the destruction of part of the city," entertained designs of burning the rest. To guard against this danger he directed that all persons must "turn out to watch when called for," to "inspect all parts of the city to apprehend incendiaries, and to stifle fires before they rise to a dangerous height." [15] He also required all the inhabitants and all persons entering the city to register their names at his office, and warned householders to give notice of the admittance of any stranger to their houses.[16]

The worst fears seemed about to be realized when, in the early hours of August 3, 1778, "a most dreadful fire broke out in the store of Mr. Jones, ship chandler, on Cruger's wharf." The firemen rushed to the scene, but they found that the 35th Regiment had preceded them and that the colonel had taken it on himself to direct all the efforts to extinguish the blaze. It was this, the citizens complained, which accounted for the loss of many houses. The fire swept over the wharf, consuming the buildings on it and on the south side of Little Dock Street, then leaped over the street to the north side, whence it caught the back buildings on Dock Street and destroyed everything in its path as far as Isaac Low's house at the Old Slip. In all sixty-four dwellings and a number of stores were consumed.[17]

As the crowds viewed the ruins the next morning, they cursed the incendiaries, who they were sure were responsible, and waited impatiently for their arrest. General Jones issued a proclamation offering a reward of one hundred guineas for information leading to the detection of the persons guilty of or "aiding in so horrid a crime." [18] It was only after careful investigation that the authorities were convinced that the origin of the fire was accidental.

In the midst of this excitement the city was again alarmed, this time by a tremendous explosion, coming from the direction of the East River. When anxious men, women and children rushed into the streets, they found that the *Morning Star,* a sloop carrying 248 barrels of gunpowder, had blown up. The crew were killed instantly, the sloop destroyed, persons walking on the docks were knocked down, considerable damage was done to windows and roofs. It was supposed that the sloop had been struck by lightning.[19]

In the meanwhile, word had got round in the city that though New York was not to be abandoned, the main military effort was to be made in the south, and thousands of troops shifted to the West Indies, to Georgia and South Carolina. The British Ministry had decided that if it could not destroy Washington's army, they might leave it stranded. It was easy for Clinton to concentrate his forces on any part of the seaboard, for all he had to do was to embark his men on transports and set sail; but for the Americans it was well nigh impossible to move large bodies of troops by land hundreds of miles over muddy roads and across great rivers. So the Georgians and Carolinians would have to rely almost entirely upon whatever forces could be raised in the south, with perhaps the aid of the French. Moreover, the southern Tories were numerous, if not active, and it was thought that they would flock in by the thousands as soon as the British had gained a foothold on their coast.

Clinton was deeply displeased at this shift in the military policy of the government, for it hurt his ego to be forced to play a minor role in the war; Brigadier Leslie, Colonel O'Hara and other officers were offended because the southern expedition was entrusted to Lieutenant Colonel Archibald Campbell, who was their junior; [20] the northern Loyalists looked upon the whole thing as an open sacrifice of their interests. So there was no enthusiasm when, in November, 1778, ships began to drop down from New York to Staten Island, until a fleet of 100 sail had been gathered there, and then put out to sea. But three months later criticism for the movement was hushed, when word reached the city that Campbell had landed his men at Savannah, and had stormed the city, driving the Georgia troops before him and capturing 450 officers and men. And later, the announcement that all Georgia had fallen to the royal forces brought rejoicing and renewed hope.[21]

But whatever encouragement Campbell's success gave was more than offset by Clinton's moves in the north, which seemed to most observers to be part of no large plan, accomplished little and several times ended in disaster. On the whole, the year 1779 was a discouraging one for the New York Tories. Typical was the raid into New Jersey in the late winter. Embarking a large force on Long Island by moonlight, Clinton landed them three miles from Elizabeth, and after some delay moved on the town. It had been his hope to surprise the garrison, capture Governor Livingston, and perhaps release Burgoyne's captive army which was on the move from Massachusetts to Virginia. But he was too late, and all he could accomplish was to destroy the American barracks, armory and stores, and make a few prisoners. He then beat a retreat while the militia hung on his flank.[22]

Later, when Clinton sent an expedition under General Vaughan up the Hudson to threaten Washington's hold on the Highlands, he did not get off so lightly. At first all went well. The transports came within three miles of the American works at Stony Point, where three regiments went ashore and then pushed forward. The Americans, seeing that they might be cut off by land and water, set fire to their large blockhouse, abandoned Stony Point and retired to the hills.[23] Thereupon the British, after fortifying both Stony Point and Verplancks

Point, left 1,000 men for their defense and retired down the river. "I have not been without hopes that Mr. Washington would risk something to recover [these forts] and that the consequences might be a general action on ground disadvantageous to him," Clinton wrote Germain.

Washington did risk something. On July 16, 1779, he sent a detachment of 1,200 men, under the dashing Anthony Wayne, to surprise Stony Point. Arriving before the fort as dark was descending over the wooded mountains and vales of the Highlands, Wayne divided his force into two parties, and waiting till after midnight stormed forward. Not a shot was fired by the Americans, for they had orders to rely wholly upon their bayonets. "Neither the deep morass, the formidable and double rows of abatis, nor the strong works in front and flank could damp the ardor of the troops, who, in the face of the most tremendous and incessant fire of musketry, and from cannon loaded with grape-shot, forced their way at the point of the bayonet through every obstacle." As the Americans swarmed into the fort, the garrison laid down their arms. The British loss was 151 killed, wounded and missing and 472 prisoners.[24]

This brilliant success greatly heartened the Americans. Congress praised the "vigilance, wisdom and magnanimity" of Washington, and ordered three medals to be struck, one for Wayne and the others for two of his officers.[25] And though Judge Smith thought this an attempt to magnify a minor success, there were those in high places who did not agree with him. "The King was much surprised and concerned to hear of the rebels' having assaulted and carried the lines at Stony Point," Germain wrote Clinton, "and yet more so at the aggravating circumstance of the loss of the whole garrison." [26]

When Germain wrote these lines he probably did not realize that they could but strengthen Clinton in his conviction that he did not have forces sufficient to garrison outlying posts and that his only safe policy was to keep within the lines around New York. In this respect Stony Point was another Trenton, and its influence on British strategy was hardly less important. Clinton at once rushed a force up the river to reoccupy the post, which the Americans permitted him to do without opposition, but later in the year he thought it prudent to withdraw.

If Clinton needed any other demonstration of the insecurity of his posts, the Americans, under General "Lighthorse Harry" Lee, provided it in the early morning of August 19, when they surprised the garrison at Paulus Hook,[27] within sight of the British headquarters. Lee's men waded through the marsh which separated the Hook from the mainland, then rushed forward with set bayonets, cleared the abatis, crossed the ditch and swarmed into the fort. There was a short but desperate hand-to-hand fight which ended in the surrender of the British. As the gray streak of dawn broke over the roofs of New York across the river, Lee gathered his prisoners and beat a hasty retreat.[28]

There was bitter criticism of Clinton for this "affront," wherever two officers got together, or when a group of Loyalists could give vent to their disgust without fear of being quoted. "Another instance of the great carelessness on our side, when, on the other hand, the military gentlemen amuse themselves with trifles and diversions," wrote Parson Shewkirk. Tryon thought Clinton might "be playing into the hand" of the enemy, and admitted that he had sought in vain to discover "what plan the general acted on." Judge Smith declared that the whole town was "disgusted and dispirited." [29]

Clinton, deeply concerned, the next day set up a court of inquiry headed by Brigadier Martin, to place the responsibility of this new disaster. The court reported that the defeat "proceeded from a general misconduct in the commandant, a total neglect of duty in the garrison and the particular shameful behaviour of the artillery in the fort and the guards in the blockhouses." On the other hand, the officers and the Hessians acted well, throwing themselves into the circular redoubt and defending it gallantly.

The gloom occasioned by the loss of the garrisons of Stony Point and Paulus Hook was in no way lessened when Tryon led a raid into Connecticut, carrying fire and destruction to several towns. The former governor began by issuing an "Address to the Inhabitants of Connecticut," in which he reproached them for their "ungenerous and wanton insurrection" against the best of kings, but promising to shield from injury all who remained in peace at their usual place of residence. Behind this verbal screen he landed at New Haven on July 5 to burn the stores there, and then turned westward, laying in ashes all of Fairfield and much of Norwalk. At this point Clinton, who had learned by experience that indiscriminate plunder and burning served merely to intensify the hatred of the Revolutionists for the

British and to alienate those who had been loyal, sent for him to come back.[30]

Some months later Clinton received a letter from Germain praising Tryon for the success of his expedition. "But I cannot help lamenting with you," he added, "that the behaviour of the rebels in firing from their houses upon the troops, rendered it necessary to make use of severities that are very painful to British soldiers to inflict." [31]

Whatever may have been the excuse, the burning of Fairfield and Norwalk was a mistake. No doubt the scathing letter which Samuel H. Parsons wrote Tryon fairly represents the view of most Americans. "I entertained some hopes of a personal interview with you in your descents upon some of the defenceless towns of Connecticut to execute your master's vengeance upon the rebellious women and formidable hosts of boys and girls who, confiding in your insidious proclamation, remained peaceably in those hapless places . . . But . . . the prudent resolution you took to suffer the town of Stamford to escape the conflagration after the arrival of some men in arms . . . prevented my wishes on this head." [32]

But the discouraging course of events in the north was offset by a very real victory in Georgia. In September, d'Estaing, with a fleet of thirty-seven ships carrying more than 2,000 guns and escorting an army of 6,000 men, arrived off Savannah. Here he was joined by General Lincoln with 750 militia and 600 Continentals. Had the two commanders assaulted the place immediately, they probably would have captured it, together with its garrison of 3,000. But the Americans and French delayed, while the British worked feverishly to strengthen their position. Finally when the attack was made the allies were thrown back with the loss of 837 men, among them the gallant Pulaski. Thereupon d'Estaing raised the siege, and reembarking his men, returned to the West Indies.

It was nearly six weeks after this victory before the privateer *Rosebud* arrived in New York with the news. "How shameful that we should be uninformed before this late day respecting the situation in the south country!" complained Judge Smith, "and that we have been so inactive here while the enemy were busy there." [33] "Nothing, surely, can be more shameful than our present inactivity during the whole summer and autumn," agreed J. Mervin Nooth. "For God's sake let us have a man of resolution and abilities."

Smith and Nooth did not realize that while they and others were hoping for some offensive move in the north, Clinton had reason to be concerned with defending what he had. With the French fleet hovering off the coast, and with Washington ready to cooperate with it should it move north, the threat to New York and Newport was not to be ignored. So it was only prudent, Clinton thought, to concentrate his forces by evacuating Rhode Island and Stony Point. He was sure that while the British remained inferior at sea, Rhode Island was incapable of making a defense of forty-eight hours against such a force as Count d'Estaing and the Americans could bring against it. "And thinking that the troops in garrison there might be more usefully employed defensively . . . on October 7th I ordered the evacuation of the place," he wrote Germain.[34]

Perhaps he did not realize how seriously these moves lowered the morale of the Loyalists, perhaps he did not care. "This week all the troops returned from Rhode Island which they evacuated," wrote Shewkirk. "This affair caused various reflections and sensations. Stony Point has been evacuated, too, so that now the city is filled with troops from every direction." [35]

But it was soon apparent that the soldiers were not to settle down to a comfortable winter, for the city became alive with preparations for another southern expedition. Troops were shifted from point to point, cart loads of provisions passed through the streets to the wharves, detachment after detachment went aboard the transports, while out in the harbor the sailors were busy getting the warships in readiness to take to sea. Finally it became known that General Clinton himself, with Lord Cornwallis as second in command, was preparing to lead a formidable expedition against South Carolina. "The admiral, Lord Cornwallis and I are clearly of the same opinion respecting the present plan . . . and I hope in a short time to be embarked," Clinton wrote Germain.[36]

The Tories were alarmed at the defenseless state in which the departure of all save one of the warships would leave the city, and were divided as to the ability of Lord Cornwallis upon whom command in the south would ultimately devolve. Despite his "unfavorable physiognomy," the "cast in his eye" and his heavy figure and awkward gait, his friendliness and high sense of honor made him personally popular. But some distrusted his zeal for the war, others thought him a "blockhead" who so overrated the power of America as to think it "impossible to crush the rebellion." Yet, on Christmas

Day, 1779, when the two commanders stepped aboard a sloop and, dropping down the bay, went aboard one of the ships as the admiral gave the signal to weigh anchor, not even the distrust concerning Cornwallis could damp the joy of the Loyalists at being rid for the moment of the detested Clinton.[37]

Those who left on the southern expedition were fortunate in escaping the winter of 1779–1780, marked as it was by bitter cold, suffering and anxiety. The oldest living inhabitant had never felt such weather as visited the city early in January and continued almost unabated until late in February. Judge Smith, seated within two feet of his grate filled with glowing coals, could not write because the ink froze in his pen. The judge shuddered when he thought of the many families who had no fuel and were without money to buy it. "We often hear of the deaths of the poor frozen in their houses," he wrote in his *Diary*. "Many reputable people lay abed in these days for want of fuel." [38]

The North River was frozen from shore to shore, the East River was frozen, Long Island Sound was frozen, Upper New York Bay was frozen solid. Three sleighs and ten horses, captured from the Americans, crossed on the ice from Staten Island to New York, a thing never before "attempted since the first settlement of the country." [39] And persons who braved the cold to venture down to the Battery were astonished to see a troop of horsemen galloping from Staten Island to Paulus Hook.[40] Three men were reported to have crossed the Sound on the ice from Saybrook on the Connecticut shore to Long Island, a distance of twenty miles.[41] In New York Harbor the ice was so thick that it was possible to haul the heaviest cannon over it.[42]

The situation was made more acute by the negligence of the barrack-master in failing to provide fuel enough to supply the needs of the city. As early as October 4, Smith had noted that though "the season of winter" was advancing, the town was destitute of firewood. This he ascribed to the "distressed state of the people in the country, the risk that their wood boats might be captured, and the General totally negligent of this matter." So, when the killing cold of January found the woodyards almost empty, thousands cursed the barrack-master and many spoke "with great freedom" of Clinton.[43]

In this emergency garden fences, old sheds, anything which could be spared and would burn were split into firewood. Sleighs and even carriages dashed out to neighboring farms to take on loads of wood, but what they brought back was but a fraction of what was needed. Madam Riedesel, who happened to be in the city at the time, tells us that "the poor were obliged to burn fat in order to warm themselves and cook their meals." Firewood was selling at £10 a cord and she herself paid a Spanish dollar for a single stick. When a Major Brown was criticized for cutting down an avenue of shade trees, he answered that it was far better to sacrifice a few trees than permit families who had served the King with zeal to suffer from the cold.[44] Tryon, himself reduced to one cord of wood, gave orders that certain old hulks be cut up, and the slips soon resounded to the sound of the axe. Judge Smith says that so great was the emergency that a vessel laden for a voyage was unloaded and hacked to pieces for fuel.[45]

To the physical sufferings of the Loyalists was added intense anxiety for the safety of the city. It was recognized by all that the water which surrounded Manhattan was its strongest rampart, the warships which floated on that water its "wooden walls." But now the solid ice which extended from shore to shore offered inviting avenues of approach, while holding the war vessels motionless in its grip. Might not Washington, calling the militia of the neighboring colonies to his aid, sweep over the rigid Hudson or the equally rigid Harlem, to overwhelm the depleted garrison of New York?

General von Knyphausen, the able German officer left in command by Clinton, did all in his power to prepare for the expected attack. Since Staten Island and Manhattan were especially exposed, he decided to concentrate most of his troops on them. So the 22d Regiment and part of the 76th were sent shivering over the ice to Staten Island, while most of the 76th and all of the 80th were added to the garrison of New York.[46] In the city men worked feverishly on the fortifications. Platforms were raised on the circular redoubt on the East River, while "Stevenson's house on the height above the shipyard," the wharves from the shipyard to the lower Battery, the "Foundary Redoubt," the "New Star Fort," and other positions were strengthened and supplied with ammunition.[47] The firing of guns a stated number of times from the posts was to be the signal that the enemy was approaching.

Despite these precautions, the Loyalists, when they arose each morning, must have glanced out over the Hudson fearfully, half expecting to see Washington's ragged veterans advancing. Hundreds went to General Pattison with the request that they be organized into companies, armed and assigned to defensive positions. Pattison not only complied, but issued a proclamation calling upon all men from the age of seventeen to sixty to enroll, and declaring that even firemen and Quakers were "expected to exert themselves in cases of emergency." Soon the streets were filled with men, marching back and forth through the snowdrifts to the command of the drill sergeant. Several hundred men from the royal navy who offered their services were assigned to the circular redoubt, while large numbers of sailors from the vessels frozen in the harbor—transports, victuallers, merchantmen, small craft—trudged over the ice, armed with pikes, to join the garrison.[48] Even the officers and artificers of the naval yard and the supply detachments of the army took up arms.

But Washington decided that zero weather, even though it opened hitherto closed passages to Manhattan, was no time for an attack on the city. It was difficult to move cannon and supplies through the snowdrifts, his men would suffer bitterly, the militia might balk at leaving the roaring fires of their comfortable homes. So he contented himself with a series of raids upon isolated posts which kept the British in a state of constant alarm.

The most ambitious of these was an attack on Staten Island, when 2,700 men under Lord Stirling with six cannon and two mortars, crossed over on the ice from Elizabeth Town Point. When the garrison retired to a strong position, protected by redoubts, the Americans contented themselves with hovering around huge fires until the next morning, when they withdrew, taking with them great numbers of cattle and several hundred sleigh loads of salted provisions, clothing, blankets and household furniture.[49] Knyphausen retaliated with a series of raids on Elizabeth, Newark and White Plains, which for the most part proved ineffective because his cavalry and his sleighs could not get past the snowdrifts which blocked many of the roads.[50]

With the approach of spring and the thawing of the ice on the rivers, the English lapsed once more into inactivity. "It begins to be surmised either that the British are tired or unwilling to terminate the war," complained Judge Smith. "If Great Britain recalled all her generals and raised her colonels, her affairs would probably mend. . . Her distresses must increase before men rise by merit for the service of the day. The apology for our present idleness is the possibility of the French fleet's appearance here . . . We are therefore fiddling in the

planting of cannon on the shores and at the same time amusing ourselves with toasts, plays, etc." [51]

But though Knyphausen's regiments were inactive, Rivington kept
up a lively propaganda offensive in his *Royal Gazette*. "I am convinced the rebellion is nearly over," wrote a correspondent, pointing
out that the dollar had depreciated, that there was "general misery
and distress," throughout the country, and that Congress composed of
"the very refuse of the people," was showing its incompetence.[52]

Another writer, in a letter not less remarkable for its prophesies than
its exaggerations, thought that all "save the blockheads who at first
excited" the rebellion must realize that France and Spain, after ex-
hausting both Great Britain and her colonies, intended to pour forces
into America to subject the people to their "merciless dominion." And
should the colonies establish an independent state, it would become
"an asylum to Europeans," so that there would be endless migrations
from the old to the new world. This, he thought, would be disastrous.
"The crowd of active and restless minds, whom the hopes of a better
fortune and the dawn of liberty in a rising state may attract to the
western hemisphere, will not fail to multiply the seeds of disorder
there; they will carry with them their vices, their avidity, their aversion
to repose as well as to useful labor, and their facility to adopt new
projects."

Moreover, he added, when America was fully populated, it would
no longer need the products of Europe. "It will then be from the necessity of things that we shall depend on them more than ever they depended on us; . . . it will be no longer by Cairo or the Cape of Good
Hope that we shall procure the treasures of Africa or the perfumed
productions of Asia, but from the factories established in . . . America."
With the power derived from "the vigor of youth and a consciousness
of prosperity" they would aim at crushing the "languid powers of
Europe," unless they should no longer seem worth subjecting to "the
possessors of the most brilliant empire the art of politics has yet given
birth to." [53]

But New Yorkers were far more interested in the events of the moment than in speculations on the fate of America and Europe in the
distant future, and awaited impatiently news from the center of naval
and military operations in the south. So there was great rejoicing when,
on May 29, the frigate *Iris* put in with word that Charleston had
surrendered with 5,500 prisoners, 391 guns and huge stores of ammuni-

tion.[54] It seemed that nothing now could prevent the total subjugation of the Carolinas and perhaps Virginia.

It was within the glow of enthusiasm created by the southern victories that General Knyphausen decided to seize the first opportunity to invade New Jersey. So when he heard that Washington's men were in a mutinous mood, that many wished to desert to the British, and that the New York troops had been sent off towards Albany to repel attacks by the Indians, he prepared to strike.[55] On June 6, his army crossed over from Staten Island and advanced in the direction of Springfield. But he was immediately undeceived as to the temper of the Americans, for they contested every foot of the way. The militia, hastening in from the surrounding countryside, poured in a galling fire from thickets, woods and ditches. The British and Hessians retaliated by plundering and laying waste the hamlet of Connecticut Farms, burning not only residences, but the meetinghouse, the schoolhouse, barns and even orchards. The next day they retired to Elizabeth Town Point.[56]

In New York, citizens and officers were still discussing this fiasco, when word came that the sails of a great fleet had been sighted through the mist standing in for Sandy Hook. Clinton had returned with a part of his army from his victorious expedition to South Carolina. At last, they thought, the period of defensive action was at an end, at last the British army could repeat in the north its successes in the south and bring the war to a conclusion.[57]

Clinton's first steps lent support to this hope. Sending one body of troops under General Leslie up the North River to force Washington to weaken his army in New Jersey, he ordered Knyphausen to renew the advance towards Morristown. But once more every foot of the way was fiercely contested, and Clinton, seeing that he had not caught Washington off guard, ordered a retreat. So Knyphausen, after resting his men an hour and a half at Springfield, set the village on fire, moved swiftly back to Elizabeth Town Point and over a pontoon bridge to Staten Island.[58] What this futile expedition accomplished is told in vivid words by a militiaman who passed over the battlefield: "The whole scene was one of gloomy horror—a dead horse, a broken carriage of a fieldpiece, a town laid in ashes, the former inhabitants standing over the ruins of their dwellings and the unburied dead." [59]

A few days later Judge Smith was conversing with General Clinton when the latter remarked that "the rebellion would end suddenly in a crash." Not suspecting that Clinton might be basing his opinion on secret information, Smith replied laconically that in his opinion it would die of a consumption.[60] Had he happened to be at headquarters one day in the following September he might have gathered that something unusual was afoot, when a certain Mary McCarthy, wife of a soldier of the 9th Regiment who at the time was a prisoner in the Highlands, came in to deliver dispatches which she had brought through the lines from West Point and which she insisted were of the utmost importance.[61] A few days later came the sensational news that the Americans had discovered a plot hatched by General Benedict Arnold with Clinton to deliver the Highlands posts, the key to Washington's position, into British hands.

It was in the spring of 1779 that Clinton began receiving letters from an American officer signed with a fictitious name, expressing a desire to go over to the British cause. He could not stomach the alliance of America with France, he said. Clinton, by doing a bit of detective work, came to the conclusion that his correspondent was none other than Arnold. But hearing that he was "in a sort of disgrace" and not apt to be assigned to a post of importance, he lost interest. It was only when it was announced that "Arnold had obtained the command of all the rebel forts in the Highlands with near 4,000 men," that he gave the matter his earnest attention. "The getting possession of these posts with the garrisons, cannon, stores, gunboats, etc., appeared to me an object of the highest importance," he wrote Germain.[62]

It was his intention at first to delay taking over the Highlands until the Americans and French were involved in some major move, so that he could catch them at a disadvantage and inflict a crushing defeat. "A French fleet and a considerable land force had arrived at Rhode Island," he wrote. "There was great reason to suppose that an attempt was intended upon New York." Washington, he was sure, would attack Kingsbridge, another force would threaten Staten Island, and the French would approach by way of Long Island. If, at this moment, Arnold turned the forts over to him, Washington, with his line of supply cut, would have to retire precipitately, and the French would be trapped. But at this point Sir George Rodney arrived with his fleet at New York, which for the time made an attack by the allies improbable, and so spoiled Clinton's plan.[63]

Yet the possession of the Highlands was in itself of major importance and Clinton decided to strike without further delay. To draw attention from the Hudson, he began ostentatious preparations for an expedition to the Chesapeake, placing 3,000 men on transports and giving the command to General Leslie. Then he drew Sir George Rodney and General Knyphausen into consultation and laid his plans before them. They both approved heartily. Rodney "most handsomely promised to give . . . every naval assistance in his power." "It became at this instant necessary that the secret correspondence under feigned names which had so long been carried on, should be rendered into a certainty," said Clinton, "both as to the person being Major General Arnold, commanding at West Point," and as to "the manner in which he was to surrender himself, the forts and troops to me," and that "it should be so conducted under a concerted plan between us as that the King's troops sent upon this expedition should not be under a risk of surprise or counter plot." [64]

Several plans were formulated for a meeting between Arnold and some officer representing Clinton, only to be laid aside as impracticable. Arnold requested that whoever was sent should have Clinton's "particular confidence" and in the end insisted upon having his adjutant general, Major John André. Finally, when all had been arranged, and both Arnold and André were on their way to the rendezvous, the former encountered a gunboat in the river and "with difficulty escaped being taken." So the correspondence was resumed and another appointment made to meet in the river a few miles below Stony Point. [65]

On the evening of September 19, there was gay laughter and the clinking of glasses at the farmhouse of Jacobus Kip, where Colonel Williams, of the 80th Regiment, gave a dinner to Sir Henry Clinton and his staff. All knew that André was about to leave on some important mission; none knew what. But they rose with alacrity when Sir Henry proposed the toast: "The health of Major André, who leaves us tomorrow to return Sir John André." [66] The next day the young officer got on board the British war vessel *Vulture* and proceeded up the river.

It had been agreed that Arnold should row out to the *Vulture* at night, but instead of doing so, he sent a message for André to come ashore at Haverstraw. Reluctantly he complied. Late that night the two officers met at the square, two-storied Joshua Hett Smith House, where they discussed their plans in subdued tones and pored over maps

Anthony Wayne, Hero of
Stony Point. The painting
is a detail from one of Ed-
win Austin Abbey's paint-
ings for the State Capitol at
Harrisburg, Pennsylvania.

The Capture of Stony Point. Americans under the command of
Anthony Wayne took the fort from an equal force of Britishers
in twenty minutes.

Lord Cornwallis
(*upper left*) and
General Bur-
goyne (*upper
right*). *Right:*
Mrs. Benedict
Arnold (Peggy
Shippen) and
Child.

The Capture of Paulus Hook by the Forces of General "Lighthorse Harry" Lee.

View from Fort Putnam. Washington made a visit of inspection to this fort only two or three hours before the discovery of Arnold's treason.

Major John André's Drawing of Himself Made while in Prison,
a Ticket for the Meschianza, and a Drawing by Major André.

West Point as it appeared during the American Revolution. A. Constitution Island. B. Chain stretched across the Hudson to prevent the passage of the British. C. Fort Clinton.

Washington's Headquarters at Tappan from which the order for André's execution was issued.

Arnold Tells His Wife of the Discovery of His Treason.

and diagrams by the flickering light of the candles. When every detail had been arranged and André was ready to return, it was discovered that some American gunboats had fallen down the river and lay between the forts and the *Vulture*. Thereupon Arnold, realizing that if André were intercepted and the plot revealed, his own life would be forfeited, insisted that he return to New York by land. André was also persuaded to change his regimentals for an old suit of homespun. Thereupon Smith, the host, rowed him across the river and left him to pursue his journey alone to New York, with incriminating papers concealed in his boots.[67]

Judge Thomas Jones, commenting on the refusal of Arnold to send André back to the *Vulture*, was bitter in his criticisms. If the major went on shore "under the sanction of the flag," and this Arnold in a letter to Washington positively asserts, why in the name of God could he not return on board again under the same "sanction?" "This odd piece of conduct, however, took place; unaccountable as it is . . . André, instead of taking the safe, easy and expeditious method, of returning on board the man-of-war . . . was advised to change his name and take a pass from Arnold . . . and to proceed to New York by land." [68]

The fate of nations often hinges upon small events—the course of the assassin's bullet, the blowing of a vessel out of its path by a storm at sea, the striking down of some great figure by disease. Who knows what important events might have happened had the solitary figure riding through the Westchester woods reached his destination in safety. The plot against the Highlands forts might have succeeded; General Washington might have been captured; the Revolution might have failed; it is even possible that there would have been no United States.

But as André was approaching Tarrytown, he was stopped by three young men who were playing cards by the roadside. Thinking they were Loyalists, he made the mistake of telling them he was British. After that, even though he produced his pass from Arnold, his captors insisted upon searching him, and so discovered the incriminating papers. Thereupon they took him to the nearest American outpost, commanded by a Colonel Jamieson. This officer, not suspecting Arnold's treason, sent him word of André's arrest.

Despite the merry blaze in the fireplace of the dining room of the Beverly Robinson House at the foot of Sugar Loaf Mountain, the company which sat down with General Arnold for breakfast on the morning of September 21 seemed overcast with gloom. Suddenly a young officer entered and handed Arnold a dispatch. Quietly the traitor excused himself, went to his wife's chamber to tell her that he must flee for his life, and leaving her in a swooning condition, mounted his horse and dashed down to the river. Here he entered a barge and directed the six oarsmen to pull for the *Vulture*. He was going there under a flag of truce, he explained, to open negotiations with the enemy. A moment later he was gliding on the bosom of the river beneath the wooded heights brilliant in the autumn colors, past Anthony's Nose, Verplancks Point, Stony Point, out into the lovely Tappan Sea, where he clambered aboard the *Vulture*.

Washington, who arrived at the Robinson House an hour after Arnold left, immediately summoned a board of fourteen officers, among them Lafayette, Steuben, Lord Stirling and Knox, to meet in the old Dutch church at Tappan, to try the unfortunate André. They found that he had passed the American works "under a feigned name and in a disguised habit," that "when taken he had in his possession several papers which contained intelligence for the enemy," that therefore he "ought to be considered a spy from the enemy, and that agreeably to the laws and usage of nations, it is their opinion he ought to suffer death." Washington, though with deep emotion, approved the sentence, and set October 1, as the date of the execution.[69]

Clinton, who seems to have had a sincere friendship for his gallant and attractive young adjutant general, did all in his power to save him.[70] On September 30 he gathered around him at headquarters a group of his most trusted advisers—Judge William Smith, General Robertson, William Franklin, Andrew Elliot and others. He began by having several letters read, one from Arnold to himself, one from himself to Washington, one from André.

As the last pathetic missive was read, Clinton was deeply affected. "Your Excellency is doubtless already apprized of the manner in which I was taken and possibly of the serious light in which my conduct is considered . . . I have obtained General Washington's permission to send you this letter, the object of which is to remove from your breast any suspicion that I could imagine I was bound by your Excellency's orders to expose myself to what has happened. The events of coming within an enemy's posts and of changing my dress which led to my present situation were contrary to your own intentions as they were to your orders and the circuitous route which I took to return was imposed (perhaps unavoidably) without alternative upon me . . . I am perfectly tranquil in mind and prepared for any fate to which an honest zeal for my King's service may have devoted me . . . With all the warmth of my heart I give you thanks for all your Excellency's kindness to me and I send you the most earnest wishes for your welfare which a faithful, affectionate and respectful attendant can frame. I have a mother and three sisters to whom the value of my commission would be an object, as the loss of Grenada has much affected their income." [71]

One wonders whether there was a dry eye in the room at the conclusion of the reading of this letter. Certainly there was a unanimous determination to try to save the writer from the fate which impended. After a long discussion, in which most of those present gave it as their opinion that André could not be considered a spy, Sir Henry withdrew to another room and penned a letter to Washington. When he had returned and Captain Smyth, his secretary, had read what he had written, General Robertson thought that it was not peremptory enough. Thereupon Robertson, himself, with Clinton's approval, went out to frame a letter after his own notion. It intimated that Washington and his board of officers were misinformed as to the facts, that if they would consult with French and Hessian generals they would set them right as to European military usage, that Clinton had many American spies in his power upon whom he would take revenge if André suffered, and finally that he was sending a commission to meet anyone Washington would delegate to confer upon the whole matter. This letter Clinton hastened over to Paulus Hook and thence by land to Tappan under a flag of truce. [72]

On the afternoon of October 1, Clinton's commissioners—General Robertson, Judge William Smith and Andrew Elliot—crossed over to Corbet's Point, near Tappan, and sent ashore to know whether the Americans were ready to receive them. They were told that General Greene, who was to represent Washington, wished to talk alone with Robertson. So while Robertson's aide, Murray, walked up and down with Washington's aide, Alexander Hamilton, the two generals discussed the tragic situation at length. Robertson pointed out that André had entered the American lines "under the cover of Arnold's flag," and he was sure Rochambeau would admit that he was not a spy, and reminded Greene that Clinton held a number of spies "whom he had forborne to execute from a desire to spare the horrors of war."

Thereupon Greene produced a letter from André to Washington in which he admitted his error in disguising himself and confessed that he had no flag. When he hinted that André might be safe if Arnold were given up, "Robertson answered with a look." [73]

Robertson's arguments did not convince Washington. Deeply moved though he was at the plight of the young officer whom fate had placed in his hands, he realized that this was no time for leniency. He shuddered to think by what a narrow margin the American cause had been saved. Let all others, Americans and their British accomplices alike, who were plotting to betray it, realize the risks they were running. He even refused André's request to be shot, and on October 2, at 12 o'clock, at a spot near Tappan, André was executed by hanging.[74] Major Benjamin Tallmadge, who was present, says: "His conduct was unparalleled on this occasion. He met death with a smile, cheerfully marching to the place of execution and bidding his friends who had been with him farewell." [75]

André had been very popular in the British army and with the Loyalists, and his tragic death created the greatest excitement. For days people could talk of nothing else. Whether in private houses, or at the coffeehouses, or in taverns, the justice of the sentence was impeached and Washington denounced. To his many friends who remembered him as among the gayest of the Knights of the Meschianza, or making an extemporaneous address on "Love and Fashion" at a gathering at the residence of Richard Deane, or delivering the prologue at a performance at the Theatre Royal, it seemed the irony of fate that he should have died on the scaffold. One wonders whether among the belles of New York there were some who, like André's faithful servant Peter, were prostrated with grief.[76]

Though Arnold's plot failed, the British kept their part of the bargain. He received £6,300 from the government, was made a brigadier and was given an important command. But he received in addition what was more nearly his desert, the detestation of the Americans and the scorn of the British. "General Arnold is a very unpopular character in the British army, nor can all the patronage he meets with from the commander-in-chief procure him respectability," declared one observer. "The subaltern officers have conceived such an aversion to him, that they unanimously refused to serve under his command, and the detachment he is to lead was, on this account, officered from the Loyal American corps." [77]

With the exposure of Arnold's plot the northern campaign of 1780, if it can be called a campaign, ended in failure. As winter approached, the British were still cooped up in Manhattan, Staten Island and parts of Westchester and Long Island. The Loyalists, though comforted by the victories in the south, thought them no excuse for Clinton's continued inactivity. And in the few moves he did make, they looked in vain for any concerted plan, any "system" as they called it. So far as they could see his only idea was to sit still behind the Hudson and Long Island Sound, or to make hasty excursions into the enemy country and then turn round and run. With his highly disciplined army, which was as large or larger than Washington's, why did he not force a decisive engagement and bring the war to an end? Some went so far as to hint that Clinton, for personal reasons, wished to "prolong the war." [78]

It might have been wise for Clinton to discuss his difficulties more fully with some of his critics. The reasons for his inactivity, as he explained them in his letters to Lord Germain, seem logical enough, and might have convinced even the most impetuous of his young officers. "I owe to my country and I must in justice to my own fame declare to your Lordship that I become every day more sensible of the utter impossibility of prosecuting the war in this country without reinforcements," he wrote on August 25, 1780.

He might conquer territory, but to hold it was another matter. "To possess territory demands garrisons," he pointed out. "If it has required 6,000 to hold Carolina where nature has traced out a defensible boundary against foes and given little resource for domestic insurrection, surely my Lord, I cannot hope with a field army of 6,000 men first to subdue and then to cover and protect the neighboring populous tracts." It was vain also, he thought, to expect from the Americans who opposed the Revolution assistance enough to "disperse Mr. Washington's army or maintain the country against him." To invade a colony and summon the Loyalists there to arms, "without we occupy the country they inhabit," was merely to add more unhappy exiles "to the list of pensioned refugees." [79]

As for pursuing Washington and forcing him to fight, Clinton had had too much experience with the American commander-in-chief to try any such thing. He was sure that Washington, who usually had ample notice of his moves, would fall back into hilly and almost inaccessible country, where all the advantages of position would be his and all the advantages of superior discipline would be lost to the British. Moreover, with Clinton drawn far from his base, the militia would come swarming in to cut off his retreat. Then there might be another Saratoga, and the war would be lost. Better by far, he thought, to hold on to what he had and hope that in time the British Ministry would send over the thousands of reinforcements needed if any real offensive was to be attempted.

CHAPTER IX

LIFE IN LOYALIST NEW YORK

AN INTERESTING spectacle presented itself to the visitor to New York from the deck of his vessel as it came through the Narrows and up New York Bay. Here were great ships of the line, their guns looking out menacingly from long rows of portholes, their masts rising amid a network of ropes; here a frigate or two, smaller and more graceful than their bulldog sister ships; here a group of merchantmen, some with small craft drawn up alongside to take off their cargoes or to load them with articles of export; here a score of transports, perhaps waiting to take on troops destined for some distant expedition; and on all sides sloops laden with firewood, or meat, or grain from the farms of Long Island, upper Manhattan and Staten Island.

As the visitor's vessel rounded the toe of Manhattan to enter the East River, the city stretched out before him—warehouses lining the lower streets or rising over the wharves, dismal stone sugar refineries now used as prisons, rows of quaint Dutch buildings, with their stepped gable-ends abutting on the street, here and there a brick house built in the Georgian style; Fort George, its bastions rising above the shanties of the fire-swept district along Whitehall, the British flag flapping in the breeze; in the distance the tall tower of the New Dutch Church, to the right the cupola of the City Hall.

When the visitor had descended into a rowboat with his trunks to go ashore at the dock at the foot of Broad Street, it needed but a glance for him to realize that wartime New York was a very busy port. The wharves and the commercial streets were swarming with busy men—merchants and clerks on their way to the counting houses; stevedores, tugging at a heavy crate or a hogshead of sugar; Dutch farmers, unloading their boats or heaving vegetables and meat in carts for transfer to the markets. And piled up on the wharves or in the warehouses were military stores, West Indian products, European manufactured goods—salted meat, barrels of biscuits, casks of powder, perhaps crates of firearms, barrels of sugar and molasses, boxes of hardware, of pewter, of cutlery, of silverware, of Cheshire cheese, of clothing, of farm implements, of books, casks of Jamaica rum, bottles of porter, boxes of soap and candles, etc.

Threading his way through this maze of human beings, merchandise, and carts, our visitor's host searches him out and conducts him to his waiting coach. When the trunks have been strapped on behind, they enter, and rattle off over the cobblestones through the crowded streets. The visitor notes with interest the street lanterns, the pumps, the markets, the taverns, the prisons, the hospitals, the coffee-houses, the mansions of the rich, the wooden shacks of the poor, perhaps the ruins of Trinity Church. The people who elbow each other on the street seem to him an ill-assorted lot—handsomely dressed and bewigged gentlemen, a group of noisy sailors, shabby children, artisans in homespun clothes and leather aprons, British officers in their red uniforms, German grenadiers, Scottish Highlanders, the wives of German soldiers strangely out of place in their peasant costumes. If the coach stops long enough for the visitor to hear what the passers-by are saying, he finds that many are conversing in a strange medley of English and Dutch, others in German, still others in good English.

If the host is a man of means, a wealthy merchant perhaps, his residence is a pretentious Georgian house, three stories high, built of brick, its windows set off with flat arches, its roof with a balustrade, the front stone steps leading to a handsome Doric door. Inside, the hardwood floors, the elaborate mouldings, the Chippendale furniture, the dining-room silver, the books of the library lining the shelves of the cabinets and safe from dust and intruders behind locked glass doors, the harpsichord, the expensive rugs, the imported wallpaper, the marble mantles all bespoke wealth, culture and good taste.

It must have seemed strange to any visitor that in the midst of war, with poverty, suffering and tragedy visible on all sides, there should be so much gaiety. Certainly the numerous balls, dinners and receptions gave deep offense to many of the more seriously minded citizens. Especially offensive was the desecration of Trinity church-yard by placing benches against the walls of the ruins, where the orchestra from the theatre seated themselves to play while handsomely dressed men and women sat under lanterns hung in the trees or strolled

along the walks. To keep them from lounging on the graves, the resting places of the dead were enclosed by a green fence. But when the
walk proved too narrow to accommodate the crowds, this fence was
moved out until the posts were actually sunk in the graves.

This "gave great offense and uneasiness to all serious and still more
to all godly men and caused many reflections, not only on the irre-
ligious turn of the Commandant, but also the rector, who it is said
had given his consent to it," wrote Shewkirk. "Profaneness and
wickedness prevaileth." [1] Judge Smith, too, was shocked. "There is
now set up . . . music every evening at the church walls. What a
medley assemble there! A horrible contrast! Ladies in the walk. The
mob in the street and funerals crossing the company to the church-
yard. The parson there officiating at the grave." [2]

Many were shocked, also, at the lavish expenditure of money to
celebrate the Queen's birthday in January, 1780. At noon the guns
at Fort George fired a salute, followed at one o'clock by another from
the ships in the harbor. "The public rooms were on this occasion
painted and decorated . . . A Doric pediment was erected over the
principal entrance, enclosing a transparent painting of their majesties
at full length, in their royal robes; over which was . . . the motto
of, Britons Strike Home, the whole illuminated with a beautiful
variety of different colored lamps." [3]

In the evening the principal officers of the army gave "a most
splendid ball," led by the Baroness Riedesel and General Pattison. At
six o'clock the Baroness seated herself in a carriage with Generals
Tryon and Pattison and drove to Hick's tavern, where they were
greeted by the rattling of kettledrums and the sounding of trumpets.
The ball opened with a minuet, continued with English dances, while
country dances began at half-past nine.[4]

At twelve the music stopped, and each gentleman, taking his
partner on his arm, escorted her to two long rooms where an elegant
supper had been prepared. To the guests it seemed that the tables had
been decorated by Flora herself, for they were covered with parterres
and arbors, made of a profusion of natural and artificial flowers, china
images, etc. The Baroness Riedesel, who represented the Queen, was
conducted to a throne under a canopy, where she offered the first
toast. And so the evening was passed in what the *New York Mercury*
described as "the most perfect hilarity." [5] It was "the most truly
elegant ball and entertainment ever known on this side of the Atlan-

tic," the editor thought. "It is said the ball cost above 2,000 guineas and they had 300 dishes for supper," wrote Shewkirk.[6]

Among those who viewed social activities during the war with a jaundiced eye was Judge William Smith. When General Pattison asked him why none in his family save his daughter attended the public amusements, he replied that he was too old. Pattison then invited him to play a rubber of whist, but Smith refused. "I never touch cards," he added, muttering under his breath: "Heaven preserve a nation of triflers." [7] High on the list of "triflers" Smith put Clinton. Perhaps he thought it undignified for Sir Henry, when he was host at the Feast of St. Andrew, to appear in Scottish kilt and plaid.[8]

All New York was excited and every feminine heart set fluttering on September 26, 1781, by the announcement that a British fleet under Admiral Digby had arrived, bringing as a naval officer the seventeen year old Prince William Henry, third son of George III. As the tars rowing the admiral and prince ashore backed water near the Kennedy House, the guns from the Battery thundered "a royal salute," while the crowd cheered. When the prince stepped ashore he was greeted by Sir Henry Clinton, Governor Robertson and a group of admirals, generals and other officers. Then, escorted by a guard of honor, the whole group went on foot to Commodore Affleck's house, where his Royal Highness dined.[9]

Two days later the members of the Council went to the prince's lodgings with an address of welcome. As they entered the house and mounted the stairs, they found the passage all through lined with officers of the army and navy waiting to be introduced. The prince stood at the right of the fireplace with Admiral Digby and Admiral Hood beside him. Thereupon Governor Robertson advanced, took out the address, and began to read. But since he had neglected to bring his spectacles and his old eyes were too dim without them to see much of what had been written, he "got through with great difficulty." The prince, apparently not minding, read his answer, after which Robertson introduced the group as they stood one by one, "down to the bottom, ending with the Mayor and General De Lancey." [10]

Later in the day the prince rode out in a phaeton "to see the island," and that evening the party sat down to dinner. At the head of the horseshoe table was the prince, seated between General Robertson and General Knyphausen, with Sir Samuel Hood, Admiral Drake, the Earl of Lincoln, Judge Smith and others, on either side. Despite the numerous toasts, in which the prince "drank down the left wing of the table," there was no disorder, and, save by Sir Samuel Hood, a native of Shropshire but "the image of a Yankee colonel both in person and stiff behavior," no loud talking.[11]

If we may believe the *Royal Gazette,* young William Henry won all hearts. "It is impossible to express the satisfaction felt by persons of all ranks from the ease, affability and condescension shown by this most pleasing, manly youth, when he appears abroad amongst the happy and approved loyal subjects of the good and gracious King, our best and firmest friend, the Majesty of England." [12]

The *Royal Gazette* would have been horrified had it known that in March, 1782, an American officer, Colonel Matthias Ogden, was planning to penetrate to the lodgings of Digby and the prince, capture them and bring them into the American lines. Washington gave the dare-devil venture his sanction, but warned Ogden against "offering insult or indignity" to either of them. When William Henry, many years later as King William IV, heard of this, he is said to have remarked: "I am obliged to General Washington for his humanity, but I'm damned glad I did not give him an opportunity of exercising it towards me." [13]

The presence of the prince made the celebration of the King's birthday on June 4, 1782, a notable occasion. "At noon a royal salute was fired from the guns of Fort George and answered by the ships of war, adorned in a distinguished manner by an infinite variety of colors, presenting a beautiful exhibition. His Excellency, the Commander in Chief, attended by a numerous procession of principal officers, waited on his Royal Highness, Prince William Henry, with their compliments of congratulation. Very elegant entertainments were given by his Excellency Sir Guy Carleton, Rear Admiral Digby and Lieutenant General Robertson. A *feu de joie* was fired in the evening, amongst many thousands of rejoicing inhabitants, and the night was closed with perfect hilarity and harmony." [14]

If the prince had imagined before coming to America that life in New York would be dull, he must have changed his mind before the end of the summer of 1782, for July and August were marked by a series of celebrations in which he was the leading figure. Of these he was no doubt most highly pleased with the observance of his eighteenth birthday, on August 21. "A very elegant dinner was given on the occasion by his Excellency Admiral Digby, to all the great officers of state;

and in the evening a splendid illumination, ball and supper was presented at Greenwich . . . where a great number of ladies, gentlemen
of the navy, army and inhabitants of the city were most politely entertained." [15]

When, several weeks later, the prince went on board the *Warwick*,
and standing on deck as the vessel moved down the bay on its way out
to sea, looked back at the cluster of roofs, chimneys and church towers
on the toe of Manhattan, he must have felt a pang of regret at leaving a place where he had been the recipient of such homage and
adulation. [16]

The British officers looked forward to the celebrations of the King's
birthday, the Queen's birthday, the anniversary of the coronation, or
of important victories in the south or the West Indies as welcome
breaks in the dullness of garrison duty. But the refugees, who watched
with intense anxiety the declining fortunes of the royal cause in
America, often wondered whether balls and festivals and fireworks
were not out of place. One day in 1780, when a group of officers and
civilians were at dinner, the former began laying their plans to celebrate the King's birthday. Whereupon Henry White remarked: "My
opinion is that the best preparation for the birthday is to beat Washington before the French reinforcements arrive." At this the officers of
lower rank smiled, but the others "hung their heads and were as silent
as birds in a thunder gust." Judge Smith, who was present, thought
this reproof of "a set of idlers" richly deserved. [17]

None the less, the celebrations continued. Typical was the observance on September 20, 1780, of the King's coronation. After a
royal salute by the guns at Fort George and the ships of the line at
Staten Island, the British troops, two battalions of Hessians, the Tory
militia and other detachments formed a line extending from river to
river, and then paraded through the city. That evening a *feu de joie*
was fired in honor of Earl Cornwallis's victory at Camden, while the
"Commander-in-Chief, the noble lords lately arrived with Admiral
Sir George B. Rodney, the governor, commandant, all the general
and other officers, British and German, with an infinite concourse of
ladies, gentlemen, etc.," looked on. [18]

For those young blades who were not satisfied with dances and
dinners and an occasional celebration, horse racing offered an exciting diversion. There were courses at Hempstead Plains, Beaver Pond
and elsewhere, but the best track seems to have been on Ascot Heath,

formerly called Flat Land Plains, on Long Island, five miles from Brooklyn Ferry. Here, on November 13, 14, and 15, 1780, were run a series of heats, one for a purse of £60, open to mares and geldings; another open only to ponies, for "a saddle, bridle and whip of £15 value"; still another for £50 to be run "in three two-mile heats." For "the races by women" there were prizes of a "Holland smock and a chintz gown, full trimmed." And as though this did not provide sport enough, fox hunts, starting at the King's Head Tavern at daybreak, were arranged for each day of the races.[19]

Even more successful were the races over the same course on April 16, 17, 18 and 19, 1781. Of the hundreds who came out from the city, some no doubt brought luncheon baskets with them, but others stopped before the booths or wagons, where vendors were doing a thriving business, to purchase food or wine or liquors. And great must have been the excitement when the jockeys, properly uniformed in silk jackets, light boots and small caps, set spurs to their horses and started around the course. On two of the days a "Country Subscription Purse" of £50 was offered, on another a "Noblemen and Gentlemen's Subscription Purse" of £100, and on the other a "City Subscription Purse" of £100, prizes well worth winning, especially if one were an officer who had lived beyond his means and was deeply in debt to the local tailors or merchants.[20]

If some of the young British officers happened not to be interested in racing, they could find diversion in a game of cricket on the elevated plain between the ropewalk and the shipyards. Here on each Monday morning at ten the contestants set up the wickets and began play. With the bowlers matching their skill against the batters, and with the spectators sipping tea in a large booth, one could have imagined that the scene was laid at Eton or Oxford. That the sport was not monopolized by the British is shown from an advertisement in the *Royal Gazette* in which a group of Americans challenged the best England could produce to a game for any sum of money the latter would suggest.[21] As to whether the match was ever played and if so, who won, we are left in the dark.

Nor was it beneath the dignity of the British officers to go out to Thomas McMullan's tavern, near fresh water pump, to witness a bull-baiting, for most of them had seen similar spectacles in Great Britain, perhaps at Cambridge or Oxford. McMullan promised them "satisfactory diversion," as the bull was "active and very vicious." [22] Equally exciting must have been the bull-baiting at Brooklyn Ferry, where, it was announced, "a bull of magnitude and spirit" would try the merit of the dogs. "Taurus will be brought to the ring at 3½ o'clock; some good dogs are already provided . . . A dinner exactly British will be upon Loosley's table at 11 o'clock, after which there is not the least doubt but that the song, *O! The Roast Beef of Old England,* will be sung with harmony and glee." [23]

But those of more refined taste, who scorned such brutal diversions, could attend or even take part in the plays at the John Street Theatre. Among the "Society of Gentlemen of the Army and Navy" there were a number capable of taking leading parts in *Macbeth, Richard III,* and other tragedies, but it was not so easy to find an Ophelia or a Portia in the families of the merchants or the refugees. In the autumn of 1779 the managers of the theatre were forced to advertise in the newspapers for ladies who were "qualified and inclined to perform on the stage during the course of the ensuing winter." [24] That some responded we know, for among those who received pay for various performances were Maria Turner, Anna Tomlinson, Jane Tomlinson and Margaret Shaw.[25]

The rehearsing, acting, keeping the playhouse in repair, painting the scenery, etc., must have kept the young thespians busy indeed. We may follow some of their activities through the pages of the old account book, which records the sums paid for scene shifting, for "washing done in the theatre," for tallow candles, for "sundry dresses," for "hats and trimmings," for "coach-hire," for music supplied by the Hessian band of fourteen pieces, for "sundry wiggs," for "suppers including liquor," etc.[26]

Typical of the notices which appeared in the newspaper was that in the *Royal Gazette* of November 1, 1780: "THEATRE. On Monday next, the 6th instant will be presented a tragedy never before performed here, called *Three Weeks After Marriage,* the characters by gentlemen of the army. The doors to be opened at five, and to begin precisely at seven o'clock. No admittance behind the scenes. No money will be taken at the door. Tickets to be purchased at the time of registering places for the boxes, for which purpose the clerk will attend at Mr. Petits, next door to the theatre . . . Box 8 s., pit 8 s., gallery 4 s."

In many of the handsome homes of the city or its suburbs, well dressed men and women sought to while away the time or seek diversion from the anxieties of the times by indulging in the pleasures of music. In one, it might be the matron who entertained her family or the guests with a performance on the harpsichord; in another the father played on the violin, while his daughter accompanied him on the harp; in still another a small music society brought their flutes, French horns, violins, etc., for an evening's entertainment. If any music lover was in need of an instrument, he could secure what he wanted from the ubiquitous James Rivington, who advertised for sale violins, guitars, German flutes, fifes, French horns, clarinets, hautboys, and harps. He charged from seven dollars to nine guineas for his violins, guaranteed, all of them, to give satisfaction.[27]

Nor was the enjoyment of music confined to those who had the skill to perform, for, in addition to the open air concerts by various military bands, there was a series of subscription concerts at the City Tavern. The officers of the navy and army, and "the gentlemen of the city" who subscribed a guinea, were to have the privilege of attending for the season, and of bringing two ladies and one gentleman, provided the latter was not a resident of the city. The concerts were held weekly.[28] That the music was of a high character we gather from the program of a benefit performance for two destitute refugee families, in which symphonies by Bach, Haydn, and Stamitz alternated with vocal solos, oboe concertos and instrumental quartets.[29]

The British officers took the lead in the social life of Tory New York; but the merchant families also entertained lavishly, patronized the theatre and attended public dances. When General Howe's victorious redcoats took possession of the city in the autumn of 1776, a number of merchants, even some of those who had been active in protesting against the Stamp Act and other repressive measures of the British Ministry, remained, took the oath of allegiance and continued their mercantile activities. To these were added a group of refugees, Scotsmen many of them, who "brought with them sufficient capital" to enter "advantageously into trade." [30] Typical of the latter was Niel Jamieson. A successful merchant of Norfolk, Virginia, when Dunmore evacuated that city in December, 1775, he placed his family on his brigantine *Fincastle* together with as much of his goods as she would hold, and escaping to New York, entered business there.[31]

Sir William Howe, Sir Henry Clinton, and Sir Guy Carleton all realized that without the activities of the merchants, New York could not maintain itself. It is true that the Cork fleet arrived every few months with food, clothing and munitions in sufficient quantities for the British forces. It is true, also, that the farmers of Long Island, Staten Island and Manhattan produced meat, vegetables and grain in considerable quantities. But it was the sugar, rum and molasses which the merchants brought in from the West Indies, and the manufactured goods from Great Britain, which prevented business stagnation and universal poverty among the civilian population of the city.

The merchants undoubtedly made this clear to Sir William Howe when he took command of the city in the autumn of 1776. At that time the Prohibitory Act of January 1, 1776, although designed to cripple the commerce of the rebellious colonies and not of a port filled with Loyalists and occupied by British troops, was still in force. This act permitted imports, but forbade the merchants to export anything without the express permission of the commander-in-chief. With this permission the merchants begged Sir William to be generous. If New York must not pay for the goods brought in from the West Indies and Great Britain with a return stream of commodities, trade would stagnate and hunger and nakedness would result. Nothing loath, Howe drew up a set of regulations for the port which seems to have been satisfactory to all, and under which trade flourished.

But when, in 1778, the merchants heard that Carlisle, Eden and Johnstone, in conjunction with Clinton, had been authorized to regulate commerce, they were greatly alarmed. Pleading with them not to enforce the Prohibitory Act, they pointed out that they had in their warehouses "a variety of articles," some imported and others which had long been stored in the city, which were not needed by the army and navy, and would be wasted if not sent to Great Britain. Of these the most important were tobacco, indigo, beeswax, flaxseed, potash, lumber, fur, dyewood and oil.[32] It was so obvious that nothing was to be gained by keeping these goods in New York to occupy valuable space, that the Commissioners readily consented to reopen trade on the old footing.

In 1780, Parliament at last passed an act laying down rules to govern the trade of the port, but when it expired in 1781 did not take the trouble to renew it. Whereupon the commander-in-chief was "obliged again to exert his authority and order trade to go on agreeable to the regulations" of the act, as otherwise "great inconveniency and even risk of necessary supplies might have been felt . . . and heavy unavoidable losses fallen upon the British merchants." [33]

In February 1781, the merchants were once more thrown into panic when Andrew Elliot, Superintendent of Exports and Imports, announced that he was going to begin collecting duties. In an appeal to Clinton, they pointed out that the war had so restricted their trade, especially exports, that to place on it the extra burden of duties would entirely disrupt it. In fact the duty on the cargoes of captured enemy vessels "amounted to more than they would sell for." But Clinton soon calmed their fears by directing Elliot to withdraw the demand for duties, and trade continued as before.[34]

Whatever hardships the war brought to New York, a dearth of English manufactured goods was not one of them. If one had the money to buy, one could procure anything from a silver teapot to a deck of playing cards. At No. 41 Smith Street, near Pitt's statue, the merchant Williams had on display, in June 1782, a typical assortment of goods, "imported in the last ships from England"—hardware, cutlery, pewter, pocket knives, razors, snuffers, buckles, spurs, silverware, pencils, swords, pistols, spoons, andirons, tongs, pots and kettles, etc.[35] If the shopper could not find what he wanted among this assortment, he could walk down to No. 873 Great Dock Street, where he would find boxes of goods piled high waiting for purchasers. Here were to be had British brandy, bar iron, knee buckles, snuff boxes, bottles, buttons, carpeting, twine, cheese, spices, wool, hair powder, playing cards, almonds, long and short pipes, needles, snuff, shoes, candles, nails, etc.[36]

If one saw displayed for sale Pennsylvania flour, or Virginia tobacco, or Connecticut wheat, or horses and lumber from Boston, there was no occasion for surprise as these things almost certainly had been brought in on some vessel captured by the New York privateers. When word reached the city in the spring of 1777, that Parliament had passed an act permitting the admiralty "to grant letters of marque to private ships of war, or merchant ships, to make reprisals on all ships belonging to the American colonies," there was general satisfaction.[37] Now there would be compensation to the merchants for being cut off from articles of export from New Jersey, Connecticut and the upper Hudson; now every prize would bring rich profits; now every sailor in town would find employment so that there would be fewer tars wasting their time and money in the taprooms down on the water front.

So for the moment the merchants forgot all their former troubles and losses in the general scramble to be among the first to equip and send out privateers. Selecting their fastest vessels, adding all the extra canvas they would carry, equipping them with cannon, gathering as crews every man who had ever seen service on the sea and some even who had not, they sailed forth to seek their prey. Even the ladies of New York, fired with enthusiasm for the royal cause and at the prospects of rich returns, armed and fitted out a fast sailing sloop, which they named the *Royal Charlotte*.[38] In the year following September 8, 1778, Governor Tryon commissioned no less than 121 vessels, almost all of them undoubtedly privateers.

King George gave all this activity his blessing, for he thought it an excellent way to weaken his rebellious subjects and to force them to return to their obedience. But Admiral Collier and General Clinton, when they heard that the masters of the privateers were enticing some of the soldiers and many of the sailors to take service with them by promises of rich profits, thought matters were going too far. In a proclamation of April 13, 1779, Collier reminded the seamen who were deserting his Majesty's service that the penalty was death.[39]

In an incredibly short time privateering had become the most important activity of New York, in which no less than 6,000 men were employed. The privateer, when she had been properly armed and manned, sailed out into the Atlantic and cruised along the coast in search of merchantmen trading between New England and the Chesapeake, or between the Delaware and the West Indies, or between Virginia and the continent of Europe. When the lookout spied a sail on the horizon, the master would order the crew to put on every stitch of canvas and the chase was on. The intended victim, if when overtaken it proved to be unarmed, had no alternative save to surrender, but should it itself be carrying a few six-pounders, it often put up a strenuous resistance. If in the end the merchant vessel struck her flag, she was boarded, put under a crew from the privateer and sent to New York.

One of the most successful of the privateers was the *Virginia*, owned by Speddin and Goodrich, two former merchants of Norfolk. On June 22, 1782, this vessel came into port bringing three prizes, the ships *George* and *Trooper,* both laden with flour from Baltimore for the West Indies, and the schooner *Eagle,* with tobacco from Baltimore for Cadiz. All three were armed. In September the *Virginia* sighted the ship *Phoenix,* mounting 16 guns, on her way from the Chesapeake to Calais with 139 hogsheads of tobacco, and captured her after a chase of forty-eight hours. A month later she took the schooner *Governor Moore,* on her way from Havana to New Bern with 207 boxes of sugar, "a quantity of gunpowder, &c." [40] Before the end of the year Messrs. Speddin and Goodrich's warehouses must have been filled with captured goods and their pocketbooks with coin.

Nor were they the only New York merchants to reap a rich harvest. Tryon wrote Germain on March 1, 1779, that the privateers had taken 150 prizes in the six and a half months since September 18, 1778. Seldom a day passed in which no prize came in. As early as March 1779, the value of the captured vessels and cargos amounted to £600,000.[41] With such wealth pouring in, it is not surprising that "numbers of very fortunate men" had sprung up "like mushrooms since the King's troops took possession of the city." [42]

Many of the captures were made, not by privateers, but by the swift sailing frigates of the royal navy, which cruised far and wide over the ocean, especially after the entry into the war of France and Spain. "Yesterday arrived the *Eloise,* a ship of 20 guns, bound from Havana to Cadiz, laden with 1,200 barrels of sugar, some indigo, hides and about 14,000 splendid dollars," reported the *Royal Gazette* of September 28, 1782. "This acquisition, with a brigantine and another vessel lately sent into our port, are on a moderate valuation estimated at £30,000, all taken by that musical son of thundering Jove, his Majesty's ship *Amphion.*" When a fleet of seventy vessels emerged from Delaware Bay late in December 1781, bound some for France and the rest for the West Indies, the frigate *Adamant* sailed into their midst and brought off the schooner *Delaware,* laden with 350 barrels of flour and 6 hogsheads of tobacco for Cape Francois.[43] Other captures were made by the *Greyhound,* the *Iris, Experiment, Centurion, Pandora,* etc.

It was a happy moment for the officers and men of a privateer or one of the King's ships, when they assembled at the office of the agent to receive their shares of the money from the sale of a captured vessel and cargo. An interesting group they must have been—old sea dogs the veterans of many a voyage, raw hands recently recruited, officers of the royal navy in full uniform—each with a smile on his face, counting the pounds sterling, or the dollars, or the pistoles as they were handed out to him. The payment made on July 19, 1782, to the officers and crew of the warship *Lion,* for the capture of the schooner *Fame,* the ship *Vengeance,* the schooner *Morris,* and the schooner *Lango Lee,* must have doubled or tripled their yearly wages. Shares which were not called for, were to be advertised for three years, and then paid over to the Greenwich Hospital.[44]

But privateering was a game in which both sides could play, and the great profits it brought the New York merchants were in part off-set by their losses to daring American raiders. It was a sad day for the owner of a brig or a ship when he learned, perhaps from the pages of a "rebel" gazette, that she had been captured and brought into Boston or Philadelphia. The Americans were leaders in the matter of ship design, some of their vessels were noted for their speed, every port had its quota of skilled seamen, and no unprotected English or Tory vessel was safe from their depredations. At times the daring of the American privateers was such that they would cruise in groups of three or four off Sandy Hook to capture incoming and outgoing merchantmen. When, in May, 1780, they took a London ship and made off with her in sight of the *Russel,* a 74-gun royal warship, the New York merchants were indignant.[45]

The *Portsmouth,* carrying twenty-two 4-pounders and 6-pounders, and a crew of 150 men, which captured the three-deck ship *Ducken-field* and a number of other vessels, was a thorn in the flesh for the British and Tories.[46] Equally successful was the privateer *Fair American,* which for two years prowled up and down the coast making captures, and always escaping the British cruisers "by her swiftness of sailing." There was rejoicing in the counting houses of New York, then, when at last she was captured by the *Garland* and brought into port.[47]

The depredations of the American privateers became a source of such danger to the trade of New York that in May, 1781, the Chamber of Commerce complained to Admiral Arbuthnot that he was not giving the merchant vessels adequate protection. "A couple of fast sailing frigates, constantly to cruise between Delaware and Block Island, as the winds permit," they thought, "would effectually protect the trade of this port from all invaders." The admiral's reply, while not very satisfactory to the merchants, was a tribute to the daring and seamanship of the Americans. "Since my return from Charleston, the greater part of my force hath been upon this coast, and during my stay at Gardner's Bay frigates have not only been cruising almost constantly off the bar, but between Montock Point and the Delaware." [48]

Despite captures by the Americans, on the whole the New Yorkers were the gainers in this legalized form of piracy. For the vessels and cargoes which the privateers and frigates brought in, there was a ready market. The schooners, brigs, ships, etc., were put into the European or the West Indian trade, or themselves fitted out as privateers; the flour, Indian corn, pork, beef, and some of the rum, sugar and molasses found a ready sale in the city markets or with the army and navy commissaries; the tobacco, naval stores, indigo and silver coins, and much of the West Indian products went to Great Britain to balance the incoming stream of manufactured goods.

As we have seen, English goods were needed, not only to supply the people of Manhattan, Staten Island and Long Island, but for the illegal trade with New England and New Jersey. Some of the merchants had agents at Southampton and other points on the east end of Long Island to whom they sent large consignments of cloth, clothing, hardware, etc. The agents in turn kept in touch with boatmen in Connecticut, who came over on dark nights to take on the goods and distribute them to New England traders. Much danger attended this business, for though the New York merchants, by a well placed bribe, were reasonably safe in getting their goods out of the city, they might be seized in the Sound by one of the King's cruisers, or in Connecticut by State officials. But the profits were so great that it paid to take the risk. [49]

Judge Jones thought that the trade to New England was "no ways prejudicial to the King's service, provided that powder, lead, flints and other military stores" were not included, for it brought provisions of all kinds to the New York market and drained the Americans of their hard money. "The merchants had a large vent for their merchandise . . . It assisted the royal army, and it distressed rebellion." [50] Apparently Congress thought so too, for it passed a resolution calling upon the States to confiscate all English goods found within their borders. "The merchants of New York and their associates in a number of these states employ every kind of means for conveying English goods through this continent," wrote one observer. "We see by the New York gazettes and by divers letters from that city that the inhabitants are enraged at the late resolves of Congress . . . This is one proof that these resolutions have struck them in a most sensible part." [51] None the less, the traffic continued until, in 1782, the approach of peace brought about a resumption of open trade between New York and Boston, Philadelphia and other American ports.

Whereas some of the refugees grew rich on foreign trade and privateering, others, many of them persons of refinement and formerly possessed of large estates, were reduced to poverty. The farmer of upper New York, or New England or New Jersey, when he fled the wrath of the Revolutionists, had to leave behind him his house, his land, his barn, his crops, his cattle and bring with him nothing but the clothes on his back. Knowing no other trade than agriculture, when he reached the city he found it difficult to earn a living. To add to his troubles, the patriots, not wishing to feed his wife and children, were sure to send them after him.

"It is impossible for any pen to describe the agonies I endured prior to my arrival here last June, since which my personal property has been confiscated and my family banished," Joshua Hett Smith wrote Clinton, in November, 1781. "What I had in this town I have indeed been put in possession of . . . but . . . it yields me no more than £140 currency per annum, so that I am every day at straits for the bare necessities of life to subsist a family of six adult persons and three children." [52]

But Smith was fortunate compared with John Harlock, a refugee from Bergen County, New Jersey. He had persuaded some of his neighbors not to bear arms against the King, so that to escape persecution he had been forced to flee with his family, leaving behind all his possessions. In the city he supported his wife and six children "by his industry," until his eyesight failed, when he was obliged to appeal to headquarters for help.[53]

Typical was the case of John Peter Lawson. The owner of a farm of 200 acres in Dutchess County, "under the blessing of God" he lived "in affluence of every good thing, having his farm well stocked with all sorts of cattle and a family of negroes." But because of his loyalty to the King he "was obliged in order to save his life to leave his family and quit all his possessions." Upon arriving within the British lines he joined the Corps of Guides and Pioneers, serving in both New York and Pennsylvania until bad health forced him to retire. When the Revolutionists heard that Lawson had entered the King's service, "they sold . . . his farm, effects, grain, live stock, negroes etc., and sent his wife with her two children . . . to the city of New York, allowing her no more but eight days' provisions to take along." [54]

John Weatherbed, an Englishman by birth, thought it his duty, "publicly or privately" to "encourage all as appeared willing to abide by their allegiance." As a result he was "insulted and threatened with death." At last he and his family fled "to avoid the fury of a body of rebel riflemen" who had orders to seize him in his bed in the dead of night, and took refuge on a British warship. To add to his misfortunes the dreadful fire of September 1776 laid almost all his property in ashes. [55]

The experiences of Sereno Edwards Dwight, of Northampton, Massachusetts, which would fit into the pages of one of James Fenimore Cooper's novels, were the most thrilling of all. "Insulted, imprisoned and threatened with death," he was obliged to "quit his native country and seek an asylum in West Florida at Natchez, on the Mississippi." But even here he was not safe, and when the Spaniards raided the place, he abandoned "a considerable property," and with his wife and children set out through the wilderness for New York 1,500 miles away. Day after day, week after week, month after month they journeyed on, weary and ragged, sleeping in the woods, exposed to the weather, trying to hush the cries of the children and "calm the preying hunger." [56] As a small compensation for his losses and suffering Dwight asked General Clinton to make him an ensign in the King's American Regiment.

It was with a sense of relief that the refugee sighted the roofs and steeples of New York, for he knew that at last he would be free from persecution. But he found that life there was to be no bed of roses. The destruction of a large part of the city by the fire of 1776, the presence of thousands of soldiers and sailors, many of whom had brought their wives and children, and the influx of his fellow refugees combined to create an acute housing problem. To some of the early comers Howe allotted space in the deserted houses of the Revolutionists, and when this proved inadequate, he granted permission to others to build on vacant lots. Mayor Matthews stated that this had been "the means of rendering great numbers very comfortable," but at best it was a makeshift. Many lacked the means to build, labor was costly, materials scarce. "Canvas town" was the name given to the collection of huts, erected by placing pieces of spars on chimneys and parts of walls and covering them with old canvas, which sprang up on parts of the area burnt over in 1776.

The situation grew worse as the war wore on. The first comers had been largely from neighboring colonies, with a group from Virginia, who accompanied Lord Dunmore when he sailed into the harbor on August 15, 1776. But with the evacuation of Philadelphia, as we have seen, several thousand newcomers were added to the crowded population. In August, 1782, after Savannah had been abandoned by the British, "most of the officers, some of the inhabitants and the sick men" were brought to New York.[57] The following January another contingent came in from Charleston. In addition to these large groups, "persons from all parts of this continent . . . were constantly coming to this city." [58] In November 1782, when it was rumored that New York was to be evacuated at once by the King's forces, the *Royal Gazette* stated that this would entail the abandoning of 60,000 persons within the British lines, who with their property would be sacrificed to "rebel resentment." [59]

When the refugee at last found a roof over his head, his next thought was to secure food and fuel for himself and his family. For this he had to go, hat in hand, to General Robertson. Clinton had thought of establishing a board to distribute the King's bounty, but "when he considered the personal dislikes, piques and provincial prejudices that appeared in the conversations he had with the most moderate of the refugees," it convinced him that it was better to have the matter in the hands of one man. If the refugee could convince the old general that his was a deserving case, he would issue orders to allow him a certain number of rations and a certain number of cords of firewood. This was better than paying out money, Clinton thought, because with flour costing from £5 to £10 per hundredweight, and wood almost unobtainable, no sum which he could grant would be adequate.[60]

For General Robertson, old as he was and charged with very heavy responsibilities, to enquire into the claims of thousands of refugees, was obviously impossible. So he was forced to turn this duty over to Colonel Roger Morris, with the title of Inspector of the Claims of the Refugees. To fill this office acceptably would have required tact, sympathy, diligence and impartiality, and Morris seems to have had none of these qualities. In January 1782, 361 refugees signed a memorial to Clinton complaining of his conduct. "His total ignorance of the character of the refugees," his "austere manners," his inhumanity and his suspicion "of his Majesty's good subjects," were defeating the King's good intentions in granting relief. They hoped, therefore, that Clinton would grant them relief by removing so extremely obnoxious a person.[61]

When Sir Guy Carleton arrived to take over the supreme command, these complaints were no doubt poured into his ears. Carleton at once took matters in hand by appointing a board of four men, headed by Robertson, "to regulate the bounty of government to the refugees." A stop was put to the practice of handing out "rations of provisions, wood and forage," and instead, those who the board thought had a valid claim, were voted a pension of £20 a year.[62]

In the closing months of the war New York became the sole refuge on American soil for the Tories, to which they flocked from all directions. If one had stopped at the board office to watch those who came in to apply for aid, one would have found that this farmer was from Westchester County, this man from New Jersey, this from Connecticut, this from Virginia, that from Georgia. In the first three months of the year 1783, the board granted pensions amounting to £9,491.-12.6 to 540 persons, of whom 212 were from New York, 105 from New Jersey, 143 from New England, 40 from Pennsylvania, 29 from the south and one from Canada.[63]

One wonders whether the refugees gained by the substitution of pensions for rations. When they went to market they found there beef, pork, bread, vegetables and fish in abundance, but at prices few could afford. The old expedient of price ceilings was tried over and over. The price of bread was fixed, the price of meat was fixed, the price of tea water was fixed, the price of firewood was fixed. A notice was put in the newspapers warning "hucksters or other persons who may be detected forestalling any provisions or vegetables," that they could "depend on being treated with the utmost rigour." But the black market continued to flourish. On November 17, 1781, Parson Shewkirk wrote hopefully in his *Diary*: "A proclamation of the governor was issued today respecting firewood, which will afford much relief, for the distress and extortion has been great." Four weeks later he added: "Weather very cold, great distress for want of wood, the proclamation of no avail."

How openly the regulations were flouted we gather from a letter by an officer of the *Black George* to a friend in Edinburgh, written in September, 1782: "Every necessary here is beyond imagination dear;

beef and mutton from 2 s. to 2 s. 6 d., and none under a general or a commissary can get a fowl or goose. I yesterday gave three dollars for a pair of shoes." [64]

It must have been with a sense of injustice that the wife of a refugee, who perhaps had once lived in plenty, watched the new rich of the city—corrupt commissaries or the owners of privateers—buy everything they needed, while she had to count pennies to keep hunger from her family. As for the many lavish dinners, the dances, the theatre parties, she was obliged to stay at home, even though she and her husband received invitations, since she could not afford a suitable dress, and it was impossible for her to return the proffered hospitality.

Living in the city was made more difficult by the prevalence of crime. With every dark corner crowded with thieves and bawds, with low dens down on the wharves handing out grog, with drunken soldiers and sailors prowling the streets at night, Andrew Elliot's police proved entirely inadequate to the task of preserving order. From time to time the citizens organized a night watch, who patrolled the streets with arms in their hands, but still the robberies and murders continued. Women could not venture out after dark without running the risk of being insulted, men were set upon by thieves, robbed and beaten. "I could narrate many and very frightful occurrences of theft, fraud, robbery and murder by the English soldiers which their love of drink excited," wrote Lieutenant Von Kraft in his journal. After one unpleasant encounter, when he went for a walk in the evening he thought it prudent to take two German soldiers to follow at a little distance. [65]

One set of sharpers hung around the market to entice unsuspecting farmers into taverns, "pretending business with them," and there defrauding them of large sums of money. [66] Even worse was the fate of Mr. Peter Ball, who one night at eleven o'clock, while walking along Broadway, was attacked by five men, who knocked him down, threatened to kill him if he called for help, and robbed him of his cash, shoes, buckles, broach, Freemason's apron, keys, etc. [67] "In this city robberies constantly take place," wrote Shewkirk in January 1781, "persons have been attacked on the streets and a woman and a Scotch officer murdered, mostly by soldiery." Although in the autumn of 1783 the police made a raid on the city dives which netted fifteen men, hardly a night passed without a robbery. [68]

Nor was the danger which honest men incurred on the streets entirely from robbers and drunken soldiers, for they ran the risk of being pressed into the royal navy. From time to time, when the ships of the line, frigates and other war vessels were undermanned because of sickness or desertion, armed groups of sailors and marines scoured the city to pick up every able-bodied man they could lay their hands on. Visiting every grog shop, every low tavern, every seaman's lodging house, they dragged off sailors of the merchant marine, local boatmen, clerks in the stores, perhaps even a few farm hands.

In August, 1780, "there was the hottest press" in New York the city had ever seen, the armed sailors taking not only seamen, "but all the refugees, laborers and merchant's clerks they came across." [69] Eight months later, when the fleet, which was preparing to put to sea, was short of sailors because many of the men were ill, "a very hot press took place by which several hundred men from the city were carried on board the fleet." [70] We can only surmise what bitter thoughts came to the man whose loyalty to the King had forced him to seek refuge in New York, as the press gang laid hold of him, or as he was rowed away to the fleet, or as he scrubbed the deck of a transport or climbed the rigging to take a hand in unfurling a sail. He may even have agreed with the *New Jersey Gazette* in thinking pressing "unexampled barbarity."

One must not imagine that Loyalist New York was given over entirely to the very rich and the very poor, for there was a vigorous middle class made up of shopkeepers, tavern keepers, artisans. Some of these had been in the city before the British occupation; others came in as refugees. It was not an easy matter, however, for a shopkeeper of Norfolk or Philadelphia or Charleston to transfer his business to New York. In the excitement and haste when the British were preparing to evacuate these places it was difficult for him to find a merchant vessel to move his stock of goods, while there was no room for them on the crowded transports. If he had brought along a little capital, or if he had friends who would advance him credit, he could open shop on a small scale, otherwise he had to look for employment or depend on the King's bounty.[71]

Yet on Hanover Square, William Street and Wall Street there were even more shops than in former days, stocked to the ceiling with all kinds of goods and filled with customers. At Daniel Wright's place, "half way between the Coffee House and Lord Howe's," one found "strong shoes suitable for soldiers and gentlemen," old rum, loaf and brown sugar, best hyson tea, bohea tea, table knives and forks, "common and plated buckles," etc.[72] Around the corner at No. 19 Wall Street, next door to Taylor and Bayard's store, Joseph Corre opened a bakery where customers could find "all kinds of confectionary and pastry." [73]

If one were looking for any article of general merchandise—shoes and boots, handkerchiefs, Irish linen, calico, satin, hose, gloves, razors, umbrellas, carpets, teakettles, hair powder, etc.—it was to be found at Alexander Lockie's, at No. 22 Hanover Square. But should the customer desire to see what Mr. Lockie's competitors had in stock, he could move on to the stores of Benjamin Waddington and Co., Joseph Brewer, Joseph Allicocke, Bell and Hill, and William Backhouse and Co. Among the leading wine merchants were Richard Yates, Edward Gould, Alexander Wallace and Richard Deane; groceries were sold by William Burton, Michael Price, Jacobus Lefferts and Isaac Winslow.[74]

For the artisan who fled to New York to establish himself was easier than for the shopkeeper. If he were a shoemaker, or a tailor, or a locksmith, he might have put his tools in his saddlebags and made the journey by horse; if a carpenter or blacksmith or cabinetmaker or saddler, a good sized chest which could be stored in the hold of a transport would contain enough saws, hammers, planes, etc. to make it possible for him to continue his trade in his new home. So among the skilled workers whose little shops lined Queen Street, there must have been a large proportion of refugees.

At No. 30, at the corner of Burling Slip, Thomas Thomas, "tin man," had on hand "tin, copper, pewter and japanned ware," such as plate warmers, stewpans, desk covers, tureens, and "signal lanterns." [75] Further along the street at No. 55, John Barr, "saddler and cap-maker," sold men and women's saddles, saddle-cloths, bridles, portmanteaux, trunks, saddlebags, whips, spurs, etc.[76] Up at No. 176, near Peck's Slip, Daniel Hartung, under the sign of the Cap and Muff, "furrier, late from London," had in stock muffs, tippets, gloves lined with fur, squirrel linings of cloaks, gentlemen's travelling caps, etc.[77] Down near the Coffee House bridge, Robert Montgomery carried on the trade of clockmaker and engraver, "in all its various branches." [78]

The increase in the population of the city during the British occupation and the presence of thousands of soldiers and sailors made it boom times for tavern keepers. The best taverns made a point of catering to officers of the royal forces, for both British and Germans were free spenders, and gave costly dinners at which wine flowed freely. There must have been many a jolly party at the Navy Coffee House, near the Battery, under the Sign of Lord Cornwallis, where the public in general and the gentlemen of the navy and army in particular, were invited to partake of the excellent food served by the host, Alexander Grant.[79] Lenox's tavern on Wall Street, noted for its sign of the Indian King, representing the celebrated Joseph Brant, was a meeting place for the Loyalists. The merchants often came in to Ashley's tavern, at No. 2 Water Street, to talk over the latest news of the West Indian market or a naval victory or the exploits of this privateer or that.[80]

For those who could not afford the prices charged by Lenox or Ashley or Roubalet, "a glass of excellent purl piping hot" could be had at the sign of the Faithful Irishman and Jolly Sailors, in King Street. Apparently some of the sailors, and others as well, became too jolly, for General Pattison had to warn tavern keepers that their licences would be withdrawn if they continued "to harbor or tolerate any riotous or disorderly companies." There were too many taverns and public houses in the city, he thought, and he was determined to limit their number to 200. In order to eliminate convivial drinking in the taprooms, he instituted a forerunner of the modern package store by announcing that licenses would be issued to persons retailing spirituous liquors in quantities less than five gallons only on condition that "the same be not drunk within their houses or sold in less quantity than a quart." [81]

One of the best known hosts was Charles Roubalet, proprietor of the famous City Tavern at 115 Broadway. Here was held the "Garrison Assembly," when every two weeks "officers of the army, navy and public departments" went through the minuet or country dances with the belles of New York. Here, also, were to be had delicious food and excellent wine. How good a place it was to spend money becomes obvious by a glance at the bill Roubalet presented Major Phillips and Captain Armstrong: For two dinners £7.4, for six plates of fruit 12 s., for tea and coffee for eight persons £1.4, for wine £18.3, for grog 1 s., for two bowls of wine and bitters £1.12, for six apples £1.4, for "segars" 8 s., for two "spermaceti lights 8 s." [82]

The Brooklyn Ferry House, renamed the King's Head Tavern by its proprietor, one Loosley, was a meeting place for persons fond of racing, cricket, bull baiting and fox hunting. Whether the sportsmen failed to pay their bills, or whether Loosley was a poor manager, he went into bankruptcy, and in November, 1782, all his household effects were sold. By following the auctioneer from room to room one learns much about the furniture, equipment and accessories of the typical tavern. Card tables, a billiard table and an organ testify to the amusements offered the guests; mahogany bedsteads, feather beds, mattresses, chintz curtains, sheets make the bedrooms attractive and comfortable; "table and tea sets of china," damask and "other table linen" were to be found in the dining room and utensils of all kinds in the kitchen; and to the reception rooms "an elegant clock in a mahogany case" and "a curious collection of well chosen paintings and pictures" added interest and charm. In the stable were a wagon, horses, cows, etc., while stored away for celebrations were ensigns and pendants and several hundred "transparent and tin lamps fit for an illumination." [83]

For the tavern keepers it was by no means all profits and good times. Among the Pennsylvania refugees who arrived with the fleet when the British evacuated Philadelphia, was John Hales, a tavern keeper. "In consideration of the losses he suffered for his loyalty," he was allotted a house in King Street by an order from headquarters, where after spending upwards of £300 to make it habitable, he re-entered business under the sign of the Tally-Ho. But a year later, to his dismay, he was ordered to vacate the house to "make room for the troops." We are not informed whether or not the ouster was put into effect, or whether he was indemnified so that he could hang out his sign at some other place, but in September 1780, he was still in business.[84]

The mistake of Henry Branett was in being too trusting of the German soldiers who frequented his tavern. In July 1783, he made a complaint to General Carleton, stating that a large sum was due him, especially from members of the Hesse Hanau Chasseurs and the An-halt Zerbst Corps. He had applied to the commanders of these corps in vain, so he now asked Carleton to deduct the money from the soldiers' wages, "or cause him such other relief" as he thought fit.[85]

And so life in Tory New York moved on toward the end, to the day when the thousands of men, women and children who for seven years had thronged its streets, turned their backs on the familiar scenes and sailed away, never to return. A strange, abnormal, almost feverish life it was, a life marked by the sudden acquisition of wealth by some, the plunging of others into poverty; by gaiety and extravagance and by cold and hunger; by bitter hatreds and cruelty; by immorality, corruption and lawlessness; by alternating elation and despair. Yet through it all men went about their daily tasks as usual, the merchant sending out his cargoes, the storekeeper offering his wares for sale, the artisan fashioning his shoes or silverware or saddles, the host welcoming his patrons to his tavern, the cartmen rattling over the streets, the water carriers going from house to house, as though no eighteenth century atomic bomb was hanging over their heads, the bomb of a peace acknowledging American independence and calling for the evacuation of the city.

CHAPTER X

THE FRATRICIDAL STRIFE

IN THE early days of the war great hopes were reposed in the military aid which the Loyalists could give to the British cause. Among the thousands who poured into New York were many young men capable of bearing arms, and whose incentive for fighting was greater than that of the British regulars and far greater than that of the Hessians. When they came to General Robertson's office asking for rations or pensions, it would be but natural for the general to ask why they did not join one of the provincial corps and go out and fight for the King.

When it was announced in November, 1777, that a plan was on foot to raise a battalion of provincial troops, Rivington gave it hearty support. "That we are involved in a war which threatens ruin to this country, I need not observe," he wrote in his *Royal Gazette*. "Everything that can be dear to men is threatened by it, your property, your liberty, your lives, your religion . . . When you see the officers and soldiers of our august and Royal Master and his allies exerting themselves in every quarter and encountering every danger for your defence, when you see them bleeding and dying that you may live in peace and security, can you possibly refuse to share the fatigue and danger with them?" [1]

Nor were the refugees unwilling to enlist. To the young men who had enjoyed wealth and position in their former homes, a commission in the King's American Regiment or the Queen's Rangers offered a fair salary, possible promotion and an opportunity for revenge. To the poor—farm hands, laborers, idle mechanics—it meant bread and butter, a warm suit of clothes and the promise of land at the conclusion of the war. So scores assembled at Mr. Waldron Blaau's, in Little Dock Street, near the Exchange; or the Bull's Head Tavern, in the Bowery; or at the Queen's Head Tavern, to put their names to the

muster rolls and receive their uniforms, swords, muskets and powder.

From the purely military point of view, the greatest efficiency
would have been attained by running the American recruits into British regiments, and to some extent this seems to have been done. But
the refugees, hungry though some of them were, could not stomach the
strict discipline, poor pay and social inferiority which was the lot of
the British private. The life in America had made them too proud, too
impatient of restraint. At the same time, it was almost out of the question for a provincial to procure a commission in the regular army, no
matter how great his influence, and no matter how much he was willing to pay. A commission was a coveted prize, reserved for the British
aristocracy.

So, from the first, the efforts of General Howe and General Clinton
were directed toward organizing distinctly provincial corps. And these,
so they thought, should not be filled indiscriminately with men from
various colonies. "When it is considered that they have resorted hither
from several rebellious colonies," it was pointed out, "which must
necessarily create distinctions and parties among them and which perhaps are subdivided by more local prejudices and animosities, it may
be difficult to combine their force so as to render it efficient." In other
words, it was thought that it would not do to have Rhode Islanders
and Carolinians fighting side by side, or Virginians taking orders from
a captain or a colonel from Boston. So the Loyalist regiments were
organized in large part by colonies, or in some cases by counties—
the New York Volunteers, the Bucks County Light Dragoons, the
Staten Island Volunteers, the Pennsylvania Loyalists, the Maryland
Loyalists, the New Jersey Volunteers, the Massachusetts Volunteers.
The same fear of local jealousies influenced Howe, in selecting the
provincial commander-in-chief, to pass over the claims of leading
colonials in favor of Governor Tryon, who though a man of wide ac-
quaintance in America, was born in Ireland.

As a stimulus to enrollment, Howe promised 200 acres of public
land, which he hoped to take from the Americans, to every noncom-
missioned officer who served two years, and to every private soldier
50 acres. Soon the streets of the city resounded to the beat of shoes on
the cobblestones and the sharp commands of drillmasters, as the
troops went through their maneuvres.[2] A very smart appearance they
must have made in their green uniforms faced some with white, some

with green, some with blue, white trousers, brown leggings, coarse felt hats and pewter buttons bearing the letters R P for Royal Provincial. Occasionally a troop of chasseurs would gallop by, in their green coats with blue facing, blue waistcoats, white breeches, high boots, blue shoulder bands and cocked hats.

And now the old dispute over the relative rank of officers of the line and provincials, which had caused so much trouble during the French and Indian War, arose again to create ill will. Two decades earlier, George Washington had protested against the regulation which placed a captain of the line on a par with a colonial colonel, and the Loyalist officers were equally vexed when the same rule was imposed on them.

Later, when Germain sent orders that provincial officers should "command according to their rank," the British in turn were offended. As for Germain's further order that no subaltern regular should be made a provincial field officer, it was ridiculed whenever two or more redcoats got together. Perhaps Germain thought that subalterns could not possibly know as much about military affairs "as any butcher or baker" he might "pick up in the country," they said. But though "every officer in the army remonstrated," the orders were not rescinded.[3]

In fact, Germain was elated at the news that the Loyalists were taking up arms to aid in suppressing the Revolution, and was determined to encourage them in every way possible. His most perplexing problem, the problem of securing men, would be in part solved if he could place ten or twenty fully equipped provincial regiments at the disposal of the commander-in-chief. So, for the moment, the provincials were his pets. He gave orders that any of their officers who were maimed were to have "the same gratuity of one year's advanced pay as officers of the regular army," that when a provincial regiment had filled its ranks the officers were to be on a permanent footing, that a bounty of twenty-two shillings, sixpence be offered for enlistments.[4]

Nor were Germain's hopes entirely disappointed. In March, 1779, of the provincials in New York, the Queen's American Rangers and Hussars numbered 480 men, the New Jersey Volunteers 810, De Lancey's Brigade 226, the Loyal American Regiment 271, the British Legion 441, the Volunteers of Ireland 494, and other detachments 425, a total of 3,147.[5] In fact, although the numbers of the various detachments varied from time to time, the British commanders usually had several thousand provincial troops upon whom to fall back in case of need.

Howe hoped that some of the Loyalist regiments would so prove their efficiency that they could be taken along on important campaigns to fight side by side with the British and Hessians. But though occasionally we find this regiment or that storming a Highlands fort or taking part in a major battle, their chief service was to act as a home guard for New York City, Long Island, Staten Island and Westchester and make raids into New Jersey and Connecticut. Now we find them crossing the Hudson to descend on the farm of some ardent patriot, now surprising a nest of privateers in a secluded harbor on the New Jersey coast, now driving down to Manhattan a herd of cattle gathered in northern Westchester, now burning and pillaging the villages of southern Connecticut.

One of the first regiments to be organized, the one which achieved the best record, and the only one which Clinton "dared send out of the continent," was the Queen's Rangers. Raised by Lieutenant Colonel Rogers, and whipped into shape by Major Wernyss, the regiment was finally put under the able Lieutenant Colonel Simcoe, of the 41st Infantry. The eight companies of riflemen, one company of grenadiers, one of light infantry, one of Highlanders, and one of hussars, with their green coats and waistcoats faced with blue, white small clothes and black leather caps, were seen on many a battlefield. They accompanied Clinton in the Philadelphia campaign, when "the whole army did ample justice to their merit and services"; they were numbered among the troops sent to Jamaica in response to Governor Dalling's appeal for help in 1779; [6] they were constantly making incursions into the neighboring states.

Typical of these raids was that of October, 1779, when Colonel Simcoe, with his Rangers and the Bucks County Volunteers, landed at Perth Amboy, and leaving his infantry at South River, galloped on with 100 horse to Bound Brook, where he destroyed eighteen flatboats and some stores. Then, after proceeding to Somerset Court House to release "several suffering Loyalists," he started on his return. But the militia had now assembled and hung on his flank to keep up a constant fire. One discharge from a wood killed Simcoe's horse, which, falling on him, caused his capture, a mishap which he thought the "very malice of fortune." Governor Livingston, though receiving him with politeness, assured him that for his own sake it was best not to grant him a parole, but to keep him in confinement so save him from insult.[7]

Very different from the hard fighting Queen's Rangers were the King's American Dragoons. Organized in February, 1782, four months after the British disaster at Yorktown, by Benjamin Thompson, the Massachusetts scientist who later was made Count Rumford because of his distinguished services at the Court of the Elector of Bavaria, its chief purpose seems to have been to give employment to young aristocrats forced into idleness by the disintegration of the regiments in which they had seen service. Thompson had no trouble in securing officers, who were "to a man American," but as late as June, 1782, he was still seeking recruits for the ranks. "Any likely spirited young lads who are desirous of distinguishing themselves by serving their King and country and who prefer riding on horseback to going on foot," were asked to apply at once at the regimental headquarters. Volunteers were to have a bounty of ten guineas and were to serve for five years, or for the duration of the war.[8]

The day of days for the King's American Dragoons came on August 1, 1782, when all the fashion and beauty of New York went out to the encampment to witness the ceremonies in which Prince William Henry delivered their standards to the regiment. The prince passed along the line of horsemen, who stood at attention, their swords and helmets glittering, while the trumpets sounded and the band played *God Save the King*. He then seated himself under a canopy while the dragoons went through their maneuvres. Then dismounting, the men formed in a semicircle in front of the pavilion, and laying their helmets and arms on the ground, knelt and with their right hands lifted, took an oath of allegiance to the King and of fidelity to their standard. After they had saluted, the prince took the flags from the hands of Admiral Digby and presented them to Lieutenant Colonel Thompson. Thereupon "the whole regiment, with all the numerous spectators, gave three shouts, the trumpets sounded, the music played *God Save the King*, the artillery fired a royal salute and the ceremony was concluded.[9]

Ardent Loyalists the original members of the New York Volunteers must have been, for, slipping away from their homes in the Highlands in the spring and summer of 1776, they made their way hundreds of miles to Halifax, where they offered their services to General Howe.

Sir William organized them into two independent companies, one under Captain Campbell and the other under Captain Grant. From Halifax they returned with the invading British army and fought gallantly at the Battle of Long Island, took part in the storming of Fort Montgomery and accompanied Lieutenant Colonel Archibald Campbell in his expedition to Georgia. From this last expedition they returned with ranks so depleted that a recruiting office was opened in Dock Street, opposite Fraunce's Tavern, and large rewards offered to persons bringing in volunteers. "As the said regiment chiefly consists of refugees from the Highlands and Hudson River," stated a notice in the *Royal Gazette*, "it is hoped that all young men from that part of the province will cheerfully join it, by which means they will have the satisfaction of once more meeting their neighbors and relations." [10] But fate decreed that most of them should never see their neighbors again, for in August 1783, we find them preparing to go aboard the transports which a few days later were to take them into exile in far away New Brunswick.[11]

Such great things had been expected of the provincials that Clinton, despite the excellent records made by some of the regiments, was deeply disappointed at the sum total of accomplishment. "It will not be out of place here to express my regret at seeing the incomplete state of the provincial corps," he wrote to Germain in December, 1779. "So many attempts to raise men have always totally failed of success, and some corps which at first promised to be of importance have remained notwithstanding in so very weak a state that there is little encouragement to undertake anything more in that line." There were many who offered themselves as officers, in fact there was a long waiting list, but the enlistments as privates were few. Experience had taught him to "distrust the sanguine hopes of gentlemen" who offered to raise new corps, especially when they expected the British chest to finance the purchase of uniforms and arms.[12]

Nor was his confidence in the New York Loyalist militia any greater. As early as 1776, twenty volunteer companies were formed to defend the city from possible attack, guard prisoners and erect fortifications. Typical was the First Independent Company of New York Rangers, numbering 120 men and commanded by Captain Christopher Benson. In their short red coats with blue trimmings, white-lined cape and round buckskin hat set off with a black feather, they made a fine showing on parade. But their duties, which consisted chiefly in guarding East Wharf, prison duty and throwing up redoubts, brought them no glory and much monotonous work.[13]

A year later Theophilus Bache wrote Clinton pointing out that there were thousands of loyal men within the British lines who could be relied upon to turn out for the defence of the city. "They should be immediately armed and organized by an experienced officer," he advised. "Each company should consist of fifty privates, one drum, two corporals, two sergeants, two lieutenants and a captain." In Queens alone there were 1,500 militia already organized and armed, and the city, as well as the other loyal counties, should follow their example.[14]

Interest in the militia lagged, however, until the reduction of the regular garrison by the sending of many detachments to the south, together with the freezing of the waters surrounding Manhattan in the winter of 1779–1780, made it necessary to put every available man under arms. It gave the people a sense of security to see the companies drilling or working on the fortifications, and even Clinton thought that they would be useful in case Washington attacked the city. But he pointed out that the militia "consisted in merchants, tradesmen and men attached to the different army and navy departments, of sailors, watermen and others" who could leave their daily employments only in times of emergency.[15] As for their numbers, he thought they had been "stretched to make a figure upon paper" and that at least half of the persons listed could not be trusted. Some 2,300 "tolerably good bourgeois" might be found who would fight to defend their property, but that was all.[16] In October, 1782, the militia numbered 2,958 Lieutenant Colonel Walton's battalion, with 651 men, being the largest detachment, Lieutenant Colonel Leake's battalion next, with 514, and Benson's New York Rangers far down the list with only 80.[17]

It was in the nature of things that the Loyalist militia played, had to play, a far less important role in the war than the American militia. Each was primarily a defensive body, made up of men who laid down the plow or the leather apron to seize their arms on the approach of the enemy. But while the patriot militia was called on over and over again, and were respected and dreaded by the British, the militia of Tory New York saw little real fighting. They constituted only the third line of defence, the first line being the British navy which patrolled the waters around Manhattan, Staten Island and Long Island, and the second line the British army. And as it happened the third line was seldom if ever needed.

Far more active, far more dreaded by the Revolutionists, were the Associated Loyalists. It was in the summer of 1779 that General Tryon wrote Clinton suggesting that groups of refugees, not in any of the provincial corps, form an independent association to carry on hostilities against the enemy. Under the presidency of William Franklin, former governor of New Jersey, they were to establish posts in New York, on Long Island, Sandy Hook and elsewhere, from which to send raiding expeditions into Connecticut and New Jersey to bring off cattle and make prisoners. But Clinton demurred. He objected to having an independent military command "alarming the enemy when he might wish to lull them into security," and drawing on the military chest when he might have other more important uses for the money.[18]

Thereupon some of the refugees went over Clinton's head by taking the matter up with Lord Germain through a memorial presented by George Leonard. The association, Leonard pointed out, would be an excellent means of employing the zeal of the King's faithful subjects in annoying the coasts of the revolted provinces and distressing their trade. Germain liked the idea; King George liked the idea. So the memorialists were made a Board of Directors and given authority to go ahead.[19]

In January 1781, the Board met to perfect their plans and to organize their forces. Each company was to consist of 46 privates, four sergeants, four corporals, an ensign, a lieutenant and a captain. When five companies had been formed they were to constitute a battalion, under a lieutenant colonel. Nor was there any lack of volunteers, for hundreds of refugees welcomed the opportunity of filling their pockets at the expense of the hated Revolutionists. George Ogilvie was authorized to raise a company; Thomas Hazard, Thomas Ward, Charles Nomfray, Edward Michaels, Jeremiah Pemberton, Michael Clarke, David Ives, Richard Lippincott were authorized to raise companies.[20]

Gathering a fleet of sloops, schooners and whaleboats, the Associators, many of whom had lived in Connecticut or New Jersey and were well acquainted with every creek, cove, river and harbor in those states, set out on raid after raid. Waiting for some dark night, they hoisted sail, and making their way across Long Island Sound or along the New Jersey coast, descended on isolated villages and farms, to capture "noted rebels" and bring off cattle, horses, hogs, poultry, furniture, slaves, clothes and anything else for which there was room in their vessels. And what they could not take with them—houses, barns and even churches—they burned down.[21]

Throughout the summer of 1781 the people of southern Connecticut, when they retired at night, did so with the realization that they might at any moment be pulled out of bed and hustled off into captivity by the light of their burning houses. On July 21, a Captain Frost, crossing the Sound at night, crept ashore and concealed his men near the Middlesex meetinghouse. The next afternoon, when the congregation assembled for worship, the Associators surrounded the building, and rudely interrupting the services, arrested the minister and fifty "notorious rebels." These, together with forty horses "ready saddled," they marched off to the shore amid a scattering fire from the neighboring militia, put them aboard their vessels and brought them over to the post at Lloyd's Neck.[22]

Not all the expeditions were so successful. When Major Hubbell led a band of raiders into Connecticut and seized a number of cattle and horses he was waylaid by the militia and a few Continentals and he and four others were wounded.[23] An expedition to West Haven, while returning across the Sound, ran into a squall which sank the brig *Sir Henry Clinton* and drowned four men.[24] Moreover, the depredations of the Associators brought retaliation which cost the people of Long Island dear. Sloops and whaleboats were fitted out in the Connecticut harbors, and filled with armed men who took ample revenge. Though they burned no churches and no dwellings, they plundered the farmers, took off cattle and destroyed sawmills which had been working for the British army.[25]

But when men indulge in wholesale plunder, when one side seeks revenge for the damage inflicted by the other and the other in turn retaliates, when hatreds become intense, it is almost inevitable that personal violence and even murder will follow. Lord Germain should have foreseen this when he gave permission to the refugees to organize the Associated Loyalists; perhaps Clinton did foresee it when he interposed his objections. As the *Royal Gazette* pointed out, in a struggle such as this "men are hurried on by prejudice, rage and resentment, to perpetrate the greatest enormities without remorse, and you might as well reason with a whirlwind as reason with them." [26] On the whole, the Associators did the British cause more harm than good, for whatever hurt they did to the American war effort was more than offset by the inflexible determination to win which their violence created in the minds of the people of the neighboring colonies.

So now stories were circulated on both sides of the brutality of the other to prisoners. The Associators complained that when they fell into the hands of the Connecticut militia, they were stripped of their clothing, or put in irons, or "buried alive" in the Simsbury mine. Oliver De Lancey hanged one of his prisoners in retaliation for the alleged hanging of one of his refugees. In New Jersey, a law had been passed making all citizens of the state who fought with the British guilty of treason, under which some of the Associators were tried and executed. General Forman, known to the refugees as Black David, "butchered in cold blood" several men "under the usurped law." [27]

It was in April, 1782, that an incident occurred which brought matters to a head and created a sensation in Great Britain as well as America. At a meeting of the Board of the Associated Loyalists, Captain Richard Lippincott received permission to take three prisoners from the provost jail in New York to Monmouth County where they were to be exchanged. Interpreting his orders in a very "broad" sense, perhaps with the sanction of some of the Board, he "exchanged" Joshua Huddy for an Associator named White whom he claimed the Americans had executed, by taking Huddy to the heights near Middletown and there hanging him.[28]

The people of the neighborhood, when they found the body hanging with a placard attached, probably as a warning to "rebels", notified General Knox, and Knox notified Washington. Thereupon Washington wrote Clinton that unless the murderer were delivered to him for punishment, he would retaliate by hanging a British captain. And when Clinton hesitated, he actually made a number of officers draw lots, the black ball falling to an attractive young aristocrat named Asgill. This put an entirely different light on the matter. For one of De Lancey's "cowboys" or an Associator from New Jersey to be strung up was not a matter of the greatest importance, but for a captain of the Guard to be threatened with such a fate was unthinkable.[29]

Clinton had Lippincott lodged in jail, charged with murder and tried by court-martial. The Associated Loyalists were furious. They could hardly believe, they wrote Clinton, that he had taken such a step because of the threats of a "rebel general." The Associators had looked to him in vain to protect them from the outrages of the rebels, and now, when one of their number had taken matters into his own hands, he was treated like a criminal. None the less, Clinton persisted, as did Sir Guy Carleton, who arrived to take command while the excitement was at its height.[30]

At the trial Lippincott first pleaded that the court did not have jurisdiction in the case, since Huddy was hanged in New Jersey. When this was decided against him, he claimed that he had acted, if not under the orders of the Board of the Associated Loyalists, at least with their knowledge and sanction. And though Daniel Coxe and other members denied indignantly that they had had any intimation that Huddy was to be murdered, the court acquitted Lippincott.[31]

In the meanwhile poor Asgill was kept in prison, fearful that at any moment he might be taken out to the gallows. But it is probable that Washington never intended to execute him, desiring only to prevent any more Huddy incidents. So, when Lady Asgill, the young captain's mother, appealed to the Queen of France, and the Queen directed the French ambassador in Philadelphia to request his release, Washington and Congress complied.

Yet Huddy's death did not go unavenged, since it brought about the dissolution of the Associated Loyalists. The Board, in putting an end to the organization, fired a last shot at Clinton and Carleton by declaring that they would "not serve in future under persons in whom they can place no reliance." And they may have been conscious, also, that many persons in New York and Great Britain alike had lost confidence in them.[32] When William Franklin sailed for England to plead for compensation for the Loyalists after the treaty of peace, there were some who feared that because he had been president of the Board he might be received very coolly by the Ministry.[33]

Long before the Associated Loyalists disbanded, military and naval events had made the British cause in America hopeless, so that their raids had become as purposeless as they were brutal. Both Clinton and Washington were well aware that the rather precarious hold of the British upon America was largely dependent upon their control of the sea. This it was which made it possible to bring reinforcements, arms and munitions from Great Britain, to transfer troops from any point of attack or defence rapidly and in safety, to use the great bays and rivers to penetrate into the heart of the country. On the other hand, if the French once wrested the control of American waters from them, their armies would be cut off from their source of supply, would be cut off from each other, would be in imminent danger of being defeated in detail or starved into submission.

Clinton was greatly alarmed, then, when in June 1781, he learned from an intercepted letter that Admiral de Grasse had been ordered to bring his powerful fleet from the West Indies to the American coast, where, if he formed a junction with the squadron at Newport under Barras, he might have a decided superiority over the British.[34]

The previous summer, in response to the earnest pleas of Lafayette, King Louis had sent a fleet to Rhode Island, with an army of 6,000 men under General Rochambeau. As the seven stately ships of the line, the five frigates and innumerable transports anchored at Newport, none of the white-uniformed men who came ashore dreamed that the foe they were destined to battle was at the moment seven hundred miles away in South Carolina, nor that they would have to march through a half dozen states before encountering him. Rochambeau and his men expected, not to fight Lord Cornwallis, but in conjunction with Washington, to drive Clinton out of New York.

But this plan failed because, for the time being, the French government had not sent enough warships to establish naval superiority in American waters. And when Admiral Arbuthnot, in conjunction with a newly arrived squadron under Admiral Graves, sailed for Newport and anchored off Point Judith, the French fleet was shut up in Narragansett Bay. This, in turn, made it necessary for the French army to remain, cooling their heels at Newport throughout the winter, lest, should they leave to join Washington, the warships would be left exposed to attack by land and sea. So Rochambeau had to restrain his impatience and seek compensation in receiving some of the leading men of New England at the Vernon House where he lodged, and giving splendid dinners. It was a graceful gesture, he thought, for Washington to unite the American cockade with the French cockade by ordering his officers to wear in future black cockades with white relief.

In the meanwhile, Rochambeau's future antagonist, Cornwallis, was having anything but a restful time. We find him marching back and forth in South Carolina, defeating the Americans under General Horatio Gates at Camden, pursuing General Nathanael Greene's little army across North Carolina into Virginia, turning back at the Dan River, fighting the indecisive and costly Battle of Guilford Court House, and finally retiring down the Cape Fear River to Wilmington.

But now the British general was in perplexity as to what to do next. Should he pursue Greene and run the risk of annihilation; or remain inactive while the Revolutionists reconquered the Carolinas; or take the "ruinous and disgraceful" decision of waiting for transports to take his army to New York? As Cornwallis pondered these alternatives, he wished fervently for directions from Clinton. But it would take six weeks to send to New York to find out whether Sir Henry was laying plans which would require his cooperation, and in six weeks it might be too late. So, when word came that General Phillips had been ordered to Virginia, he decided to march north to join him.[35]

By the time Clinton knew of Cornwallis's decision, the latter's 1,500 troops were making their way over the Carolina roads to Petersburg, where they arrived late in May, 1781. Uniting them with Phillips's army and a detachment of 1,500 men which Clinton sent him from New York, Cornwallis now found himself at the head of an army vastly superior to any Lafayette, who was in command of the Revolutionary troops in Virginia, could bring against him. Had he struck quickly by getting between the youthful French general and Steuben, who was gathering recruits near Charlottesville, and Wayne, who was hastening down from Pennsylvania, he would soon have been master of all Virginia. But he contented himself with chasing Lafayette's little force as far as the North Anna, then sweeping into Goochland County, then turning east to Richmond and on to Williamsburg. The total fruits of this 200-mile rambling march was the destruction of some hundreds of hogsheads of tobacco and some arms and supplies.

While he was making himself at home in Williamsburg where he turned the president of William and Mary out of his residence on the campus so he could use it as his headquarters, Cornwallis received a letter from Clinton ordering him to abandon for the moment the offensive, select a strong post "either at Williamsburg or York," and then detach 3,000 men from his army and send them to New York. To this Cornwallis replied that he could not spare so large a force, for to do so would reduce his army to "about 2,400 rank and file fit for duty." Moreover, instead of remaining in Williamsburg or marching to Yorktown, he crossed the James and transferred his men to Portsmouth.[36] And at Portsmouth he should have remained, for he could not have made a better selection of a defensive post. The broad Elizabeth River gave the place access to the sea, while the Dismal Swamp and the Western Branch made it almost impregnable by land.

But again Clinton interfered. After consulting Admiral Graves, who thought it absolutely necessary to have a naval station in the Chesapeake suitable for large ships, he ordered Cornwallis to "examine Old Point Comfort in the mouth of James River and fortify it." But when the naval officers who were with Cornwallis told him that post "would not answer the purpose," he decided "in compliance with the spirit of his orders" to move to Yorktown, whose harbor was the only one where he could "give effectual protection to the line of battle ships." [37] So the men went on board transports, which moved past the ruins of Norfolk, out in Hampton Roads and round the toe of the Peninsula to the mouth of the York. Here they went ashore at Yorktown and Gloucester Point, laid out lines of fortification and began the work of digging.

Such was the situation in Virginia when Washington, at his headquarters in New Windsor, on the Hudson, was thrilled by the news that the French government was planning to send a powerful fleet under Admiral de Grasse to the West Indies and thence to the American coast to cooperate with him and Rochambeau. This was the opportunity for which he had been waiting and praying. When, in 1778, the arrival of d'Estaing's fleet had given the French temporary naval superiority in American waters, the chance to strike a decisive blow had been lost by the admiral's failure to cooperate fully with the Americans. There must be no repetition of that mistake. The Continentals must be ready, Rochambeau must be ready, to strike with all their might the instant de Grasse arrived to bottle up the British fleet.

But Washington could make no definite plans until he knew just where de Grasse would come. It would be futile for him to assail New York if the French fleet were in the Chesapeake; it would be folly to march hundreds of miles to Virginia if it should be headed for Sandy Hook. It was necessary, then, for him to prepare for either alternative, holding his own men and the French army poised, ready to strike in either direction.

On May 22, Washington and Rochambeau met at the quaint old town of Wethersfield, on the Connecticut River, to lay their plans. It was decided that the first move would be for the French army to march to White Plains, where they would be in position to cooperate with the Americans, either in an assault on New York or a campaign in the south. [38] So, early in June, Rochambeau left Newport and headed west. As the Frenchmen came swinging by in their white coats and waistcoats, the lapels and collar bands differing in color according to the regiment, some crimson, some pink, some blue, some yellow, some green, the New England farmers lined the roads to wave their welcome. They were not a little surprised to find them well set up, sturdy men, who seemed quite capable of holding their own with the best the British could bring against them.

Though Washington and Rochambeau had to conform their plans to the movements of de Grasse, it was their hope that he would head for New York. "In every point of view an attempt upon New York with its present garrison, which by estimation is reduced to 4,500 regular troops and about 3,000 irregulars, was deemed preferable to a southern operation," Washington wrote Lafayette. "The reasons which induced this determination were the danger to be apprehended from the approaching heats, the dissipation and loss of men by so long a march, and the difficulty of transportation, but above all it was thought that we had a tolerable prospect of expelling the enemy or obliging them to withdraw part of their force from the southward." [39] As it happened, it was Clinton, and not Lafayette, who was destined to read this letter, for it was intercepted and forwarded to British headquarters. But so far from being of service to Sir Henry, it served only to deceive him, when later Washington suddenly changed his plans.

Exciting days followed for Washington. As he crossed the Hudson with Rochambeau, and rode along the top of the palisades to peer across at the British works in northern Manhattan, his calm face belied the quickened beat of his heart. The next few weeks might see the American flag flying over New York City, might see the final blow for independence. The island he found much changed from the days when he had fought the Battle of Harlem Heights, or when the Americans met disaster at Fort Washington. "The island is totally stripped of trees," he reported, "but low bushes, apparently as high as a man's waist, appear in places which were covered with wood in the year 1776." [40]

In New York the Loyalists were scornful of the threat to the city and glad that the long inactivity had come to an end. "Jonathan is collecting all his forces, raising Heaven and earth to besiege us in conjunction with about 4,000 French troops," one wrote to a friend in London. "On this occasion the New England Yankees seem to be very forward and turn out in great numbers in hopes of getting possession of this place. Hence we expect some warm work in about a month, as the lads are investing us on all sides. . . . However . . . from the strength of our lines and the ardour of our garrison, which, I dare say, with the militia, consists of 20,000 fighting men at least, am in hopes they will pay dear for their presumption, and may, in its consequences, put an end to the rebellion." [41]

But Clinton was not so confident. Early in July Washington had sent forward General Lincoln to surprise the post at Kingsbridge, and though the attempt failed, it demonstrated that the British were not inclined to accept the invitation to battle in the open. "Nothing could have been more alarming as well as mortifying than my situation at the present crisis," wrote Clinton. "The enemy's army parading on the heights in my front for two days and no possibility of any stirring against it, was I in ever so great force, as I had not an armed vessel to cover either of my flanks . . . and should the Count de Grasse happen to arrive on the coast in the admiral's absence, everything was to be apprehended, not only for the distant posts of my army, but even for those of New York." [42] Confident that Washington and Rochambeau were going to attack the city, Clinton decided that the best thing to do was to prepare for a vigorous defense.

It was at this moment that Rochambeau received a letter from de Grasse written at St. Francis, San Domingo, which altered the whole situation. It stated that the French fleet would sail on August 13, not for New York, but for the Chesapeake, that he would bring twenty-nine warships and three regiments, 1,000 men strong each, 100 dragoons, 100 artillerymen, ten field pieces and several cannon, and that he would return to the West Indies on October 15.

Washington did not hesitate a moment. If de Grasse was coming to the Chesapeake, he must be there to meet him with every man at his disposal. With the great French fleet blockading Cornwallis by sea and with his Continentals, Rochambeau's army, Lafayette's force, the men de Grasse was bringing with him and the Virginia militia assailing him by land, his situation would be hopeless. A lesser man than Washington might have hesitated to give up his long-cherished hopes of capturing New York, might have quailed at the prospect of shifting his bases of supplies, might have thought himself not justified in leaving the Highlands and other important posts in the north almost bare of defenders, would have drawn back at the thought of transferring a large body of men all the way from the Hudson to the James.

But Washington knew that the supreme opportunity had come; he was not going to let it escape him.

Soon reports began to arrive at the British headquarters that the armies of Washington and Rochambeau were on the move. Three deserters brought word on August 20 that the French were marching westward towards the Hudson, that the cannon at Dobbs Ferry had been taken away, that the Americans, breaking camp on the 19th, had taken the road to Tarrytown.[43] "It seems difficult as yet to ascertain the objects of the enemy from the movements they have . . . made," George Beckwith wrote Oliver De Lancey, "but be they what they will, I must be of opinion that their whole plan of operations has undergone a material change." [44] The British were still more puzzled when the allies, with their supply trains and cannon, moved across the Hudson at King's Ferry and marched southward. This was followed by word that they were pouring through New Jersey, the Continentals and the French infantry trudging over the roads, followed by the lumbering artillery, long lines of supply wagons and boats mounted on carriages.

Among the weary American troops, as they marched on or sat around the campfire, speculation was rife as to their destination. "Our situation reminds me of some theatrical exhibition where the interest and expectations of the spectators are continually increasing and where curiosity is wrought to the highest point," wrote an officer in his diary. "Our destination has been for some time matter of perplexing doubt and uncertainty; bets have run high on one side that we were to . . . aid in the siege of New York, and on the other that we are stealing a march on the enemy, and are actually destined to Virginia in pursuit of the army under Lord Cornwallis." [45]

In New York City, too, the mystery of Washington's movements was the topic of conversation in private homes, in the taverns, at headquarters, wherever two or more men met. Some thought he was preparing to attack Staten Island; others that he was heading for the Chesapeake. But all were united in criticising Clinton for his inactivity.[46] Why had he not gone out to attack the French and Americans when they were lined up in front of him at Kingsbridge? He had as many men as they, perhaps more. Could he not have left the city to the protection of the militia, and with the regulars and the provincials inflicted such a blow as would have made it impossible for the enemy to cross the Hudson and begin new maneuvres? And when, after hav-

New York's First Racecourse, a Favorite Resort of the Governors of New York and the Farmers of Long Island. The racecourse was named "New Market" after the English sporting ground.

On Monday,

The Sixteenth Inftant, *February 1778.*

At the Theatre in Southwark,

For the Benefit of a PUBLIC CHARITY,

Will be reprefented a Comedy

CALLED THE

Conftant Couple.

To which will be added,

DUKE AND NO DUKE.

The CHARACTERS by the OFFICERS of the ARMY and NAVY

Tickets to be had at the Printer's: at the Coffee-houfe in Market-ftreet: and at the Pennfilvania Farmer, near the New-Market, and no where elfe.

Boxes and Pit, One Dollar.—Gallery, Half a Dollar. Doors to open at Five o'Clock, and begin precifely at Seven. No Money will, on any Account, be taken at the Door. Gentlemen are earneftly requefted not to attempt to bribe the Door-keepers.

Theatre in Front-ftreet, between the Hours of Nine and Two o'clock: After which Time, the Box-keeper will not attend. Ladies or Gentlemen who would have Places kept for them, are defired to fend their Servants to the Theatre at Four o'clock, otherwife their Places will be given up.

Top: Interior View of the John Street Theater. *Left:* Playbill Announcing a Theatrical Performance by British Officers in Philadelphia, February, 1778.

Sir Henry Clinton.   General Rochambeau.

View of New York Harbor in 1793. Trinity Church can be seen
through the ship's rigging.

Federal Hall in Wall Street.

Washington Firing the First Gun at the Siege of Yorktown.

The Richmond Hill House overlooking the Hudson was one of New York's finest private estates while occupied by John Adams. During the early days of the Revolution, it served as Washington's headquarters.

A present-day view of the Moore House at Yorktown, scene of the Meeting of the Commissioners who drafted the Articles of Capitulation for Cornwallis's Army.

NEWPORT, October 25, 1781.

GLORIOUS INTELLIGENCE!

YESTERDAY Afternoon arrived in this Harbour, Capt. Lovatt, of the Schooner Adventure, from York-River, in Chefapeake-Bay (which he left the 20th Inftant) and brought us the glorious News of the Surrender of Lord Cornwallis and his Army Prifoners of War to the allied Army under the command of our illuftrious General, and the French Fleet under the command of his Excellency the Count de Graffe.

A Ceffation of Hoftilities took Place on Thurfday the 18th Inftant, in Confepuence of Propofals from Lord Cornwallis for a Capitulation.—His Lordfhip propofed a Ceffation of twenty-four Hours, but Two only was granted by his Excellency General Wafhington. The Articles were compleated the fame Day, and the next Day the allied Army took Poffeffion of York-Town.

By this glorious Conqueft NINE THOUSAND of the Enemy encluding Seamen, fell into our Hands, with an immenfe Quantity of warlike Stores, a Forty Gun Ship, a Frigate, an armed Veffel, and about One Hundred Sail of Transports.

We have taken the earlieft Opportunity to congratulate our Cuftomers, and our Country on this important Event.

NEWPORT, Printed:
NEW-LONDON: Re-printed by T. GREEN.

News of the Surrender of Cornwallis.

Benjamin Franklin and Richard Oswald Discussing the Treaty of
Peace in Paris.

ing let this opportunity slip, he permitted Washington and Rochambeau to sweep through New Jersey under his very nose, without making the least effort to stop them, men could hardly credit their senses.[47]

The Loyalists especially were bitter in their criticism. "Every measure of Sir Henry Clinton since he came to the command has been so
far beyond the view of vulgar capacity, that this in particular strikes
with less force and is in some degree buried amidst a multiplicity of
more unaccountable actions," declared William Franklin sarcastically.
"And we have only to lament that we have not penetration enough to
fathom the policy of his deep laid schemes. For deep laid they must be
because unintelligible." [48]

Later, when these criticisms came to his attention, Clinton defended himself vigorously. To have attacked Washington when he was
east of the Hudson would have been folly, since the allies had 11,000
men, exclusive of militia, and he not above 9,300 in all. Nor was he
deceived by "false communications into thinking Staten Island was
the object of the move into New Jersey." As to attacking the allies
there, it was out of the question. "My whole force . . . did not exceed
10,000 men, and . . . half of those would be required for the defense
of New York . . . The American general could never have entertained any apprehension from being followed by that number." Even
had he had boats enough to bring his entire force over, Washington
could have met him with four times as many men.[49]

Clinton's excuses would have been more convincing had they not
been so confused and contradictory. At one time he says he had
thought of the possibility that Washington might be heading for Virginia, at another he declared that he "could not infer he proposed
moving his whole force to the southward," though he "judged it possible he might send a detachment there." [50] Later he declared that
"when Washington began his march to the southward, Arnold was in
expedition at New London with 3,000 men, all the sailors and all the
boats," [51] leaving the inference that this made it impossible for him
to assail the enemy in New Jersey. Yet, unless Clinton's memory had
completely failed him, he knew that Arnold at that time had not
started, in fact did not start until Washington and Rochambeau were
passing Philadelphia.

Far more reliable than these excuses and afterthoughts are the
letters Clinton wrote at the time. "Washington . . . suddenly quitted
his camp at White Plains," he wrote Germain on September 7. "On

the 23d and 24th he crossed the North River and by the position he
took seemed to threaten Staten Island until the 29th when he suddenly moved towards the Delaware. At first I judged this to be a
feint, but finding that he passed that river with some of his avant
guard, and publicly talked of the Count de Grasse's being every moment expected in the Chesapeake to cooperate with him, I immediately endeavored both by land and water to communicate my suspicions
to Lord Cornwallis." [52] In other words, Clinton thought the allies
still planned to attack New York until the Americans were crossing
the Delaware, and only when Washington openly declared his intentions, were his suspicions aroused.

Then it was, and not until then, that he sent Arnold off on his
fool's errand to New London. Arnold captured Fort Trumbull and
Fort Griswold, wiped out the garrisons and burnt the town, but as a
strategic move the expedition was a total failure. It did not turn the
French and Americans back from the southern expedition, and it deprived Clinton of several thousand men at a critical juncture and made
it impossible for him to follow behind to delay Washington's movements. [53]

But while Clinton was hesitating and surmising, Washington and
Rochambeau were pushing south as fast as the roads permitted. Riding forward ahead of the troops, they entered the suburbs of Philadelphia about noon on August 30, and were escorted into town by the
Light Horse Troop. Three days later the Continentals, headed by "the
general officers and their aides in rich military uniforms" marched
through, the line of weary infantry extending two miles as they trudged
along in a cloud of dust. On September 4, the French made their
entry. "The troops . . . were dressed as elegantly as ever were the
soldiers of a garrison on a day of royal review. They . . . marched
through the town with military music playing . . . The streets were
crowded with people and the ladies appeared at the windows in their
most splendid attire." The ladies thought that the Soissonais regiment
were especially grand in their white coats with rose-colored facings,
and grenadier caps with white and rose-colored feathers.[54]

With some difficulty Washington and Rochambeau escaped the
attentions which the people of Philadelphia showered on them, and
pushing on, prepared for the embarkation of the troops at Head of
Elk. For the moment the two separated, and at Chester, when by
chance Rochambeau caught sight of Washington again, the latter

waved his hat at him with gestures of excitement and joy. When the French general approached, Washington called out that he had received word that de Grasse had arrived in the Chesapeake with twenty-eight ships of the line. "I never saw a man more thoroughly and openly delighted," said the Duke de Lauson.

But Yorktown was still over 200 miles away and if the army did not make the best possible speed the golden chance might slip. At Head of Elk Washington was disappointed to find that the boats he had counted on to transport the men to Virginia were so few in number that, crowd them though he did, they were sufficient for only 2,000 men. But he was cheered at the news that 1,800 Marylanders, many of them sons of the heroes of the Battle of Long Island, were on their way to Virginia to join his forces. "Some are riding, some are sailing, some are walking," he was told, "they will be there, general, before you are."

There was trouble and delay in crossing the broad Susquehanna, and it was September 12 before the troops reached Baltimore. Then came the welcome news that de Grasse had sent five frigates and nine transports up the Chesapeake to meet them, and twenty-four hours later the footsore troops climbed on board at Annapolis. Moving down the bay, almost in sight of the British vessels anchored in the York River, the fleet rounded Old Point Comfort and heading up the James, landed the men at Jamestown.

Two weeks before they arrived, Washington and Rochambeau, after paying a brief visit to Mt. Vernon, rode into Williamsburg. As the news spread through the town, Lafayette's men—Continentals and French—formed in line and saluted at the approach of the generals. Then Lafayette came forward, "joy painted on his countenance," to clasp Washington in his arms. Thereupon the three rode into town, while men, women and children pressed forward to show their "eagerness to see their beloved countryman." On September 27, with the arrival of the transports, the troops from the north marched through Williamsburg, flags flying, on their way to Yorktown.

In the meanwhile events of great importance were happening on the sea. When Rochambeau marched to join Washington, leaving only a small garrison and the squadron under Admiral Barras at Newport, Clinton had planned to parry by descending on that place with overwhelming sea and land forces.[55] And success seemed certain when, on August 28, Sir Samuel Hood's fleet of fourteen great ships entered the harbor to reinforce Admiral Graves' small squadron. The troops went aboard the transports and the order to sail awaited "some small repairs to His Majesty's ships," when word came that Barras had sailed away from Rhode Island. Surmising that he was headed for the Chesapeake and hoping to intercept him, Graves and Hood put to sea with nineteen ships of the line.

Arriving at the mouth of the Chesapeake Bay on the morning of September 5, the British sighted de Grasse's fleet of twenty-eight great ships anchored off Cape Henry. A few hours later the French fleet got under way and headed out to sea. This was Graves' chance. Had he circled past the head of the French line as it emerged, he might have concentrated his fire on de Grasse's vessels one by one and disabled them all in turn. But he waited until the enemy were abreast of his fleet before pouring in his broadsides. De Grasse, on his part, answered with such a blast that ten of the British ships were seriously damaged, and four of them, the *Montagu,* the *Shrewsbury,* the *Terrible* and the *Ajax,* so badly battered as to make them unfit for further fighting. The French, while losing several hundred men, killed and wounded, suffered less damage to their ships.

For two days the fleets stood watching each other, licking their wounds, when de Grasse turned about and reentered the Chesapeake. On September 11, Graves approached the entrance to the bay cautiously, sending forward a frigate to reconnoitre. In a few hours this vessel came back with the surprising news that de Grasse's fleet now numbered thirty-six ships of the line instead of the twenty-eight which had participated in the battle. Barras, with his eight ships, had slipped in unobserved. With such overwhelming odds against him, Graves reluctantly set sail for New York, where he arrived on September 19.[56]

When Graves and Hood sailed away from New York on August 31, the Loyalists realized that upon their success or failure hinged the fate of America. "A week will decide perhaps the ruin or salvation of the British Empire," Judge Smith wrote in his *Diary.* So when the fleet came limping back, some of the vessels badly damaged and the *Terrible,* which had had to be sunk at sea, missing, gloom and intense anxiety spread throughout the city. Rumors were rife. "Nothing has been published," wrote Shewkirk, "but it is reported that thirteen ships of the line were engaged, and that the French were again in the Chesapeake. The *Terrible* . . . has been lost, and ten of our ships will have to be refitted." [57] Four days later the crowds which gathered on the wharves as the damaged ships came up the river for repairs, could see for themselves the shattered spars and rigging.

What now would become of Lord Cornwallis? people asked each other. Assailed on land by the combined armies of Washington and Rochambeau, cut off from escape by sea by the powerful French fleet, his position vulnerable to attack, his provisions limited, unless speedy assistance arrived his fate was sealed. With blanched faces and bitter criticisms of the bungling which had brought things to this pass, the Tories speculated on what should be done to save the day. "My zeal and perhaps my ignorance would incline me to march with 10,000 men to Philadelphia for the destruction of every thing useful for commerce or for arms except the cattle of the implacable foe wanted here," said Judge Smith. [58]

With this Clinton did not agree. At a conference of principal officers it was decided that the only way to relieve Cornwallis was "to go to him," since "nothing could turn Washington from such an object." But as it was now too late for an army to march to Virginia, everything had to wait upon the repairing of the damaged ships and the arrival of expected naval reinforcements under Admiral Digby. "Digby! Digby! is the cry," wrote Judge Smith. "Every hour is precious to Lord Cornwallis." Later on the same day he added: "To our unspeakable joy Digby is at the Hook." [59] The three ships of the line which he brought with him, with two more which came in from the West Indies on October 11, gave Graves a formidable fleet capable of giving a good account of itself in a clash with de Grasse.

But the time was growing short. "The enemy are encamped about two miles from us," wrote Cornwallis on October 3. "On the night of the 30th of September they broke ground and made two redoubts about eleven hundred yards from our works." [60] October 5 was the date set for Graves' sailing, but the day came and went and the damaged ships were still not ready. Thereupon Clinton wrote Cornwallis that the army was ready and waiting to come to his succor, and that they would sail with the fleet by the 12th. But now news came that Cornwallis was in desperate straits. "The enemy within 600 yards. About 100 men lost by the fire from 40 pieces of cannon and 17 mortars." [61]

When October 12 came and still the damaged ships were not ready, the Loyalists could no longer restrain their indignation. Did it really require three weeks to repair the spars and rigging of a few vessels? Were the workmen putting in their best licks, or were they loafing on the job while the fate of a continent hung in the balance? [62] But at last, on October 16, when all was ready, and Clinton went on board to take command of the army, the people rejoiced. Perhaps after all the expedition would arrive in time to save Cornwallis. And then the fates turned against them. "The weather has come foul," wrote Clinton. "We cannot sail." [63] Only on October 19, when conditions were more favorable, did the great armament of ships of the line, frigates and transports hoist sail and head for the south.

Five days later, off Cape Charles, a vessel was sighted coming off shore to meet them, which proved to be the *Charon*. To the anxious inquiries of Clinton and Graves, the pilot stated that he and several other persons on board had escaped from Yorktown on October 18, and had not heard any firing there since. The next day the frigate *Nymph* arrived from New York with a letter from Cornwallis dated the 15th, whose "desponding tenor" aroused the "most alarming apprehensions." When two men in a canoe were overtaken and brought aboard one of the ships for questioning, and they too told the group of anxious officers that fighting had ceased, they could no longer doubt that they were too late and that Cornwallis had surrendered. So, reluctantly, sadly, Graves gave the order for the fleet to turn about and return to New York. [64]

They did not have to break the news there, for it had preceded them. It was on October 23 that the New Yorkers heard firing across the Hudson in New Jersey as though in celebration of some great victory, "which made the people very apprehensive." The next day, when some Americans, who came over from Elizabeth under a white flag to exchange prisoners, confirmed their worst fears, "general consternation and lamentation prevailed." [65] So this was the end. The war might drag on for a year or two longer, but eventual defeat and exile for the Loyalists were now inevitable. Some clung desperately to the hope that the report might yet prove to be unfounded. "I believed it, but many would not," wrote Hugh Gaine, "and no further account being received thereof, the report in some measure was explained away." Even when full particulars and some of the articles of capitulation arrived, there were some who would not believe.

The last doubts were dispelled, however, when the sloop of war *Bonetta* came in from Virginia with a number of refugees. In drawing up the terms of surrender Cornwallis had asked that the Loyalists under his command should not "be punished on account of having joined the British army." Washington had refused, but gave a loophole by permitting the *Bonetta* to leave for New York with such soldiers as Cornwallis should select.[66] Grateful though they were for their escape, the Loyalists, on their arrival, complained bitterly to Clinton at not being treated as regular prisoners of war. The next time one of them was captured he might be turned over to the civil authorities and hanged as a traitor. The Board of the Associated Loyalists were so outraged over the discrimination that they protested to Clinton "in most violent terms." [67]

New York City was now a very gloomy place indeed, with despair written on men's faces and the air filled with contention. So pessimistic were the merchants that many refused to open the goods received by the last fleet and others sold only for cash. Someone posted a lampoon at the City Hall accusing Clinton of sacrificing Cornwallis to his envy.[68]

On November 19 Cornwallis himself arrived on parole, and going at once to headquarters, closeted himself with Clinton. An unpleasant interview it must have been, with Clinton demanding why Cornwallis had not obeyed his instructions, and Cornwallis retorting that he might have made his escape from Yorktown, had he not received repeated assurances from Clinton that he would come to his assistance.[69] It was the beginning of a long controversy between the two generals which lasted for years, and in which eventually everyone but themselves lost interest.

When the egotistical Clinton discovered that many, both in America and England, blamed him for the failure of the British arms, he fought back with every weapon in his power, deluging Germain with excuses and explanations. When Judge Smith visited him on November 26, he launched out on a "desultory justification of his own conduct and a censure of everybody else . . . He is a distressed man, looking for friends and suspicious of all mankind and complains of the number of his enemies." [70]

Clinton would have done well had he, instead of blaming Cornwallis for the Yorktown disaster, contented himself with pointing out that the root of the trouble lay in the loss by the British navy of the control of American waters. "I have been of opinion that operations should not be undertaken in the Chesapeake without a naval superiority in these seas," he wrote Germain, "and to the want of it, and perhaps that alone, we are to impute our late misfortunes in that quarter." He had warned the Ministry of the dangers Cornwallis was exposed to without a covering fleet, and they in turn had promised him naval superiority. "We, however, had it not," he complained, "and the consequences were such as I had predicted." [71]

On December 15, a fleet sailed away from New York, taking to England two of the principal actors in the drama of the war—Lord Cornwallis and Benedict Arnold. Arriving in Great Britain six weeks later these men met with contrasting receptions, Arnold with coolness and Cornwallis with enthusiasm, if not affection. "In his way to town, he was complimented by the mayor and corporation of Exeter with the freedom of the city; and so pleased were the people with his arrival, that he was carried from the London Inn to Guildhall on men's shoulders, accompanied by an incredible number of spectators." [72]

Clinton was not long in following Cornwallis and Arnold. Months earlier he had intimated his desire to resign, and in the spring of 1781 had received permission from the King to do so. "Which I should certainly have done," he wrote Germain, "had not the circumstances of this post been such at the time as to render such a measure highly improper." [73] And now, with the London papers criticising him and with Germain intimating that he might be brought to trial for his blunders, he was determined not to give up. "He raves—calls Denbigh a fool, Germain a villain," wrote Smith after a conversation with Sir Henry. "Speaks with contempt of the Ministry. Takes care to let me know that he is not recalled and that he will not leave the country in the present condition voluntarily." [74]

As it happened he returned involuntarily. In April orders came directing him to turn over his command to Sir Guy Carleton and come home. "A fortunate event," wrote Judge Smith. A few days later Carleton arrived and went ashore at Whitehall, where he was received "by a party of horse and foot, the gentlemen of the army, most of the respectable inhabitants of the city, and a numerous concourse of people." [75] On May 10, the army officers gave a "splendid entertainment" to Clinton, at Roubalet's Tavern, which was graced by Carleton, Digby, and other "persons of distinction." Three days later Carleton, General Robertson and others accompanied Clinton to the wharf and waved good-bye, as the ship which was to take him away from the city over which he had ruled for four years, moved out into East River and headed down the bay. [76]

The Loyalists were overjoyed to be rid of him. Among the Headquarters Papers, now at the Clements Library, at the University of Michigan, is a document in the handwriting of William Franklin, which depicts Clinton as the Tories saw him. "The Commander in Chief is gallant to a proverb and possesses great military knowledge in the field, but he is weak, irresolute, unsteady, vain, incapable of forming any plan himself, and too weak or rather too proud and conceited to follow that of another . . . Since the death of André he has not had a man of abilities about him, never were there a set of men more eminently ill qualified for the offices they occupy. In consequence there is confusion in every department though offices are multiplied without number . . . If folly herself had presided at the helm, she could not take more effectual measures to overturn everything we had been doing."

Perhaps this judgement is too harsh. Clinton attributed Franklin's hatred to the restraining hand he placed on the "sanguinary and mercenary" activities of the Associated Loyalists. But there can be no doubt that Clinton, in the important post he held in America, was a failure. Despite the dictatorial powers entrusted to him, his administration of civil and military affairs was shot through with corruption. Instead of winning the friendship and hearty support of the Loyalists, he antagonized and offended them. He injured the King's cause by failing to put an end to the wholesale plundering by his troops of friend and foe alike.

The selling of commissions, which had long been a source of weakness in the British army, was carried to an excess under his command and filled the service "with captains under twenty," and blocked promotions for able officers. As a tactitian Clinton showed great ability, but he was a very poor strategist. Forever overestimating the strength of the forces opposed to him, afraid to take chances, insisting upon leaving thousands of troops to defend the almost impregnable Manhattan at the very time that he was attacking the only force which could threaten it, unwilling to face Washington save on grounds of his own choosing, quarreling with those with whom he should have cooperated, he was in no small degree responsible for the British failures in America.

CHAPTER XI

EXILE

SO GLAD were the Loyalists to be rid of Sir Henry Clinton that his successor, no matter who, would have received a warm welcome. As it happened, they had every reason to congratulate themselves upon the appointment of Sir Guy Carleton. An able soldier, an efficient and honest administrator, modest, democratic in his dealings with citizens and soldiers alike, a man of broad views, and above all intensely anxious to prevent unnecessary suffering and to bind up the wounds of war, no better man could have been selected to command in America during the last few months of the British regime. The Loyalists in their address of welcome were not indulging in mere verbiage when they called him the preserver of Quebec and praised his prudence, energy and military ability.[1] Even the Revolutionists respected him. "You were once, we are told, the master and afterwards the pupil of the immortal Wolfe," said the *Pennsylvania Packet*. "Your behavior in Canada and your general conduct, have procured you the character of a gentleman and a hero." [2]

Liberal in his views, Carleton took no pains to conceal his opposition to the reactionary measures of the British government, which had driven the Americans into rebellion. In a conversation with Judge Smith he made it clear that he "had been all along with the opposition." [3] The New Yorkers, who had grown accustomed to the inactivity and exclusiveness of Clinton, were delighted with Carleton's activity and accessibility. "He sees everything with his own eyes and hears everybody," wrote an observer. "He is up and about before four in the morning. Before the quarter part of his army have opened their eyelids, he has perhaps rode ten or a dozen miles; he comes almost every day to the parade, which is a signal that immediately after he will have a levee, where every one may tell their story, or request a private hour . . . and those who have had conversations with him go away very much satisfied with his patience and condescension. In short, his conduct has procured him the respect of the army, and the love of the Loyalists." [4]

The only persons to resent Carleton's appointment were Clinton's favorites and the numerous group of unscrupulous officials who had profited by his laxness. Some of these were resentful at the reforms which the new commander-in-chief instituted, and inclined to sneer at his economies. "In short," said one, "there are so many regulations making, the people in general get nothing. So that we shall soon, like the miser's horse, die just as we are brought to live upon one oat per day." [5] But the public as a whole rejoiced that Carleton's measures promised to make a "saving of near a million" annually. They approved, also, of the opening of the civil court of justice, of Carleton's kindness to prisoners, and above all of his sympathy with the sufferings of the Loyalists and his exertions in their behalf.

And for the Loyalists it was a time of great anxiety. From the hour that Cornwallis's surrender had been accepted as a fact, they had wondered what the effect would be upon the political situation in Great Britain. Would it undermine the present Ministry and place in power men who favored peace at any cost? Would it turn public sentiment against the war? If the government succeeded in weathering the storm, would the tremendous strain upon the Treasury permit the creation of another army by the expenditure of further millions?

The *Royal Gazette* tried to still these apprehensions. "The melancholy catastrophe that has befallen my Lord Cornwallis and his gallant army is justly bewailed by every real lover of his country. But . . . we ought not to despond or despair. The spirit of the nation is too high, its resources too many, not to urge us to repair his loss and revenge his fate. Such accidents only stimulate the powerful and brave to a further prosecution of the war." [6]

The first news from Great Britain was reassuring. On November 27, the King at the opening of Parliament had made a speech urging the vigorous prosecution of the war. "I have no doubt but that by the concurrence and support of my Parliament, by the valour of my fleets and armies, and by a vigorous, animated and united exertion of the faculties and resources of my people, I shall be able to restore the blessings of a safe and honorable peace to all my dominions." [7]

Even this was not enough to dispel the gloom in New York. "This was proof of the extreme dejection into which the minds of the Loyalists have been plunged," thought Judge Smith. "They want strong cordials, confident expressions, great promises and hoped to have heard of formidable alliances." [8]

Yet the news from England for a time continued good. "Our friends in New York may safely stand their ground," said a Londoner in a letter written in January, 1782. "Government here does not intend to give up the contest, and I am convinced they will send out all the force that can be spared from this country and Ireland early in the spring . . . So confident am I that this country will strain every nerve for the recovery of America, that I shall not think of any arrangements in my concerns which some panic struck creatures might be induced to adopt after the Chesapeake affair." [9]

None the less, the Tories, as they went about their daily tasks, glanced anxiously down the harbor to see whether the packet from Falmouth was in with news from England. When at last, on March 28, it was sighted, they were discouraged to hear that the Ministry had ordered that no further offensive war be carried on in America. Did this mean that Great Britain had come to terms with the Revolutionists? "Various reports of a peace, and some believe it," wrote Hugh Gaine in his *Journal*.[10]

Yet five weeks passed before the arrival of the *Ceres,* bringing an account of the overthrow of the Ministry. For the Tories it was an ominous story. On February 22, General Conway had introduced a motion in the House of Commons to discontinue the war. It was lost by one vote only. Five days later he came back with a similar motion, and this time it passed by a vote of 234 to 215. On March 8, Lord John Cavendish rose to propose several resolutions: "That since the year 1775, upwards of one hundred millions of money have been expended on the army and navy in a fruitless war . . . That during the above period we have lost the thirteen colonies in America . . . That Great Britain is at present engaged in an expensive war with America, France, Spain and Holland, without a single ally . . . That the chief cause of all these misfortunes has been the want of foresight and ability in his Majesty's ministers." On March 20, Lord North announced to the Commons "that his Majesty had come to a full determination of changing his ministers." [11]

The new government was headed by the Marquis of Rockingham, the wealthy and liberal nobleman who had endeared himself to the

Americans by proposing the repeal of the Stamp Act. Associated with him were Burke, Fox, Lord Shelburne and others who had opposed the policies which drove the colonies into revolt. The new Ministry pledged themselves to conclude peace with the former colonies even though peace should entail independence.

Yet the Loyalists did not give up hope. They knew that King George would hold out to the last ditch against independence; they were confident that British naval power and naval leadership would yet sweep the sea. So their spirits rose mightily late in May, when word reached New York that Admiral Rodney had encountered the French fleet off Santo Domingo and had virtually destroyed it, sinking many of the ships, scattering the rest and making the gallant de Grasse prisoner. Once more Loyalist New York could celebrate a great victory. "The artillery company with their field pieces and the two battalions of the Kingston Regiment of foot militia," paraded, there was a *feu de joie,* and in the evening the city was "most splendidly illuminated." [12]

But the rejoicing was short-lived. "Everything in this country has continued in a state of suspense . . . until last Wednesday, July 31, on which day a packet arrived from England with the May and June mails," Beverly Robinson wrote Clinton. "And, oh my dear Sir, what dreadful and distressing tidings does she bring us—the independence of America given up by the King without any conditions whatever, the Loyalists of America to depend upon the mercy of their enemies for the restoration of their possessions, which we are assured they will never grant, the greatest part of the estates that have been confiscated by them are already sold." [13]

Wrote another observer, "Never was despair and distraction stronger painted than in the countenances I momentarily see, and I do declare that I am often obliged to retire to my room to avoid hearing aspersions against my country too justly founded. The militia, who have been performing the military duties of the Crown have declined further service . . . and went to their different homes to console their wretched fates . . . Papers are every night stuck up in every quarter of the town with the most vindictive fury against those who advised our Sovereign to accede to the independence of this country." [14]

So this was the end. If the Loyalists returned to their former homes, not only would their estates not be returned, but they would be mobbed, possibly hanged as traitors. "But what, my good sir, is to become of me and my family," Beverly Robinson wrote in anguish of mind. "You well know that I can expect no mercy from them, my wife, my eldest son and myself being among those proscribed by an act of Assembly . . . by which act we are condemned to be hanged without further trial or ceremony if we are ever caught within this state . . . I must therefore prepare to go to England with my wife and daughters, and I still comfort myself with the hope that the government of Great Britain will not suffer us to starve but allow us a small pittance to support us the remainder of our lives." [15]

Rivington made an unconvincing attempt to reassure the Tories by an article in the *Royal Gazette*. "It is earnestly recommended to the Loyalists, everywhere, to suspend their opinion . . . and each in his place to continue firm to the professions he has made of loyalty and zeal for the reunion of the empire . . . Until a general peace shall be ratified we cannot know what is to be the eventual condition of this country . . . We are bound by every consideration of prudence and duty to wait the issue with manly steadiness . . . By such a conduct we shall preserve a claim to national regard and protection which it would be madness to forfeit." [16]

In the midst of the general despair, notices were sent out for the people to assemble at headquarters. Here a letter was read from Carleton and Digby to Washington, in which they informed him that the British peace envoys had been instructed to deal with the Americans, not as representatives of the colonies, but of an independent nation. As the throng listened to this disclosure, they were more convinced than ever that the King, for whom they had sacrificed so much, had deserted them. Nor were they reassured by his Majesty's assertion that he had the highest confidence that the possessions of the Loyalists would be restored to them or a full compensation made.

As the crowd dispersed every face was clouded, for the reading "made many a heavy heart." "The shock at first was so great that we thought everything lost past recovery," wrote Robinson. But hope dies hard. "Upon reading the letter over and reflecting upon it, I for my part think there is still some hope left, and cannot persuade myself that England means or intends to give up all connections with or command over this country."

After several other meetings, in which the situation was gone over fully, the Loyalists appointed Robert Alexander, Daniel Coxe, Isaac Low, Samuel Seabury and several others to draw up a letter to Carleton and Digby, protesting against independence. It was impossible for them to express the consternation with which they were struck at even the probability of so calamitous an event, which so imperiled their "peace, safety and happiness." They had risked their lives and fortunes to preserve the British dominions entire, confidently relying on the repeated assurances by his Majesty "that they should never be deserted." At a moment when British naval superiority had been gloriously manifested, when the national resources were still great, they had joyfully concluded that independence for America would have been considered preposterous. The hour of victory might be the proper hour to treat for peace, but not to dismember the empire. But should independence become a fact, the Loyalists would face "the most inexpressible misfortune of being forever cast out from the protection of his Majesty." They entreated Carleton and Digby, therefore, to explain their distressed situation to the King, so that he might save them from the "ruin and despair" which must otherwise fall on their devoted heads.[17]

Not content with this appeal, the Loyalists drew up another, and intrusting it to William Franklin, sent him to England on the packet *Roebuck* with instructions to place it in the King's hands. The former governor of New Jersey was welcomed by the new Prime Minister, the Earl of Shelburne, and the King listened sympathetically as he poured out the story of the sufferings and broken hopes of his loyal subjects in America.

In New York the next few months were filled with agonizing suspense. Would the next vessel from England seal the fate of the Tories by bringing word that a treaty had been signed, acknowledging independence without providing for their return to their homes and the restitution of their property? If so, where did the government plan for them to go? How did it expect them to live? "It is the most awful moment of uncertainty," wrote John W. Watson to Clinton. "The extreme dejection of some, the fear of others, the anxiety and suspense of all is so strongly marked it checks the ardor of the stoutest hope and forces you to participate in their alarms."

"Judge Bayard has given £300 for a cabin to transport himself and family to England. Billy says, 'God d--n them, I thought it would come to this. What is to become of me, sir. I am totally ruined, sir. I have not a guinea, sir.' Thomson, who . . . casts his eyes generally on the dark side of the picture, has worried himself into a settled illness. Coxe is struck dumb . . .Shoemaker says Providence will work good out of evil, Colonel Morris that if he had remained in the army he should now have been an old Lieutenant General." [18]

Nor was Judge Bayard the only one to close his affairs in New York and leave for England. Some of the leading merchants, disposing of their interests as best they could, loaded vessels with goods from their warehouses, put their families aboard and set sail for London or Bristol or Glasgow. "A great number of refugee families are preparing to leave," stated the *New Jersey Gazette,* of October 23. "David Mathews, the mayor, and several other active Loyalists have taken vessels for the transportation of themselves and families."

The columns of the *Royal Gazette* were full of advertisements of ships bound for Great Britain, which boasted "excellent accommodations for passengers." In the issue of October 9, the public were notified that the ship *Rosamond,* at Well's Wharf, had space for passengers; the ship *New York* had "valuable accommodation for passengers," the ship *Edward,* lying at Brownejohn's Wharf, would carry passengers. Some of the refugees, who took with them such part of their property as they could not sell in New York, ran into trouble with the trade laws. But Carleton directed the port officers to grant them "particular permissions," and wrote the Board of Treasury asking indulgence for them. [19]

But there were thousands who did not have the means to take their families to Great Britain. Some place of refuge must be provided for them, where they would be under the protection of the Crown and where they could start life over again. As the Loyalists cast anxious eyes on the map, the only British province which offered an inviting prospect was the territory bordering the Bay of Fundy. The West Indies were too far away, they were too crowded. So the region of the Acadians and the adjacent region which later became the province of New Brunswick became for the refugees the land of promise, their haven in the storm of the Revolution.

It was a strange whim of fate which made the Bay of Fundy the scene of two of the most tragic movements of evicted peoples in the history of America—the removal of the Acadians and the influx of the Loyalists. But whereas the former is known to every schoolchild, has been made famous by Longfellow's poem *Evangeline,* has elicited the interest and pity of the world, the latter remains an obscure incident. Yet the number of those who fled to Nova Scotia and the valley of the St. John's River in 1782 and 1783 was far greater than of those who were deported by the British in 1755; their sorrow at leaving their native land and their hardships in a strange country were also severe. Nor were the causes of these tragedies dissimilar, for in each case the displaced persons were paying the penalty of their loyalty to their king, the Acadians to a king even less worthy than the one whom the exiled Americans so revered.

Almost on the very day of his arrival, Carleton, foreseeing the possibility that the refugees would have to leave New York, began to look into the fitness of Nova Scotia to be their chief asylum. Early in the summer he received a favorable report of the resources of the province from a certain John Campbell. There were numerous great bays, harbors and rivers; in the marshes which lined the rivers the grass made good fodder for cattle; the upland produced white clover, wheat, barley, oats, peas, buckwheat, beans, hemp, flax, apples, pears, plums, vegetables; there was timber for shipbuilding; the woods abounded in moose, caribou and other game; the waters swarmed with cod and mackerel; though the winters were long the summers were very agreeable.[20]

Convinced that Nova Scotia was the ideal refuge for the Loyalists, Carleton wrote to Sir Andrew Snape Hammond, telling him that "upwards of 600 persons, women and children included," were preparing to migrate, and asking him to assist them by every means in his power. He hoped he would reserve for them such unappropriated lands as they should wish to settle on, granting them 500 to 600 acres to each family and 300 acres to a single man.[21]

And now Carleton busied himself with arranging for the sailing of the first group, most of them from the Loyalist post at Bergen's Point. He gave orders that each family should have provisions of all kinds supplied them from the King's stores sufficient to sustain them for one year, rations for the passage to Nova Scotia, comfortable clothing, an assortment of medicines, farm tools, and arms and ammunition for hunting and defense. So these poor people, farmers most of them, went aboard the transports, and as the ships slipped down the bay, waved good-bye to their native country which they were never to see again, and prepared their minds for the life which awaited them in a far-off and strange land.[22]

But there were thousands who remained behind to hope against hope. Beverly Robinson was sure that should Great Britain offer "a proper and reasonable constitution to America at large without having anything to say to Washington or Congress" and support it with a strong army, the people would accept it gladly.[23] And anything would be preferable to the months of anxious waiting. On March 15, 1783, Robinson reported that since January 19, no reports had been received "except flying and uncertain by way of the West Indies and by some prizes brought into this place. All of these accounts talk much of a general peace and it is the opinion of most people that it is so. We got a copy of the King's speech to his Parliament dated the 5th of December, by way of St. Thomas, and by that it appears that peace was near at hand. It is very strange that we have not had the least account from England from the date of the speech to this day. Being in this unhappy and uncertain situation, the Loyalists are greatly distressed what to do." [24]

They had not much longer to wait. On March 25, the people of the city interrupted their daily tasks to glance excitedly over a bulletin issued by Rivington's press. "Late last night," it stated, "an express from New Jersey brought the following account. That on . . . the twenty-third instant a vessel arrived at Philadelphia, in thirty-five days from Cadiz, with dispatches to the Continental Congress, informing them that . . . the preliminaries to a general peace . . . was signed at Paris, in consequence of which hostilities by sea and land were to cease . . . in America on Thursday the twentieth day of March . . . This very important intelligence was last night announced by the firing of cannon and great rejoicings at Elizabeth-Town." [25]

A few days later the news was confirmed, when the proclamation for the cessation of hostilities was read in the presence of a "multitude" of people. "When the reading was concluded, no one huzza'd or showed any mark of joy or approbation," and "nothing but groans and hisses prevailed, attended by bitter reproaches and curses upon their king for having deserted them in the midst of their calamities. The greatest despair is depicted in every countenance." [26]

As the Loyalists pored over the provisional articles to see in what way they affected their interests, what they read proved cold comfort. The fifth article stipulated that Congress should recommend to the different states "the restitution of all estates, rights and properties which had been confiscated belonging to real British subjects." By the sixth article it was agreed "that no future confiscations should be made, nor prosecutions commenced" against any person for the part he had taken in the war.

"But my dear sir," Beverly Robinson wrote Clinton, "these provisional articles are no kind of security to me, either to my person or property; for the 6th article only stipulates that there shall be no further confiscations made, nor prosecutions commenced, and does not affect those that had been made here before . . . The 5th article is much worse. A greater cruelty could not have been laid upon any set of men whatever, for we poor provincials are entirely excluded and not even allowed to be British subjects . . . My dear sir, the cruel and hard treatment we have received from the Ministry of Great Britain is ten times more afflicting and cuts deeper to the heart than all the Americans can do to us. We have made them our enemies by adhering to and endeavoring to support the constitution and government of England, for which cause we are slighted and cast off as beggars." [27]

That Robinson's agony of mind was shared by the other Tories is shown by a letter published in the *London Chronicle*. "The Loyalists in this country are most shamefully and traitorously abandoned . . . Our fears at present surpass all description. Never was there upon the face of the earth a set of wretches in a more deplorable situation. Deprived of all hope of future comfort or safety, either for themselves or their unhappy wives and children, many have lost their senses, and now are in a state of perfect madness. Some have put a period to their miserable existence by drowning, shooting and hanging themselves, leaving their unfortunate wives and helpless infants destitute of bread to support them." [28]

It did not serve to raise the spirits of the Loyalists to have hundreds of former residents of New York, who had joined in the revolutionary movement and had fled on the approach of Howe's army in 1776, come swarming back to demand possession of their houses. By April 19, it was estimated that "upwards of 2,000" were in town.[29] They were permitted "to view their estates, take inventories and unmolested or insulted to return." But many of them, taking for granted that their property would be immediately restored to them, had imprudently given up the houses they had occupied within the American lines. So they were compelled to find lodgings as best they could, and some had to "separate their families amongst such hospitable farmers" as were "able to give them shelter." [30]

The meeting of Revolutionists and Loyalists in the streets of New York, men who had for years been engaged in merciless warfare against each other, was far from cordial. The Tories thought the insolence of the Americans such that it could scarce be endured. When

Jerseymen caught sight of Captain Tilton, a notorious Associated Loyalist, whose practice it had long been "to burn grist mills and meeting-houses," they could with difficulty keep their hands off him. "This fellow walks constantly with a spear cane and talks of nothing but rebels and rebellion and such like stuff." Nor was he the only Tory "seen stalking about," and glowering at every Revolutionist he saw.

But there were few acts of violence, for sentries were placed at "almost every hundred yards," ready to arrest any who broke the newly established peace. The British soldiers were "tolerably civil and polite." But this cannot be said of Mayor David Mathews. When an American officer complained to him of some ill usage, "this father of the city treated him very roughly, and by way of shortening conversation, wished all d——d rascals to hell." [31]

Far more dignified was the conference between Washington and Carleton over the details of the evacuation of New York, Westchester, Long Island and Staten Island. Carleton sailed up the Hudson as far as Dobbs Ferry and then crossed over to the west bank where the American general met him and drove with him in a chariot to the house of a Mr. Dewint near Orangeburg. "An hour was spent in congratulations and separate chat in and before the door, when the two generals took a room," where they were joined by Governor George Clinton, Judge Smith and others. "When all were seated Washington opened the business," delivering himself "without animation with great slowness and a low tone of voice."

He trusted that in evacuating thousands of persons from New York care would be had to prevent the property of citizens of the United States, especially slaves who had run away from their masters, from being carried off. Carleton replied that he had already appointed officers to inspect the ships to prevent the "irregular embarkation of property." But as to the slaves, the British had issued proclamations promising them their freedom, and he could not honorably force them back into bondage. The only correct procedure was for his government "to pay for the Negroes," in which case justice would be done both to the slave and the owner.

To Washington's request that a date be fixed for the evacuation of New York, Carleton stated that he had already sent thousands of persons to Nova Scotia, and would do all in his power to hasten the withdrawal of the other Loyalists and the troops, but that "it must of necessity take time." At Washington's suggestion Governor Clinton expressed the hope that the British would withdraw at once from all Westchester and most of Long Island, so that the jurisdiction of the state could be extended over those regions, and the American refugees could return to their estates. "Sir Guy gave hope as to Westchester," but "as to Long Island he saw too many difficulties." There followed a general discussion, which was ended when "Washington pulled out his watch, and observing that it was near dinner time, offered wine and bitters." [32]

The difficulties which Carleton anticipated in evacuating New York were greatly increased by the violence shown those Loyalists who ventured to return to their former homes within the American lines. He had made plans for the sailing of the troops, provincials as well as regulars, and had asked for transports sufficient for the removal of a large part of the Tories, but he now found himself faced with the necessity of taking off practically all who had opposed the Revolution. "The violence of the Americans . . . increased the number of their countrymen to look to me for escape from threatened destruction," he wrote Elias Boudinot. "Almost all within these lines conceive the safety both of their property and of their lives depend upon their being removed by me, which renders it impossible to say when the evacuation will be completed." [33]

The people of the United States were determined to drive out all who had taken an active part in opposing the Revolution. The New Yorkers and Jerseymen especially, who had suffered so bitterly by the merciless raids of Tryon's provincials and of the Associated Loyalists, were in no humor to forgive and forget and welcome back as neighbors men who had so recently been burning and pillaging. Nor did they relish the thought that the Tories would certainly claim their confiscated property under the articles of the treaty and so cause trouble and the expense of legal battles. And the state governments, while themselves not taking a hand in the expulsion of the Loyalists, did little to restrain the violence of the Levellers, as the organized mobs came to be known.

It was with sympathy and indignation that Carleton listened to the complaints of those who had fallen into the hands of these men. The case of Joshua Booth was typical. A number of men had seized him near Goshen, New York, pinioned him and "carried him" to Ward's bridge, where they cut off his hair and shaved his eyebrows with a penknife, tarred and feathered his head and stuck a sheepskin cap over it. They then hung a cowbell around his neck and fixed on his forehead a paper with the inscription:

> "Look ye Tory crew
> and see what George
> your King can do."

In this condition he was forced to walk four miles, to the accompaniment of a drum and fife, to a near-by town and parade through the streets till "near midnight" amid "much mockery and insult." Finally he was placed aboard a sloop and sent down to New York City, where he was released.[34]

The treatment of Cavalier Jouett, who had taken his family to Woodbridge, New Jersey, "to speculate on the spirit of the times there," though less humiliating, was equally emphatic. When a prisoner on parole in this town some time previously the people had treated him with kindness, but they told him "the case was altered now," and that he "had no right or title to come there." So they came around him with sticks and whips in their hands, ready to give him a "continental jacket." When he asked whether he had ever injured any of them, they replied that he had proved a traitor to his country, and "that no such damned rascal should ever enjoy the benefits of the country again." At this juncture a general of the militia came up, but instead of reproving the mob, egged them on. In short, it was with "infinite difficulty" that Jouett escaped their clutches.[35]

Rather than face treatment such as this the Loyalists turned their faces to any part of the British Empire which would offer them an asylum. Fleet after fleet of transports came into New York Harbor, took on hundreds of refugees with such part of their property as they could take with them, and then headed for Nova Scotia or the St. John's River or the West Indies. One large group made a settlement in the Bahama Islands, for whom Carleton requested of the army in the West Indies six months provisions for 2,000 persons.[36] Among them was Thomas W. W. Bearans, who went to New Providence, "distressed and friendless, destitute not only of a sufficiency to carry him there in genteel character, but even to procure common necessaries for the voyage," and taking with him a "venerable mother very far advanced in years."[37]

Another group, numbering about 200 families, preferring the north to the heat of the West Indies, set out for historic Fort Frontenac to engage in the fur trade. To General Haldimand, Carleton wrote in the strongest terms, urging him to grant them lands, to remit any fees, and to supply them with provisions for a year.[38]

But the main stream continued to head for the Bay of Fundy. Day after day petitions poured into headquarters from individuals and groups, asking for grants of land and for transportation. The Associated Loyalists wanted to go to Nova Scotia, the King's American Dragoons wanted to go to Nova Scotia, the Westchester refugees wanted to go to Nova Scotia. The Reverend Charles Inglis, the Reverend Samuel Seabury and other ministers presented a plan for establishing an episcopate in Nova Scotia, for organizing of congregations and for the erection of churches and schools.

When Carleton learned that the provincial regiments wished to join the exiles, he called the officers together to ask what aid they wanted. After declaring "their detestation of that republican system which the leaders in the rebellion" were trying to establish, and pointing out that it would be "utterly impossible" for those who fought for the King to remain in the country, they made a plea for especial consideration. Many had entered the service very young, had grown up in the army and knew no other profession than that of the soldier. Their wives, "born to the fairest expectations," now faced hardship; the widows and orphans of officers and soldiers were reduced to extreme poverty. So they requested arms, ammunition, tools, building materials, clothing, provisions, three years pay and 300 acres for every private and more for officers.

Life in Nova Scotia, even for the younger men, seemed far from alluring; for the middle-aged and old, it appeared drear indeed. "I can't bear the idea," wrote one, "and it is distressing to me to think I should be drove with my wife in our old age and my two dear daughters to begin a settlement in a cold climate, and in the woods where we are to cut down the first tree. I can hardly expect to live to see the settlement so far advanced as to be in a tolerable comfortable way and then what a situation shall I leave my dear wife and daughters in." [39]

With the arrival of a large fleet of transports, the whole city seemed to be on the move. The streets were filled with men, women and children heading for the wharves—here a well-to-do tradesman, his chariot rolling over the streets, his household goods piled high in several carts, his servants trudging behind; here a Westchester farmer with his wife and children, driving before them a half dozen cattle; here a poor laborer, a bundle over his shoulder containing his meager possessions; here a company of militia, their bright uniforms belying the sadness of their hearts. There would have been endless delays at the office of the Superintendent of Exports and Imports, had not Carleton ordered him to pass every article the refugees thought necessary to take with them. So beds, chairs, boxes of clothing, kitchen utensils, farm implements, horses, cattle, went aboard the transports to occupy every inch of space not reserved for the passengers and crew.[40] On April 27, 1783, the ships hoisted sail and headed out to sea, taking with them some 7,000 persons.[41]

Present at the loading of the vessels were several American officers whose duty it was to prevent the carrying off of property belonging to American citizens. These men were not a little surprised to find that scores of Negroes were going on board, and at once protested to Carleton that this was an obvious breach of the treaty. But Carleton absolutely refused to surrender the blacks. "The Negroes I found free when I arrived at New York. I had therefore no right, as I thought, to prevent their going to any part of the world they thought proper." He was taking an accurate register, which would serve later to determine the former owner and the amount of compensation due him.[42] So when the fleet sailed, there were hundreds of former slaves aboard, who were leaving what for them had never been the land of freedom. Six months later a British naval officer, whose ship stopped at Nova Scotia, noted with interest the rapid growth of a refugee city at Port Roseway, with its population of 9,000, "exclusive of Black town," which had "about 1,200 free blacks," who had "served during the war." [43]

Even before the sailing of the fleet, additional thousands were applying for land in Nova Scotia and for berths on the transports. "No news here but that of evacuation," wrote a correspondent to the *Pennsylvania Packet*. "Some look smiling, others melancholy, and a third class mad . . . Some there are who represent the cold regions of Nova Scotia as a new-created Paradise, others as a country unfit for any human being to inhabit." [44] In the universal tragedy the individual tragedies were lost sight of—the separation of life-long friends, the breaking up of partnerships in business, the scattering of fellow commoners in lands, the severing of family ties, the plight of widows and orphans, the agony of the sick.

For some of the refugees, who had made all their preparations to sail, there were heartbreaking delays because of the inadequate number

of transports and the necessity of evacuating the regular troops. Not only
had shipping to be found for the New York garrison, but for the thousands of British and Hessian prisoners released by the Americans, who
now came pouring into the city. When Admiral Digby sent a part of
his fleet back to England, some of the regulars crowded on board, to go
with them, but other thousands had to wait. "The transports at present
destined for Nova Scotia with refugees have orders immediately after
their disembarkation to sail to the different ports in that province and
take on board all the foreign troops at present there and sail to the
Downs," Carleton wrote Lord North on June 17. By another fleet he
planned to send over "the Anspach, Waldeck, Hanau and Anhalt
Zerbst troops," followed by the Hessians. "But our present quantity of
tonnage is greatly inadequate to our various demands." [45]

Despite these interruptions, the flow of refugees to Nova Scotia
continued. On June 13, 3,000 persons embarked on fourteen transports.
By July 10, "the Hessian and other foreign troops taken with Burgoyne" had sailed, while a fleet of twenty-six transports, crowded with
refugees, was about to depart. And still the adjutant general's office
was crowded day after day with those who wished to leave, till, on
August 16, 5,339 new names were listed. [46] A month later a great fleet
went out past the Hook and headed east with about 8,000 persons, [47]
among them many of the provincial regiments—the British Legion,
the Queen's Rangers, the King's American Regiment, the New York
Volunteers, De Lancey's Volunteers, the Loyal Americans, the American Legion, etc. [48]

With the pressure to get away growing daily greater, large numbers
of brigs, schooners and sloops and an occasional ship were put into
service. On June 11, the brig *Charming Polly*, together with five smaller
vessels, their holds filled with "family effects," their decks crowded with
Loyalists, cleared for Nova Scotia. Thereafter the sailings became more
and more frequent until in August, September and October hardly
a day passed without several. On October 1, the sloop *Fanny*, the sloop
Nancy and the brig *Grace* left for Nova Scotia; two days later they
were followed by two brigs, four schooners and five sloops; on October
5, one brig, one schooner and three sloops went out; on the 17th three
brigs and two schooners left. In all there were over 175 sailings in five
months. [49]

Still, as the date of the final evacuation drew near, there were great
numbers left, whose services could not be dispensed with until the last

moment—"civil officers, artificers and laborers, armed boatsmen and seafaring people." "Besides, there will be a large embarkation of . . . merchants, farmers and mechanics and many persons of large property," Carleton wrote Governor Parr of Nova Scotia, "amounting to several thousands."

Throughout most of the year 1783 New York Harbor presented a scene of unprecedented activity. British, West Indian and American ports were scoured for transports, so that amid the forest of masts the Stars and Stripes mingled with the Union Jack. Lying peacefully side by side were privateers and frigates and ships of the line and merchant vessels, which perhaps a few months before had been facing each other in battle, or had played the hound and hare in the open ocean. Here could be seen a fleet, its decks lined with refugees, or red with the uniforms of the regulars, heading out into the Lower Bay; here a group of transports just in from Jamaica; here a score of ships, brigs and schooners, taking on a variety of commodities for the use of the exiles —food, clothing, spikes, nails, wood screws, hammers, lathing, shingles, locks, saws, window frames, sashes, medicines, even a knock-down windmill.[50]

Despite the continuous departure of thousands of persons the streets seemed as busy, as filled with people as ever, for many Americans moved in to take advantage of the business opportunities offered by the sale of Loyalist property. Down on the docks army commissaries were selling surplus stock—cattle, wagons, horses, firewood; on Queen Street there was one auction after another, as the departing merchants disposed of all goods they could not take with them; here one dealer was selling bricks, here another a pile of heavy timbers, there still another barrels of sugar, molasses and rum. It was bargain day for the buyers. "Several articles sold by auction have fallen surprisingly," noted Shewkirk, "flour, rum, molasses and coffee . . . Some men now meet with great losses."[51] A returning Revolutionist thought that some of the goods put up for sale had been taken from the Americans. "There is no end to auctions and vendues," he said, "everything is selling off, and I believe a great deal more than the venders can make a good title for."[52]

As though there was not enough of tragedy in the great exodus, fate dealt a cruel blow to one of the ships. At four o'clock on the morning of September 23, the *Martha*, a transport filled with soldiers and refugees, struck a sunken rock near Seal Island, off the coast of Maine.

The crew worked desperately to bring the vessel off, but finding that she stuck fast and that water was pouring into the hold, the master ordered out the long boat. But no sooner had it been placed in the water than the mast went over the side and smashed it. Thereupon the master, the mate and some others of the crew got into the yawl, and leaving the passengers to their fate, bore away with the wind. A few minutes later, looking back, they saw the *Martha* part asunder." [53]

In reporting the loss of the vessel, together with a list of the survivors, Carleton severely censured the conduct of the master, John Willis. But this did not bring back to life those who were lost, nor restore the property of those who were saved. The case of William Stafford was no doubt typical. After "struggling with amazing difficulties," he was "enabled barely to save his life." But he not only lost all his baggage, but the store of goods he had gathered to make it possible for him to make a start in Nova Scotia. Now he was back in New York, ill, destitute of clothing and utterly dependent upon his friends. [54] Even worse was the plight of Lieutenant Colonel Hewlett, "an unfortunate old man," the father of a large family, who was aboard the *Martha* with the greater part of his effects. The shipwreck, with the loss of everything upon which he had relied to start over in life, left him "in the utmost want, distress and misery." [55]

We cannot follow the twenty-nine thousand or more exiles in their new homes in Nova Scotia and St. John's as they cleared their fields, built their houses and barns, founded cities, became fishermen or traders. Many were the hardships they endured, many the adjustments it was necessary to make. In the building up of the great Dominion of Canada, with which the United States has so long enjoyed friendly relations, they played an important role.

Despite the reproaches which the Loyalists heaped on Great Britain for deserting them, the government was generous in granting compensation. In June, 1783, Parliament passed an act appointing commissioners to enquire into the losses and services of all who had suffered "in their rights, properties and professions" because of their loyalty to the King. Some of the commissioners sat in London, others in Halifax. By March 1790, over three million pounds had been paid, while pensions had been granted to 588 persons, most of them widows, orphans and others who had no means of earning a living. The New Yorkers fared well. Beverly Robinson, as it turned out, did not have to live on a meager pension or start life over in Nova Scotia, since the commissioners voted him £24,764; William Bayard received £19,397, Oliver De Lancey £24,940, Colonel William Axtell £9,442, Andrew Elliott £3,400, Judge Thomas Jones £5,392, the Reverend Charles Inglis £3,670, Isaac Low £5,667.[56]

While Loyalist New York was slowly expiring with the departure of the troops and exiles, the new New York, the New York of the young American republic, gradually came to life. The transformation began when word arrived that the preliminary articles of peace had been signed, it ended with the evacuation of the last British detachments and the entry of Washington's army. Houses which for seven years had been occupied by British officers, or commissaries, or army doctors, or the wives and children of soldiers, or used as hospitals or storehouses were gradually restored to their former owners. Shop keepers, who had fled at the approach of Howe's army, returned to town, secured a stock of goods from the departing Loyalists, and resumed business.

Trade was reopened with all parts of America. On May 9, 1783, alone, four vessels cleared for the Delaware, one for Rhode Island, two for Virginia, and two for Maryland.[57] So irritated were the Loyalists at the frequent appearance of the Stars and Stripes in the harbor, that on October 20 a mob boarded an American vessel, tore down the flag and carried it in triumph through the streets, "attended by a chosen banditti of Negroes, sailors and loyal leather aproned statesmen." Cornelius Bradford, "a steady patriot," who had been proprietor of the Merchants Coffee House before the Revolution, returned to resume business. Samuel Loudon, who for seven years had been forced to issue his *New York Packet* from Fishkill, announced that "the happy restoration of peace . . . invited his return to the city." When, on November 25, Washington's troops entered New York they found it a republican, not a Tory, city.

And this event was now close at hand. On November 19, Carleton notified Washington that the British troops would retire from Kingsbridge, McGowan's Pass, Hempstead and all eastern Long Island on the twenty-first. He expected, also, to evacuate Brooklyn and New York city at noon four days later, or "as soon after as wind and weather" permitted.

Already the people had been preparing for the great day. On the eighteenth "a large and respectable number of inhabitants, lately returned from a seven years exile," met at Cape's Tavern, on Broadway.

After requesting every person who had remained in New York during "the late contest" to leave the room, they pledged themselves to do their utmost to prevent disorders on the day of the evacuation and appointed a committee "to form a badge of distinction" to be worn by all patriots, and formulate a plan for receiving Governor Clinton and General Washington.[58]

The committee, at its meeting two days later, with Colonel Frederick Weissenfels in the chair, resolved that the badge should be a union cockade of black and white ribbon, worn on the left breast, and a sprig of laurel on the hat; that the citizens should assemble at the Bull's Head Tavern, in Bowery Lane, at nine o'clock; that Mr. Daniel Green be requested to carry the colors of the United States.

In the meanwhile, Governor Clinton and his suite had left Peekskill and proceeded to Edward Covenhoven's, at Tarrytown, where he was joined by General Washington. Together the general and the governor rode south, stopping at Yonkers and Harlem and finally arriving at "Mr. Stuyvesant's," just beyond the barrier, or fortified line across Manhattan. As they rode along through the farms and villages, they found the country greatly altered since that fatal September, seven years ago, when the American troops retired so precipitately before Sir William Howe's regiments. The woods had been swept away as by a hurricane, orchards had vanished, fences were few and far between, many estates formerly so beautifully cared for were run down, the mansions dilapidated.

The news that Washington was near spread through the city, and a number of patriotic persons, bringing American flags forth from their closets and chests, displayed them in anticipation of his entry. But the notorious William Cunningham, who still lingered in the city, took it upon himself to tear them down, at the same time delivering himself of "some scores of double-headed damns." He met his match on the morning of the twenty-fifth, however, when he tried to remove the Stars and Stripes from Day's Tavern, on Murray Street. Mrs. Day, a stout athletic woman, met him at the door, and when he tried to push past her, boxed his ears until the powder flew from his hair, forcing him to retreat amid the jeers and laughter of a few bystanders.

The morning of November 25 broke cold and clear, and at an early hour the streets were crowded with excited people. Up at McGowan's Pass the American troops were already stirring, and at eight o'clock started on their march to the city. When they reached the barrier, on the Bowery, near Grand Street, they halted, broke ranks, seated themselves on the grass and waited for the British to withdraw. At one o'clock the redcoats formed their column, and marching down the Bowery into Chatham and thence down Queen Street, turned off to the wharves along East River, where they were rowed out to the waiting British fleet.

No sooner had they cleared the barrier than the Americans, under General Knox, got under way. The crowds which had gathered along the Bowery, proudly displaying their union badge and cheering the troops, saw in the lead a corps of dragoons, followed in turn by an advance guard of light infantry, a corps of artillery, a battalion of light infantry, a battalion of Massachusetts troops and a rear guard. Down the Bowery they marched in the tracks of the British, into Chatham and Queen, and then, wheeling right into Wall Street, proceeded to Broadway, where they drew up in front of Cape's Tavern. Here they remained while a detail of infantry and artillery continued down Broadway to raise the American flag over Fort George.

At the fort they met with an unexpected delay. Some mischief-loving British, before taking their departure, had removed the halyards, knocked off the cleats and greased the pole. A sailor boy made three attempts to scale the pole, but each time slipped back. Then, while Washington, Clinton and the main body of troops waited, wondering why the delay, some person ran all the way to Golet's ironmongery in Hanover Square, returning with a saw, hammer and nails. After a board had been split into cleats, the sailor tied the halyards around his waist, and nailing the cleats as he went, climbed to the top and affixed the rope to the pulley. Thereupon the Stars and Stripes was hoisted amid the cheers of the crowd and the firing of guns.

It is strange that an event so momentous as the raising of the American flag over the last bit of American soil to be given up by the British should have been marked by this bit of comedy. Out in the bay aboard the royal warships, while the sailors prepared for the departure of the fleet, Carleton and his officers, as they saw the Stars and Stripes rise over the fort, could reflect upon the folly of the King and his ministers in alienating the affections of the Americans and driving them into rebellion. When George III came to the throne the colonists were proud to be members of the great British Empire, proud of their English inheritance, of the British representative system, of the common law, of their civil rights; they dressed in clothes made in the English fashion, built their houses after the Georgian mode, read English books, went to English plays. But now all was changed. Carleton knew, as he looked out over the water, that the raising of the American flag symbolized the breaking, not only of political ties, but the even stronger ties of tradition, loyalty and affection.

But it is unlikely that such thoughts disturbed the jubilation of the crowd assembled on the Bowling Green. With New York now officially in the hands of the Americans, Knox put himself at the head of a body of mounted citizens and galloped back to the Bowery to escort Washington and Clinton into the city. On their arrival the procession started. In the lead were the general and the governor with their suites escorted by the Westchester Light Horse, next came the lieutenant governor, then General Knox and a group of army officers, and then the mounted citizens, eight abreast. At the fresh water pump the column was joined by a large number of citizens on foot, who fell in behind, also marching eight abreast.

As the procession moved along there were many among the soldiers who noted with interest familiar landmarks they had not seen for seven years—the old windmill on the Bowery; the ropewalk; the Jews burying ground; the tanyard; the magnificent Walton House; the long rows of houses on Queen Street, prominent among them the Evert Byvanck House, the Robert R. Livingston House, the Isaac Roosevelt House, the Gerard De Peyster House; the City Hall and the Presbyterian Church on Wall Street; and finally, on Broadway, the ruins of Trinity Church.

Along the line of march the cheering crowds were interested first of all in catching a sight of Washington, the hero of the Revolution, the man who had kept the cause alive in the darkest hours of suffering and discouragement, the man who had outgeneraled Sir Henry Clinton and brought disaster to Cornwallis.[59] They gave a hearty welcome, also, to Governor George Clinton, the man of the people, who symbolized the new republican era that was dawning for the city. There were cheers too for General Knox and the officers who accompanied him, and for the Speaker of the Assembly.

That night Governor Clinton was host at a dinner at Fraunces Tavern, with General Washington, the higher officers and distinguished citizens as guests. Amid the clinking of glasses and the sound of animated conversation the company drank a series of toasts in appreciation of the great events of the struggle through which they had just passed and in anticipation of great things to come—to the United States of America, His most Christian Majesty, the American army, the memory of those heroes who have fallen for freedom, may justice support what courage has gained, may America be an asylum for the persecuted of the earth, may a close union of the states guard the temple they have erected to liberty.[60]

Prophetic as were these toasts, Washington and the other members of the group would have been incredulous could a vision of what the future held in store for the city and the nation been vouchsafed them —that the Dutch and Georgian houses which lined the crooked streets of New York would vanish and in their place appear great towering buildings that seemed to touch the sky; that the few thousand citizens would multiply until they could be counted by the millions; that the city limits would expand until all Manhattan, and large parts of Staten Island, Westchester and Long Island were covered with streets and buildings. They could not be expected to foresee that the infant United States would one day embrace all the vast region between the Atlantic and Pacific, and between Canada and the lower Rio Grande; that its three millions of people would become a hundred and forty millions; that its wealth would be the wonder of the world, its standard of living the highest in history. Nor could Washington have realized that the citizens of this great nation, even after the passage of a century and a half, woud revere his memory and acclaim him as the father of his country.

FOOTNOTES FOR CHAPTER I

1. Montresor's *Journal*, p. 336.
2. *Colden Papers*, 1877, (N. Y. Hist. Soc.), pp. 80–81.
3. The present City Hall Park.
4. *Post Boy*, Nov. 7, 1765.
5. Montresor's *Journal*, p. 338.
6. Between Chambers and Warren Streets.
7. *Post Boy*, Nov. 7, 1765; Montresor's *Journal*, p. 337; Mass. Hist. Soc. *Cols.*, Fourth Series, X, pp. 559–567.
8. *Assembly Journal*, II, pp. 769–773.
9. *Post Boy*, Nov. 28, 1765.
10. *N. Y. Gazette* (Weyman), Apr. 27–May 4, 1767; *Prior Docs.* (Lon. 1777), p. 163.
11. I. N. P. Stokes, *Iconography*, IV, p. 741.
12. Dec. 19, 1765.
13. Upcott Cols., (N. Y. Hist. Soc.), II, p. 289.
14. *N. Y. Journal*, Dec. 17, 1767.
15. *Post Boy*, May 8, 1766; *N. Y. Gazette* (Weyman), May 12, 1766.
16. A. M. Schlesinger, *The Colonial Merchant and the American Revolution*, p. 64.
17. *Ibid.* p. 77, *N. Y. Journal*, Dec. 17, 1767.
18. Montresor's *Journal*, p. 351.
19. *Post Boy*, Nov. 7, 1765.
20. *Ibid.*, May 30, 1765.
21. *Ibid.*, Jan. 23, 1766.
22. *Ibid.*, Apr. 24, 1766.
23. Clark, *Manufactures in U. S.*, p. 217.
24. *Mercury*, Apr. 25, 1768.
25. *N. Y. Col. Docs.* VII, pp. 795–800.
26. *Colden Papers*, (N. Y. Hist. Soc.), Sept. 2–Oct. 28, 1765.
27. Sept. 2, 1765.
28. Colden Papers, (N. Y. Hist. Soc.), Sept. 6, 1765, Colden to Gage.
29. Montresor's *Journal*, pp. 338–339.
30. *N. Y. Col. Docs.* VIII, p. 67; *Post Boy*, Nov. 14, 1765.
31. *Mercury*, Apr. 7, 1766.
32. *N. Y. Col. Docs.* VII, p. 802.
33. Upcott Cols. (N. Y. Hist. Soc.) II, p. 343.
34. Isaac Q. Leake, *General John Lamb*, (1857).

35. Montresor's *Journal*, p. 362.
36. *N. Y. Gazette* (Weyman) May 26, 1766; Montresor's *Journal*, pp. 367, 368.
37. *Min. Com. Coun.*, VII, p. 20
38. *N. Y. Journal*, Oct. 30, 1766; *Mercury*, Dec. 4, 1769.
39. *N. Y. Journal*, Apr. 16, 1767.
40. *Ibid.* Jan. 7, 1768; *Mercury*, Dec. 7, 1767.
41. *N. Y. Gazette*, (Weyman) Sept. 26, 1763.
42. *Mercury*, June 3, 1765.
43. *N. Y. Gazette*, (Weyman) March 2, 1767.
44. *Princeton Whig*, July 11, 1845.
45. *N. Y. Col. Docs.* VIII, pp. 265–266.
46. William Smith Diary, Dec. 1, 1770.
47. Clinton Papers, (Clements Library), N. Y. City Register.
48. Carl Bridenbaugh, *Cities in the Wilderness*, pp. 397–98.
49. *N. Y. Mirror*, March 17, 1832; *Memorial Hist. of N. Y. City*, II, p. 306.
50. On the site of the present St. John's Park.
51. *The Ratzer Map of N. Y. City*, 1767.
52. I. N. P. Stokes, *Iconography*, IV, p. 981.
53. M. J. Lamb, *Hist. of City of N. Y.*, I, p. 757.
54. *Mercury*, Jan. 9, 1770.
55. *N. Y. Gazette*, (Weyman) Feb. 15, 1768.
56. *Independent Reflector*, July 5, 1753.
57. E. B. Livingston, *The Livingstons of Livingston Manor*, p. 168.
58. *Ibid.*, p. 178.
59. M. J. Lamb, *Hist. of the City of N. Y.*, I, p. 644.
60. *N. Y. Col. Docs.*, VII, 795–800.
61. *Ibid.* p. 813.
62. *N. Y. Gazette*, (Weyman) Jan. 19–26, 1767.
63. Montresor's *Journal*, p. 368.
64. *Ibid.* p. 382.
65. *Post Boy*, Sept. 25, 1766.
66. *N. Y. Journal*, March 26, 1767.
67. *Post Boy*, Feb. 5, 1770.
68. *N. Y. Journal*, Feb. 8, 1770.
69. I. N. P. Stokes, *Iconography*, IV, p 805.
70. *Assembly Jour.*, 1768–9, pp. 70, 71.
71. *Ibid.*, pp. 75–76.
72. *Ibid.*, 1769–70, p. 38.
73. I. N. P. Stokes, *Iconography*, Vol. IV, p. 799.
74. *N. Y. Col. Docs.*, VIII, p. 208.

75. *N. Y. Journal,* Feb. 15, 1770, March 29, 1770; *Post Boy,* Feb. 19, 1770.
76. I. N. P. Stokes, *Iconography,* IV, p. 789.
77. *Mercury,* May 1, 1769.
78. *Ibid.,* May 25, 1769.
79. *N. Y. Journal,* June 22, 1769.
80. *Ibid.,* Sept. 21, 1769.
81. *Ibid.,* July 20, 27, 1767.
82. *Mercury,* Aug. 7, 1769.
83. *Ibid.,* Feb. 19, 1770.

FOOTNOTES FOR CHAPTER II

1. *N. Y. Col. Docs.,* VIII, p. 217. A. M. Schlesinger, *The Colonial Merchants and the American Revolution,* p. 223.
2. *Mercury,* July 16, 1770.
3. *N. Y. Journal,* July 19, 1770.
4. *Ibid.,* July 5, 1770.
5. *Mercury,* June 18, 1770.
6. G. Hunt, *Writings of James Madison,* I, p. 7.
7. *N. Y. Journal,* July 19, 1770.
8. *Mercury,* July 30, 1770.
9. *Post Boy,* June 4, 1770, Aug. 20, 1770.
10. I. N. P. Stokes, *Iconography,* IV, pp. 813, 814.
11. B. J. Lossing, *Field Book of the Revolution,* II, p. 583n.
12. William Smith Diary, Oct. 18, 19, 1770.
13. *Ibid.,* Dec. 1, 1770.
14. *Ibid.,* July 8, 1771.
15. *Ibid.,* July 9, 1772.
16. *Mercury,* March 12, 1770.
17. *Ibid.,* Dec. 7, 1772.
18. *N. Y. Journal,* June 10, 1773.
19. *Ibid.,* June 10, 1773.
20. *Mercury,* March 1, 1773.
21. *Ibid.,* Apr. 12, 1773.
22. *N. Y. Journal,* Sept. 2, 1773.
23. *Mercury,* June 5, 1773.
24. William Smith Diary, Oct. 13, 1773.
25. *Penna. Journal,* Oct. 20, 1773.
26. *Mercury,* Nov. 15, 1773.
27. *Gazetteer* (Rivington) Dec. 2, 1773.

28. William Smith Diary, Dec. 17, 18, 1773.
29. I. N. P. Stokes, *Iconography*, VI, p. 843.
30. William Smith Diary, Dec. 25, 1773.
31. *N. Y. Journal*, Apr. 21, 1774.
32. *Gazetteer*, (Rivington), Apr. 28, 1774.
33. *Ibid.*, Apr. 28, 1774.
34. *Ibid.*
35. *Ibid.*
36. I. N. P. Stokes, *Iconography*, VI, p. 853.
37. William Smith Diary, May 18, 1774.
38. *N. Y. Journal*, July 7, 1774.
39. I. N. P. Stokes, *Iconography*, VI, p. 852.
40. *Ibid.*, p. 853.
41. William Smith Diary, May 18, 1774.
42. I. N. P. Stokes, *Iconography*, IV, p. 853; *Gazetteer* (Rivington) May 19, 1774; *N. Y. Journal*, May 19, 1774.
43. *Amer. Archives*, Ser. 4, I, 343; Jared Sparks, *Life of Gouverneur Morris*, I, 23, 24.
44. *Gazetteer*, (Rivington) May 26, 1774. A. M. Schlesinger, *The Colonial Merchants and the American Revolution*, pp. 329–30.
45. Isaac Q. Leake, *General John Lamb*, p. 91.
46. *Amer. Archives*, Ser. 4, I, 300n; Wilbur C. Abbott, *New York in the American Revolution*, pp. 105–08.
47. William Smith Diary, June 14, 1774.
48. *N. Y. Journal*, June 16, 23, 1774.
49. *Amer. Archives*, Ser. 4, I, p. 307.
50. *Ibid.*, 308–09.
51. C. F. Adams, *The Works of John Adams*, II, pp. 350–354.
52. I. N. P. Stokes, *Iconography*, IV, p. 859.
53. *Amer. Archives*, Ser. 4, I, 312–313.
54. William Smith Diary, July 19, 1774.
55. *Amer. Archives*, Ser. 4, I, 319–320.
56. Jay had left two days before.
57. *Mercury*, Sept. 7, 1774.
58. Still standing.
59. C. F. Adams, *The Works of John Adams*, II, p. 394.
60. *Jour. Cont. Cong.* I, p. 58.
61. William Smith Diary, Sept. 7, 1774.
62. *History Magazine*, 2d Ser. IV, pp. 289, 290; William Smith Diary, Sept. 7, 1774.
63. *Amer. Archives*, Ser. 4, I, 804.
64. *London Packet*, Apr. 5–7, 1775.

65. *N. Y. Col. Docs.,* VIII, p. 528; *Gazetteer* (Rivington) Jan. 5, 1775.
66. *N. Y. Col. Docs.,* VIII, pp. 512, 513.
67. *Amer. Archives,* Ser. 4, I, 915, 916.
68. *Ibid.,* I, 1191.
69. *Ibid.,* I, 1243–44.
70. Gage Papers, (Clements Library), Amer. Ser. Vol. 126, Feb. 20, 1775.
71. *Amer. Archives,* Ser. 4, I, 1191.
72. *London Packet,* Apr. 14–17, 1775.
73. *Amer Archives,* Ser. 4, I, 804.
74. *N. Y. Journal,* Sept. 15, 1774.
75. I. N. P. Stokes, *Iconography,* IV, p. 880.
76. William Smith Diary, Apr. 15, 24, 1775.
77. *Mercury,* Dec. 12, 1774.
78. *Ibid.,* Dec. 19, 1774.
79. *Amer. Archives,* Ser. 4, I, 1191.
80. *Ibid.,* 1203.
81. *Assembly Jour.* (1775), p. 38.
82. *Ibid.,* p. 40, Gage Papers, (Clements Library) Colden to Gage, Feb. 20, 1775.
83. *Amer. Archives,* Ser. 4, I, 1203.
84. Gage Papers, (Clements Library), Gage to Colden, Feb. 26, 1775.
85. *Amer. Archives,* Ser. 4, I, 1180.
86. *Ibid.,* II, 242; 243.
87. *Ibid.,* 118.
88. I. N. P. Stokes, *Iconography,* IV, p. 881.
89. Upcott *Cols.* (N. Y. Hist. Soc.), IV, p. 299.
90. *Amer. Archives,* Ser. 4, II, 4.
91. *Ibid.,* 48, 49.
92. *Ibid.,* 351–358.
93. *N. Y. Col. Docs.,* VIII, p. 566. Wilbur C. Abbott, *New York in the American Revolution,* pp. 137, 141–45.
94. *Gazetteer* (Rivington) March 7, 1775.
95. *Amer. Archives,* Ser. 4, II, 12–13.
96. *Ibid.,* 111–114.
97. *N. Y. Col. Docs.* VIII, 485–6.
98. Gage Papers, (Clements Library), Vol. 127, Intelligence, March 21, 1775.
99. *Ibid.,* Apr. 19,1775. Letters from London.
100. *Ibid.*

FOOTNOTES FOR CHAPTER III

1. William Smith Diary, Apr. 27, 1775.
2. *Penna. Journal,* Apr. 26, 1775.
3. William Smith Mss., Smith to Lewis Morris.
4. Thomas Jones, *Hist. of N. Y. during Rev,* I, 39, 40.
5. I. N. P. Stokes, *Iconography,* IV, 881; William Smith Diary, Apr. 27, 1775.
6. *Ibid.*
7. *Ibid.*
8. *Amer. Archives,* Ser. 4, II, 363.
9. *Ibid.,* 448, 449.
10. Gage Papers, (Clements Library), Colden to Gage, May 6, 1775.
11. *Amer. Archives,* Ser. 4, I, 1293–1297.
12. *Ibid.,* II, 389.
13. *N. Y. Col. Docs.,* VIII, 297–298, 581; Gage Papers, (Clements Library), Colden to Gage, May 6, 1775.
14. *Colden Papers,* (N. Y. Hist. Soc.), pp. 413, 414.
15. *N. Y. Journal,* May 4, 1775; *Amer. Archives,* Ser. 4, II, 448, 449.
16. *Ibid.,* 468.
17. *Jour. Prov. Cong.,* I, 7–9.
18. Gage Papers, (Clements Library), I. Hamilton to Gage, May 25, 1775.
19. Gage Papers, (Clements Library), Hamilton to Gage, June 8, 1775; N. Y. Hist. Soc. *Cols.* 1877, p. 425.
20. Gage Papers (Clements Library), Stephens to Gage, June 24, 1775.
21. *Amer. Archives,* Ser. 4, II, 1106.
22. *Ibid.,* 1342.
23. William Smith Diary, Apr. 27, 1775.
24. *Jour. Prov. Cong.,* I, 31.
25. *New Eng. Hist. of Geneal. Reg.,* XIX, 135–136.
26. M. J. Lamb, *Hist. of the City of N. Y.,* II, 46, Gilbert Livingston to Dr. Peter Tappan; Thomas Jones, *Hist. of N. Y. during Rev.* I, 55.
27. Gage Papers, (Clements Library), Tryon to Gage, June 26, 1775.
28. *Amer. Archives* Ser. 4, II, 1297.
29. *Ibid.,* 1322.
30. *Jour. Prov. Cong.* I, pp. 77, 78, 81, 104, 105.
31. *Mercury,* Sept. 4, 1775.
32. *Amer. Archives,* Ser. 4, III. 259–260; *Gazetteer,* (Rivington), Aug.

31, 1775; *N. Y. Col. Docs.*, VIII, 631–2; *London Chronicle*, Oct. 19–20.

33. Shewkirk Diary, Apr. 29, Aug. 28, 1775.
34. *N. Y. Col. Docs.*, VIII, 632
35. *London Chronicle*, Aug. 22–24, 1775.
36. Gage Papers, (Clements Library), May 25, 1775.
37. *Ibid.*, J. F. to Gage, June 14, 1775.
38. *Ibid.*, June 15, 1775.
39. *Amer. Archives*, Ser. III, 884–5.
40. *Gazetteer* (Rivington), Sept. 28, 1775.
41. "Shewkirk Diary," Oct. 19, 1775.
42. I. N. P. Stokes, *Iconography*, IV, 905.
43. *Penna. Jour.*, Dec. 6, 1775.
44. *Amer. Archives*, Ser. 4, IV, 185–186.
45. Gage Papers, (Clements Library), Aug. 14, 1775.
46. *Mercury*, Aug. 14, 23, 1775.
47. Justin H. Smith, *Our Struggle for the Fourteenth Colony*, I, p. 257.
48. *Ibid.*, p. 262.
49. *Ibid.*, p. 335.
50. *Amer. Archives*, Ser. 4, III, 1208.
51. *Ibid.*, 1595.
52. *Ibid.*, IV, 668, 669, 707, 708.
53. *Mercury*, Dec. 18, 1775.
54. William Smith Diary, Dec. 4, 9, 1775.
55. *Gage Papers*, (Clements Library), May 5, 1775.
56. *N. Y. Col. Docs.* VIII, 598, 633.
57. I. N. P. Stokes, *Iconography*, IV, 984.
58. William Smith Diary, Feb. 4, 1776.
59. *Mercury*, Nov. 13, Dec. 11, 1775.
60. *Ibid.*, Dec. 11, 1775.
61. *Penna. Eve. Post*, Feb. 6, 8, 1776.
62. *Ibid.*, Feb. 10, 1776; I. N. P. Stokes, *Iconography*, IV, p. 913.
63. M. W. Willard, *Letters of the American Revolution*, p. 305.
64. "Shewkirk Diary," Feb. 5, 1776.
65. *N. Y. Packet*, Feb. 15, 1776.
66. *Amer. Archives*, Ser. 4, IV, 1480.
67. *Ibid.*, 1144, 1145.
68. *Ibid.* 1144, 1145.
69. *N. Y. Col. Docs.*, VIII, 674.
70. William Smith Diary, Feb. 11, 1776.
71. M. W. Willard, *Letters of the American Revolution*, p. 306.
72. "Shewkirk Diary," Feb. 11, 1776.

73. *Life of Peter Van Schaack*, p. 53.
74. *Jour. Prov. Cong.*, I, 299.
75. M. W. Willard, *Letters of the American Revolution*, p. 303.
76. T. J. Wertenbaker, *The Torchbearer of the Revolution*, pp. 166–68.
77. T. J. Wertenbaker, *Norfolk-Historic Southern Port*, pp. 68, 69.
78. *Jour. Cont. Cong.*, IV, 196, 201–4.
79. Henry P. Johnston, *Campaign of 1776*, pp. 84–90.
80. M. W. Willard, *Letters of the American Revolution*, p. 302.
81. *Ibid.*, p. 303.
82. "Shewkirk Diary," Feb. 17, 1776; *Mercury*, Feb. 19, 1776.
83. *Mercury*, March 25, 1776.
84. M. W. Willard, *Letters of the American Revolution*, p. 303.
85. William Smith Diary, March 21, 1776.
86. *Ibid.*
87. *Jour. Prov. Cong.*, I, 333.
88. *Mercury*, May 6, 1776.
89. *N. Y. Journal*, Apr. 4, 1776.
90. *Penna. Eve. Post.*, Apr. 9, 1776.
91. *N. Y. Col. Docs.*, VIII, 675–77.
92. *Writings of George Washington*, (Ford ed.), IV, 17–19.

FOOTNOTES FOR CHAPTER IV

1. *Writings of George Washington* (Ford ed.), III, 468–469.
2. Chas. M. Lefferts, *Uniforms in the Revolution*, pp. 77, 90, 91.
3. *Hist. Mag.*, 2nd Ser., V, 203.
4. *Mercury*, Apr. 15, 1776.
5. *Ibid.*, Aug. 18, 1776.
6. Apr. 18, 1776.
7. *Fithian Journal* (Albion and Dodson eds.), p. 187n.
8. Ward's Island.
9. Randall's Island.
10. *Fithian Journal* (Albion and Dodson eds.) p. 209.
11. *Ibid.*, p. 227.
12. *Ibid.*, pp. 242, 243.
13. I. N. P. Stokes, *Iconography*, V, 1001.
14. *Amer. Archives*, Ser. 4, VI, 635, 636.
15. *Fithian Journal*, (Albion and Dodson eds.), pp. 196, 197.
16. I. N. P. Stokes, *Iconography*, V., p. 999.
17. *Ibid.*, IV, p. 923.
18. *Jour. Prov. Cong.*, I, p. 568.

19. "Shewkirk Diary," June 13, 1776.
20. Thomas Jones, *Hist. of N. Y. during the Rev.*, I, p. 103.
21. Clinton Papers, (Clements Library), Henry Brevoort to Tryon, March 1778.
22. *N. Y. Packet*, Apr. 11, 1776.
23. I. N. P. Stokes, *Iconography*, IV, p. 939.
24. *N. Y. Col. Docs.*, VIII, pp. 683–684.
25. Thomas Jones, *Hist. of N. Y. during the Rev.*, I, pp. 108, 109.
26. *New York City during the Rev.* (1861), pp. 66–81; *Penna. Jour.*, June 20, 1776.
27. *Penna. Eve. Post*, July 2, 1776.
28. M. W. Willard, *Letters of the American Revolution*, p. 176.
29. Thomas Paine.
30. *Mercury*, June 10, 1776.
31. *Amer. Archives*, Ser. 4, VI, 743–44.
32. *Jour. Prov. Cong.*, I, p. 518.
33. B. J. Lossing, *Field Book of the Rev.*, II, p. 801.
34. *Penna. Eve. Post*, July 13, 1776.
35. *Fithian Journal* (Albion and Dodson eds.), p. 188.
36. Montresor's *Journal*, pp. 123–24.
37. *The Diary . . . of Thomas Hutchinson* (P. O. Hutchinson ed.), II, p. 167.
38. I. N. P. Stokes, *Iconography*, V, p. 992.
39. *Fithian Journal* (Albion and Dodson eds.), p. 190.
40. *Doc. Hist. of N. Y.* III, p. 642.
41. *Ibid*, p. 641.
42. *Ibid.*, p. 642.
43. *New England Chronicle*, July 11, 1776.
44. I. N. P. Stokes, *Iconography*, V, p. 993.
45. *Amer. Jour. of Ambrose Serle*, (E. H. Tatum, Jr., ed.), p. 28.
46. *Ibid.*, p. 62
47. *Fithian Journal* (Albion and Dodson, eds.), p. 208.
48. *Mercury*, Aug. 19, 1776; Stuart, *Life of Nathan Hale*, pp. 70, 71.
49. Thomas Jones, *Hist. of N. Y. during the Rev*, I, pp. 106, 107.
50. *Ibid.*
51. Henry P. Johnston, *Battle of Harlem Heights*, p. 217.
52. *Amer. Jour. of Ambrose Serle*, (E. H. Tatum, Jr. ed.), p. 47.
53. *Ibid*, p. 68
54. *Ibid.*, pp. 36, 37.
55. *Ibid.*, p. 31.
56. *Correspondence and Jour. of S. B. Webb*, I, p. 156.
57. *N. Y. Packet*, Aug. 1, 1776; *Mercury*, July 22, 1776.

58. Brooklyn Heights.
59. T. W. Field, *Battle of Long Island*, p. 221.
60. *Fithian Journal* (Albion and Dodson, eds.), p. 217.
61. *London Gazette*, Oct. 10, 1776.
62. Henry P. Johnston, *The Campaign of 1776*, pp. 185, 186.
63. Christopher L. Ward, *The Delaware Continentals*, pp. 38–41.
64. *Fithian Journal* (Albion and Dodson, eds.), p. 219.
65. *London Gazette*, Oct. 10, 1776.
66. *Fithian Journal* (Albion and Dodson, eds.), p. 219.
67. Henry P. Johnston, *The Campaign of 1776*, pp. 221, 222.
68. "Shewkirk Diary," Aug. 30, 1776.
69. At Varick and Charlton Streets.
70. *Writings of George Washington* (Ford ed.), IV, pp. 395, 396.
71. *Amer. Archives*, Ser. 4, V, 326.
72. *Amer. Jour. of Ambrose Serle* (E. H. Tatum, Jr., ed.), p. 104.
73. *Ibid.*
74. Henry P. Johnston, *The Campaign of 1776*, p. 234.
75. I. N. P. Stokes, *Iconography*, V, p. 1013.
76. Murray Hill, near Fourth Avenue and 36th Street.
77. Henry P. Johnston. *The Campaign of 1776*, p. 236.
78. I. N. P. Stokes, *Iconography*, V, p. 1014.
79. Dr. Jas. Thatcher, *Military Journal* (Boston, 1823), pp. 70, 71.
80. Henry P. Johnston, *The Campaign of 1776*, pp. 238, 239.
81. I. N. P. Stokes, *Iconography*, V, p. 1014.
82. "Shewkirk Diary," Sept. 15, 1776.
83. *Ibid.*, Sept. 15, 16, 1776; *Amer. Jour. of Ambrose Serle* (E. H. Tatum, ed.), pp. 104–106.

FOOTNOTES FOR CHAPTER V

1. *Conn. Gaz.* (New London), March 7, 1777; Wilbur C. Abbott, *New York in the Revolution*, p. 215.
2. *Amer. Archives*, Ser. 5, II, p. 182.
3. I. N. P. Stokes, *Iconography*, V, p. 999.
4. *Jour. Cont. Cong.* (Ford, ed.), V, 33–34.
5. *Amer. Archives*, Ser. 5, II, 193.
6. *Mercury*, Sept. 28, 1776.
7. *Ibid.*
8. I. N. P. Stokes, *Iconography*, V, p. 1020.
9. *St. James's Chronicle*, Nov. 7–9, 1776; N. Y. Hist. Soc. *Cols.* (1870), p. 275.

10. Morris Street.
11. *Mercury,* Sept. 28, 1776.
12. Fulton Street, west of Broadway.
13. It still stands, a lonely relic of colonial New York.
14. Fulton Street, east of Broadway.
15. "Shewkirk Diary," Sept. 21, 1776.
16. *St. James's Chronicle,* Nov. 7–9, 1776.
17. *Amer. Archives,* Ser. 5, II, 462, 463.
18. "Shewkirk Diary," Sept. 21, 1776.
19. *Mercury,* Sept. 28, 1776.
20. *Penna. Jour.* Nov. 20, 1776.
21. "Shewkirk Diary," Sept. 23, 1776.
22. Carleton Papers, (Colonial Williamsburg), Doc. 9388.
23. I. N. P. Stokes, *Iconography,* IV, p. 1024.
24. *Ind. Chron.* (Boston), May 17, 1781.
25. *Doc. Hist. of N. Y.* III, p. 643.
26. I. N. P. Stokes, *Iconography,* V, 1018.
27. "Shewkirk Diary," Dec. 17, 1776.
28. *St. James's Chron.,* March 22–25, 1777.
29. *Mag. of Dutch Reformed Church,* II, p. 412.
30. Thomas Jones, *Hist. of N. Y. during the Rev.* I, pp. 162, 163.
31. Clinton Papers, (Clements Library), Letter to John Leland, Feb. 12, 1782, probably written by Gov. Wm. Franklin.
32. Thomas Jones, *Hist. of N. Y. during the Rev.* I, pp. 136, 137.
33. "Shewkirk Diary," Dec. 1, 1776.
34. Henry P. Johnston, *Battle of Harlem Heights,* p. 184.
35. Clinton Papers, (Clements Library), Return of Men, Women, etc. March, 1779.
36. Pearl Street.
37. Clinton Papers, (Clements Library), N. Y. City Register.
38. *Ibid.*
39. *Conn. Gazette,* March 7, 1777.
40. Clinton Papers (Clements Library), N. Y. City Register.
41. *Diary of Jabez Fitch,* pp. 21–22.
42. *Amer. Archives,* Ser. 5, III, p. 76.
43. Carleton Papers, (Colonial Williamsburg), Memorial of John Livingston, Nov. 7, 1782.
44. Fulton Street.
45. *Diary of Jabez Fitch,* pages unnumbered after 130.
46. "Shewkirk Diary," Nov. 18, 1776.
47. *Mercury,* Oct. 14, 21, 1776.
48. Morgan Dix, *Hist. of the Parish of Trinity Church,* p. 393.

49. *Mercury*, March 10, 1777.
50. Clinton Papers, (Clements Library), Browne to Clinton, Nov. 9, 1778.
51. *Ibid.*, Inglis to Tryon, Apr. 25, 1778.
52. *Amer. Archives*, Ser. 5, II, 379–380.
53. *Ibid.*, 943.
54. *The Amer. Jour. of Science and Arts*, II, 94–100.
55. *Amer. Archives*, Ser. 5, II, 351.
56. *Ibid.*, 444.
57. *Ibid.*, 1117–1118.
58. Quoted by C. L. Ward, *The Delaware Continentals*, p. 85.
59. William Heath, *Memoirs*, pp. 73, 75.
60. Kemble's *Jour.*, pp. 90–100; *London Packet*, Jan. 6–8, 1777; Henry P. Johnston, *Battle of Harlem Heights*, pp. 229–231.
61. "Shewkirk Diary," Nov. 16, 1776.
62. *Amer. Archives*, Ser. 5, III, 811.
63. Leonard Lundin, *Cockpit of the Revolution*, pp. 141–148.
64. *Stevens Facsimiles*, XXIV, Nos. 2046, 2048.
65. Kemble's *Jour.*, p. 92.
66. *Amer. Archives*, Ser. 5, III, 601, 1169, 1174.
67. Clinton Papers, (Clements Library), Peter Dubois to Clinton, Jan. 24, 1778.
68. *Ibid..* "Report of Mapor André."
69. *Ibid.*, "Patrick Ferguson *re:* Marauding," Nov. 1779.
70. T. J. Wertenbaker, *Torchbearer of the Revolution*, p. 135.
71. Leonard Lundin, *Cockpit of the Revolution*, pp. 177–187.
72. Alfred Hoyt Bill, *The Campaign of Princeton*, pp. 44–62.
73. *N. Y. Col. Docs.*, VIII, p. 694.
74. Trevelyan, *The Amer. Rev.*, Part II, II, p. 150.
75. T. J. Wertenbaker, "The Battle of Princeton," in *The Princeton Battle Monument*.
76. *London Packet*, March 3–5, 1777; *Mercury*, Nov. 11, 1776.
77. William Smith Diary, Apr. 8, 1777.
78. *Mercury*, Oct. 28, 1776.
79. *Ibid.*, Jan. 20, 1777.
80. I. N. P. Stokes, *Iconography*, IV, p. 1045.
81. *St. James's Chronicle*, June 12–14, 1777.
82. *Mercury*, Jan. 13, 1777.
83. *Ibid.*, June 16, 1777.
84. *Ibid.*, Jan. 13, Aug. 16, 1777.
85. I. N. P. Stokes, *Iconography*, IV, p. 1042.
86. *Mercury*, Jan. 6, 27, Feb. 10, 1777; *St. James's Chronicle*, Apr. 1–3, 1777.

87. *Mercury,* Sept. 29, 1777; "Shewkirk Diary," Sept. 25, 1777.
88. *Jour. of Hugh Gaine,* II, p. 19.
89. *Mercury,* Jan. 20, 1777.
90. Münchhausen's *Journal,* Dec, 13, 1776.
91. Geo. H. Moore, *The Treason of Charles Lee.*

FOOTNOTES FOR CHAPTER VI

1. Thomas Jones, *Hist. of N. Y. during the Rev.,* I, p. 171.
2. *Parl. Reg.* (1779), XI, pp. 386–88.
3. *Hist. Man. Commission,* Report on Stopford-Sackville Mans., II, pp. 63–64.
4. William Smith Diary, II, pp. 296–97.
5. Münchhausen's *Journal,* June 11–13, 1777.
6. *Ibid.,* June 20, 21, 22, 1777; J. C. Fitzpatrick, *The Writings of Geo. Washington,* VIII, p. 281.
7. *Ibid.,* pp. 295, 298–99.
8. Münchhausen's *Journal,* June 24, 25, 1777.
9. Kemble's *Jour.,* pp. 123–24.
10. Captain Hall, *The History of the Civil War in America,* p. 297 Stevens *Facsimiles, XXIV,* No. 2066.
11. William Eddis, *Letters from America,* p. 418.
12. Thomas Jones, *Hist. of N. Y. during the Rev.,* I, p. 319.
13. Clinton Papers, (Clements Library), Clinton to E. Harvey, July 11, 1777.
14. *André's Journal,* (H. C. Lodge ed.), II, p. 34.
15. Clinton Papers, (Clements Library), Howe to Clinton, Nov. 27, 1777.
16. *Mercury,* July 21, 1777.
17. *Royal Gazette,* Oct. 28, 1780.
18. *Jour. of Hugh Gaine,* II, p. 50.
19. Clinton Papers, (Clements Library), Clinton to Burgoyne, Sept. 10, 1777.
20. *Ibid.,* Clinton Memorandum.
21. *Ibid.*
22. *Royal Gazette,* Oct. 25, 1777.
23. Clinton Papers, (Clements Library), Gates to Clinton, Oct. 31, 1777.
24. *Ibid.,* Clinton and Burgoyne, Sept. 10 to Oct. 23, 1777.
25. *Ibid.*
26. Hoffman Nickerson, *The Turning Point of the Revolution,* pp. 401–02.

27. Clinton Papers, (Clements Library), Oct. 25, 1777.
28. *Narrative of Abraham Leggett*, (C. I. Bushnell ed.), pp. 21–22.
29. *St. James's Chronicle*, Dec. 30, 1777.
30. *Ibid.*, Jan. 8–10, 1778.
31. "Shewkirk Diary," Nov. 29, 1777; *St. James's Chronicle*, Jan. 17–20, 1778.
32. Clinton Papers, (Clements Library), John Campbell to Clinton, Nov. 27, 1777.
33. Nov. 29, 1777.
34. *Royal Gazette*, Dec. 27, 1777.
35. Dec. 1, 1777.
36. *St. James's Chronicle*, Sept. 23–25, 1777.
37. Clinton Papers, (Clements Library), Mayor, etc. to Clinton, July 9, 1778.
38. *Royal Gazette*, Dec. 27, 1777.
39. May 25, 1778.
40. *Mercury*, Nov. 24, 1777.
41. *Royal Gazette*, Jan. 1, 1778.
42. *Mercury*, Jan. 5, 1778.
43. Feb. 14, 1778.
44. Clinton Papers, (Clements Library), July 9, 1778.
45. *Mercury*, Dec. 1, 1777.
46. *Royal Gazette*, Jan. 3, 1778.
47. I. N. P. Stokes, *Iconography*, V, p. 1060.
48. *Royal Gazette*, Jan. 31, 1778.
49. W. E. H. Lecky, *The American Revolution*, pp. 343–45.
50. *N. Y. Journal*, (Poughkeepsie), June 8, 1778.
51. June 13, 1778.
52. *N. Y. Journal*, June 8, 1778.
53. *New Jersey Archives*, 2d Ser., II, p. 181.
54. Stevens *Facsimiles*, V, p. 500.
55. *Ibid.*, p. 508.
56. *Annual Register*, (1778), pp. 327–29.
57. Clinton Papers, (Clements Library), Clinton on his Situation.
58. *Ibid.*, Clinton to Germain, June 5 and 13, 1778.
59. Thomas Jones, *Hist. of N. Y. during the Rev.*, I, pp. 241–51.
60. Stevens *Facsimiles*, V, p. 501.

FOOTNOTES FOR CHAPTER VII

1. Thomas Jones, *Hist. of N. Y. during the Rev.*, II, pp. 120–21.
2. O. T. Barck, Jr., *N. Y. City during the War for Indep.*, p. 53.
3. William Smith Diary, Oct. 4, 1779.
4. Thomas Jones, *Hist. of N. Y. during the Rev.*, II, pp. 85–86.
5. *Ibid.*, II, p. 121.
6. William Smith Diary, Sept. 12, 1779.
7. *Mercury*, May 4, 1778.
8. Thomas Jones, *Hist. of N. Y. during the Rev.*, II, pp. 92–93.
9. Carleton Papers, (Colonial Williamsburg), Doc. 7350.
10. Thomas Jones, *Hist. of N. Y. during the Rev.*, II, pp. 93–94.
11. Carleton Papers, (Colonial Williamsburg), Vol. 46, Doc. 5234.
12. Stevens *Facsimiles*, XII, No. 1226; *Royal Gazette*, Nov. 25, 1778.
13. William Smith Diary, Oct. 19, 1779.
14. *Royal Gazette*, Apr. 19, 1780.
15. *Ibid.*, July 12, 1780.
16. Clinton Papers, (Clements Library), Clinton to Robertson, June 27, 1780.
17. *Ibid.*, Smith to Clinton, Nov. 30, 1781.
18. *Ibid.*, Clinton Letter, Jan. 24, 1782.
19. William Smith Diary, May 27, June 17, 1782.
20. Clinton Papers, (Clements Library), André to Clinton.
21. "Shewkirk Diary," Dec. 18, 1780.
22. William Smith Diary, May 18, 1780.
23. Kemble's *Journal*, p. 167.
24. Clinton Papers, (Clements Library), J. W. Watson to Clinton, Oct. 11 and 12, 1782.
25. Thomas Jones, *Hist of N. Y. during the Rev.*, I, pp. 330–332.
26. *Ibid.*, pp. 332–335.
27. *Ibid.*, p. 336.
28. *Ibid.*, pp. 336–337.
29. *Ibid.*, pp. 333–339.
30. Clinton Papers, (Clements Library), Loyalists to Carleton, May 24, 1782; Van Boskerke to Carleton, May 29, 1782.
31. Thomas Jones, *Hist. of N. Y. during the Rev.*, I, p. 338.
32. *Ibid.*, p. 340.
33. *Ibid.*, p. 341.
34. *Ibid.*
35. "Shewkirk Diary," May 18, 1782.
36. Thomas Jones, *Hist. of N. Y. during the Rev.*, II, p. 227.

37. Carleton Papers, (Colonial Williamsburg), Doc. 4795–1.
38. *Ibid.,* Doc. 4737–1.
39. *Ibid.,* Doc. 4790–1.
40. Thomas Jones, *Hist. of N. Y. during the Rev.,* I, p. 351.
41. Elias Boudinot, *Jour. or Hist. Recollections,* p. 35.
42. *Ibid.,* pp. 9–19.
43. *Amer. Archives,* Ser. 5, III, 1234.
44. I. N. P. Stokes, *Iconography,* IV, p. 1040.
45. Elias Boudinot, *Jour. or Hist. Recollections,* pp. 9–19.
46. *Diary of Jabez Fitch,* 109, 110.
47. Ashbel Green, Life of John Witherspoon, (N. J. Hist. Soc.), p. 133.
48. *London Packet,* Jan. 13–15, 1777.
49. Elias Boudinot, *Jour. or Hist. Recollections,* pp. 9–19.
50. *Ibid.*
51. *Penna. Packet,* Sept. 4, 1781.
52. *Jour. of Cong.* (Hunt Ed.), XIX, 27, 28, 96.
53. *The Destructive Operation of Foul Air, etc.* (N. Y., 1865).
54. *Ibid.*
55. "The British Prison Ship," *The Poems of Philip Freneau,* (ed. Fred Lewis Pattee), Vol. II, pp. 18–39.
56. *Ind. Chron.* (Boston), Aug. 15, 1782. See also *Penna. Packet,* Sept. 10, 1782.
57. Carleton Papers, (Colonial Williamsburg), Doc. 5200–2.
58. *Royal Gazette,* June 12, 1782.
59. *N. J. Gazette,* July 24, 1782.
60. William Smith Diary, Feb. 1, 1783.
61. July 26, 1780.
62. Thomas Jones, *Hist. of N. Y. during the Rev.,* I, p. 352.

FOOTNOTES FOR CHAPTER VIII

1. Clinton Papers, (Clements Library), O'Hara to Clinton, July 15, 1778.
2. *Penna. Packet,* July 25, 1778.
3. July 16, 1778.
4. *N. Y. Journal,* (Poughkeepsie), Sept. 7, 1778.
5. Stevens *Facsimiles,* V, p. 504.
6. Montresor's *Journal,* p. 508.
7. Stevens *Facsimiles,* V, p. 515.
8. I. N. P. Stokes, *Iconography,* V, p. 1075.
9. Stevens *Facsimiles,* V, p. 531.

10. Thomas Jones, *Hist. of N. Y. during the Rev.*, I, p. 278.
11. *Hist. Mag.*, First Ser., V, pp. 336–38.
12. *N. Y. Journal*, Nov. 9, 1778.
13. Stevens *Facsimiles*, V, p. 543.
14. Clinton Papers, (Clements Library), Nov. 8, 1777.
15. *Mercury*, Jan. 13, 1777.
16. *Ibid.*, Jan. 20, 1777.
17. *Ibid.*, Aug. 3, 1778.
18. *Royal Gazette*, Aug. 5, 1778.
19. *Mercury*, Aug. 10, 1778.
20. Kemble's *Journal*, pp. 165–66.
21. William Smith Diary, VI, Feb. 3, 1779.
22. Clinton Papers, (Clements Library), March 1 and 2, 1779.
23. *Ibid.*, Clinton to Germain, June 18, 1779.
24. Dawson, *Battles of the U. S.*, Wayne's Report, I, p. 525.
25. *Mercury*, Aug. 6, 1779.
26. Clinton Papers, (Clements Library), Nov. 4, 1779.
27. At the intersection of Washington and Grand Streets, Jersey City.
28. W. Richardson, "Washington and the Enterprise against Powles Hook."
29. William Smith Diary, Aug. 19, 1779.
30. *Ibid.*, July 16, 1779.
31. Clinton Papers, (Clements Library), Nov. 4, 1779.
32. *Ibid.*, Sept. 8, 1779.
33. William Smith Diary, Nov. 18, 1779.
34. Clinton Papers, (Clements Library), Oct. 26, 1779.
35. "Shewkirk Diary," Oct. 30, 1779.
36. Clinton Papers, (Clements Library), Dec. 12, 1779.
37. William Smith Diary, Dec. 26, 1779.
38. *Ibid.*, Jan. 3, 7, 14, 1780.
39. *Royal Gazette*, Feb. 2, 1780.
40. William Smith Diary, Feb. 2, 1780.
41. *Royal Gazette*, Feb. 9, 1780.
42. *Ibid.*
43. William Smith Diary, Oct. 4, 1779; Jan. 3, 1780.
44. Baroness Riedesel, *Letters and Journals*, (Stone ed.), pp. 169–76.
45. William Smith Diary, Jan. 8, 12, 1780.
46. Clinton Papers, (Clements Library), Knyphausen's Journal, Jan. 24, 1780.
47. I. N. P. Stokes, *Iconography*, V, p. 1103.
48. *Royal Gazette*, Feb. 9, 1780; Clinton Papers, Knyphausen's Journal, Feb. 5, 1780.

49. Clinton Papers, (Clements Library), Sir Thos. Sterling to Knyphausen, Jan. 15, 1780.
50. *Ibid.*, Knyphausen's Journal.
51. William Smith Diary, May 10, 18, 1780.
52. March 11, 1780.
53. *Royal Gazette,* May 24, 1780.
54. William Smith Diary, May 29, 1780.
55. Clinton Papers, (Clements Library), Knyphausen's Reason for Invading New Jersey.
56. *Royal Gazette,* June 21, 1780.
57. William Smith Diary, June 17, 1780.
58. Clinton Papers, (Clements Library), Clinton to Germain, July 4, 1780.
59. Green, *Life of Ashbel Green,* pp. 120–21.
60. William Smith Diary, VI, Sept. 26, 1780.
61. Carleton Papers, (Colonial Williamsburg), Doc. 8798.
62. Clinton Papers, (Clements Library), Oct. 11, 1780.
63. *Ibid.*
64. *Ibid.*
65. *Ibid.*
66. E. F. De Lancey, *Memoir of Jas. William Beekman,* p. 11.
67. Clinton Papers, (Clements Library), André to Clinton, Sept. 29, 1780.
68. Thomas Jones, *Hist. of N. Y. during the Rev.,* I, pp. 371–72.
69. Sargent, *Life of André,* pp. 346–56.
70. Clinton Papers, (Clements Library), Clinton to Germain, Oct. 12, 1780.
71. *Ibid.*, Sept. 29, 1780.
72. William Smith Diary, Oct. 3, 1780.
73. *Ibid.*
74. Sargent, *Life of André,* pp. 390–96.
75. *Hist. Mag.* Second Ser., I, p. 98.
76. William Smith Diary, Oct. 5, 1780.
77. *Lloyd's Evening Post,* Dec. 11-13, 1780.
78. William Smith Diary, Apr. 14, 1781.
79. Clinton Papers, (Clements Library), Clinton to Germain, Aug. 25, 1780.

FOOTNOTES FOR CHAPTER IX

1. "Shewkirk Diary," Aug. 19, 1779, June 5, 1780.
2. William Smith Diary, Aug. 11, 1779.

3. *Mercury,* Jan. 24, 1780.
4. *Ibid.*
5. Baroness Riedesel, *Letters and Journals,* pp. 172–73.
6. Jan. 18, 1780.
7. William Smith Diary, Apr. 1, 1780.
8. *Ibid.,* Nov. 30, 1779.
9. *Royal Gazette,* Sept. 29, 1781; "Shewkirk Diary," Sept. 26, 1781.
10. William Smith Diary, VI, Sept. 28, 1781.
11. *Ibid.*
12. Sept. 29, 1781.
13. *Writings of George Washington,* (Ford ed.), IX, pp. 466–67.
14. *Royal Gazette,* June 5, 1782.
15. *Ibid.,* Aug. 24, 1782.
16. *London Chronicle,* Oct. 26–29, 1782.
17. William Smith Diary, VI, May 11, 1780.
18. *Royal Gazette,* Sept. 23, 1780.
19. *Ibid.,* Nov. 4, 1780.
20. *Mercury,* Feb. 26, 1781.
21. Aug. 26, 1780.
22. *Royal Gazette,* Aug. 29, 1781.
23. *Ibid.,* June 20, 1781.
24. *Mercury,* Nov. 15, 1779.
25. I. N. P. Stokes, *Iconography,* V, p. 1081.
26. *Ibid.*
27. *Royal Gazette,* Jan. 9, 1782.
28. *Ibid.,* Nov. 27, 1782.
29. *Ibid.,* Apr. 27, 1782.
30. Clinton Papers, (Clements Library), Observations on Present Situation of Refugees.
31. T. J. Wertenbaker, *Norfolk: Historic Southern Port,* p. 68.
32. *Royal Gazette,* Sept. 2, 1778.
33. Carleton Papers, (Colonial Williamsburg), Sketch of Plan, etc. Doc. 4686.
34. *Ibid.; Royal Gazette,* Feb. 28, 1781.
35. *Ibid.,* June 22, 1782.
36. *Ibid.,* Dec. 9, 1780.
37. *Ann. Reg.* (1777), p. 171.
38. *Royal Gazette,* March 3, 1779.
39. *Ibid.,* Apr. 17, 1779.
40. *Ibid.,* June 22, Sept. 14, Oct. 5, 1782.
41. I. N. P. Stokes, *Iconography,* V, p. 1075.
42. Carleton Papers, (Colonial Williamsburg), Dov. 4795–1.

43. *Royal Gazette,* Jan. 5, 1782.
44. *Ibid.,* July 13, 1782.
45. William Smith Diary, May 10, 1780.
46. *Royal Gazette,* May 30, 1778.
47. *Ibid.,* Jan. 9, 1782.
48. I. N. P. Stokes, *Iconography,* V, p. 1130.
49. Clinton Papers, (Clements Library), Geo. Howell to De Lancey, Dec. 18, 1781.
50. Thomas Jones, *Hist. of N. Y. during the Rev.,* II, pp. 13, 14.
51. *Mercury,* March 21, 1781.
52. I. N. P. Stokes, *Iconography,* V, p. 1139.
53. Carleton Papers, (Colonial Williamsburg), Doc. 4602.
54. *Ibid.,* Doc. 4661–3.
55. *Ibid.,* Doc. 4795–1.
56. *Ibid.,* Doc. 7472.
57. Clinton Papers, (Clements Library), B. Robinson to Clinton, Aug. 8, 1782.
58. Carleton Papers, (Colonial Williamsburg), Doc. 6924–1.
59. Nov. 2, 1782.
60. Clinton Papers, (Clements Library), Unsigned paper, June 15, 1782
61. Clinton Papers, (Clements Library), Loyalists to Clinton.
62. *Ibid.,* Unsigned paper, June 15, 1782.
63. Carleton Papers, (Colonial Williamsburg), Doc. 7258.
64. *London Chronicle,* Oct. 26–29, 1782.
65. I. N. P. Stokes, *Iconography,* V, 1082–83.
66. *Mercury,* Nov. 8, 1779.
67. *Royal Gazette,* Sept. 18, 1782.
68. *Penna. Packet,* Oct. 4, 1783.
69. *Ibid.,* Aug. 22, 1780.
70. *N. J. Gaz.,* May 9, 1781.
71. Carleton Papers, (Colonial Williamsburg), Doc. 10182–1.
72. *Royal Gazette,* Aug. 22, 1778.
73. *Ibid.,* May 16, 1782.
74. O. T. Barck, Jr., *N. Y. City during War for Indep.* pp. 136–37.
75. *Royal Gazette,* Dec. 7, 1782.
76. *Ibid.,* Sept. 28, 1782.
77. *Ibid.,* Nov. 27, 1782.
78. *N. Y. Packet,* Nov. 1, 1783.
79. *Mercury,* Jan. 6, 1783.
80. *Ibid.,* July 14, 1783.
81. *Royal Gazette,* Jan. 1, 1780.
82. Carleton Papers, (Colonial Williamsburg), Doc. 7951.

83. *Royal Gazette,* Nov. 22, 1782.
84. I. N. P. Stokes, *Iconography,* V, p. 1082.
85. Carleton Papers, (Colonial Williamsburg), Doc. 10135–1.

FOOTNOTES FOR CHAPTER X

1. Nov. 8, 1777.
2. *Mercury,* Apr. 14, 1777.
3. Clinton Papers, (Clements Library), Statement on Military Situation, Jan. 15, 1781.
4. *Ibid.,* Clinton to Germain, Jan. 23, 1779.
5. *Ibid.,* Return of Men, etc. Victualled in N. Y.
6. *Ibid.,* Clinton to Eden, Oct. 10, 1779.
7. *Ibid.,* Clinton to Germain, Oct. 29, 1779.
8. *Royal Gazette,* June 22, 1782.
9. *London Chronicle,* Oct. 3–5, 1782.
10. Nov. 4, 1780.
11. Carleton Papers, (Colonial Williamsburg), Carleton to North, Aug. 28, 1783.
12. Clinton Papers, (Clements Library), Dec. 15, 1779.
13. O. T. Barck, Jr., *N. Y. City during the War for Indep.,* pp. 196–97.
14. Clinton Papers, (Clements Library), Nov. 8, 1777.
15. *Ibid.,* Clinton to Germain, Aug. 30, 1780.
16. *Ibid.,* Nov. 26, 1780.
17. Carleton Papers, (Colonial Williamsburg), Doc. 5792.
18. Clinton Papers, (Clements Library), Regulations for the Associated Loyalists; André to Barry, Nov. 13, 1779.
19. William Smith Diary, Nov. 21, 1780.
20. Minutes Ass'd. Loyalists, (Clements Library).
21. Thomas Jones, *Hist. of N. Y. during the Rev.,* I, pp. 300–01.
22. Minutes Ass'd. Loyalists, (Clements Library), July 23, 1781.
23. *Ibid.,* Aug. 6, 1781.
24. *Ibid.,* Sept. 3, 1781.
25. Thomas Jones, *Hist. of N. Y. during the Rev.,* I, p. 302.
26. June 22, 1782.
27. Carleton Papers, (Colonial Williamsburg), Franklin to Clinton, Apr. 27, 1782.
28. *Ibid.,* Doc. 4485–1.
29. Heath's *Memoirs,* p. 335; Sparks, *Writings of Wash.,* VIII, pp. 262–63.
30. Carleton Papers, (Colonial Williamsburg), Doc. 4485–1.

31. *Ibid.,* Doc. 5229–3.
32. Clinton Papers, (Clements Library), Unsigned paper, June 15, 1782.
33. *Ibid.,* B. Robinson to Clinton, Aug. 8, 1782.
34. *Ibid.,* Clinton to Vaughan, June 28, 1781.
35. *Ibid.,* Oct. 23, 1783.
36. *Ibid.,* Clinton to Germain, Dec. 6, 1781.
37. *Ibid.*
38. *Ibid.,* Washington to Lafayette, May 31, 1781.
39. *Ibid.*
40. *Mag. of Amer. Hist.,* VI, p. 121.
41. *Lloyd's Evening Post,* Aug. 31–Sept. 3, 1781.
42. Clinton Papers, (Clements Library), Clinton's Observations.
43. *Ibid.,* Marquand to O. De Lancey, Aug. 20, 1781.
44. *Ibid.,* Beckwith to O. De Lancey, Aug. 20, 1781.
45. Jas. Thacher, *Military Jour.,* p. 323.
46. William Smith Diary, Aug. 31, 1781.
47. Clinton Papers, (Clements Library), W. Franklin on the Military Situation.
48. *Ibid.*
49. *Ibid.,* Clinton's Observations.
50. *Ibid.*
51. *Ibid.,* Clinton to Gray, Feb. 12, 1782.
52. *Ibid.,* Clinton to Germain, Sept. 7, 1781.
53. *Ibid.,* Clinton to Germain, Sept. 4, 1781.
54. Stephen Bonsal, *When the French were Here,* pp. 121–27.
55. Clinton Papers, (Clements Library), Campaign in North America, II, Chap. II.
56. H. J. Eckenrode, *The Story of the Campaign and Siege of Yorktown,* pp. 32–33.
57. "Shewkirk Diary," Sept. 19, 1781.
58. I. N. P. Stokes, *Iconography,* V, p. 1136.
59. *Ibid.*
60. Clinton Papers, (Clements Library), Cornwallis to Clinton, Oct. 3, 1781.
61. William Smith Diary, Oct. 16, 1781.
62. *Ibid.*
63. Clinton Papers, (Clements Library), Clinton to "My Lord."
64. *Ibid.,* Clinton to Germain, Oct. 29, 1781.
65. "Shewkirk Diary," Oct. 24, 1781.
66. *Edwards Lithoprinted Facsimiles,* Articles of Capitulation.
67. Clinton Papers, (Clements Library), Clinton to "My dear General," Jan. 24, 1782.

68. William Smith Diary, Nov. 3, 1781.
69. *Ibid.*, Nov. 19, 1781.
70. *Ibid.*, Nov. 26, 1781.
71. Clinton Papers, (Clements Library), Thoughts on Late Misfortune, Oct. 23, 1783.
72. *Royal Gazette*, Apr. 24, 1782.
73. Clinton Papers, (Clements Library), Clinton to Germain, Sept. 7, 1781.
74. William Smith Diary, March 1, 1782.
75. *Mercury*, May 6, 1782.
76. William Smith Diary, May 13, 1782.

FOOTNOTES FOR CHAPTER XI

1. Carleton Papers, (Colonial Williamsburg), Doc. 4650–1.
2. June 3, 1782.
3. William Smith Diary, May 23, 1782.
4. *London Chronicle,* July 20–23, 1782.
5. Clinton Papers, (Clements Library), Unsigned paper, June 15–Oct. 30, 1783.
6. March 30, 1782.
7. *Royal Gazette,* Feb. 12, 1782.
8. William Smith Diary, Feb. 12, 1782.
9. *Royal Gazette,* March 6, 1782.
10. *Jour. of Hugh Gaine,* Vol. II, p. 148.
11. *Ann. Reg.* (1782), pp. 173–77.
12. *Royal Gazette,* May 28, 1782.
13. Clinton Papers, (Clements Library), Aug. 8, 1782.
14. *Ibid.,* Letter to Clinton, Aug. 7, 1782.
15. *Ibid.,* Robinson to Clinton, Aug. 8, 1782.
16. Aug. 7, 1782.
17. Carleton Papers, (Colonial Williamsburg), Doc. 5267.
18. *Ibid.,* Watson to Clinton, Oct. 11 and 12, 1782.
19. *Ibid.,* Carleton to Rose, Doc. 7559.
20. *Ibid.,* Doc. 4813–1.
21. *Ibid.,* Doc. 5447–1.
22. *Royal Gazette,* Oct. 19, 1782.
23. Clinton Papers, (Clements Library), Robinson to Clinton, Dec. 19, 1782.
24. *Ibid.,* March 15, 1783.
25. I. N. P. Stokes, *Iconography,* V, p. 1158.

26. *London Chronicle,* June 5–7, 1783; *Penna. Packet,* Apr. 17, 1783.
27. Clinton Papers, (Clements Library), Apr. 13, 1783.
28. June 7–10, 1783.
29. William Smith Diary, Apr. 19, 1783.
30. *Penna. Packet,* May 6, 1783.
31. *Ibid.,* Sept. 18, 1783.
32. William Smith Diary, May 6, 1783.
33. I. N. P. Stokes, *Iconography,* V, p. 1166.
34. Carleton Papers, (Colonial Williamsburg), Doc. 9506.
35. *Ibid.,* Doc. 7625, Jouett to Carleton, May 4, 1783.
36. *Ibid.,* Doc. 9410, Carleton to Fox, Oct. 21, 1783.
37. *Ibid.,* Doc. 10183–1, Bearans to Carleton, Oct. 8, 1783.
38. *Ibid.,* Doc. 7882–2.
39. Clinton Papers, (Clements Library), Robinson to Clinton, March 15, 1783.
40. Carleton Papers, (Colonial Williamsburg), Docs. 7272 and 7553.
41. *Ibid.,* Doc. 7666.
42. *Ibid.*
43. I. N. P. Stokes, *Iconography,* V, p. 1168.
44. Sept. 23, 1783.
45. Carleton Papers, (Colonial Williamsburg), Doc. 8054.
46. *Penna. Packet,* Aug. 16, 1783.
47. *Royal Gazette,* Sept. 17, 1783.
48. Carleton Papers, (Colonial Williamsburg), Doc. 8910.
49. *Ibid.,* Doc. 9509.
50. *Ibid.,* Doc. 8631.
51. "Shewkirk Diary," Feb. 14, 1783.
52. *Penna. Packet,* Sept. 18, 1783.
53. Carleton Papers, (Colonial Williamsburg), Doc. 9419.
54. *Ibid.,* Doc. 9414.
55. *Ibid.,* Doc. 9363.
56. O. T. Barck, Jr., *N. Y. City during War for Indep.,* p. 219.
57. Carleton Papers, Doc. 5909.
58. *N. Y. Gazette,* Nov. 22, 1783.
59. *Penna. Packet,* Nov. 29, 1783.
60. *N. Y. Gazette,* Nov. 26, 1783.

INDEX

Adams, John, opinion of New York Congressmen, 38–39; at Tottenville conference, 117–119

Alexander, Robert, protests independence, 252–253

Alexander, William. (see Lord Stirling)

Allen, Ethan, takes Ticonderoga, 61

Allicocke, Joseph, shopkeeper, 218

Alsop, John, sent to Congress, 38–40; reelected, 46

Amphion, the, prizes to, 209

André, Major John, on British plundering, 114–115; confers with Arnold, 190–191; captured, 191; efforts to save, 192–194; hanged, 194

Apollo, the, storm dismasts, 175

Apthorpe, Charles Ward, Dunmore assaults, 29; flees to British, 89; Washington occupies his house, 95

Arbuthnot, Admiral, on American privateers, 210–211; blockades Rhode Island, 233

Arms, Americans practiced in, 41; imported, 41; patriots seize, 53; urged to secure, 57; urgently needed, 57–58; seized from garrison, 58; at Turtle Bay taken, 58; manufactured, 59; removed from docks, 59; Battery cannon removed, 62–63; bullets from King's statue, 85

Aristocracy, moderate attitude, 11; mansions, 15; country estates, 15–16; political interests, 17; oppose Ministry, 22; join patriots, 35–37; control Assembly, 44; many turn Tory, 49–51; some flee, 54, 89; return, 107; gaiety, 198; music, 204–205; entertainments, 205

Arnold, Benedict, Canadian expedition, 66; tricks St. Leger, 134; Bemis Heights, 135; storms Horseshoe Works, 138; plot of, 188–189; confers with André, 190–191; flees, 191–192; British brigadier, 194; expedition to New London, 239–240; sails for England, 246

Artisans, numerous, 19; refuse to aid British, 43; make arms, 59, 121; among refugees, 218

Asgill, Captain, hostage in Huddy hanging, 231–232

Ashley's Tavern, merchants frequent, 219

Asia, the, garrison retires to, 58; fails to save arms, 59; menaces city, 61–63; sailors fired on, 62; fires on city, 63; runs aground, 73; at Sandy Hook, 75; Tories flee to, 89

Associated Loyalists, organized, 229; raids, 229–231; murder Huddy, 231–232; Lippincott trial, 231–232; disbanded, 232

Association, the, Congress draws up, 40; enforcement, 42–43

Association, the New York, to preserve liberty, 56

Assembly, New York, protests Stamp Act, 3; use of taxing power, 3–4; protests trade laws, 6; erects statues, 13; lawyers rule, 18–19; denounces Mutiny Act, 22; supports redcoats, 23; protests Townshend Acts, 24; reactionary measures, 44; comments on, 45; ignored, 45–46; petitions for liberty, 52; seek peace, 67; restoration of promised, 156

Auchmuty, Rev Samuel, rector of Trinity, 18; for King, 49; returns, death, 107

Axtel, William, on corruption, 158; compensated, 266

Bache, T., warns of incendiaries, 177

Ball, Peter, robbed, 216

Ballot, secret, rejected, 17

Baptist Meetinghouse, used as hospital, 105

Barrack-masters, frauds of, 160–162